HOPE *and* OTHER LUXURIES

Also available:
Elena Vanishing: A Memoir,
by Elena and Clare B. Dunkle

HOPE

and OTHER LUXURIES

A Mother's Life with a Daughter's Anorexia

CLARE B. DUNKLE

CHRONICLE BOOKS

SAN FRANCISCO

Library of Congress Cataloging-in-Publication Data:

Dunkle, Clare B.

  Hope and other luxuries : a mother's life with a daughter's anorexia / Clare B. Dunkle.

    pages cm

  Summary: "Clare Dunkle seemed to have an ideal life—two beautiful, high-achieving teenage daughters, a loving husband, and a satisfying and successful career as a children's book novelist. But it's when you let down your guard that the ax falls. Just after one daughter successfully conquered her depression, another daughter developed a life-threatening eating disorder. Co-published with *Elena Vanishing*, the memoir of her daughter, this is the story—told in brave, beautifully written, and unflinchingly honest prose—of one family's fight against a deadly disease, from an often ignored but important perspective: the mother of the anorexic"— Provided by publisher.

  ISBN 978-1-4521-2156-7 (hardback)

  1. Dunkle, Clare B. 2. Dunkle, Clare B.—Family. 3. Anorexia nervosa—Patients—Family relationships. 4. Mothers—United States—Biography. 5. Mothers and daughters—United States. 6. Anorexia nervosa—Treatment. I. Title.

RC552.A5D875 2015

616.85'2620092—dc23

[B]

2014047354

Manufactured in China

Design by Jennifer Tolo Pierce

Typeset in Adobe Caslon

10 9 8 7 6 5 4 3 2 1

Chronicle Books LLC

680 Second Street

San Francisco, CA 94107

Chronicle Books publishes distinctive books and gifts. From award-winning children's titles, bestselling cookbooks, and eclectic pop culture to acclaimed works of art and design, stationery, and journals, we craft publishing that's instantly recognizable for its spirit and creativity. Enjoy our publishing and become part of our community at www.chroniclebooks.com.

WORKS CITED

To all the parents who lie in bed and agonize every night, thinking,
What should I do?
. . . and then get up the next morning and do it.

But especially to two of the best mothers I know,
Grace D. and Cathy A.

A NOTE TO THE READER

This is a true story. But it is also a work of fiction. Every memoir is.

Every incident, thought, and work of creative imagination in this story happened as described. But my memory doesn't work like a security camera. It records the things it notices, but it can't necessarily tell me when they occurred. During important or dramatic events, it does a better job of saving that information, but during long, similar months, it can't tell me exactly when minor events happened.

The same problem occurs when I try to remember conversations. Because I work with words, I have a good memory for conversations: I easily remember the gist of what was said, and I remember the things I was thinking about as the conversation went on. My mind doesn't record exactly what someone said, though, unless those words struck me as particularly important at the time. So, rather than stop the narrative to explain exactly what I do and don't remember, I've strung together events that I do remember as accurately to my memories as possible, and I've filled in conversations with what I think was said, even if I'm not entirely sure.

I have not intentionally moved any events, and I have not changed the sequence of events. I have not moved events closer together in order to make the story more dramatic. If the story says that three dramatic events happened on the same day, then, to the best of my knowledge, those three events did all happen on the same day.

All manuscript, book, journal, and letter excerpts are real, with only clerical changes. While all the people in this book are real, all names outside the immediate family have been altered.

A few very minor plot or physical description details have been altered solely to protect the identities of others. And very minor physical details have been created, in a few cases, where such details have been forgotten.

PROLOGUE

My daughter Elena called me up last week, crying. She's twenty-four now, and she just broke up with a boyfriend she needed to break up with. It was a good thing, but that doesn't mean it was easy.

"Can you come out to see me?" she said. "If I had some company for a few days, I know it would really help. It could be an early Christmas present."

How could I resist? What mother doesn't want to be her daughter's Christmas present?

Three days later, my plane landed in Texas, and Elena picked me up and drove me home. We walked around the house together and admired how she had decorated it. The house belongs to her father, Joe, and me, but Elena's living in it while Joe and I are stationed overseas in Germany. That way, Elena has a rent-free home while she goes to nursing school, and we have peace of mind.

After the house tour, Elena moved on to what really mattered. She introduced me to her new fish.

My daughter doesn't have just one aquarium. Depending on what's going on at the moment, she has at least four, and as many as six. She can take up to an hour to choose a new fish, although nowadays, her finest beauties have hatched out in one of her own tanks. The colors of Elena's fish are rich and brilliant: turquoise, fuchsia, lemon yellow, or blood red. Her aquariums are bold, fantastic worlds where the normal rules don't apply. In these mysterious realms, the artwork lives and moves. It drifts through its liquid landscape, rearranging itself second by second in an endless series of fascinating patterns.

I watched my daughter's expressive face light up as she explained their little quirks and habits. If her fish act like pampered darlings, that's because they are. But I wasn't thinking about the fish. I was thinking, *Elena's thinner than she was when I saw her three months ago. She's stressed. This isn't good.*

When this young woman was seventeen years old, you would have thought she had it all. She was a beautiful, cosmopolitan teenager fluent in two languages and at home in two cultures: the United States and Germany, where Joe's Air Force job had taken us when she was eleven. She made top grades among the students at the military base high school overseas, but she read her Stephen King novels in German so she could discuss them with her German friends.

By her junior year in high school, Elena was an honors student who volunteered for hours each week at the nearby military hospital. She bought the furniture for her bedroom with her own babysitting money, she knew exactly what she wanted to study in college, she couldn't wait to get started on her schoolwork each day, and she never got into trouble—*ever*.

That's a lot of reflected glory for a mother to bask in.

But Elena has anorexia nervosa, a very dangerous eating disorder. Statistically speaking, it's the deadliest of all the mental illnesses, with a death rate four times that of major depression, even when you factor in the suicides. And when I had to see my perfect honors student, howling and twisting, out of her mind, held down by two frightened nurses . . . When I sat by her frail, damaged body as she lay in the ICU, strapped to a feeding tube and a twelve-channel heart monitor . . . When I helped her withdraw from college so that she could go into a psychiatric institution . . .

. . . that's a long, long way for a mother to fall.

And what has that fall taught me?

That it hurts.

That the first time the ax falls, it feels like a fluke. That the second time the ax falls, it feels like a curse. That the third time the ax falls, it feels like the new normal, so that, no matter how long things go well, a part of my mind is always waiting for another ax to fall.

And that's why, as Elena prowled from aquarium to aquarium and did her checks on her prized and petted beauties, I was doing checks and assessments of my own.

This isn't good, I thought. *Elena is looking thin.*

Here's something I've learned the hard way as the mother of an anorexic: Anorexia nervosa doesn't just disappear. It isn't a set of bad habits that can be unlearned, and—*Whew! Glad we got rid of that!* No, anorexia nervosa is a complicated ecosystem made up of nervous tics, odd compulsions, biochemical changes, neurological adjustments, obsessive anxieties, attitude issues, comfort mechanisms, and unconscious reactions. It can fade into the background for years, but when the pressure mounts, anorexia nervosa has a tendency to reemerge.

My daughter almost certainly inherited her susceptibility to this deadly disorder. Relatives on both sides of her family tree have battled anxiety, addictions, or clinical depression. But Elena's anorexia didn't emerge for the first time until she went through an episode of severe trauma and suffered severe stress as a result.

At thirteen, Elena endured violent rape. She buried it completely and focused on perfection. As long as nobody knew—as long as she was Superwoman—she could tell herself that nothing was wrong.

At least, that was the plan. What happened instead was an eating disorder that controlled her every move.

Torn by shame and bitterness, my daughter became a prisoner, isolated within her own body—a prison she did her best to destroy. It took everything we had and everything she had to bring her back from the brink. And even now, her recovery isn't a place she's reached or a goal she's checked off. It's a path. Elena will walk that path of recovery her entire life.

So, while the glorious fish floated back and forth, and while Elena launched into small lectures about aquarium salt, swim bladders, and peas, I watched, and I listened, and I looked for ways to lower my daughter's stress. Because that's something else I've learned about having a daughter with anorexia nervosa. You can't just wait and hope. You have to *do*.

That's how I ended up where I am today.

I am driving my cat to the vet.

I hum along with the radio as I make the ten-minute drive. In his carrier beside me on the passenger seat, Tor crouches on his haunches. But his ears prick forward, and his golden eyes glow with a drowsy, benevolent light. He is as relaxed as a cat taking corners in a car can be.

Over the years, this lanky gray tabby cat and I have made many trips to the vet. He's always been fragile, and a little clumsy, too, going through his nine lives at an accelerated pace. The first of his lives was already gone by the time I met him as a six-week-old kitten, with a dog's tooth marks deep in his tiny rear end. He was alone when two tourists rescued him in a forest near France and took him to my German vet. They could find no sign of his mother or littermates.

The dog bite quickly healed, but the trauma of losing his first family has haunted Tor all his life. He suffers from separation anxiety whenever he's left alone. Once, when we went away for a week on a family vacation, Tor threw up so many times that he polka-dotted our new beige carpet with dozens of spots of bloody foam.

I've been absent for months this time. I know my old cat has been worried. But I'm beside him now, and that's lifted his spirits enough to start him purring in his carrier.

We come to a stop sign, and I reach between the bars to scratch him under the chin. He closes his eyes and revels in the attention and the affection.

Tor trusts me. He's not worried about going to the vet.

Tor is wise in the ways of vets. He's been through more than his fair share of medical procedures. Once, his claw snagged on a rug and tripped him while running, and he busted several teeth. In the middle of winter, he escaped out the back door, fell into a rain barrel, and almost died of hypothermia. He needs special food for his bladder. His delicate tummy requires antacids. One time, it even had an MRI.

Just last year, Tor almost died, and he had to go through two excruciating surgeries. They kept him alive, but they couldn't be called a success.

Considering how bad vet visits have been for Tor, the old cat has no reason to look so pleased. But he's with me, his favorite human, and we're doing something together. That alone makes all the difference to Tor. So I turn up the music as I drive, and I force myself to sing along. I focus all my attention on the road.

Tor knows me well. He'll notice if I start to cry.

What's happening now is nobody's fault. If it's anybody's fault, it's mine. I'm the one who moved back to Germany. Taking Tor along was never an option. When I left last year, he was happy to stay behind in the house and yard he already knew so well. And I knew leaving him was the right thing to do. Transatlantic travel is terrifying for a cat.

But that was before the last awful surgery. That was before Tor's recovery didn't go well. That was before Elena called me up in tears and I saw for myself how stressed she is.

Tor's care is difficult and thankless these days. He leaks urine, so he can't sit on a lap anymore or sleep on the bed like he used to. His stomach has gotten more and more sensitive, and Elena has had to give him antacid pills on a daily basis and hunt for new foods he can tolerate. As he's aged, he's started to get odd infections and abscesses. In spite of Elena's worried care, he's gotten thin and bony.

The simple truth is that Tor isn't happy with his new life. He struggles to keep himself clean, and that causes irritation. He misses curling up in laps and napping on the sofa, and that triggers his separation anxiety. Elena does what she can to make him feel loved and included, but it isn't easy with his new limitations. She feels his unhappiness, and that stresses her. She wishes she could do more for him, but no one can give him what he really wants: the comfort and health he's lost as he's gotten old.

Elena loves Tor. She would never for a second think of asking me to do this. That's why I'm doing it without her asking—to carry that burden for her. Because that's something else I've learned as the mother of an anorexic: This disorder isn't about weakness or laziness. Anorexia nervosa is a burden so painful that it drives many of its victims to suicide. Life with anorexia nervosa requires tremendous courage.

For Elena, eating is an act that can trigger panic so severe that the effects of it have landed her in the emergency room. It's like taking an agoraphobic to a crowded shopping mall. It's like locking a claustrophobic up in a closet. For an anorexic, eating means facing terror and despair—again and again and again.

I know how brave my daughter is. She's brave every single day. I'm glad I can do this for her. I know it will help.

The vet's office is in a low brown building next to a small, dusty asphalt parking lot. Six lanes of heavy traffic crawl by it every morning. It's such a modest establishment that most of the commuters probably don't even notice it. Nevertheless, this place looms large in the history of the tabby beside me. Even the smell of it alarms him.

But he rubs his face against the tips of my fingers and relaxes. Lucky for him, he's got me.

Tor's carrier is heavier than I expect it to be. I hold it away from my legs so he won't have to bang into me at every step. Then there's the job of getting the office door open. I keep up a cheerful stream of talk as I navigate these obstacles.

The smart, sassy receptionist greets me with a solemn face, and for a second, the pain in my chest stops me cold. But I give myself a shake and smile at her. *We're only here for shots*, I tell myself. *Be happy. We're only here for shots.*

How many times have I buried my feelings for the sake of those around me? For animals and children, so they wouldn't be frightened. For a grumpy family, so they could let go of a bad mood. For two hysterical teenagers, so their world could stay safe and stable while they learned how to handle their emotions. For the strangers I've met who didn't need to know that I was having a rough day.

Explore your feelings—how does a mother do that exactly? What we feel, the whole family feels. A mother's private bad mood can almost instantly turn into a screaming fight between two preschoolers. It can turn into raised voices, slammed doors, and miserable evenings.

So I don't explore my feelings. I force them down. I smile.

Just shots, that's all, I remind myself. *Just shots.*

"Room 2," says the receptionist, and I take the carrier into a small, square room about ten feet by ten feet. It smells strongly of pine-scented disinfectant, but that's better than any of the other strong smells it could have. It has no windows. Frightened animals try to launch themselves out of windows. It's loaded with hard surfaces: stainless steel, linoleum, painted cinderblock.

Persian rugs wouldn't last very long at the vet.

"Hey, Tor, want to go exploring?" I ask as I hoist the carrier up onto the narrow table. Tor strolls out and stretches as I rub his skinny shoulder blades. His purr starts up again and fills the quiet space.

"You'll be good for the doctor when you get your shots, won't you?" I tell him. "You know you have to be good." *Because that's what we're here for*, I insist with stubborn optimism. *Animals read body language. Be calm. Feel the calm.*

The door slides open, and the receptionist leans around it.

"Do you want to check out now?" she says in a low voice. "So you don't have to . . . after?"

A wave of emotion breaks over me, but I hold firm. I don't just keep the smile on my face. I keep the optimism in every single muscle.

"Later," I tell her.

Because later, it won't matter how I feel. But right now, I'm busy with a living, breathing, adoring tabby cat. Nothing else matters but him.

This long stripy kitty is the smartest cat I've ever owned. Joe accidentally taught him to roll over at mealtimes; he gave the command jokingly, but before two weeks were up, Tor could roll over faster than the dog did. From then on, Tor learned every trick the dog knew, from sitting up and begging to lying down on command. He knew he was clever, and he enjoyed that advantage. While our ragged little terrier, Genny, was struggling to master a trick, Tor would do it over and over just to show her up.

"Well, old boy," I tell him, "you're quite the cat."

Tor pads over to rub against me, and his purr gets even louder, a hum of contentment in the quiet room.

Tor's purr lasts all the way to the very end. He bears the vet no ill will. He likes the tech. Gently, peacefully, he slides into a furry heap on the examining table. His purr sputters once. And then it's gone.

My cheerful resolve breaks down at the very same instant. I surprise myself by wailing out loud. Sobs rack me so viciously that I struggle for breath while the vet presses a Kleenex into my hand.

It's all right. I'm with friends. I can let myself grieve for the loss of this small, faithful companion, this unique little life that has left the world forever.

There will never be another Tor.

Out in the car, I wail again and beat on the steering wheel with my hands. I let myself feel the pain Tor deserves—this intelligent, accepting, trusting creature whose companionship I banished. I keen and sob over the difficult years we had together and the way it had to end.

I could tell myself that Tor's life was painful. Yes, it was. I could give myself false comfort with the platitude that the poor, fragile, chronically ailing beast is finished now with medicines and surgeries. But the truth is different. The truth is that my love for my sometimes-fragile cat crossed my love for my sometimes-fragile daughter. And a mother's love crushes everything in its path.

I can cry, but I know: I would do more than this. To spare my daughter pain—to make her well—I would do *so* much more than this.

Because, at the end of the day, life with an anorexic isn't about triggers and causes. It isn't about reasons and right or wrong or blame. It isn't about success (although I pray for that) or failure (although it haunts my dreams). Strange as it sounds, it isn't even about life or death.

Love: That's what life with an anorexic is about.

I love my daughter absolutely as much as I am capable of loving. Each time I feel my strength giving out, I love a little more. There is nothing love can give that I wouldn't give for her health and happiness. There is nowhere my daughter could go that love won't lead me after her.

Love.

That's all.

It's the only thing that matters.

That's what I've learned as Elena's mother.

CHAPTER ONE

One day, when Elena was seven or eight, she beckoned urgently for me to bend down so she could whisper in my ear. "I've found love," she told me solemnly.

I looked around in surprise. We were sitting in a Burger King. It wasn't my idea of the best place for life-changing emotions.

"Really?" I asked. "Where's love?"

"At the next table," she breathed.

I glanced over to find two very young, awkward teenagers sitting at the table beside us. They were sharing an order of fries in silence.

"Oh, really?" I murmured back. "How do you know it's love?"

My little daughter looked very grave, as if she were in a cathedral instead of a place equipped with deep-fat fryers.

"Because she looks at him when he isn't looking, and he looks at her when she isn't looking. And when they both look at the same time, they look away."

Elena is one-quarter Italian, a legacy from Joe's mother, and that Italian is all on the top. She's dark-haired, dark-eyed, passionate, and excitable, given to strong loves and equally strong dislikes. When we visited Rome, I kept losing track of her. My dark, thin, nervous girl melted right into the crowds of dark, thin, nervous Romans.

When Elena sits perfectly still, she's pretty, with a lean, attractive face and an adorable figure. But, unless she's sick or sleepy, Elena doesn't sit still. Her eyes light up and snap and sparkle, her hands wave in the air, and her expressive face changes like a kaleidoscope. Surprise—joy—annoyance—laughter—incredulity—sly wit—these expressions and many more flicker across her face in a matter of minutes.

And when that happens, Elena isn't just pretty anymore. She's beautiful. She's unforgettable.

I'm reserved. I put together arguments the way I put together logic puzzles: if A means B, then C means you're a jerk. In temperament, I'm more like Elena's older sister, Valerie, whose most damning comment, uttered in a deceptively casual tone, is "Hey, do whatever you want, it doesn't matter to me."

To say that both sisters have brown hair and eyes is to make them sound the same, but to my eye, they don't look at all alike. Valerie's toffee-colored hair glows with warm highlights, and her eyes are the large, gentle eyes of a deer. Easygoing and cheerful, Valerie thrives only among friends and family. Without that sense of home around her, she quietly wilts.

Valerie was a calm baby, content to smile at her adoring father and me and occasionally laugh—when she wasn't blissfully asleep, that is. She talked extremely early and walked extremely late, and even then, only if she had a hand to hold. Walking wasn't exploration to little Valerie. It was a chance for the family to do something together.

Then, twenty months after Valerie came along to bless us with her sunshine, Elena ripped into the family like a tiny tornado, indignant from the very first moment of life over the ignominies of babyhood. And from that day to this, Elena has had the gift of the Italians: to love, hate, laugh, cry, work, and play with all her heart, and often within the same five minutes.

But if Elena inherited her fierce nature from her hot-tempered father, she inherited something very precious from me. I'm a storyteller. It's my central characteristic. It's how I see the world. Beethoven's brain worked in melody and harmony. Mine works in stories, little and big. All day long, my imagination shows me pictures and snippets of film no one else has ever seen.

When I was a little girl, the grown-ups around me often talked about the end of the world, when all the nuclear missiles would fly at once. Sitting quietly in a corner of the room, I could see the whole thing: the searing explosions, the rubble, the carnage, the hideous mutations, the breakdown of society, the looting and rioting . . .

I didn't sleep that well when I was a little girl.

Elena was just the same. From the time she was old enough to speak, I discovered that her imagination, too, was both a blessing and a curse. No matter how I tried to shield her, she got macabre ideas into her brain. A few Halloween masks in the grocery store or a casual joke from an acquaintance would be enough to set her vivid imagination churning with frightening images.

When Elena was very small, those half-understood hints about complicated subjects often took her into a fantasy world. Following my little daughter into her story-worlds back then could feel downright eerie.

"The man in the next car is a gangster," she would announce ominously from her booster seat.

"Oh, yeah?" I would say. "How do you know?"

"Because he's a murderer," she would state with absolute conviction. "He killed his wife, and he's running away from the police."

Where does she get this stuff? I would think. *She's in preschool, for God's sake! The scariest thing she's allowed to watch is* Mister Rogers*!* But there it was: I'm pretty sure that, a few centuries ago, my four-year-old daughter would have gotten people burned as witches.

And God help us when Elena's grade school sat down to watch videos. The unimaginative staff there had no idea what kind of terror an old movie like *A Christmas Carol* could unleash in a sensitive six-year-old. I had to sit by Elena's bedside to save her from the ghosts, and she cried herself to sleep for several nights. Monsters in stories were more real to her than the trees outside her window. We routinely found her in bed in the morning with Valerie.

But at the same time, Elena's vivid imagination brought her in touch with the feelings of others and inspired in her a boundless curiosity. And even in early childhood, she began to detect true stories, beautiful stories, in the commonplace world around her.

I would like to be a rose, she wrote on a school worksheet when she was six. *I would like to be a rose. It would be fun. I would hope a person would water and care for me and never pull me out of the earth. I would try not to get into a person's way, but I did! I loved to get pruned. I loved it in the soil, it felt good. I did not like it when the kids pulled off my leaves, but I lived with it. I loved being a plant. I loved to watch the kids swing. I loved the soil. I loved the earthworms. Then I died a sad death. The end.*

Elena was the kind of child who saw a human soul in everything. She had conversations with ladybugs. She rescued injured bees. She once drew eyes and whiskers on a sweet potato that looked like a seal. Then she couldn't bear to let me cook it.

One spring afternoon when Elena was seven or eight, she and Valerie sat down at the kitchen table to sort through their Easter baskets. After a few minutes of digging through the crinkly green plastic grass, Elena mournfully announced, "I'm out of candy."

Valerie, my prudent, practical girl, who asked for things like coats and desks for her birthday, had had the foresight to ration her treats. Now she took pity on her impulsive sibling. "Here," she said, and she handed Elena a marshmallow-filled candy egg with a hard sugar shell. It was about an inch long, sealed in clear plastic, and it was bright blue.

Elena was delighted.

"Come here, little candy!" she ordered, marching it up her arm toward her mouth. "No, no!" in a high squeal, and the candy turned around and darted back down to the table.

This continued for several minutes. The candy ran away and hid behind the salt shaker and the napkin holder; it leapt into Elena's sweater pocket. Finally, in desperation, it begged for its life. As I remember, it was very eloquent.

Valerie watched this little romp with increasing irritation. "Are you going to eat that or not?"

"I can't," Elena admitted. "It would hurt its feelings." And the candy nestled trustingly in her hand.

"Well, then give it back! I'll eat it."

"Nooo!" screeched the candy, bolting to the safety of Elena's shoulder, where it huddled, shaking.

"Don't worry," Elena crooned, petting it. "*I'll* save you! *I'll* keep you away from the evil giant!"

And Valerie appealed to a higher power:

"*MOM!*"

But what could I do? Solomon couldn't have settled that one. It was the collision of two different world views.

As playmates, the girls weren't well matched. In fact, they couldn't have been more different. Elena was the queen of the split-second decision. Valerie liked to ponder and weigh and debate. In group play, Elena was quick to take offense and raise her voice, but if Valerie got her feelings hurt, she usually left without making a fuss and went home to have a quiet cry. On the other hand, it was Valerie who remembered these slights and acted on them for months. Neighborhood children wondered sadly why she wouldn't play with them anymore, long after they had forgotten about swiping a toy from her or refusing to help her tidy up after a game.

When Valerie was in fifth grade, she became interested in chess. Its complexity impressed her, and its unbending rules appealed to her practical nature. She got to be quite good at it—she could certainly beat me. But I didn't have much time to play, so Valerie decided to teach Elena the game.

Chess became the source of endless conflict.

It wasn't that Elena couldn't learn it. She did that pretty quickly. It was just that the chess pieces couldn't be chess pieces to her. They had shapes and titles and social status. They lived in their own little world.

Before long, every single chess piece had a name—including two pawns who were named Boogity Boogity and Shoo. Each piece came complete with a lengthy backstory. It had its own hopes, fears, likes, and dislikes.

So, when Valerie and Elena sat down to play, the game went something like this: First, Valerie would move. Then Elena's pieces would all huddle together and discuss.

"Did you see that? It's happening again! They're creeping up on us!"

"You're lucky! You're big and strong. We're half your size, and you've stuck us out here in front!" This was a common complaint from the pawns, who seemed to have their own union.

"Don't worry, my little ones. Nothing bad will happen to you. Butter Fat will save us." Butter Fat was one of the knights.

Thusly appointed, Butter Fat would sally into the fray, and Valerie would move another piece.

"It's the queen! The evil queen! Queen Tiger Lily is coming! She'll turn us into statues for her garden!"

"Elena! Would you just shut up and *move?*"

Another couple of exchanges, and Elena would lose her knight.

"Aaaauuugh! The evil queen killed Butter Fat! She carried him away with her magic spells!"

"You have to protect us! We nominate you. You have to face her in single combat!"

"No, no! Don't make me go out there! Don't make me go out there *aloooooone!*"

And Valerie would lose her patience.

"MOM!"

In spite of the difficulties of the refereeing process, watching my girls play together was one of the greatest joys of my life. Hearing their careless voices laughing or chattering healed a part of my soul that had been damaged long before they were born.

If I were to sum up my own childhood in one word, it would be *lonely*.

I was the last of three children born to a busy engineer and an absentminded English professor. My parents had both been perfectly happy to call their family complete with the two boys they already had. My brothers were close to one another in age but substantially older than I was, so for most of my growing-up years, I was barely an annoying blip on their radar.

My father commuted two hours a day in addition to his work time, and his own projects out in the garage involved activities like sawing and welding—not safe undertakings for someone watching a toddler. This threw me back on my mother's company, and she took a novel approach to the problem. Rather than do what some mothers do—set aside her career and life goals in order to look after this last small child—my mother did exactly the opposite. She taught me how to sit quietly and amuse myself with some small toys, and then she took me with her everywhere she went.

I went to appointments, meetings, and events. I went to faculty parties and long evenings with my mother's friends. I went to the enormous university library, where I sat next to the copy machine and colored while she copied endless pages, and into her office, where I played carefully with a sheet of carbon paper while she typed out exams and met with students. I went to movies far beyond my understanding. I sat through *2001: A Space Odyssey* when I was three. At four, I was attending my mother's summer-school Milton course, sitting in a desk at the back of the room and taking it all in.

It must have seemed strange to the other adults that the small me had such flawless manners. Those manners were flawless because I understood one simple fact: they were essential to my happiness. If I were to break down and have tantrums, my mother would have to leave me at home, and I didn't want that to happen.

I loved spending time with my clever, pretty mother. She treated me with respect, and she shared her life and her friends with me. When I asked her questions, she took them seriously and did her best to explain. As little notice as the rest of my family took of my existence, it was worth hours of silence to have the chance to go places with her.

My mother spent hours each week with her closest friends. Unused to children, those friends treated me like an odd but surprisingly thoughtful little adult. They greeted me fondly and made me feel at home. I identified with them more and more as I grew past my toddler years, and although I couldn't understand much of what they talked about, the images my imagination showed me while they held their scholarly discussions were absolutely enthralling.

By the time I was five, I was listening avidly to everything the grown-ups said, and I stored up questions to ask my mother on the way home. I could read the emotions of adults as they turned from earnest argument to angry sarcasm, and I could follow the details of their complex debates. Needless to say, my vocabulary skills were off the chart.

It seemed to me by this time as if I had been born understanding how adults thought. It was understanding children that I had trouble with. Their silly dramatics often surprised and baffled me. They didn't understand my big words, so I couldn't have meaningful conversations with them, and they changed from hot to cold in a flash. My best friend in the morning might be swearing she'd never speak to me again by noon, and then the next morning, she'd want to be friends again.

Adult friends didn't do that sort of thing. They were loyal. They could be trusted.

As first grade crept by, I learned how to get along with my peers. I had a boyfriend and a group of friendly classmates who listened to my ideas about what game to play next. I grew to love recess in first grade. I ran and shouted and skipped rope and had a great time.

Nevertheless, the people who really mattered to me were the people I had grown up with. My mother's close friends meant more to me than the other members of my own family did. They had been a constant presence in my life, and they noticed my ups and downs. They asked how I was doing, and they listened to my sober explanations of my childish adventures.

I felt sure that these were people who really loved me.

Then, when I was in second grade, my mother went through a religious conversion of sorts, and she and her closest friends had a falling-out. From one day to the next, those friends were gone from my life.

And my strange little world blew apart.

Like any happy child, I had taken love for granted. But now, as I kept my vigil by the front window and waited in vain for the phone or the doorbell to ring, I finally faced the new truth of my blown-up world: these people my mother and I loved must never have loved us back. Her bright conversation and my perfect manners had been for nothing.

Thrown back into my family again, I realized once more just how unimportant I was. My middle-school brothers didn't even remember how to play. They certainly had nothing in common with me.

Drawing from old habits, I would bring a stack of books into the hall and sit quietly outside their door for hours, but this time, I could feel that I wasn't included. Busy as always, the other members of the household stepped over me or around me. I was the afterthought of the family, ignored and unneeded.

My proud, well-mannered heart broke into pieces, but no one seemed to notice. God himself seemed to have other things to do. At school, I stopped playing games on the playground. I stopped doing much of anything. It didn't matter anymore what I did.

The only thing I knew how to do anymore was what I had always done: sit quietly and amuse myself. So I withdrew. My days dragged. My life was empty.

My only emotion, other than misery, was a strong feeling of protection toward my pretty mother. I was sure that she needed an ally. Her friends had broken with her, and she was plainly hurting over it. That's how my mother got used to talking to me about her interests and concerns and I got used to asking her helpful questions. It didn't occur to either of us that I was only eight or nine and lacked an adult's understanding. My mother had always treated me like an adult, and I valued that respect from her. Besides, I had lost the trick of being a child.

One day, my mother confided to me that the miniskirts in fashion back then worried her. She thought we women should wear more modest clothing, so she had decided that she was going to wear nothing but long dresses. I knew that my father didn't like to see her in clothes like that. He could be sarcastic and hurtful. I couldn't let my idealistic mother take that plunge alone, so I told her I wanted to do what she was doing.

That's how I ended up wearing dresses down to my ankles—for four long ghastly years.

Being nine at the start of it all, I didn't have any idea what I was getting myself into. My busy mother, occupied with her college classes and her research, didn't have time to find flattering styles for me, and it wasn't as if we had a lot to choose from anyway. Most of the long dresses I wore came from Goodwill, the relics of long-outdated fashions. Some were adult clothes, altered to fit me. That spelled the end of running and jumping on the playground, even if I still had the heart to try it.

As I walked through stores or down hallways in those unusual clothes, I could feel the eyes of strangers assessing me. I could look in the mirror and see for myself how freakish and ugly I looked. My school days became a special kind of martyrdom. There was nowhere I could let down my guard and just be a child.

It was official: I was the Weirdest Kid in School.

I think there may have been abortive attempts to bully me back then. I was too deep into depression to pay much attention. The bullying didn't work because bullies assume that there are things they can take away from a victim—things like acceptance, comfort, and safety.

Me, I wanted nothing from my schoolyard peers, and they soon learned that there was nothing for them to take. I didn't change expression even when they socked me in the stomach, and that seemed to frighten them. Their other weapon, the playground insult, didn't work on me, either. Their insults were so sadly juvenile, so badly stated. With a professor's vocabulary stored away in my brain, I already knew what I was.

I was a changeling child, old and shriveled up before my time. I was unlovely. I was unloved.

Meanwhile, my vivacious mother had moved on. She had found new enthusiasms and new friends. Once again, she spent long hours with other adults, engrossed in conversation. But now, more often than not, I stayed in my room.

This time, I knew better than to take these new friends of hers into my heart. Instead, I let them take her away from me. But it wasn't easy to watch my one ally pass beyond my reach. While she chatted, I grieved. I grew even more bitter.

"Why didn't you have more children?" I asked her one evening. "Why couldn't it have been like my brothers, two of us? Why couldn't I have had a sister?"

"You did have a sister," she replied absently, grading papers. (She was always grading papers.) "You had a sister, but I lost the baby. She died a few months before you came along."

My hungry imagination burst into life at this unexpected news. It blossomed into splendid, colorful images of the good times my sister and I would have shared. We would have slept in bunk beds in the same room. We would have stood up for each other. We would have swapped clothing and stories and held late-night whispered confidences in the dark.

I wouldn't have been so lost if my sister had been there. I wouldn't have been so . . . ugly.

"Oh!" I cried. "If only she had lived!"

My mother laughed. "Silly! If *she* had lived, then *you* wouldn't be here."

I know I was old enough to understand what my mother was telling me, that there weren't enough months for both of those pregnancies to occur. Certainly, that was the conclusion an adult would draw from that statement, and my mother thought of me as an adult.

But I wasn't an adult. I was still a child, and I felt as shocked as if she had slapped me across the face. My absentminded mother had done what the bullies couldn't do. She had taken something away from me.

I tried to withstand the rush of painful thoughts, but they crashed over me in a wave. There wasn't room here for two giggling, gossiping girls. This family had no time for two small children. Let's face it: my sister had chosen the better option. I was in the way, and I had been in the way ever since the day I was born.

In silence, I crept from the room. I was right: I was unlovely and unloved. And later, I dreamed that my busy mother, tired of being interrupted at her work, told a group of soldiers to machine-gun me to death so she wouldn't have to answer any more questions.

Stories were what patched me up and put me back together over time. Unable to bear the friendship of real children, I made friends with the children in books. Most readers know Emily Brontë's Heathcliff as a surly, savage man, but he was the boy I played with in the pages of *Wuthering Heights*. Heathcliff was a strong-willed, proud, neglected child who, like me, couldn't be bullied. No matter how hard he was beaten, he never cried. I learned not to cry either.

A better companion, perhaps, was Sara Crewe, the Little Princess. She, too, had worked hard on her perfect manners, manners that weren't just a surface polish but a philosophy of life. She, too, had been abandoned by careless adults, but she had refused to let that change her. She had maintained her poise and self-control even when she was wearing rags. I learned from Sara Crewe to hold my head up, and I held on to my manners, too. They became an important tool to help me navigate a hostile world.

Time itself did its work in helping me heal. Gradually, the depression began to lift.

As the outside world came back into focus, I discovered other school-yard misfits waiting for me, other oddly gifted, oddly burdened children. Several of these became friends. One of them still is. She's my oldest and dearest friend.

While our classmates skipped rope or tossed balls around us, this friend and I held deep philosophical discussions. We confessed our loneliness to one another, along with our bitter belief that this world had no room for people like us. As the years passed, we learned we could go to one another whenever life threatened to break us down. We didn't have to be alone anymore with those overwhelming feelings of sadness. We gave each other a safe place to cry.

Little by little, after much absorbed study, I mastered the trick of sounding like my peers. I learned from snide comments not to wear the same clothes too often, to pluck my bushy eyebrows, and to use concealer on my broken-out face. I even found ways to keep my unruly hair under control.

At the start of eighth grade, my mother came to me and said she thought that clothing styles had improved and that maybe we should try wearing regular dresses again. That's how I ceased to look like a freak. Perhaps my mother had been watching me struggle through middle school with my burdens and felt pity for what she saw.

I don't know. I didn't ask.

By this time, it was too late for her or anyone else to try to soften my outlook. This once-happy child had been a miserable freak too long. I had long ago fallen into the habit of blaming my busy mother for my freakishness and depression. I was sure I was the only person in the entire world who cared about what happened to me.

For the rest of my teenage years, I looked more or less normal, but that hard shell remained. I was cruel to my mother. I manipulated her shamelessly for the things I wanted. Meanwhile, she stayed gentle and respectful toward me, even when I made her cry.

I don't think she ever realized what had gone wrong.

Only when I began to take on the responsibilities of an adult myself did I understand the difficulties my mother had faced as a scholar and career woman before the days of convenience foods and after-school programs. By this time, I had learned to be grateful to my mother for sharing her love of books and learning with me, and I looked back on my teenage behavior with shame. Once again, my mother and I became close friends.

But experiences like mine leave scars.

To this day, I have to fight against a carefulness inside myself, a scrupulous attention to emotional detail. Underneath any warmth and spontaneity I feel is a nearly impenetrable layer of watchful reserve. Past my wholehearted love of life, family, and friends is a part of my heart that I still struggle to unlock. And sometimes in the mirror, peeping out of my comfortable, middle-aged face, I still meet the wary eyes of that changeling child.

That's why the chatter of my daughters' young voices, tumbling over one another, whether in argument or in play, was the most precious sound that I could ever hear. I would stop to listen, and the happy clamor was like a beacon of light that shone deep inside me, all the way to where that lonely, lost little child hid.

They'll never have to go through what you went through, I would tell myself. *They'll never have to find out what happens when the whole world blows apart. They'll never have to go through the pain of finding all the pieces and putting them back together again the way you did.* And I would feel relief—blessed relief and happiness, all the way through my scarred and damaged soul.

But I was wrong.

CHAPTER TWO

could feel my daughters' eyes on me as I hung up the phone. I looked up. Anxious eyes.

"Who was that?" Valerie wanted to know.

"That," I said, "is the headmistress of a girls' boarding school near Cologne." I paused. "She's a nun."

Valerie and Elena exchanged glances. Fourteen-year-old Valerie had shot up several inches the year before, and she was now taller than I was. Twelve-year-old Elena looked to her to lead in times of stress. Elena was looking to her now.

"Whatever, we can talk about the nun later," Valerie said. "But I heard our names in there. What's that about?"

"Sister learned about you American girls working so hard on your German. So she called to invite you to visit her school for two weeks as a kind of cultural exchange."

"Two weeks!" said Valerie. "In a foreign school. In a foreign language. With a bunch of foreign girls."

"Yep," I said. "Starting next week."

"You're kidding!" she said. And then, when I didn't respond, "Come on, Mom. *Please* tell us you're kidding!"

Almost exactly one year before this conversation, Joe had come home from work, very excited. "The boss wants me to take a job in Germany," he said. "But it won't be forever. These Air Force jobs overseas are only for about five years. It seems like a lot of hassle, but it would be great to be able to fool around in Europe. What do you think I should tell him?"

"Yes. Yes!" was my answer. "Let's go!" So we had moved to Germany. We had said good-bye to friends the girls had known all their lives, rented out our house in Texas, packed up our belongings, shipped our car, put our family and dog and cat onto a plane, and landed ourselves in the middle of Europe.

The girls had been pretty happy about it—until now.

I had been teaching Valerie and Elena German at home. We had spent hours poring over foreign comic books together, with extra-sharp pencils and dictionaries close at hand. In the evening, after Joe got home for the day, the four of us had worked through dozens of language tapes together. We had made friends who spoke no English, we had shopped in foreign stores, and we attended a German-language church every Sunday. All that effort had paid off handsomely in this generous invitation.

Two weeks of language immersion! I couldn't have been more thrilled. I had attended intensive language courses myself in the past, so I knew what that kind of exposure could mean for my daughters' comfort in this new language. They would return with more confidence, as well as the skills they needed to start meeting their peers out in the community. It was like jumping into a pool: a shock at first, but the quickest way to start swimming.

Valerie and Elena weren't thrilled at all. In fact, they were horrified. But in the end, they both agreed to go.

Joe and I drove our girls to the school, a two-and-a-half-hour trip on highways winding through bright green fields and dark pine forests. We found the school in a tiny village at the top of a high hill, at the end of a steep one-lane street, where an old convent had been converted into a dormitory for one hundred and twenty girls. The rich, lively voice I had heard on the phone belonged to a tall nun in long black robes. Sister greeted us in her office, where an enormous fuzzy cat snoozed on her desk, stretched on his back with all four paws in the air.

Next, Sister and her head housemother took us on a tour of the school, talking in a halting mix of English and German. Curious girls stared at us from doorways and windows. Valerie and Elena stared back.

Then it was time to say good-bye.

Valerie and Elena were too stiff to hug me. They looked as if they might pass out. I felt butterflies in my stomach as we pulled away and the housemother herded them off to their rooms.

"Do you think we did the right thing?" I worried to Joe on the way home. "*I* think it's cool," Joe said.

The next morning, I occupied myself with punitive busywork. I sorted laundry, filed papers, balanced accounts, and tried not to think about what might be happening. But—what had I done? My poor children must be terrified!

That day, my overactive imagination outdid itself. It played me endless disastrous vignettes: Elena, cornered by a gang of vicious school-girls. Valerie, weeping in a bare little room. Over and over, it played me hysterical phone calls: Valerie had left the property and was walking home, all two hundred and fifty kilometers' worth of highway. Elena had locked herself in a closet. Valerie had fainted. Elena wouldn't stop crying.

After all the practice I had had with these nonsensical worst-case scenarios, you'd think I would have been ready for the real thing. But when the phone rang that evening, shrill and shattering, the unhappiness in my daughters' voices blew away my self-control.

"They hate us!" sobbed Valerie.

"They're so mean!" sobbed Elena. "Come get us! We want to go home!"

I would have grabbed the car keys right then, but Joe stepped in and took the phone. Unlike the girls and me, Joe was a veteran of the new-school experience. The son of an Air Force sergeant, he had lived on three different continents by the time he was ten, and he had changed schools over and over.

"You can do this," he told the girls. "I know it's hard, but I know you can do this. You'll be disappointed in yourselves if you leave. Then, the next time you need to try something new, you'll be afraid to try it. You need to see if you can stick this out."

I could hear their voices quavering on the phone: "All right, Dad."

"Now, you can't just wait for the other girls to make friends with you. You need to find ways to make friends with them. Let them tell you about themselves. Let them talk."

"But we can't understand them!" they wailed.

I was sitting beside him, listening, but I was no help at all. Inside me, the lonely changeling girl had woken up and filled my mind with self-loathing.

From the day I had first found out I was pregnant, I had promised myself that I would learn from my own childhood, and I wouldn't let myself get too busy to notice how my children were doing. If bad things started happening, I had sworn to myself that I would step in and fix them.

When the girls were little, I was a busy career woman, just as my mother had been. I was a university librarian, managing staff and working to earn tenure. It was a dream job, but the whole time I was there, I felt conflicted. I tried to convince myself that my work had meaning, but I couldn't shake the sense that my most important work was being set aside.

The fact was that our house didn't feel like a home to me back then. It wasn't our safe haven; it was only a place to stop on the road to somewhere else, a bus station of sorts, strewn with the trash of our chaotic lives. We didn't live there; we just paused there long enough to heat up something out of a bag or a box, tackle the dirty dishes, pull a few wrinkled clothes out of the dryer, and climb into bed for a little sleep.

Back then, I worried that I was depriving my girls of their family, but what I felt most keenly was that I was depriving myself. As I sat in my library office and did my work, some other woman was raising my little girls. Some other woman had the pleasure of sitting with them and playing games with them and helping them learn to read.

And me? I was actually paying that woman! I was giving her money to take these wonderful moments away from me.

For years, Joe and I talked about the daunting changes we would need to make to give up my income, so it wasn't until Valerie was twelve years old that we finally took the plunge. I'd felt a new urgency about the issue at that point. The girls' school wasn't challenging them. We had fallen into a rut. Joe and I were exhausted; it seemed as if we spent all our spare time just trying to catch up with the housework. And Valerie and Elena were about to reach their teenage years—on the verge of leaving for good.

So I gave up my career. And I never once looked back.

Now, as I sat by Joe and listened to the stress in my daughters' voices, all those conflicted feelings rose to the surface again. It was my coming home from the library that had allowed us this opportunity to move to Germany in the first place. The whole idea had been that we would grow as a family, not split up. What had I been thinking of, sending my daughters out alone to face such pressure? What kind of mother *was* I?

But Joe kept on talking, and I could hear Valerie and Elena brighten up.

"Hang in there," he said. "Remember, you won't ever have to see these girls again after two weeks. Two weeks? Not even two weeks now. And ask yourself this: Could any of these girls step into an American school if the tables were turned? Could they do what you're doing?"

"Yeah!" Elena said. "Their English is awful!"

By the time Joe put down the phone, he had done it. Both girls had cheered up and started making positive plans. I tiptoed through the next couple of days, keeping busy, unpacking boxes we hadn't gotten around to since the move, but no more hysterical calls came through.

Maybe it was going to be okay.

Then the letters started—long letters, sometimes two in one day. They reflected deep homesickness and stress. As the days passed, the stress eased, but the homesickness remained. *I can't wait till you get us out of here!* they said.

My stomach hurt, and I alternated between elation and misery. I was so very proud of what the girls were accomplishing! It was bound to make them walk taller; if they could do this, they could handle anything. But then I would receive another unhappy letter in the mail, and I would punish myself with more joyless busywork. This was trauma, that's what it was, and it was all my fault. I had talked my daughters into wretchedness and trauma.

At the end of fourteen long days, Joe and I made the trek once more to bring back our triumphant warriors. They had done it: they had slogged through the hardship and pain, and now it was time for them to have fun. At home waited all their favorite activities and desserts. I was looking forward to spoiling them.

Once again, Joe steered the car through the narrow lane to the top of the hill and pulled up in front of the erstwhile convent. This time, we were led into an oak bookcase–lined parlor, our shoes tapping soberly on the black-and-white tiles. Then the head housemother opened the door. She wore a ruffled apron, and her blond braids were tucked up into rolls on either side of her face. She was smiling.

"Your daughters have something to say to you," she said in crisp, practiced English, and she reached back to beckon them in. There they were, my two brave girls, a little hollow around the eyes, and maybe a little thinner, too, but their faces were lit with shy smiles. The housemother led them forward, an arm around each. She said, "Now, what was it you want to say?"

"We want to stay and go to school here," Valerie said.

"We want this to be our new school!" Elena said.

I thought my jaw was going to bounce off the black-and-white tiles.

It's temporary, I told myself as we walked out to the car together. *It's the desert island effect, the same kind of community building that happens whenever humans form a small group and go through an intense experience together. It won't last, though. The girls will shake it off and change their minds in an hour.*

And I could tell by the look and the smile Joe gave me that he was thinking the same thing.

But all the way home, Valerie and Elena chattered to us about new friends and new experiences. Their eyes were shining, and their eager sentences spilled out in fountains of excited words. They told us hilarious stories and heartrending stories. They gave us character sketches of heroes and villains. And their German! Their German had improved amazingly.

As the girls gushed about the school, I began to see the appeal of joining such a lively, boisterous group. Here were no "twelve little girls in two straight lines," in Ludwig Bemelmans' famous words. It sounded more like a three-ring circus. With one hundred and twenty girls in one great big dormitory, there was always something crazy going on.

The weekend passed, but Valerie and Elena didn't stop talking about the school. They held long and elaborate discussions about which girls they wanted to room with and which girls would make the nicest friends. I hadn't seen them so enthusiastic in years.

Soon we all got caught up in the idea. Joe and I sat down to work out the finances while Valerie and Elena made long lists of things they would need—or at least would want. Finally, I called Sister to discuss plans. It was already spring. Should we just wait until the next school year?

"No, bring them back as soon as you can," she advised, "before they have time to lose their nerve."

The days flew by in a mad rush. We had to track down all kinds of supplies that we had never known existed before: laundry labels and little zippered pencil cases, special graph paper and school fountain pens. (German schoolchildren still write with fountain pens.) By the time we drove Valerie and Elena back to school, we were all riding high on a wave of adrenaline.

Once there, Joe and I hauled in suitcases while the girls vanished into the busy dormitory like drops of water falling into a pond. Then he and I drove home in the dark, with the sudden silence ringing in our ears.

We wouldn't be seeing our girls again for three weeks.

The following morning was completely different from any day that had preceded it. Since Valerie's birth, the welfare of the children had shaped every one of my days. Now they weren't here, and I wasn't worried about them. My day seemed to have no shape.

Joe sensed this.

"What do you think you'll do with yourself today?" he asked me over breakfast.

The thought completely baffled me. I felt simultaneously lighthearted and numb. I felt as if I might be walking in my sleep.

"Maybe I'll do some cleaning," I said. "Maybe get a little ironing done."

"My shirts are starting to pile up," Joe agreed, getting up to rinse out his coffee cup.

I kissed him good-bye at the door, and then I took my own cup of coffee and wandered the empty rooms. Nothing moved, and nothing made a sound. The old Dalmatian was asleep on his rug. Our old cat might as well have been a couch cushion.

For the first time in fourteen years, I had no children to plan for or care for. I had no job, no schoolwork, no errands, and no projects. I had not a single thing, in short, that *had* to get done. It was a phenomenon I could barely comprehend.

I'll clean, I thought as I drifted through the silent spaces. *Now that I'm alone, I can get this house whipped into shape.* But I didn't—because, with the imagination I have, it turns out that I am never alone.

When I was little, my imagination terrified me with glimpses of disaster, but it also helped me escape my lonely childhood. I spent days at a time shut away in my room, staring at the wall while my imagination played its movies. Every book I read, I moved into and took over, and I turned my own characters loose in that world to see what would happen. I played with other worlds the way some children play with Legos.

That was fine when I was young and lonely, but once I grew up, I decided that my imagination was a waste of time. All it did was steal energy and attention that ought to belong to others: my family, my home, or my employer. I realized that I must be the only manager in the library who spent half her break time staring at a blank wall.

Through careful attention, I slowly learned to conquer my imagination. It was like stopping any bad habit—like getting a handle on nailbiting. I would catch my mind as soon it started to wander, as soon as I saw those first few seconds of new film. Then I would stamp a neon-green *X* over the image.

But now, as I sat on the sofa in my empty house and drank my cup of coffee, that mischievous imagination crept up on me unawares. Little by little, a forest of tall, twisted trees wove itself around me. It grew until the walls of my living room faded out, and I could see that it spread for miles: wild, verdant woodland, engulfing tumbled hills and rugged boulders. Beneath its mossy boughs, narrow paths wound away into the shadows.

What is this place? I wondered.

England. Northern England. At the edge of this forest stood an old English mansion. Nearby, sheer cliffs fell to the surface of a deep blue lake.

Who lives here? I wondered.

And two people walked out of the forest, hand in hand—a young woman and a girl.

Who are they? I wondered.

By this time, I had forgotten about cleaning my house. I had forgotten that I even *had* a house.

The two girls were sisters, Kate and Emily, and they wore dresses with the empire waists and long, trailing skirts of Regency-era England. They appeared to have stepped out of Jane Austen's *Pride and Prejudice*, and I realized that Kate, at least, would have loved to find herself in *Pride and Prejudice*. But, bad luck for her, this was not a Jane Austen world.

There were surprises waiting for the two sisters in this tangle of hoary trees. I glimpsed a large black cat with huge golden eyes—I could tell right away that he wasn't a regular cat. I spotted a short, ugly gypsy woman who read palms and told fortunes—I was positive that she wasn't a regular gypsy. I saw a tall, stooped man with a black hood over his face—I was sure that he wasn't a regular man. He was a brilliant magician and a magnificently ugly monster. He was Marak, my goblin King.

I had sensed Marak's presence in that twisted old forest even before Kate and Emily had stepped out of it. As soon as I saw that land, I knew it belonged to him. I am fond of every single character in each of my books, including many of the villains. But the goblin King is the oldest and best beloved of all my character children.

That day, Marak's story unspooled itself before my eyes, a movie that was playing just for me. The first time Kate, my Jane Austen girl, got a good look at him, his ugly face was peering at her out of her own mirror. While Kate stared at him, I forgot entirely that I had breakfast dishes to wash. I forgot that I had promised Joe I would iron him some shirts. I even forgot that I should probably make at least some sort of effort to defrost dinner.

What does a goblin look like? I wondered. *What does Kate see?*

Long hair—rough hair, like a horse's mane. Shrewd eyes in two different colors, one eye green and the other eye black. A lean, pinched face, bony forehead, sunken temples, deep-set eyes, and pointed ears that flopped at the tips like a dog's. Shiny gray skin, brown lips, and dark pointed teeth—teeth like tarnished silver.

Marak's hair was all one length, brushing his shoulders in a shaggy mane. It was pale beige. Or was it? The image came into clearer focus, and

I saw a palm-size patch of black hair growing in a cowlick over the green eye. That black hair cast long sooty streaks over the pale hair below.

While I sat and studied this brilliantly ugly monster, a sudden sound jarred me out of my reverie. The front door. The front *door*? It couldn't be! But it was. The workday was over, and Joe had come home to admire his newly cleaned house and ironed shirts.

"Oh, hey!" I called, jumping up. "So, I was thinking of French toast. How does that sound to you?"

Over the dinner we threw together, Joe said, "I thought you were going to clean today." But he said it philosophically—almost dispassionately. After fifteen years of marriage, he had learned not to count too much on my homemaking skills.

Joe and I had met while I was earning my master's degree in library science and he was a young engineer working for the Navy. Like Valerie and Elena, he and I were opposites in almost every way: I had gotten degrees in Russian and Latin, with a strong focus on literature, while he had managed to steer clear of the liberal arts almost entirely. He was practical but hot-tempered; I was dreamy but reserved. He thrived on routine; my student days had no order whatsoever.

We fell head over heels in love.

Throughout our years of marriage, Joe has been the anxious nest builder, the one who says, "Where's the money going to come from?" And over the years, I've been the flighty adventurer, the one who says, "If not now, when?" Joe and I trust one another completely, but we also know what we can count on each other to do. If Joe calls home from a business trip and says, "I want to read poetry with you," I know that he's telling me he misses me, not that he has a sudden burning desire to read Keats. And when I tell Joe the first time or two that I think I might get to the ironing, he knows that I'm about as likely to follow through and do that ironing as he is to sit down with that book of Keats.

So, that first evening the girls were away, I felt comfortable knowing, as Joe munched on his French toast, that he hadn't really expected ironed shirts *just* yet. Nevertheless, I felt I should explain.

"It's this new daydream," I said. "It's keeping me from getting any work done." (And was that a circle of ancient oak trees on that hill?)

"What's the daydream about?" Joe asked.

"I don't know. A goblin King." (A king of what, exactly? And why *were* his eyes different colors?)

I didn't expect Joe to ask any more questions. He had heard me make similar complaints for years. I had been at war with my imagination for our entire marriage, and I had complained about it the whole time. Joe is reassuringly immune from this weakness, so I didn't expect goblins to interest him particularly, much less where they lived (jeweled caverns? Yes, and the twilit, indigo-tinted lands below the lake) or what they ate. (Sheep? Yes, sheep probably made the most sense.)

But this time, Joe surprised me.

"Why don't you write it down?" he said.

The idea didn't immediately appeal to me. It sounded suspiciously like work.

"Why?" I asked. "Who would bother reading it?"

"I would. You're always complaining about daydreams, but I never get to see what they're about."

That made me feel grateful and more than a little guilty. Maybe I *would* get the shirts ironed after all.

The next morning, after I kissed Joe good-bye at the door, I took my coffee cup and wandered the house again. I paused for a couple of seconds by the ironing board, but then I went to the computer. There was work, and then again, there was *work*.

I sat at the keyboard and pondered. I thought about daydreams. I thought about stories. Writing is a bridge between two people, the writer and the reader. Who would be my reader? That reader would shape every single word.

Well, Joe, of course. After all, he had promised.

But would Joe really get around to reading a story? He was a busy manager, and I had never known him to read a work of fiction. He was just being kind.

(I really should get that ironing done.)

But if Joe wasn't my reader, who was? Who would actually enjoy this story?

Of course! Valerie and Elena!

The girls had loved the little stories I had made up for them when they were younger. Now that they were off exploring the world and having their own adventures, I could still reach out and share an adventure that belonged to us alone. I would send them their own story in letters, a chapter a week—a story no one else had ever read.

Working on that story was slow going at first. I hadn't written fiction in almost a quarter of a century, not since I'd had fiction assignments in middle school. As much as I had always loved books and writing, I had hated to share my stories. They weren't for the outside world. They were the very things that kept me safe from that outside world.

Now, as I watched this movie in my head, I struggled to find the best way to capture what I was seeing in words. "Not right," I muttered as I backspaced over half an hour's hard work. "The sentences don't lead into one another. They stutter. The image they create is blurry. And right here, the word *dark* is too . . . flimsy. I need a heavier word."

Because writing isn't just a question of setting down accurate images, as I had known from birth, and possibly before, if doctors are right that unborn children listen to their mothers' voices. There was the rhythm of the sentences to consider, the pauses for breath, and the placement of critical words. As a story unfolds, the words have to flow like a river. That's how a good book casts its spell. That's how the words and pages disappear completely and the reader falls into the writer's world. My literature-loving mother had taught my writer's ear to listen for balance.

As those spring days slowly passed, I sat at the keyboard and marveled at what was happening on the screen. I would agonize for hours, barely coming up with more than a page or two of prose, and the whole thing would seem like a hopeless waste of time. But the next morning, I would read those couple of pages, and the scene would unfold before my eyes, just as if I myself were reading a book I'd never read before.

What happens next? I asked myself each morning when I came to the last sentence. *Let's get to work. I want to see what happens next!*

That's how the first couple of weeks passed: hours of struggle followed by moments of sheer excitement. Then the goblin King stepped in, and I lost myself in the story. He was so much fun to write!

My new hobby enchanted Joe. He sat down with that day's new pages the minute he walked through the door each night.

"I don't know how you do it!" he gushed. "This is the best novel I've ever read!"

"It's just about the only novel you've read," I pointed out. "You know you've never been a fiction guy."

But that didn't make the compliments any less fun to hear.

Valerie and Elena were thrilled. They adored getting their letters. They called me up and pumped me for information about goblins, as if I were a paparazzo who followed around living people rather than a writer who made things up. Kate and Marak were as real to them as their own friends were—as real as they were to me, in fact.

"When I get a letter," Elena told me on the phone one night, "I run off with it to where it's quiet. And then, as I read, it's like you're telling the story into my ear. I can hear your voice reading me the words."

That brought tears to my eyes.

"Write lots!" she begged me as she said good-bye. "Write lots!" echoed Valerie as she took the phone.

After I got off the phone with my girls that night, I sat with that conversation for a while. I leaned in close and warmed my heart at it. Even though it seemed as if my daughters were far away, I could still sit by them in their rooms and whisper my story to them. We weren't apart while that happened. We transcended time and distance. We were a family.

By the time the girls came home for summer break, I had written hundreds of pages and made my way like a machete-wielding explorer deep into the crisis of the story. Writing had surprised me yet again: I was not remotely in control of this process. My characters were the ones who were in control. It took all I had to keep up with them.

Nothing about who these people were or what they did seemed to be my decision. All I could do was spy on them relentlessly, until I learned things about them that even they barely guessed. Along the way, those characters taught me lessons about hope, endurance, duty, and forgiveness. Their lives were a very serious matter to them. How could they mean any less to me?

Each day that summer, Valerie and Elena dashed by my computer as they played their high-spirited games—sophisticated teens they might be now, but they still were young enough to play. As they passed, they leaned over my shoulder to read the new paragraphs. "Write lots!" they shrieked as they dashed away.

The short German vacation was over in just six weeks. Full of excitement, Valerie and Elena packed their bags again. They gossiped merrily as we made the trek to take them back to school, and they joined the boisterous groups of girls without hesitation.

"Write lots!" they clamored as they hugged me good-bye.

A few more weeks of quiet passed, with just the sleepy dog and cat for company, and the goblin King's story was complete. I printed it out and read the whole thing through on a train to Paris while Joe watched sunny fields rolling past our window.

"What do you think I ought to change?" I asked Joe as the train rocked us gently back and forth.

"Why should anything change? It's a great story."

"I just don't know if this is it yet, though. I need help with it."

"But how could it change? It's finished. It's all already there."

"No. That's only one way the story could be." And I tried to convey to his tidy engineering brain how the story felt in my mind: like a map, maybe, or like a country covered over with dozens of different paths. Just as the train and the highway both connected our city to Paris, so one story path instead of another would cause the whole feeling of the story to change. But somehow, it was still the same place in my mind. The same country. The same world.

"I don't get it," Joe said finally. "I wouldn't mess with it. I think it's fine the way it is."

"Well, what do you think I should do with it, then?"

He looked very serious. "I think you should send it somewhere."

"It's not a bad story," I conceded. "I studied teen literature in library school, so I know what a young adult novel should look like. And I don't think I'm bragging here, either. It's really not bad."

"Then do it!" he said. "Get it published. You could be a famous author and make me a million dollars. That would be amazing!"

"Oh, please!" I said. "It doesn't work that way. Everybody wants to be a famous author! Do you know how many people are trying to get published right this minute? Everybody's written a book."

"I haven't."

"Well, everybody else has, and they're all fighting to get their name into print. That takes years of hard work, rejections, begging, letter writing . . . You know me—I don't have that kind of patience."

"Publishing doesn't look that hard," Joe said. "I was on the web the other night, and there are these publishers all over the place who say they can help you get published. One of them could turn your story into a book."

"So I could—what? Use it as a paperweight?" I countered. "That's not the way to get a book to readers. The publishers who get their books into bookstores aren't waiting to hold my hand. They're the big places in New York City: Scholastic; Simon & Schuster; Holt; Penguin; Harcourt; Little, Brown . . ."

As I said the names, they echoed back to me from my earliest childhood, from long summer days spent sitting in the corners of offices, listening to the literature professors talk. I had heard many conversations about the New York publishing companies, about their mergers and ruptures, their tastes and trends, and their triumphs and disasters. In my childish mind, these institutions had loomed large but mysterious: the venerable guardians of society and culture, like noble families lodged in great castles. Their logos—the farmer scattering seeds, the sprinting torchbearer, the boxy double *H*—had seemed to me no different from the quaint images on knights' shields in my mother's old books.

There was the House of Tudor, and there was Random House. The main difference, to my young mind, was that Random House seemed to use its wealth more wisely.

But all of this was lost on Joe. He had spent his childhood playing Little League.

"Well, aren't writers supposed to get agents or something?" he asked. "The agent does the letter writing and begging for you, right?"

"I have no idea," I said. "I don't know anything about agents. I guess I ought to find out how this works."

When we got back from vacation, we both turned to the Internet. I looked for information about agents while Joe went through a stack of YA books from the girls' rooms and searched the websites of their various publishers.

"There's this book that lists all the agents," I told him when we reconvened. "But it's not at the library, and it's not in our bookstore, either. I can ask my mother to copy the young-adult agents' pages and send them to me."

"Well, it looks like that's the only way you'll get published," Joe said. "The publishers in this stack won't give you the time of day unless you've got an agent. Except one—they'll look at your manuscript as long as you give them a couple of months to do it. It's"—he pulled out a Post-it note and consulted it—"Henry Holt and Company."

"Holt? Oh, that's nice," I said. "They published Lloyd Alexander's Prydain series."

Even to the engineer beside me, that comment had meaning. Lloyd Alexander is my hero. I'd loved his Prydain books so much as a child that when the girls were old enough for them, I'd sat the whole family down, including Joe, and we had read them out loud together.

"What great books!" Joe said, his eyes dreamy. "Wouldn't it be great if your book could come out from the same place that published his?"

I laughed. "It's not going to happen."

Nevertheless, I had nothing to lose except the cost of a box and some printing paper, so the next morning, Joe posted a bulky package to New York City. Then I got on the phone with my mother to request the photocopies.

A thick packet of copied pages arrived a couple of weeks later. I brewed an extra-strong cup of coffee and sat down to read through them. Page fees, commissions, percentages, extra charges, instructions on what *not* to send—my heart sank as I slogged along.

This wasn't my idea of the venerable guardianship of culture. It felt more like selling a used car. This was exactly that uncaring world, that shark-toothed, dog-eat-dog world that was the antimatter to my worlds of imagination.

Market analysis and genre breakdowns . . . what did *that* have to do with magic and wonder?

Oh, well, I thought. *At least I gave it a look.* And I set the stack of photocopies aside and did other things. I think I may even have finished the ironing.

Weeks went by. The photocopies started to gather dust. Meanwhile, Joe kept talking about publishers and contracts.

"Did you find some people to send your story to?" he asked.

"Not today," I said. "I don't know. Maybe tomorrow." And *maybe tomorrow* is exactly where my publishing career would have stayed. But that's when it happened: that's when something so extraordinary took place that it could have come right out of my dreamworlds.

The email materialized in my inbox late at night, like a disembodied voice from another dimension:

> Dear Ms. Dunkle,
> The Hollow Kingdom managed to fall into the hands of the editor here at Holt who would most appreciate it. I am a big fan of this kind of fantasy, and I very much enjoyed reading your novel . . .

Was I asleep? Was I actually reading this?

Here was no hard-bitten analysis of fees and markets. This was the voice of a friend, a kindred spirit, telling me what was great in my story—and what could improve. As I read her suggestions, I felt them fall into place in my mind. Of course! I had known those were problems, hadn't I?

"If you'd like to discuss anything I've said (or haven't said)," that magical letter concluded, "please feel free to email or call me." And there followed the contact information of a real, live editor ensconced in one of those semimythical castles of my childhood—the actual number of an actual phone that rang on an actual desk halfway up an actual skyscraper in the heart of really-truly New York City.

Joe's proposal of marriage didn't sweep me off my feet the way that midnight email did. I wandered to bed in a rainbow-colored haze, in a cloud of pure, blissful romance. I was every bit as happy and giddy as any girl who ever went to a ball. All I needed was a rose to hold as I drifted off to sleep.

The school year went rattling by as my editor—*my* editor!—and I worked on perfecting Marak's story. And every three weeks, Valerie and Elena rode the train home from school, changing at the huge Cologne train station. Germans from northern Germany heard them speak and thought they might be from Bavaria. Germans from southern Germany thought they might be from up by Bremen. But no German could tell that they were foreigners anymore, a fact that brought them endless amusement and delight.

Each free weekend, the girls would burst back into our lives and fill them with color and excitement. "Guess *what!*" Elena would announce breathlessly as she flung herself down the steps onto the platform at the train station. And, no matter how hard I tried, I could never guess.

If I was growing through my writing, both girls were growing through their experiences at school. Untidy by nature, Valerie was learning to enjoy the order and routine of her contained little world. She was laid-back and well liked, and her language skills were brilliant. It annoyed Elena to no end that Valerie seemed to learn German by effortless osmosis.

But Elena, too, was changing in amazing ways. Given before to anthropomorphizing objects and living a rich imaginative life, Elena had turned her attention outward, and her lively sense of compassion had blossomed into real goodness to those around her. She tucked homesick little girls into bed at night. She helped the older girls study English. Like Don Quixote, she couldn't resist tilting at windmills: she took frightened classmates directly to Sister to plead their causes, and she fought pettiness and injustice in any form. Every penny of her allowance went to thought-ful little gifts.

A whole group of girls had flocked to Elena and nominated her their leader. Lively and creative, she set the tone for their free time: if she took up jogging, they all took up jogging. When I pointed out to her that she could be an influence for good, she announced that they would all attend daily Mass, and they lined up next to her in the church pew like lambs.

"It's a lot of responsibility," she confided to me with distinct satisfaction. "I think they would help me commit murder if I asked them to."

By the time Valerie and Elena came home again for the short summer break, I had written three complete stories for them, and my editor and I had polished the first manuscript to a fine gloss. And late in August, in the middle of the night, I woke up my entire family one by one to tell them the news: The same house that had published Lloyd Alexander's Prydain series was going to buy and publish my first book.

"That's great news," Valerie murmured. "You deserve it, Momma." And she closed her eyes again.

"That's great, Mom," Elena said blearily. "Now you can make us a million dollars." And she rolled over and went back to sleep.

As I tiptoed back to bed in the middle of that peaceful night, my heart brimmed with happiness.

I'm so lucky, I thought. *Except, there's no such thing as luck.*

When I was a young loner of a teen, I used to help my mother get everything ready for Mass. Priests would fly in every week to say the old Latin Mass for our small congregation in any venue we could provide: a hastily converted hotel room, or, later, a small recital hall. In those days, the Latin Mass was frowned upon as old-fashioned, and the local bishop disapproved it. The priests who looked after our congregation were a small missionary order, and each priest had a territory that covered several states.

One day, I was loitering outside in the parking lot, and I found a penny. I saw this week's priest nearby, walking slowly back and forth as he read his breviary. Having nothing else to do, I brought the coin over to him.

"Here's a penny for luck," I said as I held it out.

His eyes twinkled.

"There's no such thing as luck," he said. "But I'll be happy to have the penny."

That caught my attention, and I took a closer look at him. The missionary priests were practically interchangeable to me; they wore their long black habits, and they no longer looked like people—they weren't regular people anymore, they were priests. But this priest was only a young man, and in spite of his smile, he looked exhausted. He had flown in that morning from Oklahoma City, and he would fly out again in another few hours. He spent half his life crammed into small commuter jets on monotonous airline flights.

While other men his age were waxing their cars and taking out girls, this young man was spending all his time bringing the sacraments to congregations like ours. And what could we offer in return? We didn't have the money to provide a pretty church. We barely had the money for his airfare. He lived out of a small suitcase, and the nicest thing he owned was his breviary. No wonder he was happy to have the penny.

I watched him walk away, turning the pages of that breviary as his lips moved silently to the ancient prayers. It hit me why he was doing that work on his feet. If he sat down, he would be asleep in seconds.

He's telling the truth, I thought with a sudden flash of insight. *He doesn't believe in luck. No one chooses a life this hard if he believes in luck.* And in that moment, my small, lonely, bitter world stretched and became a little bigger. I wasn't quite the same person I had been, thanks to that young priest.

And a decade later, when Joe and I got married, he officiated at our wedding.

So now, as I was falling asleep again, a real author with a real book contract, I gathered peaceful, happy thoughts to myself as I snuggled down into my pillow.

We're so lucky, I thought. *Except, there's no such thing as luck.*
There's no such thing as luck.

CHAPTER THREE

A few days later, Elena was sitting on a high stool at the kitchen counter, talking to me while I cleaned the kitchen. Listening to Elena talk was an occupation that demanded just as much energy as the cleaning. An Elena talk was a rapid-fire barrage of new ideas, and I enjoyed it every bit as much as she did.

Just now, she was educating me in popular culture.

"So, I read an article about the Lord of the Rings actors," she said. "Did you know they all got the same tattoo? Even Gandalf!"

"You're kidding!" My imagination tried to produce images of Gandalf with a tattoo. Nope! I couldn't do it.

"High school and college girls pick Orlando Bloom as the actor they'd want to date," Elena continued. "But women your age pick Viggo Mortensen."

"My age?" I inquired, still struggling with the tattoo.

"Well, you know, old women. The ones out of college."

"Old! Okay, got it," I said. I gathered up the breakfast dishes and ran a sink full of suds.

"So, anyway, the article said Elijah Wood is most popular among preteens and thirteen-year-old girls. That's so mean! Think how he must feel. I'll bet they tease him for it. And anyway, I don't think it's fair. *I* think he's really cute."

"Hmm," I said as I scrubbed oatmeal out of bowls. "And you're— how old?"

"Thirteen," Elena replied. "Hey!" And then she laughed. "Oh, well, I'll bet I'd think he's cute anyway. But it's a shame! The article said he's a *Kettenraucher*."

"A *Kettenraucher*? What's that?"

"I dunno," Elena said, helping herself to some Hershey's Kisses. "I don't know that word in English."

Languages have always been a passion of mine, and it doesn't matter much to me which one I'm learning. It's the thrill of absorbing new structures of thought that I love, the thrill of matching a familiar idea to a new one. It's all those beautiful new words to pick up and marvel over, like ocean-washed seashells on a beach.

Like *Kettenraucher*. As I wiped the kitchen counter, I took the word apart in my mind. *Ketten*. My imagination showed me steel links, rattling together and making metallic music. *Raucher*. Now my imagination sent me chimneys, incense holders, and spicy, heavy meats.

"*Chain smoker!*" I cried, and I felt that little frisson of joy that comes from seeing something ordinary from an entirely new point of view.

"Whatever," Elena said as she dropped a handful of candy wrappers onto the counter. "Anyway, *I* think he's cute, and so do all my friends."

"Speaking of which," I warned, "you'd better get to packing." And Elena, who did nothing by halves, flung herself out of the room and up the stairs, yelling for her sister in a messy mix of two languages.

The summer was ending, and Valerie and Elena were getting ready for another academic year. September had just started, and tomorrow afternoon, my girls would be headed back to school. I felt wistful and a touch melancholy at the thought of the quiet days ahead, but the girls were feeling no such pangs about leaving me.

All that day, the house was in an uproar. The old Dalmatian saw suitcases come out of the closet and grew nervous and started licking his paws. The old black cat assessed the situation and got out of the way. Late that afternoon, I found her curled up in a patch of sunshine in the garret room at the top of the house.

"Where did that stack of photos go? They're for the pinboard on my locker."

"You know we still need to go to the store, right? I need refills for my pens."

"Oh, no! We forgot to sew my name into my new shirts! Mom, can you help?"

"Where did my sour straws go? Did you eat my sour straws?? I swear, if you ate my sour straws—!"

By dinnertime, the suitcases were full, and only a couple of piles of clothes still waited next to our German washer. No matter how rushed we might feel, there was no hurrying that washer. It would get to those clothes in its own sweet, leisurely time.

I was sitting on the couch in the living room, sewing laundry labels into things, when Joe came home. I heard the front door open downstairs. Only one of the many oddities of that house was the fact that the living room was on the second floor.

Joe appeared at the top of the stairs, unknotting his tie. "They threw me out," he complained. Behind him, from the kitchen below, came the clatter of metal pots and the sound of girlish chatter.

"They wanted to make dinner," I explained. "Alone."

Joe paused, his tie still half undone. "Um . . . Do we know what it is?"

"I think it's going to be spaghetti."

"Oh, good!" he said, resuming work on his tie. "It's hard to mess that up."

As if in answer, a loud crash sounded from the kitchen. I dropped my sewing.

"Is everything all right?" I asked.

"Don't come down! Don't come down!" called Elena's voice.

"Just a teeny situation," added Valerie's.

And then both voices joined in shrieks of laughter.

A few minutes later, the girls called us downstairs and ushered us to the table, where four green salads waited in bowls. The spaghetti was excellent, and Joe and I refrained from asking if any part of the meal had landed on the floor.

"Gotta finish packing!" Elena cried, darting up from the table as dinner drew to a close.

"Cooks don't have to clean up!" Valerie reminded us joyfully as she followed her sister up the stairs.

Joe and I stayed behind to face the kitchen, which looked as if it had never been clean before in the history of the world. Towers of pans and bowls created their own skyline on the counter, and red splotches accented the tile on the walls. Not for nothing do they call that tile a backsplash.

"Did those two make another dinner that we don't know about?" Joe wondered mournfully.

The next day, we drove Valerie and Elena back to school. The whole trip was one long, animated gossip session. It would have been easier for Joe and me to follow if half the girls hadn't had overlapping names.

"Wait!" I said. "Is that the Gabrielle who slipped on the grass last year and dislocated her thumb?"

"No, no!" Elena replied. "You're talking about Gabrielle Theiss. This is Gabrielle Hermann, whose brother Timo is the sailing instructor."

"Okay . . ."

"You remember," Valerie prompted. "You know about Gabrielle. She's the one with the baby brother who hit his head on the—"

"Frau Hermann is hilarious!" interrupted Elena. "Gabrielle told me she sat the kids down one day and told them she'd read an article that teenage boys think about sex every seven seconds. And she says, 'I want to talk to you all about this,' and the girls, you know, they're giggling, but the boys are just *bright* red, just staring a hole through the wall like they're getting tortured. And Frau Hermann waits, but they don't say a word, so she says, 'Timo? Matthias? Well, what do you think?' And Matthias jumps up and says, 'I am *not* having this conversation,' and he bolts out the door!"

That made me laugh. But then I registered something unusual. Both girls had actually stopped talking. I glanced at the backseat and found that they were looking at me expectantly.

"Well?" Elena prodded.

"Well what?"

"Well? *Do* boys think about sex every seven seconds?"

Joe flicked a glance at me out of the corner of his eye, but I knew he wasn't about to field this one. I thought for a minute. It was my policy to try to give a good answer to every question, if only so that the girls would keep asking me things.

"Think about Matthias's reaction," I suggested. "Think about what the boys did."

There was a pause. Elena said, "I don't get it."

"Well," I said, "did they deny it?"

"Criminy! You're right!" Valerie said. "If it was wrong, they would have just *said* it was wrong. They would have said, 'Hey, Mom, that's stupid.'"

"So it's true?" Elena said. And she and Valerie burst out laughing. "Oh, I can't *wait*," Elena said, "I can't *wait* to tell Gabrielle!"

We drove through massive Cologne, over the wide gray Rhine River, and took the turn off the highway onto curving country roads. Once again, we threaded our way along the steep little street—more of a driveway, really—up to the top of the hill.

"Once, Mona and I sneaked outside after lights-out," Elena told us as we were walking up to the dormitory, "and we surprised a hedgehog on the side of this steep part here. It rolled up into a ball, and the next thing we knew, it rolled out of sight! We could hear the poor thing squeaking all the way down the hill. Hey! Hallo, Andrea!" And Elena went racing off to give one of her friends a hug.

As Joe and I lugged suitcases and boxes from the car to the new dorm rooms, throngs and knots of girls swept by and robbed us of one or the other daughter. Then, a few minutes later, another little crowd would sweep by and bring that daughter back again.

"This is Birgit," Valerie announced. "Birgit, *meine Mutter und Vater*," and our hands were shaken, and German sentences whipped by our ears faster than our brains could decode them. Joe and I did our best to look knowing and thoughtful and not make too big a fool of ourselves before Birgit and Valerie headed off down the hall together and we could sigh in relief and recommence lugging.

"It's really impressive," Joe said. "I mean, I *know* they speak great German now, but here, you really get to see what that *means*."

I watched my two girls, happy and animated, chattering away with their friends. *My daughters are popular*, I thought in amazement. *They are actually popular at school.* I realized that even if I told them what school had been like for me—about how it had felt to be the school freak for years—they wouldn't be able to understand.

That was a strange feeling for me, both happy and sad.

Finally, the last bag was up in the room where it belonged, and Joe and I felt the welcome needlessness of our presence. So deep were our girls in catching up with their friends that they had to make an effort to remember we were there.

First, I went to Valerie's room and hugged her good-bye.

"Look after yourself, Mom," she said with her usual wisdom. "And hurry up and send me that new chapter."

Then I made my way down to Elena's room and hugged her.

"I love you, Mom," she told me. "Write lots!"

"And you will, too, won't you?" Joe said as we walked to the car. "Write lots, now that they're back at school."

I gave a little sigh of happiness.

"I certainly *hope* so."

The atmosphere of the house reverted to quiet. The cat moved back down to the living room sofa. The dog caught up on his rest. I missed my girls, but I had a new youngster to worry about now: Paul, a woodcarver who lived in the Middle Ages in the Highlands of Scotland.

> There was a fragile quality to his hands as they turned the wood. They were bone-white, the fingers long and slender. There was a fragile quality, too, to the hunch of his lanky shoulders. Shaggy black hair fell into his face as he bent over his work.

Like the changeling child of my own early years, Paul was an outcast. He was carrying a terrible secret. His kind—the werewolf kind—kill the people they love . . . if they aren't killed first, that is.

When the first free weekend of the school year came along, neither one of my girls came home. Elena wanted to go stay at her friend Mona's house, and Valerie went home with her roommate.

"You understand, right, Mom?" Valerie said, sounding a little worried. "Hey, you just had us for a whole summer."

"No problem," I said. "Dad and I are happy that you like to spend time with your friends. That's what growing up is all about."

"Okay," she said. "And by the way—if that woodcarver's story doesn't have a happy ending, I'm going to be really upset."

Aha! My reader was hooked!

"You know I can't tell you how a story ends," I reminded her.

"I know," she said. "I'm just saying."

When I drove to the train station three weeks after that, I couldn't wait to see my girls. Even with a tragically afflicted werewolf for company, I had found six whole weeks without their lively chatter a little bit too boring and lonely. It would soon be over, though, and the hour-long ride back to the house would be an excited, colorful, jumbled download of everything that had happened since the very first second of the school year.

The problem wouldn't be getting those two girls to talk. It would be getting them to talk in turns.

I was waiting on the platform when they climbed down from the train. I waved, and they spotted me, but their faces didn't light up. Valerie's expression was distant and guarded, as though she were thinking private thoughts. Elena's looked like a thundercloud. She looked furious.

Uh-oh. Something must have happened on the train.

The girls were quiet on the walk to the parking lot. I was surprised at Elena's reserve. She usually had trouble getting a polite distance away from a crisis before she started filling me in on the details. But there it was—she was growing up and learning discretion. There would be no more comments about *that man over there* while he was still within earshot.

As soon as we get to the car, I thought, *she's going to launch in and tell me all about it.*

But Elena didn't. She put her suitcase into the trunk and sat down in silence. I pulled out of the parking space, and we made our way into traffic.

No stories. No chatter. No nothing.

I glanced in the rearview mirror. Each girl was staring out her side window, with no particular expression on her face. Had they been fighting? Maybe. But even if they were having an argument, silence wasn't their style. Toe-to-toe shouting matches: that was more what I was used to from them.

"Is everything okay?" I asked.

"Oh, sure," Valerie said.

"Why shouldn't it be?" said Elena.

"It's just that you're both so quiet."

A long pause.

I glanced in the mirror again. Valerie was staring at the back of the seat in front of her. Elena was glaring at the world outside her window and chewing on her bottom lip.

"Everything's okay, Mom," Valerie said in the same calm, patient tone of voice I had once used to soothe frightened preschoolers. I knew what that tone meant. It didn't mean things were okay. It only meant that she didn't like to see me worry.

"Elena, how was your birthday?" I asked next. Elena had had her fourteenth birthday a couple of weeks before. It still seemed strange to me to have the girls gone on big days like that.

I was sure that this question would break through Elena's bad mood. She had given me extensive rundowns of school birthday parties in the past. Germans love birthdays, and I was sure that the girls had gone all out to make hers special.

But today, Elena only shrugged. She said, "It was okay."

"Oh . . . Well, I've got a cake ready for you at home. We're going to have our own celebration."

I waited, but Elena didn't respond. Valerie spoke instead. "That's nice, Mom."

Puzzled and worried, I lapsed into silence, too. We were back on the highway now, climbing up the tall, steep cliffs that closed in the Mosel River valley. Two thousand years ago, the Romans had planted these dizzying slopes with grapevines. The Romans were gone, but the grapevines were still there.

"So . . . ," I said. "So . . . What's new at school these days?"

Another pause. Then Valerie spoke up. "It's about the same."

"Elena? What about you? What's new for you this year?"

One word from Elena: "Nothing."

Nothing? *Nothing?* Six weeks of new experiences, and that was all she had to say? This bubbly, sparkly chatterbox, who could turn a ten-minute trip to the store with her father into twenty minutes' worth of stories for me?

"You're sure nothing's happened? Not a single thing has happened?" I prodded, trying to joke. "Come on! Don't you have any stories for me?"

Valerie spoke up then. She volunteered a few observations about how her new classes were going. But what I heard from Elena was . . . nothing.

Elena was sick, I decided. That must be it. She was getting sick. She just didn't feel good. So, half an hour later, as we walked into the house, I laid my hand on her forehead.

To my surprise, she whipped around and jerked out of reach. "What are you *doing?*" she snapped.

"All I was doing . . . ," I faltered, cut to the quick by her reaction, "I was just trying to see if you had a fever . . ."

"I'm *fine*, Mom!"

She clattered up the stairs.

I turned back to the door. Valerie was standing there, looking at me with something like sympathy.

"She's kinda been like that to everybody."

"Do you think she's sick?"

"I don't know. I thought maybe she'd had a fight with Mona. I don't think their weekend together went very well."

Valerie stayed in the kitchen with me while I prepared dinner. Freed from her little sister's glowering presence, she loosened up and shared her thoughts about the new school year.

Valerie's all right, I thought to myself while we chatted. *It's just Elena. Something's wrong with her.*

Elena's mood didn't improve all evening. Even her birthday presents failed to put a smile on her face. And as for the celebration dinner I'd prepared for her, Elena barely touched it. All she did was move things around on her plate.

That night, I couldn't fall asleep. I lay in bed and worried.

This was a habit I'd taken away from my librarian years. Back then, every waking minute had been stuffed full of activity, but I had sworn to myself that I'd stay in touch with how my family was doing. So, after bedtime, I would lie awake and go back over the day. This was when I pinpointed problems and brainstormed solutions to try out the next morning. This was when I got all my best mothering done.

A good day could roll by in five minutes. But a bad day took time. This day had been so unexpected and awful that I went over it again and again.

Maybe it was housemother trouble. Elena often butted heads with certain housemothers. The mothering she did of the younger girls interfered with their own brand of mothering, and she was such a vigorous crusader against injustice that she often stirred up trouble for those authority figures who liked to play favorites. Elena despised bullying in any form. Under her care, the misfits and the weak girls had a chance.

And then there was the simple matter of culture shock. Elena might be a veteran of the school now, but that didn't mean she had let it change her character. I recalled a conversation with one of the housemothers during a visit to the school last year.

"Please talk to Elena about her negative behavior," she had said to me in crisp *Hochdeutsch*. "When we tell her a rule, she wants to know the reason."

"Oh," I had answered. "I'm not quite sure I understood that. So, you tell her a rule and she asks why?"

"Yes."

"And . . ." I could feel myself floundering. "And you said something about negative behavior, too?"

"Yes."

"Please, exactly what is she doing wrong?"

A dent had appeared between the housemother's eyebrows. "What I just told you," she had answered. "When we tell her a rule, she wants to know why!"

I had gasped, "Oh, I see!" And I did. But there wasn't very much I could do about it.

Now, as I lay there in the dark, pondering this and other possible explanations for Elena's unusual behavior, I heard small sounds coming from the other side of the living room. I pulled on my robe and went to investigate.

It was Elena. She was pacing the room in the dark, scanning the bookshelves by the weak light from her cell phone.

"What are you doing?" I whispered. "It's one in the morning!"

"I can't sleep," she whispered back. "I was looking for something to read."

I felt her forehead again. At least this time she didn't jerk away as if I'd tried to slap her. But it was cool.

"Are you sure you're not getting sick?" I asked. "Sore throat?"

"No."

I sat down and watched as she prowled the room in the dim light, bending close to read the titles of books.

"So, what's wrong?" I asked.

"Nothing."

Nothing? *Really?*

In the years I had known this child, I had heard many explanations of what was wrong. She had told me once, eyes filling with tears, that she was sad because her father would die one day. She had told me that she was afraid thieves would target her window out of every possible window in the house to jimmy open in the middle of the night. She had told me that crickets have been known to get lodged in people's ear canals and that we swallow eight spiders per year. Over and over, she had told me she'd had a bad dream. Cross an anxious, excitable temperament with an overactive imagination, and the result is that I had never *once* heard that nothing was wrong—

Until now.

"So . . . Really? Nothing's wrong?" I prodded. "Nothing at all? Everything's fine?"

"Mm-hmm."

I watched her continue to prowl.

"How's Mona doing this year?" I asked. "Is she managing to keep out of trouble?"

This was a blatant fishing expedition. Raising the topic of Elena's roommate was usually enough to start a good half hour of entertaining talk. Like Elena, Mona had a larger-than-life spirit, coupled with a lively distaste for rules and routine. That and her unsettled and somewhat tragic home life made her a great character for Elena's stories.

But not this time. This time, Elena just said again, "Mm-hmm."

She chose a book and went back to bed.

For the whole weekend, Elena stayed preoccupied and silent. And for the whole weekend, I worried. Each day, I alternated between giving her alone time to sort out her troubles and giving her opportunities to confide them. Valerie stayed away from her, too. On her own, Valerie was cheerful and relaxed, but she tensed up around her sister.

I heard no happy voices raised in chatter that weekend.

Silence was so unlike Elena that I could think of no precedent for it. Even when she had had the flu last year, she hadn't stayed in bed. She had continually bundled herself up and come to find me to tell me stories. But now she barely spoke, she barely ate, and she barely slept.

Elena was one raw nerve.

I'll wait until the next free weekend, I thought. *Maybe things will have worked themselves out by then.*

Three weeks later, my girls came home again. This time, they both seemed subdued and touchy. Elena was thinner. I could tell she wasn't eating well. Once again, I cooked her favorite foods, and once again, she barely touched them.

But at least this time, Elena had some stories for me.

She told me that she and Mona were storing beer on their windowsill. It was the perfect windowsill for it, she boasted, because no other window overlooked it. One of the older girls had brought her stash of beer to Elena and begged her to hide it. The housemothers knew there was beer in the dorm, so they searched high and low. One of them even stood right by the window. All she had to do was push aside the curtain! But she didn't. They didn't find the beer. They had no clue.

Needless to say, this story didn't thrill me.

"Why are you doing a thing like that?" I said. "It's wrong, and it could land you in serious trouble."

Elena rolled her eyes. "Oh, *please!*" she said. "Everybody does it."

Since when had this creative, confident girl cared about what everybody else might be doing?

"So there's this new housemother," she went on. "She's really young, and she doesn't have much of a brain. Maybe she's even, you know, a little *behindert.*"

I did know. That was the German word for *disabled.*

"So anyway, her door was open," Elena said. "So Mona and I sneaked into her room and read her diary."

I frowned. "What did you do a thing like that for?"

Elena shrugged. "Why not?" she countered. "She shouldn't have left it where we could find it if she didn't want it to get read. Anyway, turns out, she has this huge crush on this guy in the choir, and all the way through the diary, she calls him her *bunny.* Can you believe it?" She laughed. "'My *bunny!*'"

As laughs went, it wasn't very nice.

"The French call each other little cabbages," I pointed out.

"That's stupid, too," Elena said. "So, Mona and I followed her around, and we kept talking about bunnies. 'Am I your *bunny*? Can I be your *bunny*?'" Elena giggled again. "And finally, this stupid woman figured out what we were talking about. She busted out crying, and she ran out of the room! Can you believe it? Bawling like a baby!"

I turned around and stared at Elena. She had many faults, I knew that perfectly well, but cruelty had never been one of them. Weaker characters had always flourished around Elena: she sheltered the loners, and she tutored the slow ones.

And now, here she sat, this warmhearted, idealistic girl, telling me about a heartless prank.

"Elena!" I said. "How *could* you?" And I really meant it. How was this even possible?

Elena's mouth set in a hard line.

"She's a housemother. She deserved it!"

I saw the look in my daughter's eyes, and God help me, I understood. I had seen that look a thousand times in my own mirror. The jaded, bitter look of the changeling child stared at me out of my daughter's face.

Elena's world had blown apart.

"Elena! What's wrong?" I said. "There's something wrong! You can tell me."

"You mean, *besides* the fact that the school is hiring *behindert* housemothers to look after us?"

And Elena walked away.

Several weeks later, I got a phone call from the boarding school, but when I answered, I didn't recognize the voice. A very polite-sounding young German woman was on the line, speaking in English.

"My name is Anna Anton," she told me. "I am in the twelfth class at your daughters' school."

"Hello, Anna. I think I remember you. Didn't I get to meet you last year?"

"Yes," she said, sounding a little pleased and relieved, but still very serious. "My call is because . . . I am the *Tischmutter* at Elena's table."

Tischmutter. That meant *table-mother*, the student who was in charge of making sure the younger girls ate a good meal.

"I am worried about Elena," Anna went on. "She doesn't want to eat. She is sick all the time."

"Yes," I said. "I've been worried, too." And that question dug into me again: *What* was wrong?

"I am afraid," Anna said, "that Elena doesn't want to live."

WHAT??

I was out of the house ten minutes later. I drove all afternoon to get to the school. I met with the housemothers. I met with Sister. And then we all met with Elena.

"Hi, Mom!" she said as soon as she saw me. "What are you doing here?"

In light of this scary phone call, I tried to see my daughter with new eyes. Yes, Elena was thin. But then again, she'd always run a little thin. She hadn't grown a single centimeter all year. But she looked more relaxed than she had the last time I'd seen her, and when she heard why I'd come to the school, she laughed.

"What are you *talking* about?" she said with an amazed smile. "That's ridiculous. I'm fine!"

And when she left the room, I could see her friends surrounding her in the hallway: "Leni, what was it about? Are you in trouble? Can I help? Do you want some of my candy? Do you want to come on a walk?"

As I drove home through the darkness, I tried to decide what to do. Over the years, I had read a number of books and seen a number of documentaries about childhood trauma, and the victims had all said the same thing: "I needed professional help." This resonated with me now as I thought back on my own childhood. Professional help was probably what I had needed then to help with the rejection and depression.

"Something's wrong with Elena," I told Joe that night when I got home.

"She's different," Joe agreed. "But it's not like we can force her to talk to us."

"That's true. I think we need to get her to a professional."

So Joe and I talked about options, and the next day, I called the only psychiatric professional we knew of. His name was Dr. Eichbaum, and he was a child psychiatrist who came once a week to work with several of the girls at the boarding school. Elena had told me how he had counseled her friend Anita, who had had trouble eating due to stress. Finally, he had ordered Anita to be removed from the school, and he had sent her to an eating disorder treatment center.

The next time Joe and I went to the boarding school, we visited Dr. Eichbaum. His office waiting room was full of parents and patients, and he impressed us with his open, interested manner.

"It may be bullying," I told him.

"Except that she seems to be popular with her classmates," Joe put in. "And we thought it might be trouble with the housemothers, but we've talked to them, and they say everything's fine."

"I'll talk to the housemothers," Dr. Eichbaum said. "I know them well. There may be something they can tell me in confidence. And we'll bring Elena to the office here, away from the school environment. We'll run a full set of tests. It takes several hours, but you won't be charged my rate for it; I have my assistants do quite a bit of it."

"No, that's all right," Joe said. "Do whatever you need to. We don't mind the charges."

A week later, the phone rang. It was Dr. Eichbaum, calling with the results.

"We had your daughter here in the office for about three hours," he said. "I enjoyed meeting her very much. Elena is very ambitious." He chuckled. "And very dramatic! But then again, what teenage girl isn't?"

"And did you find out what the problem is?"

"Oh, there isn't really a problem here, Mrs. Dunkle," he said in a friendly tone. "This is just adolescence. Elena's fourteen now."

"Yes, I can understand that," I said. "I don't expect her to be an angel. We have an older daughter, you know, and when Valerie hit the teenage years, we saw some irritability there, too. But this seems different."

Dr. Eichbaum's voice radiated confidence and authority. "As intensely as Elena lives her experiences," he said, "I would expect her adolescent mood changes to be more intense as well. Don't be concerned, Mrs. Dunkle. Your daughter is completely normal. You have nothing to worry about."

Nothing to worry about. I let myself feel the relief of hearing him say that in his friendly voice. *Your daughter is completely normal.*

But if I hoped my relief would help me find a better way to deal with Elena, that hope turned into disappointment.

As the weeks passed, Elena's moods didn't improve, and Valerie wasn't doing much better either anymore. Each time they came home, they filled the house with fights and bitterness. And Elena's letters had already quit telling me stories. Now they quit coming altogether.

I still sent my stories to my girls, a chapter a week. But that became a new source of pain. Holt had bought four manuscripts from me now. I was a real professional author. But, far from being pleased at my new success, Valerie and Elena seemed to find it particularly galling. It was as if, in their unhappiness, they hated to see me feeling happy.

"I thought you wrote those stories for *us*, Mom," Valerie told me in a scathing tone.

"Well, of course I did, you know that. They're dedicated to you. They have your names in them . . ."

"Oh, sure. Big deal!"

I lay awake and puzzled over these grim changes and ugly comments. But I didn't talk them over with Joe anymore. A new commander had showed up. So horrible was that man that he became a legend at our base. Joe was now lucky if his workday stopped after a mere twelve hours. Some days, it went on longer than that.

But this new work schedule didn't seem to be something Joe regretted when the girls were at home. I could feel him withdrawing from them, hiding away in naps and computer time.

What was happening to us? What had gone wrong?

Intense experiences . . . adolescent moods. Your daughter is completely normal.

It must just be the school year, I decided. The girls were in high school now, in a foreign language, and for some reason, this year was just harder. They were getting burned-out. It would get better when they had their summer break. They could rest and recharge. They could re-center.

But when the summer break came, it brought us no relief. Valerie and Elena scarcely interacted. They were restless but had no energy. They found nothing interesting to do. Their rooms were little islands of boredom, and if they spoke, it was to fight.

One morning, I sat at the computer in the office and tried to write. Just last year, I had sat in this same spot and listened to happy voices laugh and sing together. "Write lots!" those voices had begged me . . .

Could that memory really be just one year old?

As if in answer to my gloomy thoughts, an argument broke out, rising in volume until I could make out the words.

"I *told* you! I told you not to mess with my stuff!"

"*Bitch!*"

"Hey!" I called. "Watch your language!"

I heard Elena stalk away and slam the door of her room.

I got up and went to the door that was still open. Valerie lay on her bed, reading a Stephen King novel. *Sie*, read the German title. Distracted, my imagination proposed different images to match it—the word could mean *it, her, them,* or *y'all.*

I shook off the linguistic puzzle and focused on what mattered.

"You need to not fight with your sister!" I said.

Valerie turned a page. "You heard her, Mom. She was fighting with me."

"I know that. But you need to think before you go answering and calling her names. She's your sister. She's the only sister you'll ever have!" I thought about how empty my life had been, with my own sister dead. "She's family. You're so lucky to have her!"

Valerie set down her book and held it open with one hand. "Come on, Mom," she said with devastating practicality. "It's not like Elena and I have a single thing in common. I don't like her, and she doesn't like me."

"But you look after each other!" I insisted. "Different or not, that's what sisters do. You're friends at school, right? You told me once that you and Elena had the same friends."

Valerie appeared to weigh her words. I had the sense that she was the older one here.

"No, we're not friends," she finally said. "Elena doesn't speak to me at school. And because she doesn't do it, her friends don't do it, either. None of them ever speaks to me."

"What? That isn't right . . ."

I thought about visits home in the past, when I'd heard my two girls merrily gossiping about their friends. It had been a long time since I'd heard talk like that.

But—not talking at all?

"That can't be right!" I said. "Not ever?"

Elena used words like *ever* and *never.* But Valerie wasn't my dramatic girl. Valerie didn't exaggerate the truth.

"We're not friends, Mom," she concluded. "I don't care if we're sisters or not." And she lifted the book and went back to reading.

I stared at the enigmatic cover. *Sie* in big green letters. *Her. You. It. Y'all. They.* That cover was short-circuiting my brain.

Without a word, I slunk back to my keyboard.

It wasn't right. It was wrong. It was terribly wrong. Moods were one thing, but not pushing away a family member—not shutting her out completely . . .

Your daughter is completely normal.

I sighed and went back to my writing.

An hour later, Elena emerged from her room, rumpled, sleepy, and cross.

"Hey, there," I said with false good cheer. "Do you want to read this new short story? I just finished it."

"Oh, God, Mom!" she groaned. "I'm not a child anymore!"

And she walked away.

I couldn't speak for the sudden pain that flooded through my soul. It wasn't just the hurtful words. It was her look—that lost, sick look.

The look of the changeling child.

Your daughter is completely normal.

Normal.

The new normal.

CHAPTER FOUR

When the summer ended, I tried to have meaningful talks with each of my daughters. But those talks didn't get very far.

"Are you sure you want to go back to the boarding school?" I asked.

"Why wouldn't I?" Elena murmured. "I need to go pack now." And she slipped away.

Valerie was a little more amenable to conversation, but when I asked her, she just shrugged. "It's as good as anywhere else," she said.

This time, I drove them to school alone. With the maniac commander running things, neither Joe nor his bosses could afford to take time away from the office. And that wasn't the only change, either. There was no happy chatter from the backseat this year. Each of my daughters had earbuds in her ears and was listening in silence to her own music.

I guess they don't need me anymore, I thought sadly. *They don't need to talk to me or ask me things.*

But that didn't turn out to be true.

A couple of weeks after school started, I got a call. "Hey, Momma, it's Valerie."

"Hey, hon, how are you doing? What's up?"

"Nothing," she answered. "I just wanted to hear your voice."

I waited, but Valerie seemed to have nothing further to add. So I filled her in on the small amount of news around the house—until the silence unnerved me, that is.

"So, how's class going?" I asked.

"Fine."

"Do you like your new room?"

"It's okay."

"How's that roommate of yours working out?"

"Okay, I guess. She doesn't spend much time in the room."

I paused to give Valerie space to talk. But once again, the space just filled up with silence.

"So, how's your sister?" I asked after a minute.

"Okay, I guess." Valerie's tone of voice indicated that she neither knew nor cared.

"Honey, what's the matter?" I said. "Something's wrong."

Finally, a little color came into the voice on the other end of the line. "Nothing," Valerie said, sounding slightly surprised. "Nothing's the matter, really."

"So, what's going on, then?"

"I just wanted to hear your voice. Bye, Momma."

I pondered the call that night as I lay in bed and reviewed my day. Maybe Valerie had had an argument at school. Maybe she'd gotten a bad grade and just needed a little comfort.

But a couple of weeks later, I got another call. And another one the week after that. Each time, they followed the same pattern—a pattern of emptiness.

"Please," I said. "Honey, please. I know something's wrong. Please just tell me what's wrong!"

And each time I asked this, Valerie seemed just as surprised. "Nothing's wrong," she assured me. "Don't worry, Momma."

But I did.

At least Valerie still called on occasion. I didn't hear from Elena at all. Gone were the days of gushing letters full of news. But when the girls came home for their weekends, I could see that Elena, too, seemed to be running down to a stop, like a music box that needed rewinding. She didn't flare up in anger or bitterness that often anymore. It seemed to be too much trouble. Her white, pinched face seemed to be set permanently in a look of disgust—my chatterbox girl who had once been so in love with life.

"Do you know what's wrong with Valerie?" I asked her.

Elena curled her lip. "All she does at school is sleep!"

"You mean Valerie doesn't go to class anymore?"

"She goes to class, comes back to the room, and sleeps."

This didn't sound good. Not at all.

"Honey," I said to Valerie, "Elena says all you do at school is sleep."

"So what? Momma, stop worrying!"

But I couldn't. Night after night, I lay awake, sifting through the evidence, pondering what I knew.

Your daughter is completely . . .

Well, fine. If my daughters were normal, then there must be something wrong with the school.

When I offered to take Valerie and Elena out of the boarding school, they both seemed glad to come home. Warmhearted and concerned, Sister tried to talk me into leaving them in the program there, but I could see from some of the housemothers' faces that they weren't sorry to see Elena go.

Maybe it was housemother trouble after all, I thought hopefully. *Maybe this will finally get better.*

Both girls seemed so exhausted and miserable that I decided against enrolling them in another school right away. They could finish out the school year doing correspondence classes at home. Valerie was so close to graduation that she needed only a few more credits anyway.

I imagined the three of us, sitting in the office together, my girls and me. Valerie and Elena would be at the big worktable at the center of the room, bending over their schoolbooks, while I sat at the computer desk and typed out my prose. The loudest sound would be the scratch of a pencil or the clicking of the keyboard. The mood would be quiet, absorbed, and content. How could that not be pleasant?

It didn't turn out to be pleasant. Not at all.

From Day One, the girls' correspondence-school lessons were miserable for all of us. Elena tackled her work with reliable perfectionism, but she was grim and war-weary, and her eyes were full of shadows. The only thing that remained of her former bubbly idealism was a harsh and constant sense of frustration that nothing ever went right in this world.

Valerie appeared brighter and more accommodating, but I soon learned that this was just an act. Underneath Valerie's surface of cheerful nonchalance churned savage, vicious anger. If I left her alone to do her work, she did absolutely nothing. Even when I nagged her, she did as little as possible.

"This is garbage, Valerie," I said one morning as I proofread an essay of hers. "Take it back and do it over."

"It's fine," she said. "I'm good with it. Send it in."

I grappled with my outrage and disappointment. This was my brilliant girl, my sunshiny baby. I had believed in her for years. My belief in her was so powerful, in fact, that it was almost a part of my religion. Valerie and Elena were going to be better people than I was—better in every way.

"Have a little pride!" I said. "Show what you can do!"

"I know what I can do," she said. "I don't need to show anybody. Why should I care what some mythical teacher in Washington State thinks about me? Seriously, Mom! What difference does it make?"

I couldn't even answer. Not to do one's best work—how was that even possible? I wouldn't have been able to do shoddy work if I'd tried.

"Do it over!" was all I could say. "And do it right this time, or I take away your phone, and you're grounded."

She snatched the essay out of my hand and sat back down at the worktable. Elena, doing her algebra on the other side of the table, didn't say a word, but I saw in her eyes the warm glow of schadenfreude. It seemed to be the only enjoyment Elena took from life these days.

Sighing, I set the grading folder aside and pulled up my email. A new message was waiting there, from "your biggest fan." Perking up, I opened the email. It included six questions about my goblin world and a pencil drawing of Marak, stripy hair and all.

You know, I thought, *that's really not bad!*

A warm glow of pleasure spread through me. It was obvious that my world really lived for this young woman, and her questions made the world live again for me, too. I clicked reply and started thinking through the answers, typing as I went:

> Concerning Question 1, about the cut on the goblin
> King's arm: it isn't a part of the marriage spells . . .

"Mom! What are you doing?"

Surprised, I glanced up. For a few minutes, I'd forgotten my daughters were there. Now I found that they were staring at me with accusing eyes.

"I'm just answering this reader," I said. But my heart sank.

Valerie and Elena hated my reader mail. I didn't bother mentioning it to them anymore, but they were good at catching me at it. Just now, they must have been able to detect a change in my expression. I must have looked . . . happy.

"It's a waste of time!" Valerie scolded. "You tell *us* not to waste time. Why do you want to spend all that time on strangers when you ought to be spending it on *us*?"

Because they're nicer to me than you are, I answered in my heart. *This is the only part of my day I still enjoy.*

But I didn't say that. Instead, I set aside the fan letter. Valerie wasn't right, but that didn't change anything. I couldn't enjoy it anymore with the two of them glaring at me.

"I don't get it," I said to Joe that night as he ate dinner. "Why do the girls hate my readers so much? You'd think they'd be glad people want to buy the books. Wouldn't you think they'd be glad?"

Joe had worked a very long and very horrible day. It was eight o'clock at night, and he had just come through the door.

"You could answer a fan letter in five minutes," he said as he spooned up stew. "Those things take you forever."

"Well, they ask such interesting questions," I pointed out. "Do you know, so far, no one's asked me a question I haven't already thought of and been able to answer. That's pretty good if you think about the fact that these readers have gone through the book over and over. One girl wrote that she'd read it twenty-eight times."

Joe ignored this happy bit of self-congratulation. Given the day he'd had, I couldn't really blame him.

"You should create form letters," he said. "You should let me take over. I could answer all of your mail in five minutes."

I left him eating, trudged up two flights of stairs, and pushed open the door of the garret room. Discarded stacks of games still congregated in this former playroom, silent witnesses to the fact that my children had once been close friends. Needless to say, no one touched those games anymore.

I pressed the power button on the old PC and waited a ridiculous amount of time for it to start up. My werewolf book was finished and would be coming out the following year. It was time for me to write something different. So, targeting the only reader I had left—Joe—I had decided to write a science fiction story.

I created a new Word file. It would be the future home of Martin, a thirteen-year-old boy. He looked like my husband had looked at thirteen, and he lived in a kind of parallel future. That was almost all I knew about him.

Now, I stared at the white Word page and waited for my imagination to take over. *What is Martin's world like?* I wondered.

I could answer all of your mail in five minutes.

I shook my head like an Etch A Sketch to reset the movie playing there. Not my world. *Martin's* world!

Vague patches of color began to blossom in my mind and block out the view of the white screen. Bright colors. Grape soda. Gummy candy.

Jell-O—that was it! Bright Jell-O colors.

Almost the first thing I see, when I start to work on a book, is patches or pools of color. These colors set the palette for the whole book. Kate and Marak's story had started with clear forest greens, along with deep-hued satin and the sparkle of gems. In spite of its gloom, it was a rich, sumptuous world.

My werewolf's world had been smudged and gritty, with gray peat smoke, flickering firelight, and the bright red of spilled blood.

Martin's world was going to be colorful, I could see that already. It was too colorful, in fact—highly artificial. It was clean, I could see that, too. I took a closer look into the patches of color. Now I could see bright plastic flowers stuck on window glass.

What are they doing here? I wondered.

It was spring. That's why those flower stickers were there. This world had no trees, no flowers, no bugs. That was all this world had left of springtime.

And now I could see brick around that window. A brick wall. A garage door. A front door. It looked like the door of an apartment or condo: a flat metal door with a peephole.

What's inside? I wondered.

A living room. A little living room. Here was the easy chair, here was the couch. And over here were stacks of papers to grade—I had so many papers to grade! And unfriendly, angry eyes.

Why should I care what some mythical teacher in Washington State thinks about me?

Again, I squeezed my eyes shut and gave a little shake. Not my world! I needed to see Martin's world! Hadn't this been easy once upon a time? Hadn't I had to fight to keep my dreamy head in the real world? Now I was having to fight to keep the real world out!

Slowly, the living room came into focus again. The biggest thing in it was the television. It was on. It had no switches or buttons. It couldn't be turned off. It was the most exciting thing in the whole boring room— the most passionate thing in Martin's whole world.

"The ALLDOG!" the television shrieked. "Large or small, sleek or fuzzy—all the dogs you ever wanted rolled into one!"

What does a computerized dog look like? I wondered.

Images flashed through my imagination. Exactly like a real dog, full of energy. Boundless energy and hopeful enthusiasm.

I needed some hopeful enthusiasm right now. I started typing.

A large object struck Martin in the chest, knocking his chair to the ground. Something heavy proceeded to dance on him. He gave it a shove and got a look at it. A big golden-coated collie was attacking him in a frenzy of affection, licking his face and yelping ecstatically.

I smiled. I loved that dog. I loved the affection.

"He's all yours, son," Dad said, helping Martin to his feet. "They had us send in your photo and a dirty sock and programmed him right at the factory."

I laughed. It made sense, practically speaking. But it also tickled my fancy.

> The collie, unable to contain itself any longer, began swimming forward on its belly. When its nose rested on Martin's sneaker, it toppled sideways and began running in place. Its warm brown eyes never left his face for a second.
> "'The Alldog,'" read Martin's little sister Cassie, "'is the perfect pet and particularly good with children. Do not place your Alldog in a strong magnetic field. Some assembly required.'"

"Mom?" came the voice from downstairs.

It was Valerie. But Valerie and Elena had had me all day, and they had snapped at me all day. Surely I could have a little time to myself. I kept typing.

Now I was in Martin's room, and he and Cassie were talking, but things weren't so happy anymore. Martin didn't like his dog, no matter what kind of dog it changed into. It kept switching dog breeds to try to please him, but nothing worked.

Because that's what warmth and enthusiasm bring you these days, I thought sadly. *They don't necessarily win you friends.*

Footsteps sounded on the stairs, and the garret door pushed open.

"Hey, Momma," Valerie said as she came in and sat down on the floor. "Did you ever play the guitar?"

"Um . . . No."

> A little cream-colored Chihuahua came crawling out from under the bed, whip tail curled between skinny legs. Its large ears lay against its round head

like crumpled Kleenex, and tiny whimpers rose from it at every breath. Its enormous brown eyes practically held tears.

I had it all: the feel of it, the sound of it, the way the room looked, the emotions, the next four or five paragraphs. But it was slipping. I could feel it slipping. I squinted with concentration.

"I used to play Gabi's guitar," Valerie said. "Do you know the band Echt?"

"Uh-uh," I muttered, still typing.

But the Chihuahua began to look more and more like Kleenex, and that looked like crumpled paper. Stacks of school papers gathered in drifts in Martin's room. I could see that they hadn't been graded yet.

"Before I left the school, I bought a Toten Hosen CD," Valerie said. "Do you know the Toten Hosen?"

Toten Hosen? Dead pants? A pair of black pants went walking through Martin's room, stepping over the stacks of school papers.

"Dead *pants?*" I heard myself ask. "What kind of a band name is that?"

"They were supposed to be the Roten Rosen, the Red Roses," Valerie said. "But a drunk fan called them the Toten Hosen."

Now the black pants walking through Martin's room had bold red roses embroidered on their pockets. The Chihuahua was a crumpled-up essay because *Seriously, Mom! What difference does it make?* The collection of words waiting to be racked into the next several paragraphs dripped and flowed into messy, sticky clumps of phrases with no meaning.

Then it was over. I was back in the garret room.

But did it even matter? Who would want to read this book, anyway? Joe didn't have time these days. And let's face it: my whole family thought that my writing was a waste of time.

Or maybe they just hated to share me.

That reminded me of my own mother, tucked away out of reach behind ramparts of college papers. She had never had time—not for anything.

I had certainly hated to share her.

So I closed the file. *Good-bye, Martin. I hope I see you tomorrow.*

And I said, "So, tell me about these Dead Pants."

can't stand it!" Elena wailed. "I hate my life!"

I'm not surprised, I thought. But I didn't say it.

Valerie had finished her few credits and was done with high school. Now Elena was stuck doing schoolwork by herself. Even though she didn't get along with her sister, she hated the loneliness even more. The girl who had once been at the center of an adoring throng now had not a single friend.

"Let's go to base right now," I offered. "We can enroll you today, and you can start class tomorrow. It won't take you long to make up the work."

"No way!" Elena answered. "The semester started weeks ago. They've all already made their friends. Nobody would talk to me."

"But Elena, it's a military base! Students move in and out all the time. New students show up at that school every single day and have to make friends."

"No!" And she reached for her stack of textbooks to emphasize her decision.

"Elena, think! How could it be worse than this?"

She flipped open her Latin textbook and pulled out a sheet of paper. "It could be worse," she said.

The frustration I felt drove me out of my office chair to pace the room. We had this same argument almost every day. I couldn't understand why Elena wouldn't see reason. She had started from a different culture at boarding school, for goodness' sake! That hadn't kept her from making friends.

I stopped by the bookcases and stared out the window. Valerie was strolling down our village street. At least Valerie seemed to be doing better. She was out and about every day now, making friends with all the village widows. They absolutely doted on her.

"Look at our couch potato," I said, "out soaking up a little sunshine."

"It's because she's smoking," Elena said with gloomy satisfaction. "You think she's walking to get fresh air and meet new people, but what she's really doing is smoking and then walking long enough that you can't smell the smoke when she gets home."

"Elena!" I said. "Why do you have to be so hateful about your sister?"

If there was one bad habit I despised, it was cigarette smoking. It combined the worst aspects of hedonism and self-loathing. Its contribution to society consisted of stains, stink, trash, and slow, unnecessary death. It was foul, that's what it was—foul!

And here Elena was, throwing around accusations about it. She knew how much I hated smoking!

"I'm not lying, Mom," Elena said. "She's stealing money to smoke. I'll show you."

She slipped out of her chair. A minute later, she was back with the euro coin holder in her hands. It had round slots to hold each kind of coin from every euro nation. We had bought it several years ago, when the euro first came out, so that we could collect the designs from each European Union country.

I opened it up. All the little change was there. But all the one-euro and two-euro coins were gone.

I set the holder down on the table and ran my finger around the empty circles. So many memories came up: checking change at the museums in Vienna, squirreling away coins in the bottom of my purse in Rome. They were happy memories from family vacations. This had been a family project.

Or had it been? Wasn't it really just me, admiring the interesting designs, wanting to do something as a family?

Check your coins. Which countries did you get? Oh, good, that's a new one!

At that moment, it all felt so trivial and silly, so sad, almost painfully embarrassing. There I had been, exclaiming over shiny, pretty coins. The Greek owl. The French mask. The odd Italian coin that looked like a skater wearing bricks strapped to his feet. They had meant something to this happy-go-lucky woman, out on vacation with her workaholic husband and two grumpy teens. But the coins weren't special. Not special at all. They were nothing but cold, hard cash.

"Look," I murmured. "The Portuguese euro is gone. When am I going to see another one of those?"

But it was a rhetorical question. I knew my coin-collecting days were over.

Valerie didn't deny it when I confronted her. Instead, she yelled at her sister. "You're such a little sneak!" she shouted. "You're such a hypocritical little shit!"

"You're a liar and a thief!" Elena shouted back. "How does it feel to steal from your own parents?"

My girls are amazing, I reminded myself as I lay in bed that night. *They're just going through an ugly stage. They just need time. They need the right guidance, that's all.*

I was spending a lot of time lying awake.

It wasn't just the smoking. Valerie had changed a great deal while she was at the boarding school. The darkness she felt on the inside was starting to show on the outside. She favored black nail polish and dramatic eye shadow. When she couldn't find the clothes she wanted in her closet, she raided her father's closet and started wearing his old black T-shirts.

Valerie was eighteen now. She had her diploma. It was time for her to figure out what to do with her life. But, no matter how nicely Joe or I tried to bring it up, we couldn't get Valerie to talk about the future.

"I've found you a list of good careers," Joe told her at dinner that night. "It's put out by the Department of Labor. Why don't you see if there's anything that interests you?"

"Sure," Valerie said brightly.

But the next night, when he brought it up again, she hadn't looked at the list. No, she hadn't lost it. It was right on her bed. She just hadn't found the time to get around to it.

"What was she doing?" he asked me after dinner. "What does she have to do?"

"Let's see. Singing. Listening to her music. She was out for several hours, walking." *Or*—I felt my heart ache—*maybe just smoking.*

"Well, she needs to sit down and do this." And before he left the next morning, he asked me to remind her about it.

I did remind her. Several times, in fact. "Do you want me to look at it with you?" I asked.

"No, Momma," she said. "I've got this."

But that night at dinner, she admitted that she didn't.

"What the hell is she doing?" Joe worried to me as we got ready for bed. "Why isn't this on her radar? I had my career figured out by the time I was a senior in high school."

"I don't know," I confessed. "I couldn't wait to leave for college. I had everything lined up, got myself into the school I wanted, won my scholarships, packed my room into boxes . . . I even gave my mother an inventory list so if she needed to look for something, she'd know which box it was in. But Valerie's not that way. I feel as if she breaks rules just so I'll ground her, as if that's what she wanted all along. Then, while she's grounded, she's as sweet and cheerful as anyone could want." I paused, trying to put my finger on what it all meant. "It's as if she makes a great child. But she makes a terrible adult."

"Well, she needs to get with the program," Joe said. "She's an adult whether she likes it or not. Get her to look at that list and think about colleges."

A day or so later, I noticed Valerie's hand. I stopped and took a closer look. It wasn't the alternating blue and black nail polish on her fingers. I was used to that by this time. Joe threw out her bottles of dark nail polish, but she kept getting her hands on new ones.

No, this was different: a round red scab. It looked odd. It looked . . . wrong.

"Valerie!" I said. "What happened there?"

"Oh, that," she said. "It's no big deal. It's just a burn." And then, looking oddly pleased: "It doesn't even hurt."

Doesn't hurt? What kind of burn doesn't hurt?

"Is that—Valerie, were you smoking? Is that a cigarette burn?"

"Yeah, Momma, but it wasn't me, it was Matthias. Just an accident—you know, talking with his hands."

"Oh. Okay . . ."

That afternoon, I went up to the garret room and tried to spend time with Martin. I stared at the keyboard and tried to go to his colorful, artificial world. But instead, it was another character my imagination kept showing me, a beautiful auburn-haired girl, richly dressed, with a Mona Lisa smile on her face. Her brown eyes were cool and worldly, but her fingers, quick and nervous, were ripping away at torn skin.

> It was an old habit. Miranda had hoarded her injuries even when she was very small for the pleasure of watching Marak heal them. Later, she had sneaked the nursemaid's scissors to administer her own cuts. It made her proud to bear pain without a murmur: she felt that she had mastered herself. Some days, when the household was particularly harsh to her, it seemed the only thing she could control.

I hadn't intended to write about this topic. It was Miranda's own idea. But I could pinpoint the exact moment when I had learned her secret. I was watching her carry on witty conversation with the goblin King. Her face was a perfect mask, smiling and beautiful. But down at her side, her fingers—those nervous fingers—

Miranda's a cutter! I had said to myself with that shock of true discovery that comes when a character does something unexpected. *Of course! She's under so much stress, she has to have an outlet. Pain brings her a little relief.*

And when I had said that—was I remembering myself as a little grade-school freak, tearing open scabs of my own?

> The pain was like a friend, sharing her silent vigil . . .

Oh, yes. I had understood.

Now I left my computer and went to find Valerie again. She was sitting on the couch, strumming her new guitar.

"So, about that burn," I began. And I looked at it again, the ugly maroon hole in the pale skin of her hand.

It was so round. So perfectly formed. So . . . deliberate.

"Yeah, Momma?" Valerie said with amiable good cheer.

I could ask. I could cross-examine her, make her tell me again and again. But would it do any good? And an image of the euro coin holder drifted through my mind: all those empty brown circles.

"I just wondered," I said. "Would you talk to somebody if I got you an appointment? A psychologist, psychiatrist, somebody like that?"

"Sure," Valerie said. "Will they give me pills?" And she left the room, singing softly.

I watched her go, both worried and comforted, while my mind chanted in a soft singsong: *Better to be on the safe side, the safe side, the safe side . . .*

It provided the background music to my plans.

I dug out the base phone book. There it was: the phone number to the psychiatric department at our local military hospital. Except for Elena's one visit to Dr. Eichbaum, nobody in the family had ever seen a psychiatrist before. I had no idea how it was all supposed to work, but it felt like a positive step.

Know thyself. Isn't that what psychiatrists and psychologists help us do? How could that knowledge ever be a bad thing?

"This is Mrs. Dunkle, and I need to make an appointment for my daughter Valerie to see somebody in your department. Yes, we're civilian dependents. No, she's over eighteen. Well, yes, I do know about the confidentiality rules. I'm not asking questions, just trying to get it set up. Yes, of course I'll hold."

Long pauses. Other questioners. The same questions.

"Yes, we are, we're civilians. No, she's too old for the child psychiatrist. I understand, I know you're busy with the war, but I think she may be cutting herself. Well, not cutting, burning . . . Yes, I can hold."

More blank spaces on the phone. More unhelpful questions and unhelpful answers.

"Yes, this is Mrs. Dunkle. Yes, I have our insurance card right here. No—really? You don't have a single appointment time this whole month? You mean you don't set time aside for emergencies? Well, yes—I mean no—I mean, it's not a *serious* burn, not this time, but it *could* be. Well, no, I'm not *positive* . . . No, no, I see your point. I do. Yes. Yes, of course I'll hold."

In the end, holding was all I could do.

Meanwhile, Joe continued to try to brainstorm ways to get Valerie involved in her future. "Maybe you should talk to the recruiter on base," he told her. "You could take the test, at least, and see where your aptitudes lie."

"Sure," Valerie said. "Why not?"

So the next morning, I drove her to base.

The recruiter was thrilled with Valerie. Here was a straight-A honors student—bilingual, no less!—as well as strong and healthy. Maybe Valerie was a procrastinator, but the recruiter wasn't. He soon had her finished with the basic forms.

Then Valerie knocked the top off the ASVAB test. The recruiter just gushed about her score. Joe was pleased. Even Elena was impressed. And Valerie seemed as serene as always.

"But do you want to do the Air Force?" I asked her that night. "It's a lot of structure."

"I can give it a try," she said.

I let Valerie's calm reaction comfort me. It seemed as reasonable a plan as any. Since she was so hazy on what she wanted out of life, maybe a few years in the Air Force would help her focus.

Then her recruiter upped the ante. He signed her up for the language training program at Monterey Bay. That took away my sense of comfort. I had been through the pressure cooker of intensive language programs, but Monterey Bay was something else again. It just didn't sound like the right place for my easygoing daughter.

"Are you sure you're ready for that?" I asked her. "That program is a killer! Long, long days, hard work. You'll really have to toughen up to get through it." *No more lazy days with the guitar*, I thought to myself. "It's just—I'm not sure it's for you, Valerie. Do you even *want* to do it?"

"Sure, why not?" Valerie said with even-tempered carelessness. Then she wandered off to listen to her music.

When Joe came home, I called the girls for dinner. Valerie came downstairs, humming. Her long, straight brown hair hung like satin over her shoulders, down to her ripped, ragged black shirt.

She had covered the backs of both hands with third-degree burns.

If my life really is going to flash before my eyes as I die—if every single memory of my life will play out again as it dissolves into a gentle mist of nothingness—then I think this moment will be the very last one to go. Not the first time I held my babies. Not the day I first met Joe. Not the news that my books were sold, or the first time I held a copy in my hands.

This moment. Because it changes everything.

Valerie had literally decorated herself with burns: *decorated*, like some mad, evil artist. The suppurating red dots had something of the style of henna tattoos. They were like flourishes from Persian art.

She couldn't seem to understand why we were so upset. She herself seemed to find them thrilling. It was as if these sores were not injuries she had inflicted but messages that had emerged from deep within. Their mysterious patterns seemed to reveal to her an unexpected ability to find beauty in pain.

Only one good thing came out of this horrific damage. At least now I was able to get her an appointment with the psychiatric staff.

"They put me on drugs," she said as she came out to the psychiatric waiting room. She waved the paper at me. "Zoloft!" she said, smiling.

I smiled back. Zoloft is an old family friend.

Before our children were born, Joe and I didn't have a single argument. He was witty and funny, and the two of us were madly in love. But when two small children came along to add their unpredictable demands to our days, Joe's personality seemed to change. He became a coiled spring. He simmered with anger. And we never knew when that anger would erupt.

It wasn't as if my young husband was abusive or controlling. He wasn't trying to scare me, and he didn't. I found Joe's outbursts more of an annoyance than anything else. To me, they were a breakdown, a loss of control.

But the little girls found his yelling episodes terrifying, and that upset all of us.

"I'll fix it," Joe said whenever his temper got away from him. "There's nothing to say. I'll fix it." And if he could have, he would have. He tried even harder to keep control—which only wound the spring even tighter.

One morning when Elena was about eight years old, Joe stopped by my office at the library. In his hand was a plain brown paper bag.

"Do you want to go have lunch?" I asked, reaching for my purse.

"It's from the doctor," he said.

I looked in the bag. It was full of Zoloft samples.

"We were talking about my chest pains," Joe explained, "and the doctor asked about my stress level. I started to tell her about the projects we've got going on right now in California. And then she said to me, 'Are you happy?'"

I looked across the desk at my husband. Joe didn't look happy. His mouth clamped shut in a tight line, and his eyes flicked around my office as if he were hunting for the source of an aggravating sound. His knee bounced in a nervous tic, and his fingers drummed on his pants leg. He kept picking things up off my desk, turning them in his hands, and putting them back down again.

"Well?" I said. "What did you tell her?"

"I said, 'My wife asks me that all the time.'"

I reached into his paper bag and pulled out one of the sample packs of Zoloft. It wasn't a drug I'd ever heard of.

"This says it's for depression," I said. "You don't look depressed to me."

"I told her I get angry all the time, and she said, 'I think you have anxiety problems.' This stuff also helps with anxiety."

Anxiety? A light bulb seemed to blink on in my brain. I said, "That actually makes a lot of sense."

So Joe decided to try the Zoloft. We agreed that he could stop at any time. He washed one down at the water fountain on the way out of the library, and I went back to work.

Saturday morning two days later, I was in the kitchen making a cake. It was a chocolate cake. I was beating the frosting. Joe wandered into the kitchen and sat down to watch me. After a minute, he started talking.

"Did you ever have a crush on an actor when you were a kid?"

I kept beating the chocolate. I held on to my poker face.

Okay, I thought. *This is weird . . .*

Because back then, my husband didn't just stop by to chat. Every second of his day had a purpose. He got upset if we were five minutes late to a party. He went to work even if he was almost delirious with fever. He had rearranged his cubicle so that his coworkers would stop saying good morning to him. "Do they think I have time for that kind of thing?" he had fumed.

And yet, there he was, this type A workaholic, sitting at the kitchen table, watching me frost a cake and asking about celebrity crushes.

It was the beginning of something wonderful.

Thrilled at the change he felt, Joe started telling me over the next few weeks what life with anxiety had been like. It had been shameful and isolating. The more he'd tried to control it, the worse it had become— because how can you clamp down on a feeling?

"I was always either angry, about to get angry, or coming down from being angry," he said. "The happiest part of my day was my commute to work."

But Zoloft had changed that almost overnight. It was like a puzzle piece that exactly fit whatever was missing in his brain. Years later, I heard him tell a relative, "I spent two days worrying that I was going to lose my personality. And I've spent the rest of my life afraid I'll get it back."

So now, as Valerie waved the prescription at me from across the psychiatric waiting room, I couldn't help but feel relieved.

Maybe it will fill a chemical need for her, just as it did for her father, I thought. *Maybe it will ease the stress she's feeling.*

I called up the recruiter when we got home and let him know that things weren't looking good for Valerie's Air Force career. But the recruiter got on the phone with Valerie and told her not to worry. Burns or no burns, Zoloft or no Zoloft, he knew just which doctor would sign the paperwork to get her into the service.

"Sure," Valerie said cheerfully. And then she hung up the phone and went off to play her guitar. But she was looking less and less like a successful recruit to me. People gasped and stopped talking when she walked by.

"I hate it," Elena told me after Valerie left. "I hate the way people stare at her now. Did you see how she's scribbled words all over her other pair of jeans? I walked by her room last night, and she was working on them with a pair of scissors. 'I'm customizing them,' she said."

Elena had started volunteering several afternoons a week at our local military hospital, welcoming the wounded soldiers and working in the emergency room as well. Her supervisors loved her. She was a natural, they said. She loved the work, and her sense of compassion began to revive.

But now that Elena had a life again, she also had something to protect.

"The people at the hospital think I'm an only child," she confided to me. "They don't even know I have a sister."

My heart sank. It did that a lot these days. I could actually feel it sink. I could feel the weight of that heart pull down my shoulders and bring my chin slumping toward the floor.

My girls are amazing, I said to myself. *They will be better people than I am.*

But that wasn't the message that came from my heavy heart. It whispered that something here was very wrong.

I went upstairs to find Valerie sitting on the living room couch, strumming her guitar and singing softly. Valerie had a lovely voice, husky but clear. When I looked at her, I could still see my own beautiful daughter, even under her thick black eye shadow and ripped clothes and angry scabs. But when I sat down nearby with a stack of Elena's correspondence school papers to grade, and I was feeling Valerie's presence rather than looking, I had the sense that my own child sitting in the room with me was almost a ghost.

Valerie had emptied out. Her lovely voice had lost its color. Something had eaten the life out of her, a shadow that clung to her and crippled her. It was rising to the surface through her sliced clothes and punctured skin.

"I dreamed I burned myself until I was ashes all over," she told me a few weeks later, and I felt the hair prickle up on my arms.

"Did you tell the psychiatrist that?" I asked.

"Yep," she said. "That's why he upped my Zoloft this time. That stuff doesn't do shit."

In fact, in some weird way, Zoloft seemed to have taken the brakes off. Now, Valerie was even more careless in her dress and language. She had even less interest in the future.

That night, she burned a smiley face into her shoulder.

Dear Lord, what can I do? I begged. *Where is this going to end?*

Thank God for Elena, my completely normal girl. Her matter-of-fact bitterness began to feel like a comfort to me. Seeing how hard it was for me to get Valerie out the door to her appointments, she started helping me do the work of "minding" her.

"Valerie!" she yelled one morning. "You've got an hour before you need to leave!"

"Stay out of my business!" came Valerie's response from the depths of her room. She didn't raise her voice to me, but she felt no such need to coddle her father or sister.

"It *is* my business!" Elena answered. "I'm going, too. Wear something halfway normal this time so people don't stare at you."

"I don't give a shit if people stare at me! They can do whatever the hell they want!"

"Valerie! Language!" That was me, adding my ineffective two cents to the fray.

"I feel like we have to keep track of everything!" Elena told me angrily. "Valerie just coasts along because she knows we'll get her where she needs to be. *She's* the one joining the Air Force, but *we're* the ones doing all the work. I'm sixteen, and I feel like I'm thirty-five!"

"I know," I said, and I meant it. I had never felt so old in my life. My nights of restful sleep were nothing but a memory.

A tension-filled hour later, all three of us were in the car and on our way to the hospital. Elena was volunteering in the emergency room that day, and Valerie had another psychiatric appointment. As Valerie crossed the waiting room after this one, she was waving another prescription form.

"He told me I could take this whole bottle of pills," she gloated, "and it wouldn't even kill me!"

Well, isn't he a genius! I thought.

That was the day before the Fourth of July weekend. A colleague of Joe's had invited the whole family to a get-together. The next morning dawned sunny and breezy. All our friends were going to be there. Even Elena wanted to go.

But Valerie said she'd rather stay home.

I waffled, and Elena waffled. What kind of trouble would our black sheep get herself into?

"No, go on! I'll be fine," Valerie told us. "Jeez, Lanie, quit fussing! It's not like I'm twelve. I'll take a nap and listen to my new music." And when I still hesitated in the doorway, she said in a kinder tone, "Go have fun, Momma. You deserve it."

So we went.

At first, Elena and I met in corners every half hour or so to call home and assess. But as the beautiful day glided along, our worry ebbed away. Elena watched over the little children. I sat in a lawn chair in the shade and drank a glass of wine. Joe played raucous games of foosball with his colleagues. And by the time the sun was going down and we were toasting marshmallows with our friends, we actually felt peaceful and happy.

It's when you let down your guard that the ax falls.

The phone rang while we were on the way home. Valerie sounded hysterical. It took several heart-stopping seconds before I could make out the words.

She had swallowed the bottle of pills.

I don't know what I said or did. I can't remember getting home. But I can still see Joe's tense white face staring out over the steering wheel and hear Elena's voice from the backseat, sharp with stress. Most of all, I can hear Valerie's ragged sobs: "Tell them, Momma! I wasn't trying to kill myself! Remember? He said I could take the whole bottle!"

By the time we got through the hospital paperwork and could join our daughter in the ER room, Valerie was already asleep. The doctor had made her drink a mixture of charcoal, and it had stained her mouth and her teeth black. She lay tucked between turquoise hospital sheets, with her long toffee-colored hair fanned out around her. Under the artificial lights, with her pale face and black lips, she looked like something right out of a dream.

Like a beautiful monster.

Like a nightmare princess.

Like a postapocalyptic zombie Sleeping Beauty.

Elena sat between Joe and me, and she didn't say a word. I felt sure Elena was seeing familiar faces. She had worked so hard at the hospital to build her reputation of dependability and order, and she had given the impression that she was an only child. Now, Valerie's chaos had rolled right in like a tidal wave to embarrass Elena in her home away from home.

The three of us sat by Valerie's bedside in the ER all night long, watching the jerky sine waves of the heart and breathing monitors. Elena played with her phone. Joe barely spoke. I called the Air Force recruiter's answering machine and told him once and for all that Valerie wouldn't be joining the service.

Around three in the morning, a psychiatrist came in and roused Valerie enough to sign the intake forms. Our semiconscious daughter got wheeled away to the psychiatric ward, and Joe and Elena and I stumbled outside into the first pink flush of dawn.

"Yesterday, I felt like I was thirty-five," Elena said dully. "Today, I feel like I'm fifty."

She was sixteen—sweet sixteen. But it hadn't been that kind of year.

That afternoon, the three of us made the pilgrimage to the hospital again, this time to the psychiatric ward upstairs. There were heavy steel security-locked doors in front of us. Was this real? Was this a dream?

Did a child of mine really need this?

Then there was the long bare white hallway beyond, highly polished, absolutely clean. A little further, and Valerie stood with a group of other patients, all alike in their mint-colored hospital scrubs. Her long honey-brown hair was the closest thing to color and life in that sterile place.

Valerie saw us: one quick glimpse of her big dark eyes and pale oval face turned toward us, blurred slightly, like a reflection in water. Valerie saw us. And then she turned away.

"*We're* her family!" Elena snarled a few minutes later as we walked back out the double doors. "*We're* her family! She didn't even *want* us there!"

Dr. Petras, the child psychiatrist, had been called in to consult, even though Valerie was over eighteen. He was a young doctor with dark sympathetic eyes and a little Edgar Allan Poe mustache.

"Your daughter has borderline personality disorder," he told us. "I'd like to send her to a psychiatric institution in England if one of you can make the trip with her."

Joe nodded and glanced at me.

"Of course," I said. "I can go."

"But, for this borderline disorder," Joe said, "what's the prognosis? What's happening to her?"

"To be honest," Dr. Petras said, "it's not all that good. After a decade or so, some of the patients seem to age out of it."

A decade! Valerie? Our practical, levelheaded girl, the same young woman who had earned good grades in high school—in a foreign language? But there was no time to grieve. I had plane tickets to buy.

The ax had fallen—the new normal.

Valerie and I traveled together to the psychiatric institution in England. It looked like a country manor, and Valerie loved it at once. Celebrities were known to stop their globe-trotting and come here in order to rest up from their cocaine addictions. It was the kind of place that served its patients afternoon tea.

The next morning, I flew home by myself. I felt as if I were walking in my sleep. *There is no blueprint for where I am in my life anymore*, I thought. *There is no blueprint for what my family has become.*

Valerie stayed at the psychiatric institution for two months. Her psychiatrist there called me regularly to update me on her progress. He had that perfect educated Oxford accent that absolutely inspires trust. I felt better just listening to him, even when he didn't have good news.

"We're having some difficulty stabilizing her," he said. "She hasn't responded as well as we'd hoped to the new medication."

"Is there a special medication for borderline personality disorder?" I asked.

"Who told you she has borderline personality disorder?"

"The psychiatrist who saw her here, after the overdose," I said. "He told us that's what she had."

The British psychiatrist was silent for a moment. "I wouldn't go that far," he said at last. "No, I wouldn't go that far."

"Oh. What do you think my daughter has, then?"

"Depression."

And his perfect accent made the word sound almost jolly.

He was certainly right that they were having trouble stabilizing Valerie. I got a call from a staff member a few days later to inform me that Valerie had been cutting herself. She'd cut herself quite badly, in fact. Would I authorize them to take her to a hospital for stitches?

It was the full heat of summer, and all the windows were open. Like most German houses, ours had no air-conditioning. But when I heard this, I felt clammy and chill. I found the nearest chair and sank into it.

"How?" I managed into the phone.

"She's been using razors, ma'am," the staff member told me.

"But why—for God's sake! Why are you letting her have razors?"

"We don't like the patients to feel constrained, ma'am. We have better outcomes when they feel that we trust them."

"Yes, but . . . I mean . . . trust?" My mind boggled for a few seconds. "Look—can I talk to my daughter?"

Valerie must have been right next to the phone. "Hey, Momma," she said in her cheerful way. She sounded like she always used to—like my wise, practical girl.

"So, what's this about these razors?" I asked, as if she were the sane one here and it was the orderly who was crazy.

"Yeah, sorry about that, Momma. I was kinda bored. I got a teeny bit carried away."

"But, Valerie . . ."

I trailed off. What to say? How to reach her?

"So, it's not helping?" I finally said. "It's not helping, you being there?"

"I dunno." Valerie's voice still sounded cheerful. "That depends on what you call *help*. Anyway, it's kind of funny: the staff is freaking out. My therapist says they're afraid I'm going to kill myself."

I froze.

I felt as if some giant predator was hunting me, moving closer and closer. I could feel it, this huge invisible hunter. It was snuffling, turning this way and that . . .

I couldn't breathe. I had to hold my breath.

"I'm not gonna say I haven't thought about it," Valerie went on in that same breezy tone. "Sometimes, it really sounds like a good idea. But I've told the staff that option's off the table. I said, 'I would never do that to my mother.'"

I didn't answer. I couldn't answer. I couldn't speak for the lump in my throat.

"So anyway, I'll talk to you later, Momma. Love you! Bye."

I hung up the phone.

And I cried.

CHAPTER SIX

M rs. Dunkle, this is the school counselor calling. I'm worried about your daughter, Elena. She's a little underweight. Is she eating well at home?"

I pondered the question.

"No, I'm afraid she isn't," I said. "In fact, to be honest, I don't think any of us is eating well right now."

It was October, three months after Valerie's overdose. Elena was finally attending the high school on base. She had let me enroll her there as a junior when the new school year came along. And she loved it. Already, she had made good friends.

No, it wasn't the school that was the problem.

It was Valerie.

Valerie had come home at the end of August, and we had seen improvements in her outlook: she had voluntarily enrolled herself in university courses on base and was making As. She had also found a job on base. I was driving her there every morning and picking her up every evening. It was great to see her getting out of the house and staying busy.

But when Valerie was at the house, she kept to her basement room and avoided us.

This galled Elena. Once upon a time, Valerie had been her guide, the one she had looked to for guidance and help. Now, the gulf between them couldn't be bridged.

"*We're* her family!" Elena said to me day after day, her voice savage with anger. "All she does is go on about her loser mental friends!" But at the same time, Elena didn't seem to be entirely comfortable being Valerie's family.

"Do you have to *look* like that?" she yelled at Valerie as we drove home from the base. "Do you have to wear clothes that look like they've been in the *trash*? Did you see the way they all *stared*?"

Valerie snorted. "Like I give a rat's ass if they stare."

"*I* care!" shouted Elena. "I hate going anywhere with you. I don't even want people to know you're my sister!"

"I'm sorry Miss Neat Freak can't deign to acknowledge my presence," Valerie said. "Did I *ask* to be your sister?"

"Can we please just calm down?" I heard myself saying yet again, as I had heard myself say a hundred times before. And then, as the voices got louder, "Stop it! Stop it! Just—*please*! Just shut *up*!"

That night, again, I lay awake and promised myself—really *swore* to myself—that tomorrow, I would keep my cool and help my family stay balanced and cheerful. But by the end of the next day, all four of us were standing outside Valerie's bedroom door, and all four of us were shouting.

No wonder the school counselor was worried about Elena's weight.

"Elena's always been a picky, nervous eater," I told the counselor now. "She's such a perfectionist that even back in grade school, stress and nerves could choke off her appetite. She always had trouble eating breakfast if a big test was coming up, so I'm not surprised, with all the stress in the house, that she's having trouble now."

"But Mrs. Dunkle, Elena's quite thin," the counselor pointed out. "Stress is one thing, but she's less than ninety percent of the expected weight for her height."

Guilt flashed through me. Had I noticed this?

Yes, I'd known that Elena was thinner than the other girls in her class. But members of my family tend to run thin until old age, even though we eat everything in sight. I've always baked with butter, and I've always baked a lot, but I was still wearing a favorite high school skirt when I reached forty. And Joe, too, was practically a spaghetti noodle until he was in his thirties. He couldn't put weight on back in high school no matter how much he ate.

So it hadn't surprised me that Elena was staying thin. She seemed to be running true to type. But was she? Or was this something more serious?

"Elena has been slightly underweight ever since she hit adolescence," I said. "But her weight doesn't vary by much. It's not as if she does anything extreme. You know, I was worried about her, too, for a while—she seemed so nervous. But we took her to a child psychiatrist a couple of years ago, and he and his staff tested her extensively."

"What did you find out?" asked the counselor.

"Oh, that everything was fine," I answered. "There was nothing that teenage moods couldn't explain."

"Well, maybe you could encourage her to bring snacks with her to school," suggested the counselor. "If she's not eating well at home, maybe she can eat more here. She could stop by my office to have a snack. It's usually pretty quiet."

"Yes, I'd imagine that things are calmer there than they are at home," I said.

This may have been the understatement of the year.

That afternoon, when Elena got home from the bus stop, I tried to see her with fresh eyes. She was that same quick, nervous girl she'd always been. Maybe she was a little thinner this year, but her eyes were sparkling, and she still had a curvy figure.

"The school counselor called today," I said. "She's worried about how well you're eating."

"I have been pretty stressed," Elena admitted.

"What would you like to eat tonight?" I asked. "We'll eat whatever you want."

She brightened. "Could we order a supreme pizza? There's this pizza at the food court that I really love."

"No problem," I said. And we ordered supreme pizzas pretty often after that.

As the semester progressed, Elena stopped by the counselor's office frequently to talk and blow off steam, and whenever she did, the counselor checked her weight. Elena was consistently running about ten pounds below median weight for her age, but at least the numbers were stable, and they didn't fall into an unhealthy range. And Elena continued to do well in school and in her volunteering at the hospital, too. No longer did she wail that she hated her life. She was having real fun with her new friends. She was the most engaged she'd been in years.

But the stress in the house wasn't getting better. In fact, it was getting worse.

I threw the front door open one morning as Valerie came walking up the sidewalk to the house.

"Valerie! I was up half the night!" I said. "Where were you? I checked your room at two in the morning, and you were gone!"

"Oh, sorry, Momma! Rick was having a tough time, so he came by and picked me up and we sat in his truck and talked. He's been afraid ever since he was in the psych ward with me that they're gonna kick him out of the Air Force. Seriously, Momma, we were just down the street, just talking."

"But I called and called!"

"Sorry about that, I didn't have my phone with me. It's somewhere in my room."

I followed her down the stairs into the gloom of the basement. At one time, this had been a separate apartment, but the landlord had rented it to us along with the rest of the house. He had been apologetic about the scratched-up walls and battered and stained blue carpet. "I'll fix it up for you," he had promised.

But I had known Valerie would have these rooms. "No, please—it's perfect," I had told him.

Now, great drifts of Valerie's belongings covered up that stained carpet: crumpled stacks of sheet music, a broken coffee table, a metal coil of loose guitar strings, broken tubes of mascara.

"But I didn't hear it ring," I said. "If your phone was in here, why didn't I hear it ring?" That was better than saying what I wanted to say, which was *Why did you let me go through that, dialing your number over and over and hoping each time that I'd finally hear your voice?*

"It's on vibrate," Valerie said, scanning the rubble as she strode into the room. Her hiking boot landed on a music CD, and it gave an unmusical snap. "Oh, hell!" She stopped in the middle of the drifts of trash, gave one last look, and shrugged. "Anyhoo, it's around here someplace."

"But, Valerie, you can't keep doing this to me!" I said. "I can't keep losing sleep like that, I was so worried, I almost called the police! The other night, you *promised* me—you *promised* me! Besides, you were grounded."

"Oh, that's right!" Valerie said in a tone of discovery. "Still, it wasn't like I went anywhere fun. I was only down at the corner, Momma, really. We just talked because Rick's having a hard time—all we did was talk."

And the thing is, I believed her. I believed that Valerie didn't mean to cause me trouble and heartache. It was as if she had developed some strange superpower, some knack for creating chaos wherever she went.

She's backsliding, I thought. *She's losing the progress she made in England. We need to find a way to help her hold on to the ground she gained there.*

So I came up with the idea to send Valerie back to England for follow-up visits with her therapist. It was expensive, but if it helped her hold on to the progress she'd made with him, it would be worth it.

Valerie loved the idea, and the first couple of visits seemed to help. But then the sessions with her therapist seemed to get overshadowed by the partying she did with her psych-hospital friends. She came home from one visit sporting an eyebrow piercing. And when she wound up missing a flight due to a lost weekend in London, we called the experiment off.

That meant Valerie was back to regular sessions at the military hospital again. But those doctors moved in and out to support the soldiers downrange. Valerie had gone there six or seven times, and I didn't think she'd seen the same doctor twice.

We're starting all over, every time, I agonized. *Every two weeks, a new guy starts from zero. Maybe a German professional could help us. It's a shame Dr. Eichbaum is so far away.*

So I found Valerie a German psychologist. "How did it go?" I asked her afterward.

"Fantastic!" she said. "He told me there's nothing wrong with me smoking cigarettes."

"*What?* You've got to be kidding me!"

"No lie, Mom. He says smoking is only bad for some people. Since our family doesn't have any cancer or lung stuff in it, he says you can tell it wouldn't be a problem for me. It makes sense if you think about it. You know Grandma smoked forever."

"No, it does *not* make sense!"

I thought she must have misunderstood him, so I asked the psychologist myself. He was a little man with round pink cheeks and a bullet head and a habit of bouncing forward onto his toes as he talked, like an ex-gymnast. He smoked cherry-flavored pipe tobacco, a habit I might have found endearing if it weren't for the grave lecture he gave me on how to tell if smoking was right for your body type.

I declined to schedule another appointment.

That night, I once again lay in bed and worried. Valerie had lost her job on base that day, and Joe was so furious about it that he practically steamed. He saw her self-destructive behavior as a willful refusal to grow up, but I was sure it was something else.

She's sick, I thought. *She needs regular care. She's not going to get better if we can't find her the right professionals. Just the three of us, trying to guide her—really, just yelling at her—we can't make her well.*

Valerie needed careful, thoughtful, sensitive professional care from a psychiatrist and a therapist who could truly get to know her, just as they had done in England. It seemed like such a simple thing, the obvious first step. But I couldn't manage to find it for her here.

She could get it back in Texas, though.

I lay in bed and pondered this idea. It wasn't my first choice, but it had a lot to offer. Valerie could go to college back in our home city, and with our contacts in the area, we could find her great care. She still had friends in the area, too. We had a support network there. She just wouldn't have us. We wouldn't move home for another year and a half.

She needs a doctor more than she needs her family, though, I told myself. *All we do these days is fight, and that's just giving her a reason to backslide. Valerie seems to thrive on alienating her father and sister. We're all spinning our wheels.*

The book I had written about Martin and his computerized dog had just sold for a very good price. The whole family rallied around to take me out to dinner to celebrate. It was a chain restaurant on base: bright Mexican tiles and big American portions. In honor of my celebration, Valerie was looking less rumpled, and we were actually not fighting for once.

I glanced at Joe across the appetizers: *You bring it up.*

No, you bring it up, his eyes told me.

"Valerie, do you think you might want to try college back home now?" I asked. "You could start in January."

"I thought we were stuck here for another year and a half," she pointed out. "Dad's contract and all that."

"I'm talking about you going home first. Dorm life."

We discussed it as a family over our entrées while we ate my celebration meal. Perhaps it was the fact that we were out in public where no one could shout, but we actually had a reasonable conversation. Somewhat to my surprise, Valerie liked the idea. She liked it very much.

"I think it's time for me to grow up," she told us.

Over the next few weeks, Valerie began to make more of an effort in the college courses she was taking on base. This seemed to be a promising sign. She talked often about the move to Texas, and I found a great psychiatrist for her only a few miles from the dorms. Dr. Harris came highly recommended, and when I spoke to him on the phone, I felt better at once. He specialized in treating college students, and his mild, interested manner reminded me of Dr. Eichbaum. I thought he would be a good match to Valerie's laid-back temperament.

But as the weeks went by, Elena opposed the idea more and more strongly.

"She's tricking you, Mom," she said. "She doesn't want to grow up or get better or anything. She just wants to get away from us where she can fall apart without us bugging her about it. This is going to be a disaster!"

I sighed. Why was Elena always so ready to see the worst in her sister?

"I don't think it'll be a disaster," I said. "Remember, Valerie will have a very good support network there. And you know things aren't working out for her here. She needs the kind of professional help she can't get."

"She won't get it there either, Mom. She won't go."

"Don't you think you're being a little extreme? Valerie did excellent work with her doctors last summer. She's never missed an appointment."

"Yeah, and she did excellent partying with her psycho friends, too."

"Well, sending her to England alone was probably more temptation than most young adults could handle. Look, your sister is finally doing what we've been asking her to do now for a year: she's finally working toward a life goal. I have to show her that I trust her and respect her desire to improve."

"She hasn't improved, Mom," Elena said. "She's excited for all the wrong reasons. She just wants to get away from you, so she can go crazy without you calling her on it all the time."

"So, what you're saying is that she needs a psychiatrist," I said. "Again: This is the only way to get her one."

"It won't help. She won't go. This is going to be a disaster."

Typical Elena! I thought with a sigh.

Christmas came, and we flew back for our once-every-two-years trip to the States to visit our relatives. Then Valerie and I stayed behind in Texas for a week, getting her settled into her classes and dorm room. We shopped for practical organizers and nice dorm furnishings, and she and I had a great time.

It was fun to be with Valerie without her father and sister around. She relaxed and became sunny and happy again. And she really seemed to be committed to this. She even stopped smoking.

"Dr. Harris is nice," she told me after their first appointment. "He reminds me of my therapist in England."

This seemed like a particularly good sign.

At the end of the week, I flew back to Germany, almost buoyant with hope. A new year was starting. The old, dark year was gone. This was going to be a better year—better for all of us.

But it wasn't.

Almost from the moment my plane landed in Germany, I began to get bad news.

"I didn't go to class today, Momma. It's the crowds."

"You're—what? You're afraid of crowds?"

"They all stare at me!"

"But, Valerie, you used to say you couldn't care less! Did you tell Dr. Harris? What does he say?"

"He gave me new pills."

"But what did he *say*?"

"He said take them."

I hung on to hope wherever I could. Unlike Elena's gloomy predictions, Valerie was going to all her psychiatric appointments. And Dr. Harris was wonderful. He was seeing Valerie every week, and he had arranged for her to see a therapist twice a week: a psychologist who specialized in adolescent disorders.

"Valerie is a little chaotic right now," he told me when I called, but his tone seemed reassuring. "We just need to help her find her balance."

Comforted, I hung up the phone.

But the next night, another frantic phone call would come through: "I can't face the cafeteria. I'm living on microwave popcorn."

And the night after that, another one: "I hate the history professor. She glares at me when I come to class. I don't like to go to class anymore."

And another one: "I slept through my exam."

It was all very hard for me to comprehend. I, too, had had my ups and downs in college, but I had graduated in three years. Joe had had his ups and downs and lost weekends, too, but he had survived the pressure-cooker classes to get his engineering degree. Melting down was something one did at home—not when working on one's chosen future.

Still, it was time to face facts. Regular psychiatrist or not, this experiment just wasn't working—

This very expensive experiment.

"Valerie," I said late one night, "I think you'd better withdraw from class and come home." I always seemed to talk to her late at night because that was afternoon back in the States.

"No way!" she answered. "I'm not doing that."

"Well then, you'll have to find a way to make this work. Talk to Dr. Harris. You can't just not go to class."

"No, you're right, Momma. I can do this. I'll get it together. It's not like I'm not handling it, either—I have As in my other two classes."

"Good for you! You need to build on that success then."

And I hung up the phone and went to bed to stare at the ceiling, overwrought and jittery with stress.

I got no writing done anymore. I barely managed to push myself through my days, too tired to stay awake but too upset to go to sleep. I felt like a puppet, never knowing when I would be jerked up or down.

Then, a week or two later, a call came through from a number I didn't recognize. The voice on the phone was crisp and businesslike.

"This is Valerie's therapist."

And I could hear Valerie in the background, sobbing.

"Valerie has to go back into residential care for six months at least," the therapist told me. "She needs structure; she can't handle life on her own at this point. I've spoken to your insurance company, but they won't cover it."

"Okay . . . ," I said, faint from breathlessness. "Okay . . ."

Six months! Six *months* of care?

Valerie took the phone. She was weeping with shame and fury. "She's lying! Momma, I'm fine! I've got this!"

I knew which one of the two I believed.

"Honey," I said. "Honey, it'll be okay . . ."

"I won't do it!" she said. "I won't go back into treatment."

"But . . . But you loved treatment. You know you did."

Six *months*? Tens of thousands of dollars!

"This is bullshit, Momma! You don't need to pay for me to sit around and have tea on the lawn. I trusted this woman! I shouldn't have talked to her. She promised not to tell!"

Valerie's therapist took the phone again.

"Confidentiality is important," she said. "But I believe Valerie is a danger to herself."

A *danger* to herself? Sleeping through class was one thing, but—*danger*?

Stress crawled up and down my body like prickly-footed centipedes, tightening my shoulders and raising the hair on my arms, and I felt like that puppet again—punched, jerked around, completely helpless . . .

A *danger* to herself! A *danger*!

But Valerie refused to go into treatment. And because she was over eighteen, there was nothing I could do.

When I told Joe, he was pale from stress and grim with disappointment. "If she won't do what the doctor recommends, then she can come back here," he said. "She needs structure? Great! *We* can provide structure." And he drew up a daunting list of rules.

That was the end of the argument.

"Good-bye, Momma," Valerie said on the phone. "I'm not letting anybody run my life. I'm leaving Texas. I don't need this shit. I've got friends."

"Friends? What friends do you have outside of Texas?"

"Buddies from the forum."

"Valerie! You can't mean—from the Internet? You don't know anything about them!"

"I do, too. They're great guys. They came out to visit me. We went to the movies together."

I couldn't believe I was hearing this. It had to be a nightmare—one of the many nightmares I'd had this last year, where I was trying to reach her, trying to call out to her . . .

"Valerie, that's not knowing somebody!" I cried.

"I knew you wouldn't understand."

I took a breath and tried another tack.

"Do you even know where these great guys live?" I asked.

"Yep."

"Where?"

Please give me a name. Please, please! Something to go on . . .

"That's my business. Bye, Momma."

No, this wasn't happening, not in real life. This was like the script from some hideous crime forensics show or some bad horror movie. It wasn't real, it couldn't be real that my daughter was actually saying, "I need to go now. They're busy loading up the car."

This wasn't happening. This couldn't be happening!

"Valerie!" I heard myself scream. "For God's sake, *no!* At least give me a zip code! What will we tell the police?"

Then the phone clicked. And she was gone.

I don't know how Joe or Elena took the news. I don't know if they could eat that week or couldn't. I don't know what demons Joe wrestled. I don't know if Elena lay awake and thought, *I told them! I warned them!* She certainly could have.

All I know is what happened to me.

After everything I had done for Valerie—after everything I had tried to do—I couldn't believe that it had actually ended like this. I could believe that Valerie would do this to her father and sister. Both Joe and Elena had built up their distance and stayed behind their walls of disapproval. But me? I had no walls. I had no protection.

I had only hope and love.

It was to me that Valerie had come over the course of her long, strange illness, and it was to me that she had confided her confused hopes and dreams. "Listen to this song," she had told me countless times. "Listen, Momma. It describes exactly how I feel."

And I had listened. I had listened, and I hadn't judged. I had tried to be with her wherever she was. I had followed my lost sheep so far away—so far away! As far as she would let me. And I hadn't asked for perfection. I hadn't asked for health. All I had ever asked—the most I had ever asked—was that she take one step toward health, toward goodness. One step back to me.

One step back toward the light.

My daughter is an amazing person. It was my mantra. It was my faith. *My daughter will be a better person than I am.*

And now my daughter was gone.

I crumpled. I did. After a solid year of worry, of anguish, of panicky insomniac plans for how to drag my family whole and entire through the next day—the next week—the next year—I curled up under a mound of blankets and shut down.

I had no more thoughts. No more hopes. No dreams.

I lay motionless and watched gray blobs float across the salmon-colored dusk inside my eyelids. Or I opened my eyes and watched the flimsy shadows of tree branches slide across the cool blue wallpaper of the bedroom. Occasionally, stripy cat Tor might jump up and make a warm nest at my feet. Occasionally, a bird might sing outside. In the evening, Joe or Elena would come in and stand by the bed. But when I heard the door open, I would pretend to be asleep.

I hid my injured soul away inside my safest, most comforting daydreams. I lay in bed, and my imagination brought me other worlds where characters lay in bed. They lay between crisp sheets in a tuberculosis hospital, surrounded by snow and fir trees and the clean, clear, ice-cold mountain air. Or they lay paralyzed in rose-scented hot baths while encouraging attendants massaged their shattered limbs.

The best doctors and nurses tiptoed in and out of my daydreams and brought my characters relief and care. But they couldn't get better because I couldn't get better. We would never get well again.

A part of me was missing now, torn out of my soul. Call it trust. Call it hope for the future. Whatever it was, that piece of my soul had kept me going through all those anxious months.

But it wasn't there anymore. My daughter had taken it with her.

And my daughter . . .

My daughter was gone.

CHAPTER SEVEN

Joe and Elena teamed up and applied themselves to sleuthing on the Internet. Elena cracked Valerie's passwords and found out where she was. She was living with a fundamentalist family in Georgia. They had taken her in because they thought we had kicked her out. They thought she had nowhere else to go.

"I've had it with her!" Elena told me, sitting on the edge of my bed. "I never want to speak to her again."

She's safe, I thought. *My wayward child is safe.* And all those pictures my imagination had been showing me—dirty bones poking out through a pile of mildewed leaves, white fingers rising like mushrooms from muddy ground—grayed out in a tear-soaked haze of relief.

When Elena left, I got out of bed and padded into the bathroom. The late-afternoon sun was shining in. A real-life hot shower felt so much better than any number of imaginary rose-scented baths.

"Tor!" I heard Elena cry. "Not again!"

"I'll take care of it," I called.

My poor stripy kitty had started throwing up again. His delicate stomach couldn't handle the stress of my worrisome absence. *Antacids,* I thought as I pulled on clothes. *Six small meals. Just a teaspoon of food at first.* I stopped to put in my contact lenses, and suddenly the world had clarity again. It had hard edges and purpose.

I walked back into the bedroom and saw dirty clothes to pick up.

I walked into the kitchen and washed dirty dishes.

Time passed. Our house was quiet. There was no reason to fight anymore. Elena spent her time at school or at the hospital, and Joe worked his long days at the office. Once again, I wandered through silent rooms, as I had after the girls had left for boarding school. Once again, I had no job. I had no projects.

But I was different now. The piece of my soul that Valerie had taken with her when she left—that part of me stayed lost.

My isolation was absolute. Why would I want that to change? What could I say to the people I knew?

"My daughter is gone. She dropped out of college and disappeared."

"What? Valerie? Isn't that your brilliant, funny girl, the one who seemed so wise when she was a child? Didn't you say she graduated from high school with honors? Didn't you say she was making As in college?"

"Yes, but she's ill. She's been ill for a long time."

"Ill how? You never really explained that."

"Just ill. Unhappy . . ."

"Unhappy how? You never really told us what was wrong."

"She never told us what was wrong, either. Depression, maybe. The doctors weren't sure. But why are we even talking about this? She's gone."

"Gone? But why? Why is she gone?"

Why *was* she gone?

Why?

That was the question I lived with every second. It pulsed through my arteries with every beat of my heart. I breathed and ate and slept that question. I couldn't possibly bear to hear it spoken out loud.

So I let the walls of my house define me. I had no intention of reaching out for a life beyond their limits. I was content to remain alone. But when it comes to the imagination I have, I am never alone.

As I sat and drank my tea at the dining room table, I found an old friend sitting beside me. She had an oval face like Valerie's, and dark hazel eyes, and like me, she, too, had felt no desire to leave home. She had long brown hair put up in a bun and terrible handwriting like mine, and more than anyone else, she understood what I was going through.

This hazel-eyed woman was the Victorian writer Emily Brontë, the creator of my childhood playmate, Heathcliff. She died of tuberculosis in 1848. But when we are truly great, we never really die.

Delicate kitty Tor was welcome in her shadowy company. Emily's own animals had filled her house and occupied the first place in her heart. She had once told a classroom full of her pupils that she preferred the school dog to any of them.

Nor were my spiritual bruises over the loss of my daughter any obstacle between me and Emily's presence. "Well, some may hate, and some may scorn," Emily told me with casual grace, and it was obvious that she couldn't care less if they did. Her own beloved, talented brother had drunk himself to death right in the same house with her, but she was strong and independent, a remarkable woman who had achieved remarkable things, and my imagination brought her to me now as a kind of sister.

I had looked up to Emily Brontë since I was a little girl, when my mother had first told me stories about her. I remember hearing, breathless with wonder, how she saved a child from a rabid dog—and then walked home and cauterized the bite she'd received with a red-hot poker. The world as Emily knew it was a harsh, brutal place, but she had faced that world without flinching. And her antihero, Heathcliff, true child of his powerful author mother, had helped me face my freakish childhood without flinching.

Now, vulnerable and lonely, as I tried to pull myself together again, I reread her classic novel, *Wuthering Heights*, and I found its barren, windswept world a safe place to be. No one there looked down on my crippled spirit. No one there was whole.

New characters began to walk with me on the edges of *Wuthering Heights'* stormy world. Half of those characters were already ghosts. I built a new world for them, and as I began to write, I poured all the pain of the last two years into my story:

> Deep in the nighttime, when not a spark gleamed indoors, nor a star without, the dead maid stood by my bedside again and summoned me from sleep. She shook me as if to rouse me and take me with her, those chilly fingers sliding down my arm.

And that bleak, savage story healed me.

It sounds strange to say that something so grim and brutal could help heal the damage I felt, but it happened because my characters themselves refused to give up hope. Even in that grim world, they found compassion in unexpected places, and those moments of compassion shone out in the darkness there like lighthouse beams. Step by step, they guided me back to serenity and forgiveness.

As the darkness and confusion drained out of me and into my dark, tumultuous story, I began to rouse myself to look after my family again. Joe's work was still exhausting, but he seemed to be finding his way back to his old self. The commander who had made his workdays such a burden was finally retired and gone. And Valerie, out of touch though she still was, seemed from the hints we could glean online to have found some sort of balance. At least it was clear that she was safe.

It was Elena who worried me now. Outwardly calm and successful, as well as popular with her friends, she was carrying a seething cauldron of anger within. And since Elena was keeping the secret of her torn-up family to herself, she had no one else besides me to talk to about it.

I began to worry that Elena's successful school days weren't just a reflection of her love of learning anymore. Elena still seemed to be trying to differentiate herself from Valerie. She was wearing herself out in a fierce competition with her "deadbeat" sister, even though Valerie had left the playing field.

Maybe this pointless competition was the only way Elena had found to keep her absent sister in her life.

But it didn't seem healthy. It wasn't bringing her any relief. Unlike my story, which had taken me through the darkness to the light, Elena's strategy seemed to be keeping her from moving forward.

"Why don't you talk to somebody about all this?" I suggested. "Maybe work out some of that anger."

"Are you kidding?" she said. "I don't want anybody to know that Valerie even exists!"

I had heard this so often that it didn't even hurt anymore.

"No, I mean a counselor. They have to protect your privacy, right? A counselor would keep anything you say confidential."

So Elena talked to the school psychologist, Mr. Temple, and he suggested that she go to grief counseling at the military hospital. Once again, I mentally rolled up my sleeves and tackled the phone system in the military psychiatric department. But here was some good news: since Elena was a minor, she wouldn't need to deal with their busy staff. She would see Dr. Petras, the child psychiatrist who had been called in to consult about Valerie.

Elena and I went in for the first appointment with him in mid-May.

"I don't really think I need it, though," Elena said as we waited outside his office. "Mr. Temple gave me some good advice, and anyway, the school year's almost over. I'll get a nice break and rest up and forget about this sucky year. Barbara and I have plans to work on our tans and do the summer reading list together."

"Well, why don't you go anyway?" I said. "After all, it can't hurt."

So Elena went off and talked to the social worker there. Then, after about half an hour, Dr. Petras saw us in his office for a few minutes. I was glad he had helped us through Valerie's hospitalization. It meant that he would understand why Elena was so upset.

"I'd like to put you on Zoloft," he told Elena. "It takes a few weeks to start working, so how about I see you again in a month?"

"Sure," Elena said as she handed the prescription to me. It was par for the course at this hospital: more pills. But then again, sometimes those pills helped. They hadn't done much for Valerie, but they still meant a lot for Joe's peace of mind.

And maybe the Zoloft did help. Little by little, Elena seemed to relax. Even though she started the summer with a million frenetic plans, as the weeks passed, she began to let perfection slide and started having more fun. She slept in a little later in the morning and badgered me to order pizzas in the evening. She and Barbara worked on their tans, and she got Barbara interested in volunteering at the hospital.

Slowly, the mood in the house tilted back toward happy, even without Valerie's soft singing and sunny smile. Joe began to look glad to be home again as he walked through the door at night. He and Elena watched angst-ridden reality TV shows together and wagered cheerfully over who would be the rudest contestant. I finished the rough draft of my tribute to Emily Brontë and decided that she would have liked it.

Then, on the evening of my birthday in June, a one-line email popped up in my inbox:

> hey momma happy birthday! i'm in georgia now, don't know if you knew. sorry about everything, miss you and love you so much, val

I read it over and over. I realized that I was sitting perfectly still, as if a butterfly had landed on my hand.

Elena's second monthly grief-counseling session came up that same week. Now, she felt even more ambivalent about it. "He upped the Zoloft," she said afterward, "but he barely talked to me. Most of the time, it was that social worker again. Anyway, how can somebody with a mustache that stupid possibly help me overcome my problems?"

I laughed. "It does look pretty silly. But it's a rare privilege to be able to keep facial hair in the military, so I'm sure he wants to show it off."

"He looks like a sad, noble dog," Elena said. "He looks unhappy in his own skin. He looks like he thinks people are whispering behind his back, but he's too well-mannered to listen."

"And look," I said. "We are!"

Now it was Elena's turn to laugh.

"*I'm* not whispering," she said with mock aggression. "I'd say it to his *face!*"

By the time the third grief-counseling appointment came around in early July, we were all back to living life again. Valerie and I were corresponding regularly. Joe was down to eight or nine work hours in a day. Elena was out almost constantly with her friends, not just going through the motions but having real fun. And I was on the final read-through of my Brontë manuscript—the one with all my darkness buried in it.

Tor and our black cat, Simon, and I were in the garden room, a tiny scrap of a room just off our kitchen. It was so small that two overstuffed brown chairs filled it to capacity. Tor lay in the shadow of my armchair, protected from the afternoon sun, but Simon lay in the full force of golden rays so intense that his dusty black coat was the color of bittersweet chocolate. It was a wonder he didn't burst into flames.

I glanced up from my laptop as Elena walked by.

"Pizza tonight?" I offered.

"Meh," she said, opening the fridge and pouring out some juice. "I've got that stupid psychiatric appointment tomorrow. It's a waste of time. We ought to just call and cancel it."

"Well, you wanted to go to the hospital anyway to do some volunteering," I said. "And it seems polite to go see him one last time, even if all you do is tell him you don't think you need to see him anymore."

Elena frowned at her juice glass. "I *guess* so," she said. Then she put the empty glass in the sink and walked away.

We've done it, I thought as I went back to my work. *My family and I have survived the darkest days of our lives. With a little luck—except, there's no such thing as luck—this manuscript will be the only evidence that those dark days even existed.*

It was July again, just over a year since Valerie's overdose. And it finally seemed like a long time ago.

Pizza tonight, I thought. *That's easy. I'll have this manuscript on my agent's desk by Friday. And we should take a vacation before school starts next month. Maybe England. Maybe the south of France.* And as the warm summer sunshine came streaming through the windows, I meditated on pleasant futures, near and far.

It's when you let down your guard that the ax falls.

CHAPTER EIGHT

The next afternoon, I was sitting in the very same spot, curled up in one of the big, overstuffed brown chairs with my laptop open on my lap. But, although sunshine flooded the garden room with light, I was seeing another place entirely. It started between my ears, at the top of my head, and slowly grew outward, increasing in size and color until the world in front of me blurred out. Then, although I was still dimly aware of Tor twitching his paws in his sleep, that other place was all I saw.

Rough stone walls had risen out of my mind and obliterated the sunlight. I was looking down a gloomy hallway in a bleak, dismal old house, half castle and half barn. The scent of stale air rose from dank, unopened places. It made me want to hold my breath.

Shadows congregated in this dim hallway, and dust, and cobwebs, until I found myself squinting to see. As my eyes adjusted to the gloom, I could make out a figure standing in the shadows: a gray-faced girl in a ragged black dress.

This girl had been the very first of all this story's ghosts. Her life had ended long before she came into my world. Everything that had made her human had fallen away. She had lost her fears and her joys. She had lost her eyes.

This poor little once-upon-a-time human had never shocked me, not even the very first time I saw her. But, no matter how many times I studied the empty black circles in her gray face, I never stopped feeling sad.

At the moment, I was rereading her grim story with great care, matching the image the words raised in my mind with the image the way it had looked when I had first dreamed it. If the words were wrong, they would form a fuzzy double exposure, and the image and the feelings it raised wouldn't come into focus. But if the words were right, I could read the story just the way my readers would, and I would see exactly what I was supposed to see. Then my mind wouldn't have to work to bring the image to life. The words would do it for me.

> She stood very still in the dusky passage where the light was poorest. Like me, she wore the black dress that proclaimed her a maid of the house, but where mine was new, hers was spoiled by mildew and smears of clay. Thin hair, dripping with muddy water, fell to her shoulders in limp, stringy ropes. This was my companion of the night before—and she was dead.

I could see it all: the long, limp, wet hair and the mildew-spotted black dress. But wait a minute—was that right? Mildew was black, wasn't it?

Could mildew be white? Or was it always black? Could mildew show up on a black dress?

Probably. Possibly. I didn't know. And I didn't want to wait for a copyeditor to ask. I clicked away from the Word file I was reading, pulled up Google, and typed *mildew* into the search box.

The phone rang: a double interruption. The eyeless ghost flickered and grew faint. I grabbed the phone with my free hand as I scrolled through the Google results, willing the ghost to stay where she was.

"Hello," I said, scanning. This stuff was all about mildew in houses. But there, at least the Wikipedia article mentioned clothing.

"Hello, this is Dr. Petras. I have your daughter Elena here."

Dr. Petras? Right, the child psychiatrist with the silly, droopy mustache. I had dropped Elena off at the hospital two hours ago, and she had intended to walk upstairs to her appointment after she did some volunteering. He must be calling to confirm that she wouldn't be coming back to see him. Maybe he needed to talk about her prescription.

Did Elena still need that Zoloft? Her feelings about Valerie weren't as raw now as they'd been a few months ago.

At the thought of Valerie, the eyeless ghost standing in front of me changed. Now my absent daughter stood in her place. Long hair, pale oval face, black eye shadow, ragged black clothes. The impression in my mind—the wistful sadness—remained the same.

But it's getting better, I reminded her. *You sent me an email just yesterday. You're crazy about Clint, your new boyfriend, you told me. You wrote to say that you love me.*

Meanwhile, in my ear, Dr. Petras had charged ahead. His voice was stern, like a reprimand from the boss. After listening for a few seconds, I realized that I wasn't sure what he was talking about. Ghost in the room, ghost in the Word file, ghost in my family circle—I couldn't break free from it all quickly enough for him.

"I'm sorry," I blurted into the flow of stern words, "but what is this about?"

"Your daughter has anorexia nervosa."

Anorexia nervosa?

What?

The shadow of the lost Valerie slipped away like a raindrop. Headlines lit up in my mind. Somewhere in there was Karen Carpenter's strong, expressive voice, half laughing, half crying, saying she had the blues.

"Anorexia?" I heard myself say stupidly. "My daughter? You mean . . . Elena? You do mean *that* daughter, don't you?"

But . . . she's the one who's completely normal! I thought.

A woman came walking through my memory. Her pelvic bones were sharp points under a green minidress. Her knees and elbows looked like knots, and her rough skin sagged into hollow places and dipped from neck bone to shoulders. That memory blurred into another one: a ratty horse with hipbones jutting under its hide. "Bonny's thirty," a voice drawled over the image of the horse. "She can't keep flesh on anymore."

Was that anorexia? What *was* anorexia? Wasn't Elena *normal*?

Dr. Petras had taken off again while I was caught up in my own confused thoughts. His tone was hard—almost rude. More than the words, the tone captivated me now. What could it mean?

"Anorexia nervosa," I repeated, pulling out the one thing I felt sure of so far. "Okay."

Because it *was* okay, wasn't it? Wasn't it always good to put the right words to something? If they *were* the right words, that is—and the skinny-horse woman loomed in front of me again. But that didn't make sense. Elena didn't look a thing like that horse and that woman. She had an adorable figure. For heaven's sake, her bras were a bigger cup size than mine!

"So—anorexia nervosa," I ventured again. "Are you sure?"

"This is very serious!" Dr. Petras said in answer. He sounded as if I was confirming his worst suspicions.

Suspicions about what?

Was Elena all right? Had something happened?

Anxiety surged through me, the anxiety that I had lived with every day—every minute!—for a solid year. The anxiety that was just now—just these last few weeks—beginning to go away. And the gray-faced ghost that was really my missing daughter drifted back into the room. She stared at me mutely. Accusingly.

Without eyes.

Muscles tightened in the back of my neck and sent fingers of tension crawling down to my shoulder blades—the tension that I had once thought would never let me go, the tension that had just started to release—just a little. And the warm, drowsy room, the blissfully unconscious cats, the almost-finished manuscript—the entire day, in fact, began to wobble in my grasp.

I could feel it shift. I could feel it start to slide down—

Dr. Petras said, "I'm putting Elena in the hospital, starting right now. I want you in my office in fifteen minutes!"

And the sunny day smashed into pieces.

CHAPTER NINE

There we were, half an hour later, gathered together in Dr. Petras's office: Elena, Joe, and I. Joe had been in the middle of a series of meetings, and the stress showed on his face. Even without the crazy commander, his workdays were still long and hectic. It was obvious that Elena didn't want to be there, either. This appointment I had asked her to attend as a courtesy had turned into a disaster.

And me? I was doing my best to be a logical, reasonable person. I had a firm belief that psychological sessions were useful things, and I was well aware that I had kept Elena from canceling this one. I had no desire to hate Dr. Petras, either. That wasn't a logical, reasonable feeling to feel.

But when I looked at my daughter's face, I had to struggle not to hate *somebody*.

Elena looked as if she were undergoing a prisoner interrogation. She was staring past us at the far wall, her face carefully and completely blank. After everything we had endured over the course of the last year—after things had started to get better!—the sight of that expressionless mask on Elena's face made me want to stand up and scream.

Absolutely nothing about this enforced surprise office visit was pleasant. It had ripped all three of us out of our routines. It had brought back tensions we had just shaken off, and it had raised memories we had just started to forget. In fact, the situation was so dramatic that it felt like a deliberate manipulation. And I don't like being manipulated.

"I'm admitting Elena to the hospital today," Dr. Petras announced. "She has anorexia nervosa."

Again, I found myself overwhelmed by a feeling of indignation. Just like that—out of the blue—he was deciding care for our daughter. What about discussing options first? What about explaining this surprise diagnosis?

"Do you think you have anorexia nervosa?" I asked Elena.

Her answer was an angry, explosive "No!"

For several reasons, this situation was hitting me at a weak point. Or maybe—

Maybe it was hitting me at a very strong one.

When I was a small child, around two or three, I was very close to my father. He worked nights back then, and he babysat me while my mother worked on her PhD and taught classes. I have precious memories of those long-ago days, of my father saying to me, "Well, fussbudget, what are we going to do today?" I even remember the sight of my own white diapers flapping on the clothesline.

Around the time I was four or five, my father had to take me to the doctor. He himself was sick with the flu, and I remember him shivering as he carried me to the car. I remember the sight of him huddling down in his chair as we waited in the waiting room.

He had brought me to the doctor because I had a headache.

Even back then, my headaches weren't your standard "I have a headache" headaches. I would lie still in breathless agony with my hands clamped over my eyes. Every little sound sent jolts of electricity through my overwrought frame, and I thought my right eye was going to pop out of my head. The headaches came on with very little warning and lasted for hours. Sometimes, I ended up vomiting from the pain.

On that day long ago, my pediatrician, Dr. McKinney, came smiling into the room. He examined me and listened to my father's explanation. He was still smiling as he delivered his verdict.

"It's hypochondria," he said. "Some children just want a little attention. Has anybody else in the family been sick?"

And I could hear how upset my father was when he answered, "*I'm* sick!"

"There! You see? She just wants to feel included." And Dr. McKinney went smiling back out of the room.

Preschoolers aren't supposed to understand words like *hypochondria*, but I knew what that word meant. It meant that the doctor didn't believe me. It meant that he thought I had lied—as if a small child really *could* lie about pain like that, lie about the need to stay perfectly still in a dark room, with tears leaking out of the corners of my eyes.

"I do have a headache," I said.

My father didn't answer. He was furious. I could feel his anger. As miserable as my father was, it must have been a special blow to feel that he had gotten himself out of the house for nothing.

He didn't speak to me on the car ride home.

I remember the indignation in my father's voice as he told my mother about it, how upset he was at the thought that I'd taken them in. But my mother disagreed. Headaches ran in her family, and my older brother had them, too. My father and mother ended up arguing about it, and that made a lasting impression. My father adored my mother. He hated to fight with her. In his mind, I had caused that fight.

Maybe this all would have blown over if I could have stopped having the headaches. But that was something I couldn't do. And every single time I had to drag myself off to bed, my father was sure I was trying to play him for a fool. He heckled me. "There she goes again!" he would say, as if I were a baby throwing a temper tantrum. And when my mother scolded him for it, his annoyance hardened into a grudge.

Pretty soon, my father started picking on me for other things, like leaving the milk top open or standing too long at the refrigerator door. *You have it easy*, his stern eyes told me. *Your mother coddles you. You don't deserve her trust.*

And before long, my father and I weren't close anymore.

Throughout my childhood, as I spent days in pain, I felt the weight of my father's angry disapproval and disbelief. Sickness became a shameful thing to me, a sign of weakness and bad character.

Dr. McKinney continued to be my pediatrician, and every year or two, my mother would bring up my headaches again. "Sinus," Dr. McKinney would say since I was older and in the same room, but his eyebrows would communicate something different. *Hypochondria*, they would convey with a knowing little smirk. *But we mustn't upset her, must we—hysterical little attention-seeking child.*

It was one more factor in my years of bitter isolation.

When I was sixteen, I went to a general practitioner for the first time, and it took all of thirty seconds for him to diagnose me with classic migraine and to prescribe preventive medication that broke the cycle of pain I had been in since I was old enough to talk. As I grew up and made my way in the world, I won back my father's respect, and he and I are once again close.

But I have never forgotten the terrible price I paid thanks to a doctor's hasty and incorrect diagnosis. I need facts from doctors now. They have to convince me that they know what they're talking about.

Dr. Petras already had one strike against him. His dramatic diagnosis of Valerie hadn't been backed up by the other psychiatrists who had treated her. So, faced with a second dramatic diagnosis, I wanted a real medical consultation: explain yourself, give me your supporting evidence, and let's talk about treatment options. That's how my doctors and I had worked through what to do when I had had cancer. It seemed to me to be a perfectly logical approach.

Whenever I feel threatened or emotional, I reach for logic. It calms me down. I work those "If the German in the blue house plays the clarinet, who owns the fox?" puzzles for fun, and I turn to logic in moments of argument or stress.

At that moment, I felt very emotional and, on behalf of my family, quite threatened. This doctor whom I barely knew had called us all into this sudden meeting to announce a drastic course of action. He had put Joe and me at a distinct disadvantage: we had had almost no time to educate ourselves and prepare to participate in such an important decision. I had taken five minutes to do a couple of quick Internet searches, but that was all I'd had time for.

"So, if I understand you," I said now, "you're basing this diagnosis of anorexia nervosa on three monthly weigh-ins."

"She's underweight," Dr. Petras confirmed.

"But what else supports the idea that she has anorexia?"

"She lost eight pounds in one month," he said.

"But she gained four pounds in one month, too," I pointed out, "from the first month to the second month. Both of those first weights were within the normal range. Isn't anorexia nervosa a chronic condition? How chronic can it be if she was at normal weight two months out of the three?"

If Dr. Petras had attempted to educate us, I wouldn't have felt so emotional. But his manner was very stern—almost hostile. I felt that he was keeping things from Joe and me and deliberately saying as little as possible. But why? We were Elena's caregivers. We had to be involved.

"She lost eight pounds in one month!" he snapped. "Doesn't that mean anything to you?"

"Of course it does!" I said. And really, why was I even having to say that? "But I'm still not getting from there to anorexia nervosa. There could be a serious medical issue behind weight loss like that. Don't you need to rule out physical factors first? Have you contacted Family Practice to schedule blood work?"

And I thought of my cancer. It had triggered weight loss.

"No, I haven't scheduled blood work," he said. "I know what she has."

But how? How could he know what she had before he ruled out medical factors? Was this another Dr. McKinney, reaching for that "hysterical child" diagnosis?

Logic . . . I told myself.

I started over.

"If I understand you," I said, "you're not saying that Elena told you she hates to eat. In fact, you haven't told us that you've learned anything about her eating habits. Has she told you she's been trying to diet?"

"She lost eight pounds in one month. Of course she's trying to diet."

"And she *told* you that," I said.

But Dr. Petras didn't answer.

"So," I said after a minute, "she *didn't* tell you that."

He gave a shrug. "Well, it's obvious."

Was it really obvious that Elena was on a diet? Did this man know how hard it was for that girl—and for her family members, too—to manage to hold on to weight? Did he take her family's naturally high metabolism into account? Or did he just assume she had been dieting because we women, all we want to do is diet, right?

How I hated that hysterical female crap!

Logic . . . Logic . . . This isn't helping . . .

"What about the Zoloft you put her on?" I asked. "She's been on it for two months, and you increased the dose last month. Could it have caused her weight to vary? Could it have caused this sudden weight loss?"

"No, it couldn't," Dr. Petras said.

Yes, it absolutely could. Loss of appetite and weight loss are common side effects of Zoloft, especially in children and adolescents. It isn't unusual for Zoloft to cause a child to lose more than 7 percent of his or her body weight. But I didn't know this then. I hadn't had time to educate myself.

"Look, I'm not going to argue with you," Dr. Petras continued. "Your daughter has anorexia nervosa. I'm putting her in the hospital until she gains weight. And that's how it's going to be!"

I felt completely bewildered. I hadn't realized we were having an argument. Silly me, I thought we were consulting together to try to determine the best medical course of action to help one of the three most important people in my life. But it felt as if Dr. Petras had deliberately forced me into a position that would allow him to say this.

Could he actually put Elena into the hospital, even without our permission? I wasn't sure. Our status in Germany, connected to a military base overseas, did put us into a somewhat vulnerable position. Overseas military doctors have greater latitude than civilian doctors do back home. It could be that Dr. Petras was within his rights to do this, and he certainly acted as if he was.

But in one way at least, this hospitalization wouldn't be a bad thing. It would give us the chance to bring other doctors into the picture very quickly. Putting Elena into the pediatric ward automatically meant having her care overseen by the ward pediatrician, and that pediatrician was bound to order the important medical tests I was thinking of, tests that could take weeks to order in this busy wartime hospital if Elena weren't an inpatient there.

Eight pounds of weight loss in one month might mean a very serious medical condition: lupus, hepatitis, a metabolic disorder, or even leukemia. The sooner we knew if one of these conditions was present, the better.

So Joe and I exchanged glances, and we wordlessly agreed: we wouldn't fight Dr. Petras on this. A couple of days in the hospital might bring us important answers. But I looked at the expressionless expression that shouldn't be on my daughter's face, and I felt torn and deeply distressed.

For another adolescent, this might not be an issue at all. A few days of pampering in the hospital might seem like a spa vacation. But not for Elena. She hated bullies. And this was the girl Dr. Petras was forcing into care, against her will and over her parents' authority.

He had bullied her entire family at a single blow.

When Elena was barely old enough to stand up, I took one of Valerie's toys away from her. Little Elena didn't cry. She picked up a wooden block and toddled after me. She followed me around the coffee table, clutching its edge for support. I stopped to pick up another toy, and Elena managed to catch up—and she whomped me in the back of the knee with her block.

When Elena was in grade school, she had a teacher who bullied a little boy in her class. The boy wouldn't answer back, but his ears would turn bright red from humiliation. And whenever Elena saw those bright-red ears, she would see red herself, and she would launch into a verbal attack on the teacher. For a grade-schooler, she came up with some truly insightful insults.

"Mrs. Dunkle," the teacher would tell me, "you need to talk to your daughter!"

I did talk to Elena. I asked her if she wanted me to tell the teacher what I thought of an adult who took out his own unhappiness on small children.

"No," Elena said. "That would make it worse. Last week, he lectured us for fifteen minutes about not carrying tales to our parents."

"But if he knows I know what this is about," I said, "then at least he won't punish you anymore."

"Punish me!" Elena laughed. "He sends me to the library! I get to sit and read books while everybody else is outside in the cold."

Bullies didn't just make Elena angry. They awakened in her an idealistic drive to rebalance the universe. I knew that if she saw this as a bullying situation, she would fight it with everything she had.

Joe and I went down to the food court to order Elena her favorite pizza. By the time we brought it back to the pediatric ward, she was sitting on a hospital bed, wearing a pair of green nurse's scrubs as pajamas. She hadn't pulled the covers up. It was as if she would be on that bed only for a few minutes. She set the pizza aside, smoking hot and deliciously cheesy, without so much as a glance.

"I'll be fine, Mom," she said firmly as I hugged her good-bye.

I was afraid I knew what Elena meant when she said this. She meant that she would show not one speck of weakness. Worries rose up and buzzed around me like a cloud of gnats. How could a child psychiatrist understand so little of this child's nature?

"Please eat," I told her. "It's for us, not for him. I'll miss you! We want you home."

Elena sat like a statue. The blank mask was still on her face—that expressionless expression that had no business being on her face at all.

"I'll be fine," she said again in that same firm, even tone.

Which wasn't the same thing as *happy*.

Or *well*.

CHAPTER TEN

Joe and I walked out to the hospital parking lot together. He was worried, too, but he was more practical than I was.

"A week, max," he said, half hoping and half predicting. "It can't take her long to gain weight."

Then he kissed me and drove back to his stressful workday.

I got into my car and took the familiar turns on autopilot. Part of my mind was watching the sparse traffic on the German autobahn, but the rest of it was a chaos of emotion.

I'm a storyteller. I have to have a story to tell. That means I have to have some sense of where things have come from and where they're going. But at that moment, I had absolutely no story to tell about the events of our lives.

The family's going through a rough patch right now . . . My girls—well, they're brilliant, but they do have their moments . . . Oh, sure, we have issues like everyone else, but we're all right, really . . .

No, none of those. All I had were worries and questions.

The more I thought about the meeting we'd just been through, the more confused and upset I felt. I went back through it, trying to find the moment where we had miscommunicated, the moment where we had gone from consulting to arguing. I couldn't find that moment, so I went back through the phone call. I couldn't find the moment there, either.

From the very beginning, Dr. Petras had been hostile. He had maneuvered from the first as if he were facing enemies, people he didn't respect. But why? When he had consulted with us about Valerie, he had been warm and sympathetic. Why had he changed?

My heart whispered the answer:

Because one *child might have problems, sure. But what can it mean if* both *do?*

And I remembered Dr. Petras's unfriendly eyes:

What did you do *to them? You bad mother!*

I am tremendously proud of my mother. In the years before career women were common, she became a professor at quite a young age. And later, when the head of her department pointed out that professors ought to have a PhD, my mother went out and earned her PhD. She's a scholar from the tips of her typewriter-key-blunted fingers to the depths of her vertical file cabinets. To this day, she proofreads manuscripts for publication. She's spending her retirement straightening out footnotes and block quotations.

My mother is an extraordinary person. But when I was young, I was determined to outdo her. I was going to become an extraordinary *mother*.

Long before I brought my babies home from the hospital, I had already decided that I would be an amazing mother. My children would be read to and sung to; they would hear nursery rhymes and attend story hour; they would go to the scientifically best preschool and have the scientifically best backyard play set. They would have the right kinds of toys and the right kinds of friends. They would learn and grow and blossom in ways I had only dreamed of.

My children, I vowed, would never once enter the doors of a huge public school, to be bullied and bored the way I was. They would have early education, small class sizes, and homework help, and they would grow up confident and loved.

From the moment I found out I was pregnant, I began reading the right books about education. On the backs of Joe's and my dedicated frugality, we sent our girls to the best preschool in town. We bought them gender-neutral toys and games. We let them watch only age-appropriate shows. I read books on nutrition and, with my limited culinary skills, I worked to prepare nutritionally dense meals.

No sodas in my house! Sugar was a drug. No cable TV for us! We were building neurons. It would have been hard work if watching my girls grow up hadn't been such a joy.

But now . . .

What did she do *to them—that mother? What did she* do *to those girls?*

The morning after Valerie's overdose, Joe and Elena and I couldn't just hide at home and lick our wounds. Joe's squadron had prepared a picnic, and as its deputy, he needed to attend. As an officer's wife, I had helped with the preparations, and there were things I had agreed to bring. All the people who were important in our social life were there: colleagues, associates, subordinates, bosses, babysitting charges, and friends.

So we showed up just long enough to do what we had to do. And we said it. We faced the world, and we said it:

"We were up all night with Valerie in the ER. No, Valerie wasn't in an accident. She overdosed. She took a bottle of pills."

Somehow, the hard, grinding reality of hearing those words out loud under the sunshine and blue sky felt more real to me than the long hours we had spent the night before by Valerie's bedside. Is that because I'm a storyteller, so focused on telling stories that telling my own story felt more real than living it?

"No, Valerie hasn't been released. She signed herself into the psych ward."

Because lies don't help. Lies create vulnerability. The truth carries its own severe, Spartan pride.

Did I see it in their eyes that day—that stern, hostile look? *There she is, that mother—that bad mother!*

No.

I heard, "Look after yourself, Clare. Get help if you need it."

It's the only thing I remember.

The wife of our group commander was at our squadron picnic. Her husband oversaw our squadron as well as another one, and as the full colonel who commanded us, he ranked as royalty in our small world. Among the officers' spouses, so did his wife.

I knew her, of course, but we weren't friends. One didn't befriend royalty.

Petite, slim, and pretty, with bright black eyes and hands that fluttered in the air as she spoke, she had always reminded me of a songbird.

Her daughter was beautiful and talented, earning top grades at the university. But her son had disabilities so severe that he couldn't speak.

That fresh July morning after Valerie's overdose, she came to stand with me, very close. She looked me in the eye, as if the two of us were the only people there.

"Don't be afraid to get help," she said. "I had to get help myself for a while."

When I think back on that precious gift of kindness, it still brings tears to my eyes.

So, no, I didn't see that look in the eyes of our friends and colleagues—that harsh, judging look. I didn't hear that cruel whispered voice. But that didn't mean I had escaped it. I couldn't escape it.

That voice came from me.

A cutter? Do you know what kind of pain it takes to become a cutter? What kind of mother would put her child through so much pain?

An overdose? Has anyone helped that girl? Does her family even notice she's there? How could her family let her live with such desperation?

And now, as I drove away from Dr. Petras's stern presence, I heard that voice again. It was my own voice, from four or five years ago.

It was the voice of that extraordinary mother.

Two children in the hospital? What sort of home is she running? Thank God that's never going to happen to me! My girls know that they're loved.

The me of four years ago had daughters who were at home on two continents. They laughed and sang and prattled all day long in fluent English and fluent German. They led prayers. They helped others. They didn't have a single cavity. They were beautiful. They read Shakespeare for *fun*.

Good girls have good mothers. Extraordinary girls have extraordinary mothers. But deeply troubled girls? Oh, the old me knew all about them.

Too much violence on the television. (Sad head shake.) *Too much sugar.* (Wise nod.) *Too much pressure to leave childhood behind. Not enough laughter. Not enough fun.*

The old me had read the parenting books. The old me had an answer for everything. Dropping out of college?

Not enough involvement in the early years. Not enough help with goals.

A runaway?

Too strict. Too judgmental. Teenagers need respect. You can't just lecture them and sock them with punishments. You have to listen. You have to be ready to let them do the teaching.

And anorexia nervosa? The old me had the answer for that, too.

Unrealistic, hyperperfect Barbie dolls. Photoshopped models in magazines. Overly sexualized clothing and gender-stereotyping toys. I wonder if that poor girl was wearing nail polish in preschool. I wonder if she had a cell phone in grade school.

Oh, yes, the old me had *all* the answers.

But during the last few years, what had happened to these brilliant, beautiful girls? What had happened to their laughter and creativity?

What had happened to their mother—that extraordinary mother?

She let them down, that's what she did. She must have been too strict.

But I wasn't! I didn't dictate. I loved to hear their ideas. They read to me more than I read to them. "Hey, Mom, guess *what!*" How many times did I hear that? I learned so much from my girls . . .

Two daughters in the hospital—she must have never let them breathe! I'll bet she ran their lives and gave them no room to grow. I'll bet she had no life of her own, so she lived through her children. That's what she did—she dominated those poor girls.

No, that's not right! I had my own goals, my happy marriage . . . I had my imagination, my book career . . .

But I couldn't shut it off. I heard that stern, unrelenting voice echo in my mind all the way home, and I found no comfort against the dull shame that ached inside. But did the shame I felt come from knowing what I was now? Or from knowing what I used to be?

Well, that poor mother! But that's what happens when parents are selfish and uninspired. That's what happens when they just react *to things and don't take time to* think. *No, thank God! This isn't* my *problem. It has* nothing *to do with me.*

It hurt me to hear what kind of person I'd been back when I was an extraordinary mother.

CHAPTER ELEVEN

The following morning, I drove back to the hospital and met the pediatrician in charge of Elena's care. He was a young, well-educated doctor straight from the States, and unlike Dr. Petras, he seemed neither stern nor disapproving.

"I'm trying to understand this anorexia diagnosis," I told him. "My husband and I spent a couple of hours last night looking up data about it, and the official diagnostic criteria clearly states that the anorexic must be at or below eighty-five percent of normal weight. But Elena's always been above that level, even last school year when we were under so much stress. I know because the school counselor and I kept checking her weight."

The pediatrician frowned. "I know," he said. "I don't think your daughter has anorexia nervosa at all. If it had been up to me, she wouldn't be in the hospital, but I'm not the doctor who admitted her."

This made me feel simultaneously more hopeful and more worried.

"If she's not anorexic, then what do you think caused her weight loss?"

"I'm ordering blood work," he said. "It'll help us rule out a whole host of things."

After the appointment, I stayed behind to visit with Elena. The pediatric ward was almost empty, and she had already made friends with the nurses and techs. She greeted each one by name as they dropped in to check on her and, one by one, she introduced them to me. Then, after they left, she filled me in on their gossip. It took twenty minutes of lively chatter to summarize all the interesting things she had learned.

Reassured by the sparkle in her eyes, I relaxed. Elena wasn't taking this so hard. Yes, as a child, she had resisted bullies to Quixotic lengths, but she was older and more mature now. She wasn't that same idealistic crusader. She could be practical, too.

But then I lifted the lid off the lunch tray by her bed and discovered that she hadn't even touched it.

"Hey! When are you going to get to this?" I asked.

"Never mind that," Elena said. "It's a mistake. That's the standard tray. Dr. Petras says I'm supposed to get a special diet, so I'm waiting till it gets here."

"But Elena, if you don't eat," I pointed out, "you're not going to put that weight on."

She curled her lip. "Well, I'm certainly not eating two lunches!"

Worried that Elena was missing her meal, I went out to check with the nurses sitting at the station. No, they hadn't heard about a special tray, but they promised to call and check on it for me.

I stayed there for another hour. No special tray showed up.

"I think you ought to go ahead and eat this one," I said. "It looks as if the special diet might not start till tonight."

"Nah, I'm not hungry right now anyway," Elena told me. "I've been snacking on pudding. You should grab one, too; they're free. They're in the fridge next to the nurses' station."

I was starting to get hungry. A pudding sounded good. "But I shouldn't be eating the hospital's food," I pointed out.

"Mom!" Elena said. "You wouldn't even be here if the doctor they hired hadn't been a maniac. Eat a pudding, for God's sake!"

Okay, she had a point. And besides, maybe she would split it with me.

I went out to the refrigerator by the nurses' station. The whole thing was packed with soft drinks and pudding cups. It did look as if they could spare one. I chose a vanilla and closed the fridge door.

"For Elena," I explained a little sheepishly to the nurse sitting nearby. "She's been loading up on the puddings, I guess."

"Not that I've seen," the nurse said. "Why, are we running low? What's missing?"

I opened the door again.

The fridge was full. No puddings were missing except for the one I was holding in my hand. And those prickles of worry started up again.

When exactly had Elena been snacking on pudding?

The next day, when I came to visit Elena, she was too tired or too bored to tell me stories. But that was okay. She had found something else for us to do. The pediatric nurses had brought her a VHS player and a stack of Disney tapes.

"Oh, hey, Mom, watch this video with me," she said when she saw me. "It's a *Beauty and the Beast* Christmas special. I think you'll like it."

"You know I don't like the Beast, not once he turns into that wimpy-looking blond guy," I said. "If I were Beauty, I'd want my money back."

By this time, I'd written four books with monsters as main characters. When I watched Peter Jackson's Lord of the Rings movies and his hideous orcs came into the frame, I would feel a burst of nostalgia and affection. *Oh, how nice!* I would think to myself. *The ugly dears look so much like my goblins!*

"I know you like the Beast better, and that's why you'll like this," Elena said. "It's from when he's still a Beast." So I settled down to watch the Christmas special with her. It turned out to be better than I expected.

But as the minutes passed, I sneaked glances at Elena. She wasn't looking so good. Her face was pale, and purple smudges had formed under her eyes.

"Are you feeling okay?" I asked.

"Uh-huh," Elena said. "I just stayed up too late. It's hard to sleep in this place. Do you know how many horror movies start in a hospital at night?"

"That's why I don't watch them," I said. "It's crazy that you do."

"Yeah, well, too late now."

The nurse came in with Elena's lunchtime tray, but Elena pushed it aside without a glance.

"Isn't that your special diet?" I prodded. "Do you want me to unwrap it for you?"

"Once it cools," Elena said without taking her eyes off the screen. "You know I don't like food when it's too hot."

"Hospital food is a lot of things," I observed. "But I have never known it to be too hot."

"Shh!" Elena said. "This is a good part." And we went back to watching the video. But I don't think either one of us was paying attention.

It had happened—I could see that. It had happened, and I didn't know what to do. Elena was on a hunger strike. She had gone to the mattresses. She was locked in a war of wits and nerve with bullying Dr. Petras, and I couldn't figure out how to convince her to stop.

I had never once seen Elena back down from a fight—no matter what the cost.

"Come on!" I pleaded after a few minutes. "If you don't eat, you're never going to get to come home. *Please?* The house is so quiet now. It gives me the creeps!"

Elena shrugged. She didn't try to play dumb. She knew exactly what I was talking about.

"So come see me here," she said firmly. "And bring nail polish next time—fun colors."

I didn't answer. I was trying to think of the right thing to say, the perfect argument. If I was so good with words, why couldn't I ever seem to find the right words to persuade this strong-willed young woman to change her mind?

The *Beauty and the Beast* Christmas special ended. Mentally, I congratulated the scriptwriter who had thought of making a pipe organ into the villain. After all, a pipe organ—how gothically creepy is *that?*

"Have you seen *The NeverEnding Story?*" Elena asked.

"I've read it," I said. "And so have you. It's one of the most insightful allegories in all of fiction, and the best explanation of the joys and pitfalls of the creative-writing process."

"Yeah, *well,*" Elena said. "The movie's okay. Here, pull it out of that pile there, and I'll show you the best part."

I pulled out the video and put it in for her, debating what to say next. How could I talk her into eating again?

The NeverEnding Story movie was awful. It was like watching Barney the dinosaur do Shakespeare. But maybe that was just my anxiety spoiling it for me.

"I know you don't want to make Dr. Petras happy," I ventured after a while. "But couldn't you make Dad and me happy instead? We need to be a family again."

"Hey, this isn't *my* fault," Elena said bitterly. "*I'm* not the one who messed up this family. I wouldn't even *be* here if it weren't for Valerie."

And at the look on her face, I fell silent again.

If only Dr. Petras were like one of the monsters in *The NeverEnding Story*. If only he would act like a fairy-tale villain: "Gather all the leaves in the forest for me. You have until nightfall." At least fairy-tale villains taxed a person's ingenuity, and when they got defeated, they sometimes exploded or melted, or even obligingly tore themselves in half. Elena might meet one of those challenges just to show that she could and to see how creatively the villain was going to die.

But Dr. Petras had acted like a real-world villain instead. He had said, "Do what I say because I'm stronger than you."

There wasn't a snowball's chance in hell that Elena would do that.

Two more days passed—two more anxious, worry-racked days. I don't think Elena ate a single bite of food. Far from looking ready to leave her hospital bed at any moment, she now looked as if she couldn't get out of it. She didn't try to talk much anymore. She just lay silent, a shell of her former lively self.

Her pediatrician confirmed that she had lost weight over the last five days, since being admitted to the hospital.

"There's not much we can do," he said. "This isn't a hospital with a psychiatric protocol. We're not equipped to force a patient to eat. I've ordered an IV. At least we can keep her hydrated."

"I know why she's losing weight *now*," I told him. "Elena has always resisted strong-arm tactics. But have the tests turned up any medical problems that would explain the weight she lost *before* the hospitalization?"

"Not really," he said. "But her EKG reading has changed, and it's showing irregularities now. I've contacted the cardiology department and scheduled an echo exam of her heart."

The room where the echo exam took place was very dark and quiet. The only thing that stood out was the computer screen, and even that was in black and white. Grainy shapes quivered and jumped there, like some old Atari game featuring a blizzard.

No matter what I've looked at on these sonogram monitors over the years—baby, kidney, stomach, you name it—not a single image has made sense. This one didn't make sense, either. It didn't look a thing like a heart. But as the test proceeded, I could tell that the cardiologist was becoming more and more concerned.

"See this? That's the septum." She clicked keys, and little white *x*'s appeared. "You can see—here to here—how thin it is. And see this? See that bulge? This chamber is enlarged. Your daughter has cardiomyopathy. If her heart gets worse, it could rupture."

I went cold to the tips of my fingers. This was real and terrifying physical damage. One of the old ladies at church had cardiomyopathy, and she could barely walk five steps at a time. Cardiomyopathy killed people. It could kill my daughter!

Anxious questions tumbled through my brain. How had this happened? Would it heal? What would help it heal? Would Elena live a full life? Did she really have anorexia nervosa?

"Did anorexia cause this?" I asked.

"I don't know," the cardiologist said. "Maybe. We do look for this in anorexics, but I haven't seen a heart this bad in an anorexic before, and I've done lots of these exams over the years. I've performed this exam on patients who were much thinner than your daughter, but they didn't have a heart like this."

A heart like this.

A deadly condition!

The cardiologist couldn't tell me anything more. She wasn't being cagey; she was being honest with me: she just didn't have the answers.

"We're not the right kind of hospital to deal with this," she said. "Our resources are very limited. We need to evacuate your daughter to the States and get her to a good children's hospital, to the specialists who can run more sophisticated tests and find out exactly what's wrong."

Evacuation to the States. Good! We had a plan to deal with this. I diverted all the anxiety I was feeling into working on that plan.

I walked beside Elena's gurney back to the ward. We didn't speak about the diagnosis on the way. Elena had become so passive and silent over the last several days that I didn't even expect her to speak at that point. And me, I was in full absent-while-present mental overdrive, focusing on the plan.

Would insurance cover Elena's transport to the States? Would it cover mine? How long would we be gone? How soon could we leave? How much would all this cost?

Dr. Petras met me as I was leaving Elena's room. The cardiologist had called him with the results. I hadn't seen him since the day he had admitted Elena to the hospital, and his friendly manner now surprised me.

"I want to call a meeting with Elena's entire care team," he told me. "And I want Elena to attend. We can hold it in the ward conference room tomorrow, right here," and he gestured toward a room we were passing. "Mrs. Dunkle, can you and your husband both attend?"

It was nice to be asked. The last time Dr. Petras had met with us, it had been a command performance.

"Of course," I said. I wrote down the time, said good-bye, and drove home.

And then I got on the phone.

When I was in second or third grade, I read a biography of Florence Nightingale, one of the founders of modern nursing. Before I was even finished with her story, I had already bandaged up my motley collection of dolls and turned them into wounded Crimean War soldiers. In Florence Nightingale's time, women were thought to be unsuited to nursing because of their delicate emotional natures. She had triumphed over this stereotype and epitomized action over reaction and sensible hard work over hysteria.

Nothing about my childhood had encouraged emotional displays of any kind, but it was Florence Nightingale who taught me to be proud of this. She and my other friends from the pages of British literature encouraged me to cultivate their famous stiff upper lip. I learned from them that having a good cry was a luxury, like having a manicure or a massage. It was something to indulge in only after all the hard work was over.

So now, having just learned that my daughter's heart was mysteriously and perhaps irrevocably damaged, I did what Florence Nightingale had taught me to do all those years ago: I drowned my terror in hard work. And, thanks to Valerie's crisis, I knew exactly what to do.

The first thing I did was go to my files and pull out the big paperback booklet guide to our insurance benefits. Then I studied the index and the table of contents until I had read every benefit I could find that related to the transportation of patients.

Yes, I knew I could have just called the toll-free number and talked to a benefits coordinator. But here's what I also knew: sometimes those coordinators are wrong. And here's what I knew about who has to pay the bill when those coordinators are wrong. That's right: it's *not* the insurance company.

Once I had reviewed the guide, I called the toll-free number to double-check my research, and the benefits coordinator confirmed what I had already discovered on my own: Insurance wasn't going to pay for that evacuation flight to the States.

"Be sure you know who's picking up the tab for that," the coordinator warned me. "A medical flight with a full emergency care team can cost tens of thousands of dollars."

Tens of *thousands*?

Stunned, I hung up the phone.

Next, I followed our benefits system to its source. Joe is a federal employee, so that meant calling Washington, DC. I spent an engrossing half hour trying different members of the Office of Personnel Management and listening to a variety of voicemail messages. Every so often, I broke through to real people, and they were very nice and as helpful as possible. But the question of an international ambulance flight was something they couldn't advise me on, so they kept directing me elsewhere.

This wasn't their fault. I knew that. For a few miserable, humiliating months, I had held a job answering phones for an electric company. The lesson I had learned there was not to take my problems out on the person who answers the phone. That never helps, and besides, it's cruel. (I lived through some tearful moments at the electric company.)

So now, I worked on my insurance problem with all the patience and absorbed attention of a fisherman unsnarling a bucket full of bait worms. And eventually, I wound up talking to a particular kind of expert at a particular military base somewhere, and lo and behold, he knew exactly what to tell me. (*Somebody* out there knows the answer to *every* single question—that's another lesson I live by.)

"Of course your daughter can take that flight," this man told me, "and you can go with her, too. It has nothing to do with insurance. It's part of your husband's agreement with the government. Emergency medical transport home is one of the benefits we extend to the families of our employees overseas."

I was so thrilled to hear this that I instantly suspected it might be wrong.

"Are you sure?" I asked. "Is there someplace I can read this for myself?"

"Absolutely," he said, and he quoted me chapter and verse of the *Joint Travel Regulations*. He then told me who to talk to at my local base, gave me a list of keywords to mention when I got there, and told me which form they would need to give me at the end of the process.

I hung up the phone, immensely relieved.

After dinner, Joe and I sat down to learn about Elena's cardiomyopathy. We looked up as much information as we could find in our reference books and on the Internet. We weren't able to learn much about it, but what we did learn scared us even more.

Cardiomyopathy in children and teens was a mysterious condition. And, yes, this condition could kill.

Once again, in order to fight down my panic, I took shelter in logic. What are the steps to dealing with a problem? Education, planning, execution. So, as Joe and I did our research, I wrote down a list of questions for the conference the next day. And that night, as I was falling asleep, I ran through that list over and over:

- Is this condition curable? Will the heart repair itself?

- If so, what will it take for that to happen?

- If not, what is the prognosis?

- What might be the possible causes of this damage? If it isn't anorexia—and the cardiologist sounded skeptical about that—then might it be some sort of autoimmune disorder?

- Unexplained weight loss is a symptom of a number of systemic conditions. Do any of those conditions also cause heart damage?

- What kinds of tests will another hospital be able to run, and what sorts of results might they be looking for?

As Joe and I drove to the hospital together, we talked through our list of questions again. Then I sat back and took a breath. It was all very scary, but I had the insurance issues worked out, and I had a rudimentary understanding of Elena's condition. I knew what we knew and what we still needed to learn. Overall, I felt as well prepared as I could be for the upcoming conference.

I wasn't.

Nothing in my life up to that point had prepared me for what was about to happen.

CHAPTER TWELVE

Dr. Petras was pacing up and down in the hallway outside the conference room. He appeared to be agitated. As soon as he saw us, he herded us into the room. The pediatrician and the cardiologist were there, but not our daughter.

"Where's Elena?" I said, stopping. "You said you wanted her to be at this meeting."

"Elena won't be attending," Dr. Petras said.

"I want her to attend," I said. "She's almost eighteen years old. She ought to participate."

But Dr. Petras waved me to my seat. He remained standing.

"It doesn't matter!" he snapped. "There's nothing to discuss. Elena's getting evacuated out of here on the next medical flight to be put into a psychiatric institution in the States."

"Into a *what?*" I said. "But no—the cardiologist said she's going to a children's hospital, a medical facility! Why an institution? What's going on? Has something happened?"

Joe and I turned to the other doctors. The cardiologist just shook her head. The pediatrician said, "We're sending Elena to a good children's hospital. It's a teaching hospital. They'll be able to figure out what's wrong."

"She'll be better off there," the cardiologist said next, speaking to us in a low voice, as if to exclude Dr. Petras from the conversation. "We don't have the resources to diagnose her here."

"We already know her diagnosis!" Dr. Petras said loudly. "She has *anorexia nervosa*! She needs six to nine months of residential psychiatric care!"

Six to nine *months* in a psychiatric hospital?

My mind reeled. I could swear that the room started spinning. Valerie had been *so* sick, burning and cutting herself, while staff at this same hospital had sent her home time after time with nothing but prescriptions for pills. Even when she had finally overdosed—a risk to her life, for heaven's sake!—she had stayed in the psychiatric hospital for only two months.

But Elena—our bright, responsible, busy girl—our honors student, our arrow-straight hospital volunteer, who had a million friends and a million projects, who served as an officer of the Future Business Leaders of America—*that* girl needed to be locked away for half a year?

How had this happened? For God's sake, a week ago we were getting *better*!

Logic! I needed logic. It was either that or burst into tears. "We . . . we have questions," I stammered. "About the cardiomyopathy—about what causes it . . ."

"That's the *anorexia*!" Dr. Petras stormed. "We know *exactly* what caused it!"

"But the cardiologist said . . . ," I began. Then I looked helplessly at Joe, and we both looked in mute appeal at the cardiologist.

"Honestly, I'd save your questions," she told us in that same low voice, "until you can talk to the doctor who's heading up her care team in the States."

"That's right," said the pediatrician. "I've written down his name for you so you can ask for him as soon as you get there."

Maybe because they were ignoring him, or maybe because he was finished with what he had wanted to say and had no interest in hearing from anyone else, Dr. Petras appeared to decide that our conference was at an end. He walked out of the room. Joe stayed to finish up with the other doctors, but I followed Dr. Petras.

Why I did this, I wasn't sure. Maybe I had some sort of idea that in a different setting, he would be more rational. Or maybe I instinctively guessed what he was going to do.

Dr. Petras made a beeline for Elena's room, only a couple of doors away. She must have heard the noise of our "conference" because she was already sitting up in bed.

"You're going back to the States," Dr. Petras told her, "to be treated for anorexia. You're going to spend at least six months in an institution."

I saw the stricken look on Elena's face. It must have matched the one on my own.

"We don't know that!" I hastily interrupted. "We have to see what the doctors in the States recommend."

But Dr. Petras didn't even acknowledge that I had spoken. He certainly didn't acknowledge what I had said.

"You can forget about seeing your friends again," he continued. "You won't come back to Germany. Your father will have to give up his job and take an early return to the States."

"You're going to make my father lose his job?" Elena cried.

"Hey, wait a minute," I said. "That's not true!"

"You can't take away my father's job!" Elena said. "You haven't given me a chance to gain weight on my own. If you'll give me a few weeks— if you gave me a chance—"

"It's too late for that," Dr. Petras said—and am I right that he sounded triumphant? "You won't have that senior year with your friends. You'll be in an institution for the next six to nine months, with a tube up your nose to feed you!"

At that point, Elena stopped talking. She lay back down and closed her eyes. Dr. Petras continued talking for several more minutes. The more she ignored him, the louder and more insistent he became.

"You're getting bussed to the airstrip and put on a medevac flight tomorrow, whether you like it or not! Forget about that senior year. You won't graduate with your class. You'll never see Germany or your friends again!"

I couldn't believe it. I absolutely could not believe what I was hearing. This man may not have understood my daughter well enough to find a strategy that would heal her, but he certainly knew how to turn her most vulnerable, vital dreams into a message of anguish and despair.

But if Dr. Petras had wanted to see tears—and he certainly *sounded* as if he did—then he might as well have saved himself the trouble. Short of hitting Elena's kneecaps with a hammer, I don't think there's any way he could have gotten them. Elena lay motionless, eyes closed, until he blustered his way to silence. Then he left the room without talking to me or acknowledging me in any way.

As soon as he left, Elena sat up.

"So, about what to pack," she said, as if Dr. Petras and his furious threats didn't even exist.

"Elena, I just want you to know," I said, "that he's wrong about where you're going. You're going to a medical hospital. It's for your heart."

"Sure, whatever," she said quickly, in a tone of voice that stopped further discussion. As upset as I was, I respected her desire not to prolong that unpleasant scene.

For twenty minutes, Elena and I discussed which items to take, and she told me where to find her favorite clothes. Then I left to pack, reassured that at least one of the parties to that discussion had acted like a reasonable adult.

I was up very late that night. First, I packed. Then I finished my read-through of my *Wuthering Heights* story and sent it off in an email message to my editor and agent. If, just a week ago, I had been thinking that it felt out of place in our lives now, a relic from a darker time, that day's display of ruthlessness had made the story live for me again.

Emily Brontë was right. This world is a brutal place.

The next morning was transport day. I was up very early, even though I had barely slept. And in spite of my anxiety, I was interested to see how the transport would go. After all, I told myself, how many civilians get to ride in a real military medical evacuation flight?

At this time, the height of both Mideast wars, the military hospital transported wounded soldiers home on two flights each week. Elena would be only one member of this flight's group of casualties. Her nurse wheeled her outside on a gurney to wait in the early morning sunshine for the blue medical buses to come pick us up. One gurney after another came through the double doors of the emergency room, bringing wounded soldiers to wait with us on the curved asphalt driveway.

Joe stayed with us until the blue buses showed up. He was completely miserable. He had no idea when he'd see us again. But I refused to be miserable. I insisted on seeing this as an adventure. With the long, chaotic day that stretched out in front of me, misery was one more luxury I couldn't afford.

Elena's bus was for stretcher patients and nurses only. I rode in a smaller bus with a few other family members and personnel. But at each stage of the orderly process of checking us in, getting our luggage sorted, and transporting us to the airplane, I was allowed to visit with Elena. She seemed to be in good spirits, and I knew that she liked the young nurse who was traveling with her.

Elena's fellow evacuees were Army and Marine personnel who had been badly injured downrange. Rather than rehabilitate them in Germany and send them back to the front, the hospital was sending them home to be healed and then discharged from service. The soldiers were looking forward to getting back stateside, and as they waited on their gurneys, they joked with one another. I was looking forward to getting to a stateside hospital, too. I felt that we were escaping from a dangerous and possibly unbalanced man.

The worst is behind us, I told myself as I looked out the window of my bus. *From here, things can only get better.* Maybe this new doctor in the States would know just what was wrong and would tell us that Elena's heart could still heal.

Our buses pulled onto the gigantic concrete taxiway and stopped next to a big gray C-17 aircraft. Its wide back end was open for loading. Uniformed personnel were carrying the patients up into its metal belly one at a time, teams of six soldiers to each stretcher. Then they came over to our bus, took our luggage, and told us we could walk onboard.

I looked around with curiosity as I walked up the metal ramp. This wasn't just an exhibit at a museum or an air show. This was an actual working warplane! Cryptic numbers in black stencil lettering ran along the panels overhead, and charcoal-colored nonskid tape striped the floor in chevron patterns.

The wide belly of the C-17 could haul anything it needed to haul. That day, it was flying home wounded soldiers, and their stretchers had been linked together to form several rows of broad, open temporary shelves down the center of the plane: a series of upper and lower bunks held together by special poles. Once we arrived in the States, personnel would carry the stretchers away, and the poles that had held them together would come apart. Then the belly of the aircraft would be empty again, and it could bring back trucks or pallets of cargo or whatever else the war machine downrange needed.

The young nurse who was traveling with Elena waved me over to where Elena's stretcher was racked into the open-shelf framework. Beside her stretcher, built into the outer hull of the aircraft, was a line of airplane seats. I wouldn't be facing forward for the flight; I would be looking into the interior of the plane. But that didn't matter. The plane didn't have any windows, so it wasn't as if I was missing out on a view.

Elena's stretcher was a "lower bunk" for the flight. I sat down in the nearest seat, snapped my belt, and stowed my purse and paperwork at my feet. Then I leaned over to say hello.

My daughter's eyes were closed. She appeared to be asleep. She must be exhausted to fall asleep so quickly. That was the result of a week of hunger-strike starvation, I thought, and I spent a few seconds worrying about her damaged heart.

"Hey, hon," I said. "How are you feeling?"

Elena's foot was sticking out from under the green blanket. It was moving just a little. It made slow, rhythmic swings back and forth.

"Hey," I said again. "Elena?"

No response.

Elena's hands, clasped close to her chest, began to twitch. As I watched, puzzled, the foot that stuck out from under the blanket rotated in a slow circle.

The nurse walked up to greet me with a bright smile.

"Did you give Elena any medication?" I asked her. "She seems to be asleep." How, I didn't know—the back of the plane was still open, and medical personnel were dragging in metal crates of supplies. The engine noise was so loud that I practically had to shout.

"No, we were just talking outside," the nurse said, surprised. "Elena!" She leaned down and gave Elena's arm a shake.

Elena's eyelids flickered. *Oh, good, she's waking up*, I thought. But no: her eyes were rolling in her head. And now her hands were twisting at the wrists, describing their own slow circles.

The nurse turned and yelled something to the rest of the medical crew, and my daughter's body disappeared behind green-camouflaged backs. They pushed, called, poked, picked up hands and feet, and dropped them again. They leaned down and shouted into her ear.

But Elena didn't wake up. She lay completely unresponsive, with her hands and feet gently circling.

Dr. Petras had made good on his threat to force her to leave Germany. He had stripped her of power and control. But Elena had gotten the last laugh. She had slipped beyond his reach.

She had slipped beyond the reach of everything.

CHAPTER THIRTEEN

Ambulance! Now!" yelled a gray-haired man in fatigues. "I'm sorry," he said, turning to me, "but I have to order her off this flight."

Elena's stretcher was already being quick-marched down the ramp. Stunned, I grabbed my purse and paperwork and scurried after it.

"What's wrong?" I demanded as uniformed stretcher-bearers loaded Elena onto one of the small blue buses. Elena's nurse and I climbed in behind them. "What's wrong?" I asked again. "What's happening? Is it her heart?"

But Elena's nurse didn't know. Her eyes were frightened.

As we started back to base, she and another nurse stood over Elena, and between the two of them, they tried to hold her down. But they couldn't manage it. They weren't strong enough.

Elena's body jerked and twisted. The circling of her hands and her feet became more violent. She started to breathe in long, rattling gasps.

"Elena!" shouted the nurses, trying to pin her wrists, but they couldn't slow the rapid circles.

Red lines appeared on my unconscious daughter's face and neck. Her circling fingernails were tearing into her skin. Her head was back, and the muscles of her face were rigid. Her eyes rolled under half-closed lids.

Did she have epilepsy? Did she have a heart attack? Was she losing oxygen? Was she going to *die*?

"Elena!" cried the nurse. She broke smelling salts under Elena's nose, but nothing worked to bring her around.

My hands were shaking and jerking, too. I almost dropped my cell phone. From a long way away, I heard Joe's voice.

"What's wrong?" he was asking.

What was wrong? I didn't know. Maybe Elena's heart had burst. Maybe a blood clot had reached her brain.

The ambulance stopped, and techs threw my daughter's flailing body onto a gurney. Her cheeks were bleeding from the scratches, and her gasps had become long groans. Somebody thrust an oxygen mask over her face, but her circling hands caught its straps and tangled them.

The team of techs raced the gurney down the hall. I ran along behind it, like an extra in my own personal horror movie. The only memory I retain from that journey is the shocked expressions on the faces of people jumping out of our way.

Elena's groans were wails now, long wavering howls with absolutely no mind behind them. Her eyes were open, rolling so violently in their sockets that nothing showed except the bloodshot whites.

The techs and nurses had rushed us up to the pediatric ward. Now somebody came out to meet them. "Not here!" he shouted. "Emergency room!" So we turned around and rushed away again.

I discovered that we had collected Joe at some point during this hideous parade. As we crashed through the swinging doors of the ER, staff came running up to meet the gurney, and it disappeared into a room at the end of the hall. Joe and I weren't allowed to follow, so now it was just the two of us, standing outside, panting, trying to process what we had just seen.

Was Elena dying? Did she have brain damage? Was she *dying*?

The ER doctor stepped out of the closed room to talk to us, looking remarkably calm and completely in charge. His composure steadied my wrecked nerves. "It's a panic attack," he said. "I've administered Ativan to bring her around. In the meantime, we're going to leave her alone in the room. Holding her down or interfering with her just makes it worse. We'll call you from the waiting room when she's ready for visitors."

"A—a what? A panic attack?" Joe and I asked, almost in unison. "What do you mean, a panic attack? Are you sure? What's that? What about her heart?"

"Her heart's fine."

"But a panic attack? She's never had those before. She's never done anything like this!"

"It's either a panic attack—or a psychotic break," amended the doctor. "We'll know which one it was when she comes around. Go on out to the waiting room now. We'll call you when you can come see her."

Joe and I sat in the waiting room for an hour. It was truly an hour from hell. Our only distractions were the military information pamphlets and CNN on the waiting room television.

What I thought about during that hour, I have no idea. I don't know that I thought at all.

By the time we were called back to see Elena, she had been moved upstairs. We found her lying in the intensive care unit (ICU), next to an impressive bank of machines and monitors. An oxygen sensor clip had taken over one of her fingertips. A clear plastic feeding tube snaked out of her nostril, and the fabric tape that held it in place clung to the tip of her nose like a permanent drip. She lay motionless. She didn't know we were there.

This was my daughter—my bright, fierce, idealistic daughter, who never stopped moving, planning, talking, *doing* things, from morning until night. Now, Elena lay absolutely still. She had stopped completely.

The black screen of the monitor illustrated Elena's state of deep rest: long, slow yellow loops for her breathing, widely spaced green blips for her heartbeats. Everything about her sleep was perfectly even and regular, as if she were on life-support machines that none of us could see.

I dropped into a chair beside Elena and once again set down my purse and the packet of paperwork. My first impulse was to burst into tears. What lay here was only the outer shell of the person called Elena, the part that didn't matter so much. The other part was her lively eyes, her ever-changing expression, and the millions of shades of emotion in her voice as she jumped from topic to topic: "Guess *what*!"

But that part was gone.

"Don't worry," the ICU nurse told us. "Your daughter was sitting up a while ago. She was talking to me." But she didn't sit up and talk to us, even though Joe and I sat by her bedside all evening.

Periodically, Elena would stir, like a dreamer disturbed (all the colored loops and blips clustering together and becoming uneven), and whisper something that might or might not make sense. I couldn't tell if she had any idea where she was or how she had come to be there.

Elena's pediatrician came by to see her. He could offer no insight into what had happened. But I knew. In my heart, I knew.

First, there had been the week in the hospital—the week of the hunger strike. Elena had refused food so steadily during this enforced period of "refeeding" that it must have stressed her body severely.

Then, after this week of stress, there had been the all-out attack. There were the threats, and there was the yelling: "You won't have that senior year! You won't ever see your friends again!"

As I sat by my daughter's still, frail form, those harsh sentences echoed in my mind, and I knew—I just *knew*: This had happened the very second those threats began to come true. After all the pain and grief she had gone through with Valerie and after her hesitation to try a new school, she had finally begun to take risks again. She had found a new group of friends and had made a new home for herself by volunteering at the hospital. Then, out of the blue, came this imprisonment and forced exile, and Elena couldn't bear it. She couldn't bear to go through any more grief.

So they had put her on the plane, and Elena had fought back. She had fought back the only way she could.

And me? I had let that man lock up and threaten my daughter. After all those years of swearing I would be an extraordinary mother, I had stood there and listened to that dangerously unbalanced quack as he had practiced his shady power plays on my child.

There were no words for the misery I felt.

After an hour or so, two nurses came in with a tall blue pump stand and told us that Elena would be receiving a balanced, nutrient-rich liquid diet. This mysterious medical formula turned out to be strawberry-flavored Ensure.

That made me feel a little better. It was a relief to think that Elena would be taking in nourishment at last.

The nurses filled up the clear bag connected to the pump and started it grinding away. First, the bag was soft pink. Then the tube was soft pink. Then soft pink fluid flowed out of Elena's mouth and puddled on her pillow, and she choked and gagged, and the nurses ended up having to stop the pump. They couldn't figure out what was wrong, but they thought that maybe the tube had a wrong bend.

That was the end of Elena's nutrient-rich diet.

When nighttime came, Joe went home. He had to face another long workday in the morning. But I couldn't bear to leave my daughter alone again. I already regretted so very painfully the nights I had left her here.

As a child, Elena had been afraid of many things. Her vivid imagination had brought to life all sorts of monsters. Now, she might wake up and not know where she was. I didn't want her to feel frightened.

Or maybe I was the one who was afraid.

So I stayed behind when Joe left. The ICU nurse found me a recliner chair and moved it next to Elena's bed. I settled in to watch my daughter sleep. But I didn't sleep.

When we had brought Valerie to the ER after her overdose, one floor below and one year before, I had felt angry, helpless, and afraid. Now, sitting beside the silent wreck of my second daughter, I felt far beyond those things. I felt so much that it seemed as if I felt nothing at all.

My sharp, scheming brain couldn't offer up a plan. It couldn't reach abstract thought. It couldn't seem to progress beyond its immediate surroundings. It fumbled in a dreary round over the lighted monitors, the electronic beeps, the chilly air, the still form on the bed, the unfamiliar feel of the recliner chair, and back to the monitors again. The few images my imagination served up were dreary memories of these same things: hospital walls, electronic beeps, lighted monitors, chilly air.

It was as if the entire universe had narrowed down to just this slender fragment of experience.

On the day Elena was born, I almost died. I couldn't stop bleeding. Not even in horror movies have I seen that much blood. The flowing red tide took everything away with it as the hours passed: my joy and my worry, my awareness of what people were doing, and my attentiveness to what they said. Color itself seemed to flow out of the world, and I lost track of the reason I was in the hospital. The next morning, we would learn that half my blood was gone.

As that fuzzy gray day of Elena's birth faded into shadowy night, one single solitary needle-sharp thought pierced the cotton-wool fog of my brain: *If you fall asleep, you will never wake up again.*

That thought grew and grew until, as weak as I was, it forced me out of bed. That thought forced me to walk, barely able to see, hanging onto the handrail that stretched along the corridors.

I staggered through the hospital halls that night after my daughter's birth, drunk on severe blood loss. Only the handrail kept me on my feet. When I had to cross a hall, I paused to make long and dubious calculations. Would my legs hold me up while I took that many steps alone? Would the floor be cold if I fell?

Only one image from that night is clear: I am looking through the picture window of the newborn nursery at the babies in their bassinets. Only one baby is awake: Elena stares out at the world with a look of fierce determination. It seems ominous that my new baby does not cry.

I am standing and thinking: *Does she know about me? Can she tell that her brand-new life has already gone wrong? If I die, what will happen to Elena? Who will cuddle my baby?*

In that very second, for the very first time, I felt love for this new human being. But that love was cut through with fear. My first memories of my daughter are full of pain.

Now, as I sat beside Elena's bed in the ICU, I remembered that night. Like fumbling fingers rubbing a worry stone, my mind kept reaching out and touching it. It was the only other time Elena and I had been in the hospital at night. In the seventeen years between these two complete disasters, she hadn't been sick enough to need a hospital stay.

Beeping monitors. Chilly air. Dim hospital walls. Worry and pain. My mind couldn't process thoughts about these things. It could only stumble past them again and again, on an endless, monotonous round.

In some dim way, I sensed that I had become impaired. Whenever the nurse came by and spoke to me, I had to think carefully before I could answer. My tongue tripped over itself as if I were drunk.

A pediatric nurse came down from Elena's old ward with a stack of her favorite VHS tapes. Then—and I am not quite sure how anymore, whether a nurse asked me or whether I managed to do this on my own—a movie started playing on the television monitor in the corner of the room. I don't think Elena had any idea that the movie was on. I don't think she stirred once. But I watched that movie. I watched it over and over.

The movie was *Peter Pan*, by director P. J. Hogan. I had never seen it before, but it was as familiar to me as the contents of my purse. This was the world as I had known it in the days of my earliest childhood.

Some of my oldest memories involve my mother and her friends talking about strange myths. To sophisticated professors, these tales were about comparative anthropology and the history of civilization itself. But to the preschool me, it was the concrete details that mattered: a gigantic warrior, towering over the battlefield, with one enormous red eye; a young girl, fleeing in terror, frozen in seconds inside a skin of bark and leaves.

I was too young to know that these mythic events couldn't happen. My mother and her friends discussed them as seriously as if they had. So demigods and demons and ghosts became as real to me as my own family history. To me, they were as real as the disasters on the evening news.

When my mother's friends disappeared from my young life, they left these strange mythical monsters behind them. I couldn't go to those friends' houses anymore, but I could still get to Asgard and Olympus. I played there among the warriors and gods, and they taught me their secrets. In third grade, I couldn't have told you the rules of baseball, but I could have told you how to escape from an angry Cyclops.

If we dream about what is oldest and closest to us in our lives, then it makes sense that I write fantasy. The people in my dreamworlds walk through mirrors and hide themselves in mist. They shape-shift and work strange spells. They are what those mythic childhood companions were: colorful and misshapen.

Monsters and I are very old friends.

Now, during that lonely vigil by my daughter's silent body, Peter Pan came flying in through the window like my very own guardian angel. With him came all things magical—and to me, that meant all things familiar: mermaids and fairies, skeletons, lost children, deformed pirates, mythic warriors, and a ticking crocodile with a taste for human flesh. It was as if all the monsters in all the stories I'd ever loved had come to my rescue.

God bless P. J. Hogan. I'll never be able to repay him.

The next morning, Joe showed up very early and took me for a walk outside. By then, I had recovered enough to become aware on some level that it was a beautiful day. But as the hours passed, our stricken daughter stayed out of reach. She did almost nothing but sleep, and she communicated in the vaguest of whispers. Occasionally, she opened her eyes just a crack, as if she were lying in very bright sunlight.

Then the cardiologist stopped by to check Elena's heart monitor, and she brought with her a sense of brisk, healthy purpose that blew into the ICU room like a strong, fresh breeze. Elena still needed to get to the hospital in the States, she said, and this episode only demonstrated that the sooner she could get to the experts, the better. Our orders had been updated to put Elena on a flight the following morning, and an ICU nurse would accompany her this time. If this problem happened again, he would know what to do.

So it turned out that there was still a plan in place, and it seemed to be a good one. It required nothing of Joe or me, which was good because we had very little to give. The cardiologist left, but the sense of purpose that she had brought with her stayed behind and continued to blow fresh thoughts into our traumatized brains.

Getting out of this hospital—that felt like a very welcome idea.

Dave, the ICU transport nurse, came by to meet Elena shortly afterward. He had white hair but a youthful face and the dark golden eyes and cagey, confident expression of an alpha wolf. He talked to me for a while about his battlefield experience, about medevac flights of the past, and about the two children he didn't get to see more often than a couple of times a year. He had been through a lot, and he loved what he did. He was glad to be able to help.

The pediatrician came by to ask if we had met Dave. He checked on Elena, and she opened her eyes a tiny slit and gave him a half-asleep smile.

"Is she still getting drugs through her IV line?" I asked. "She seems so out of it!"

"No," he said. "She's had no medication since yesterday afternoon."

He didn't volunteer a reason why Elena might seem so incapacitated, and I didn't have the strength to ask. But his manner was cheerful and encouraging, and I took that gift with gratitude.

During the two long days that Elena stayed in that ICU bed, Dr. Petras didn't come to check on her once.

By that evening, the nurses and I found that we had settled into a routine. It seemed as if Elena had been in the ICU for weeks instead of only a day, and what had seemed strange and ominous the previous night now felt normal and safe. Maybe tonight I could finally close my eyes and get some rest.

But just when I was ready to nod off, a problem came up to rumple my routine. A young soldier with serious injuries needed the recliner. Did I mind trading it for a regular waiting room chair?

Of course not! Anything to help the wounded.

But now—how was I going to sleep?

The waiting room chair didn't offer much in the way of support. It was a modern chrome-and-fabric type with no arms and only a low sling-style rectangle of cloth across the back. I couldn't rest my upper body in it at all, so I decided to borrow part of Elena's ICU bed. The bed had bars down both sides to keep its patient from rolling out, but there wasn't a bar near the bottom. So I pulled my chair forward, crossed my arms on the blanket by Elena's feet, and put my head down on them, just like I remembered doing during rest time in grade school.

My body was so tired that I immediately drifted off.

For about five minutes.

The ICU bed had a "smart" mattress. It was forever inflating and deflating parts of itself with purposeful breaths and long sighs, rearranging itself so that a critically ill patient wouldn't get bedsores. And this smart mattress quickly outsmarted me. It knew that nothing heavy should be lying across its very end, below where a pair of feet should be, so it emptied all the air out of the part of the mattress I was resting on. Before long, my arms and cheek were flat against its hard metal platform, and the metal edge of its framework was digging into my stomach.

I gave up. I couldn't sleep sitting up in the waiting room chair, and that meant I couldn't sleep at all. So I turned on the television, but with no sound, and I stared at whatever showed up on the screen.

A bunch of golfers were playing a tournament in Liverpool: gray skies and a brown golf course. I watched them wander through that rough, tawny seascape in stupefied amazement. It hadn't occurred to me before that golf courses came in brown.

As the hours wore away, the television screen developed a hazy glow around it, until the sober-faced golfers and the tall sea grasses and wind-driven coastal clouds all blended together into a bright smear. The night began to feel like a long transatlantic flight: lights were dim throughout the quiet ICU, like an airline cabin over the ocean, and nurses slipped in and out with drinks and blankets.

I leaned my head on the metal bars that lined Elena's bed and counted the steady beats of the monitor. *We'll get there*, I found myself thinking over and over. *Even the longest flight ends.*

Morning brought a gurney into the room, and the bustle and noise of transport. But I went through it this second time on autopilot. Not until I walked onto the plane did I really register where I was. My thoughts started there because so did my fear.

Elena was in a different place on this flight. She was on the top bunk this time. A bulky heart monitor squatted on a shelf at her feet. This time, I wasn't surprised that she was unconscious.

During takeoff and the initial ascent, Elena didn't move or open her eyes, but I watched her heart monitor with obsessive dread. First, her pulse was eighty. Then it was a hundred. Then it was a hundred and twenty.

I could feel my own heart pounding.

What if the cardiomyopathy put Elena into some sort of crisis? What if she started howling and wailing again? Would Dave be able to handle her? Would I have to watch him try to hold her down while her eyes rolled again under half-closed lids?

When I was in first grade, I got stung by a wasp. It was my first bewildered impression of attack and severe pain. For several years after that, I watched for wasps in the landscape with single-minded dread. A wasp in the room with me, bumping lazily along the ceiling, would absorb my attention entirely. I would see nothing else. I would hear nothing else. For hours.

Now, I feared the hideous apparition of my flailing, mindless daughter with just that same childlike sense of alarm. Up until two days ago, it had never even crossed my mind as a possibility. Now, it was the most terrifying thing I knew.

But as soon as the plane leveled off, Dave came to stand by Elena's stretcher and watch over her like her own personal, faithful wolf. He was so clearly in charge of the situation that my fears rapidly dissipated. Once again, optimism flickered like a match flame in my heart.

As bad as things have been, I'll bet we've finally hit bottom, I thought. *Things will get better from here.*

As my worries eased, I began to take an interest in the unusual situation I was in. Contact with Air Force bases had accustomed me to properly pressed uniforms and neatly kept beige buildings, and life on a NATO base had presented me with a fascinating assortment of camouflage patterns. But that was all very different from the sight of an actual transport of wartime wounded.

Every new experience feeds a writer's imagination. After two days of static, dreary awfulness, I could once again feel my writer's mind begin to stretch itself as it explored and catalogued the scene in front of me.

No wonder they called this the belly of the plane, I thought. It really was just a big tube. Rows of strong steel rings lay embedded in the metal floor panels, and arrays of canvas tie-down straps lay in neat coils in alcoves in the walls. Every color in the hollowed-out body of the plane seemed to have been chosen for maximum ugliness. Mustard-yellow wires snaked down the curved walls next to pale gray-white paint, and bright crimson ductwork ran next to foil-wrapped insulation panels.

Despite the interior's odd shape and bizarre appearance, it felt more like a room in a community center than it felt like anywhere else I'd been: like an anonymous space quickly adapted for a temporary use. The nursing staff didn't look like nurses, either, to my untrained eye: they looked like soldiers because they were wearing their camouflage uniforms.

The patients, young men and women from the war zones, lay on their stretchers, tucked up under dark green blankets in their upper and lower bunks. Many of them had one or more white casts sticking out from under the blanket. A couple of critical-care patients had all but disappeared under what looked like small mountains of old PC monitors.

Despite the loud engine noise, or maybe because of it, the flying ward felt quiet. No one cried out. Nobody appeared to be complaining.

We handful of family members who were accompanying the wounded sat bolt upright in our line of seats set into the wall of the aircraft. The seat on my left-hand side was empty. A Middle Eastern woman sat on my right. The flight crew, wearing their jumpsuits, came by to issue us sack lunches, also a green blanket of our own because the aircraft was cold.

Somehow, despite its kinship with baby onesies and toddler rompers, the military flight suit manages to be the most macho uniform.

Elena's hands and feet began to dip and circle occasionally, even though Dave had loaded her up with sedatives. He was still standing beside her, watching her carefully. He had a little notepad with him, and he was taking notes.

"What makes her do that?" I asked. "It's what she was doing before, when they had to take her off the plane. It's like some kind of slow-motion seizure."

"I don't know," Dave admitted. "I've never seen a patient do that."

For a while, her lazy movements held my attention and raised my apprehension again the way wasps had done in my childhood. But I was older now. I could be reasonable. Dave was on duty.

Once again, I took an interest in what was going on around me.

The young wounded woman who had the bunk underneath Elena's was tanned and muscular, with very short blond hair—almost fuzz. The side of her neck had a hole in it—not a scab or a cut but a straw-size, dried-out hole bored straight through the skin, deep into what appeared to be beef jerky. This was the site of a battlefield IV, and it wasn't hard to see why she had needed it: an enormous cast buried her leg from hip to toes in thick white plaster.

She told me that she was Army and that a roadside bomb had rolled her transport and shattered her leg. She knew she wouldn't be able to return downrange, and that was a real grief to her: the members of her unit were like brothers and sisters, her constant companions for over a year, and she hated the thought of leaving them to face hardship without her help. She was upbeat and cheerful, but over and over, she worried about her friends downrange. She had left them in the lurch, she said—as if the powdering of her leg bones was a humiliating character flaw rather than a physical injury.

The Middle Eastern woman sitting next to me looked very pretty and girlish, even though she was older than I was. According to Western culture, she was overweight, but it wasn't that simple: her ample frame was somehow abundant and healthy, and it only added to her charm. Her husband was lying very still under one of those mountains of monitors. Only the sine waves and flickering numbers showed that he was alive. But still, the woman could smile, although her black eyes were worried. Her smile was an act of will and a beautiful thing.

We were heavily involved then in the war in Iraq, but the woman told me she wasn't Iraqi. I think she may have been from Jordan. Her husband had worked as a translator for the Americans for many years, and when the war came, he had felt that he should help. So he had uprooted his wife, now a grandmother, and had moved her away from her family into troubled Iraq. She was frightened from the first, but he had considered it a point of honor, she said: he had always been proud to work for the United States, and he felt sure that the Americans would look after them.

The enemy had lain in wait for him and caught him. Whatever they had done to him had been very bad. Fortunately, his American commander had lived up to that good man's trust and code of honor. He had made this flight happen by sheer force of will, and the medical care in the States, too, when bureaucrats in Washington had tried to prevent it.

While the woman was telling me this, Elena stirred and mumbled. Dave leaned over to listen but then looked at me with a shrug. So I stood up and leaned my ear close to my daughter's lips to try to make out the words.

"Makeup bag," she was whispering. And her emaciated, birdlike fingers were plucking at the blanket, searching.

This bag and her glasses were the two things Elena had kept by her pillow during the whole stay in the hospital. Her black makeup bag seemed to have become some kind of security blanket: she spent long hours with it clutched in her hand. Now I found it for her, a few inches away from her fumbling fingers, and instantly, her uneasiness subsided.

Very, very slowly and mechanically, she unzipped the zipper and felt through it. She didn't even open her eyes. Then, very, very slowly, she pulled out her powder compact and began patting its little round sponge across her face.

She never once looked up at us. She didn't seem to be awake. But she thoroughly, painstakingly powdered her face, replaced the sponge, put the compact away, and zipped the bag shut. Then she unzipped it again, felt around, found the compact, took out the sponge, and powdered her face again.

She did this over and over.

As I watched her, the tiny flame of optimism in my heart guttered and went out. Who *was* this skinny young woman? I didn't know this person at all. My daughter—my ally—my friend!—where *was* she?

The Elena I knew didn't back away from a fight. She loved to go up against the mighty. Dark eyes dancing, wry smile on her face, she found humor in the most unexpected places. What had happened to that bright, witty girl? Was she ever going to come back?

I felt a rustle in the seat next to mine as the Middle Eastern grandmother leaned toward me. "What is wrong with your daughter?" she asked me kindly. "Such a pretty young girl!"

"Her heart," I answered. "Something's wrong with her heart."

As if it could really be that simple.

CHAPTER FOURTEEN

couldn't sleep on the medevac flight. Seats embedded in the walls of an airplane hull don't recline. By the time our plane landed in the States, I hadn't slept in about thirty-six hours.

But when they let down the big ramp at the back of the airplane, the sunshine revived me, and an ambulance waited on the concrete only a few steps away to take Elena and me to the children's hospital.

I had no idea where I would be sleeping that night. I had been in this city only once, at a conference downtown. It's on the East Coast, thousands of miles away from my home in Texas.

Normally, this would be worrying me. I would be asking questions and trying to put together a plan. But the stress of the last few days had slowed me down. I couldn't put together plans anymore. So I rode in the front seat with the ambulance driver through sunlit streets, and I gave no real thought to where we were going.

The golden light of late afternoon sparkled off the windshield and the stones in the roadway. *Everything will be all right,* those hypnotic sparkles seemed to say. *Don't worry. It's all taken care of.*

We pulled up to a special entrance and almost immediately stepped into a large elevator. I followed Elena's stretcher down wide bright hallways and into her room. After the stark, utilitarian ICU back in Germany, this hospital room seemed almost pretty. It had a big window partially covered by a dark blue curtain, and another curtain beside the bed, with pastel fish swimming across it. Accustomed to double-occupancy rooms in other hospitals, I was happy to discover that this room held only one bed.

While the techs settled Elena in and hooked her up to a new set of machines, I wandered over to the window. A small desk and office-style chair were there, pushed up against the wall, and a low, comfortable-looking foam chair occupied the floor beside them. I sank down onto the foam chair with a feeling of relief, leaned my heavy head back into its softness, and watched the parade of nurses, doctors, students, and techs come by to check on my daughter.

The change of venue seemed to have been good for Elena. She was actually half awake now. She still kept her eyes slitted against the light, but she was talking in a low voice and even joking a little.

I felt myself sliding closer to sleep. *Life is good*, I thought.

Elena's parade of visitors comprised every ethnicity and skin tone, from rich, deep ebony to warm coffee brown and light olive tan. *This is America*, I thought as I drowsed on the foam chair. *This is one of the most wonderful things about America.* And, even though I was thousands of miles away from my own state, I thought, *This is home. I've come home.*

A nurse approached me. "Will you be staying with your daughter?" she asked.

I roused myself to answer. "I'd like to stay as long as I can. I don't know what your policy is on that. But I do need to get my hotel sorted out. Do you know where I can get a list of hotels nearby?"

"This is a children's hospital," she said. "We expect a parent to stay in the room. You're welcome to stay if you like."

"For the night?" I asked, feeling confused and a little stupid. "But how—where can I sleep?"

"For as long as your daughter is here," she answered with characteristic patience. "That chair you're on folds out into a bed."

A bed! All my remaining problems, solved in one friendly sentence. I found that I couldn't speak. I actually couldn't speak. My eyes were full of tears.

The nurse understood. She didn't wait for me to answer. She said, "I'll bring you sheets and a pillow."

A bed! I washed my face, spread out the sheets, took off my shoes, and lay down. A bed. A horizontal surface! My exhausted body sagged into the cushions, and I lay there, happy beyond all expectation of happiness at being horizontal at last.

"Elena," I heard the nurse say. "Elena?"

Her tone of voice prickled through my peaceful drowsiness. Her tone of voice was distressingly familiar.

"Elena!"

I dragged myself up from the foam mattress and came over to the bed.

The nurse was rolling my daughter back and forth. "Answer me!" she said loudly. The nurse was doing things, hurried things: patting and prodding. Then she hit the alarm.

Instantly, the room was full of staff. "She won't respond," the nurse told them. "Elena? Elena!"

Half asleep, half petrified, I tried to gather data. No, Elena's heart hadn't stopped: her monitor still sounded the steady, reassuring beep of the heartbeats. I tried to take in the details of the scene, but the details were eluding me. Was that a needle in someone's hand, or was it just a pen?

"Elena!" the person said, stabbing it at her arm. "Elena, wake up!"

"Get her to CT scan," ordered a firm voice. "Now!"

Then a gurney was in the room, and the gurney went rushing out the door. I just had time to slip on my shoes, grab my purse (why my purse?), and follow it. The hallway had no more golden sunlight in it, or kind faces, or rich colors. It was grim and gray and poorly lit, and I had done this before—oh, God! I'd done this before!

Then I was standing on the other side of a glass wall, locked outside, while a big machine ran tests on Elena's brain. What was wrong? Was my daughter dying? Was she *dying*?

A technician came out. I saw no face. I only heard a voice. "The CT scan is normal," the voice said.

"Why?" I asked. "Why is she doing this? What's happening to her?" I wanted to grab him and make him look me in the eye, but there seemed to be no faces anymore.

"I'm afraid I can't answer that," said the voice.

Now I was shuffling after the gurney again, down more half-lit, blurry hallways. We crowded into a big elevator with shiny white walls, and I couldn't see the lights that told the floors. That's when it hit me: my contact lenses were in their case inside my purse. That's why nobody had a face anymore.

Elena's gurney stopped in a vast room without edges that I could see. A white shape detached itself from the vague scenery and approached me.

"You can't stay here," the shape told me. "No parents are allowed in the ICU at night."

Completely bewildered, I tried to process this unexpected information. My brain felt for the edges of this new obstacle, but nothing like a useful idea came back. I couldn't stay here: a big blank wall that my thoughts couldn't get past. Dead end. It was a dead end. I was at the end.

"Where can I go?" I blurted out. "Where do I go?"

"There are waiting rooms and sleeping lounges," answered the shape. Then it walked away.

I was standing beside the gurney. The only thing my poor eyesight could decode was the still form lying on it. Only my sleeping daughter had a face, half bad vision and half good memory: that face I had known and had watched for every quicksilver change of mood—for how many years now?

Forever.

That face was the only familiar thing left in my scary world.

I leaned in, close enough to see the face clearly. My sparkly daughter. My youngest child. But the face didn't move. It didn't respond.

I didn't think I could bear it. My heart was going to break.

"Elena," I whispered. "Elena! Please come back."

My daughter didn't stir. She was breathing quietly, frowning slightly: still, remote, and utterly impassive.

I couldn't help myself. I started to cry.

"Elena, please don't leave me like this!" I whispered. "I'm alone here. I'm all alone. Please don't do this to me. Please don't leave me here alone."

Elena's eyes didn't open. But she rolled over, like a sleeper who has been disturbed. One thin hand reached up to touch my face.

Then the white shape was back. "You need to leave now," it said.

So I went.

I blundered out into deserted hallways, where featureless black night pressed up against the windows. Somewhere in this building was a foam bed with sheets on it, all made up for me, but I had no idea where that foam bed was. It didn't occur to me, in my sleep-deprived state, that I could go back to that room and that they would let me sleep there, even though Elena was somewhere else. It didn't occur to me that I could go to the front desk and ask for my daughter's room number. I was beyond such practical thoughts.

So, once again, I wandered hospital halls, as I had done on the night Elena was born. I met no one. I recognized nothing. Nothing disturbed the misery of that journey.

Dark glass windows lined the wall to my left. Night. I glanced outside. But I wasn't looking outside, I was looking inside, into an unlit room. My bad eyes could just make out rows of foam chairs like the one in Elena's room by the window.

For a little while, my slow-moving brain computed. Then it spit out an actual thought:

This is a sleeping lounge. It's here for people like me.

I found the door and tiptoed inside.

One other person was using the room. A man lay cocooned under a dark blue blanket nearby, on a foldout chair of his own. He had the blanket pulled up over his face. I tiptoed past him, found stacks of those same blue blankets near the wall, and located a pile of pillows as well. I took a set, tiptoed to a chair that seemed a suitable distance away from the sleeping stranger, and arranged myself for the rest of the night.

My waistband pinched. I hadn't taken off my shoes. But I couldn't do anything about that now. I had gone as far as I could. I rolled onto my side, hugged my purse like a teddy bear, and closed my eyes.

No one was there for me—not my family and not the collection of kind staff members I had left back in Elena's hospital room. That hospital room now seemed like a star hovering in the dark sky nearby, and it formed a constellation with the other star, the room without edges that held Elena's motionless body. I felt those stars, not intellectually, but viscerally, as points of reference toward which I could navigate. But my exhausted brain and body both agreed: I had no strength to reach them. Not anymore.

Those stars were sealed off from me. I would find no comfort there. So, in a last blind, muddled attempt to shield myself from bone-shaking loneliness, I reached into my mind, toward the characters who had been my friends and companions over the years.

But even my characters wouldn't meet me halfway. They stood around the walls of the pale gallery of my imagination, half wax doll and half astonished, so influenced by my own state of shock that for the first time, they had no life in them.

Only Marak, the old, ugly goblin King, the oldest of my character children, still had the strength to come to my rescue. Only Marak, that brilliant, pitiless schemer, still had a mind of his own. He assessed me through his tangle of rough, striped hair, slightly amused and a little worried and very, very wise. Then he came and lay down beside me and wrapped his strong, bony arms around me, and I could feel his hands with their knotted fingers clasping my own hands as they clasped my purse.

I'm safe now, I thought with more optimism than logic. *Marak will protect me. He'll do the planning for me. That brilliant mind is never without a plan for long.*

I closed my eyes and sank without a trace into the dark, sad, featureless night.

CHAPTER FIFTEEN

When I woke up, both the goblin King and the sleeping man were gone. The man had left his wrinkled blanket behind on the foam chair like a cast-off cocoon, so I did the same with mine and stumbled off to find a sink where I could wash my face.

Blurry people were in the halls now, and the hospital had a different tempo than it had before, a quicker step and more noise. Sure enough, I discovered through a line of square windows that the sun had come back. It lit up a vague gray wilderness of roof.

In the restroom, the cold water felt bracing and wonderful against my face. Then I put in my contacts, and the world became a manageable place again, and the insurmountable difficulties of the night before resolved themselves almost automatically. There were signs in the hallway. I could read them now. There was a sign for the ICU. I followed it to the big white room that held my daughter.

This time, I was cheered to learn that I would be allowed to sit by Elena's bed. But when I saw her, that sense of cheer froze at once. Elena looked no better. She lay inert on yet another special ICU mattress, her head and hands rocking and gently circling.

"Elena," I said. "Hey, Elena! Are you awake?"

But my daughter didn't respond.

Maybe she would never respond again.

I sat down in an empty chair by the head of the bed and watched Elena's hands swing slowly on the pivots of their wrists. Every now and then, they caught the IV line and gave it a jerk. I saw that the IV had been moved during the night. The old site was bloody under a clear bandage.

"How did the night go?" I asked Elena's ICU nurse.

The nurse was sitting in a chair by the foot of Elena's bed. She was young, overweight, and annoyed. She grumbled out a noncommittal reply that didn't translate into words. Maybe she didn't like visitors near her patients.

"Elena," I murmured again to the silent form on the bed. But again, there was no answer. Elena had been in bed for ten days now. Maybe she would never get out of bed again.

We were in a very large square room with a nurses' station in the center and hefty ICU beds ranged around the walls. A couple of pastel curtains on either side of each bed gave the illusion of privacy, but nothing screened the beds off from the nurses' station in the middle.

I sat quietly and watched the staff bustle to and fro past the end of Elena's bed. It was better than looking at my unconscious daughter.

It's true, I thought, insofar as I was capable of thinking. *It's true: we do have souls.*

I was thinking this because I could feel mine hurting.

My soul felt like one large, soft bruise. It was a diffuse, gentle ache that extended up my neck to the base of my skull and down both arms into my hands. My ribs cradled my aching soul, which swirled around my spine like a cloud of tears and drooped down to my knees. My feet were soulless little machines, but the rest of my body wrapped up and hid away my damaged soul.

Maybe Elena would never laugh again. Maybe she would never tell me another story. Maybe I would never again see her eyes go wide with mischief as she told me, "Guess *what!*"

"You have a merry heart," Shakespeare's prince tells Beatrice. Both Valerie and Elena had been born with merry hearts. I thought about all the times they had torn through the house, shrieking with laughter. They had made me laugh thousands of times.

One Halloween, a large plastic tarantula had found its way into our house. It was vividly realistic. Immediately, the girls adopted it, and it went away to live out innumerable fantasies on the same shelves that held their stuffed animals and model horses.

I walked by those shelves one day to find the tarantula transformed. A multicolored silk sash decorated its waist. All eight legs ended in brace-lets of gold or bright beads.

"What's up with the tarantula?" I asked the girls.

"He's a gypsy!" they said. "He's a gypsy spider."

The memory made me smile, but I knew better than anyone that imaginations like that come with a danger of their own. I remembered my days lost in Marak's thick, tangled forests, and the days I'd spent walking with ghosts in the House of Dead Maids. And I knew this: Elena didn't need reality. She had a storyteller's other hidden worlds to escape to.

"Wake up," I would tell her in the morning. "Time for school."

"Not now," she would say. "I just need to finish this dream first."

Elena's dreams were glorious.

Where was she now? What dream was she in? I sat and looked at my broken daughter. Long, long black lashes lying against fragile olive-shadowed skin. Long child-thin arms lying over the blanket. Stern expression. No movement. The barest rise and fall of breath.

Maybe that's why she won't come back, I thought. *She's found the perfect dream.*

Maybe she would never come back to me again.

The busy routine of the ICU was humming along around us. The nurse juggled a lapful of charts and wrote down things I didn't under-stand. Two techs went around the room, pushing a rolling scale and getting weights on all the patients. The scale was a large contraption that weighed the whole bed.

Eventually those techs worked their way over to us. One tech hooked up the scale and read a number out to the nurse.

No, that's way off, I thought idly when I heard it. *That's off by about fifteen pounds.*

But Elena's brown eyes snapped open—fully open, for the first time in days. They were bloodshot and sunken, but they gleamed with fierce determination.

"Then I've gained weight!" she said. "I can go home!"

The overweight nurse shot Elena a look of loathing—a look of pure contempt. She left us to confer with the ICU doctor, and an hour later, Elena and I were back in our regular room.

Nobody there mentioned going home, of course. Even Elena didn't mention it again. She let them settle her back into bed and helped them hook up all her heart leads. Then she lapsed again into unconsciousness, or sleep.

But I was left with the pain and longing of that unguarded sentence, straight from my daughter's own damaged soul. That cry from her injured heart: *I can go home!*

It weighed me down like a stone.

I was carrying so many of these stones now, so many painful moments, that it seemed almost a miracle that I could still stand. I felt them burdening me, dragging on me, as I wandered out of the room to find breakfast. I walked slowly down the wide hall, bowed down by their weight. I couldn't manage to look up far enough to meet the eyes of the people I passed.

But by the time I had eaten a hot meal and had a cup of coffee, I was seeing things differently. All around me, parents were wheeling their children in wheelchairs. I saw a baby with bandages and a feeding tube. As I walked back upstairs, I spotted signs for the burn ward and the oncology department.

We're the lucky ones, I thought. *Except, there's no such thing as luck. Other parents are dealing with things that are so much worse.*

As I passed the nurses' station, one of the staff flagged me down. "Dr. Costello is looking for you," she said.

Dr. Costello turned out to be a very short, trim man with a lean face and thoughtful gray eyes.

"I've ordered an EEG test for your daughter," he told me, "and another echo exam of her heart. As long as she's here, she'll be on full bed rest, and the psychiatrists are putting together an anorexia protocol."

"Do you have any idea whether something medical might link her symptoms?" I said. "The weak heart, the weight loss, and the blackouts?"

"I can't really speculate on that," he said. "But I'll be interested to see what the tests will turn up, and I'll share them with you as soon as I get them."

Then he hurried away.

Did I just make that busy man state the obvious? I thought. *Yes, and he did it with good humor and patience. That's a kind man. I think I like him.*

The psychiatrists came into the room an hour or so later, and they came in a set of three. They didn't seem like individuals. They seemed like a perfect team. Only the middle one spoke, but the faces of the other two expressed calm agreement with every word.

The middle psychiatrist asked me to leave the room for a few minutes so they could talk to Elena. Then he talked to me while Elena dozed nearby. He explained about the mechanisms of anorexia. I listened with interest and tried to keep an open mind. He talked about a constant obsession with food. That didn't fit very well with what I had seen of Elena's nervous hit-or-miss eating.

"I just haven't known her to be like that," I said. "She's never been all that interested in food one way or the other, and yes, she'll skip meals when she's under stress. But she's glad to eat when she's feeling relaxed and her favorite foods show up. She'll snack on them all day long."

The psychiatrists listened politely but didn't respond. I got the impression that they didn't believe me. And the middle psychiatrist talked in elusive generalities, even when I tried to talk in particulars.

Anorexics rigorously dieted, he told me.

"*Is* my daughter rigorously dieting?" I asked.

The middle psychiatrist shrugged and spread his hands, as if to say, *Would she be here if she isn't?* But he didn't actually answer the question. It was as if I couldn't be trusted with what he knew, and he couldn't trust what I knew.

This baffled and frustrated me. My daughter was a minor, and I was her caregiver. If she was exhibiting life-threatening behaviors, I needed to know about them, not hear a lecture on how anorexic patients generally behaved.

"How could rigorous anorexic dieting have allowed her to reach normal weight last month?" I asked. "She was at full normal weight just one month ago. And even during last year, although she was a few pounds underweight, she wasn't in the anorexic weight range. She's lost weight faster in the hospital than I've ever known her to lose weight before. She hasn't been at this weight in years."

The psychiatrists didn't answer me, but again, I sensed their polite disbelief. Why? I couldn't understand it. Elena's weight on a scale wasn't the hysterical imagining of a parent; I had been with her at the doctors' offices each time she'd gone in for an appointment, so I had seen for myself what her weights had been. This was data I had asked Dr. Petras to look at, too; he could have pulled it together from the data in the hospital computer. But he, too, had declined to look at the facts.

Didn't psychiatry concern itself with facts at all?

"What I'm getting at," I said, "is that Elena's weight hasn't been within the anorexic range before, and it was normal one month ago. From what I've been able to tell, that weight range is one of the main diagnostic criteria for anorexia. So, how does the fact that she hasn't been at anorexic weight before agree with her being anorexic?"

"She's at anorexic weight now," the psychiatrist pointed out.

"Yes," I said, "after the stress of an enforced hospital stay during which she staged a well-documented hunger strike, followed by several days of unconsciousness, during which she could eat very little. But isn't anorexia nervosa a chronic condition? How does this concentrated, rapid weight loss match up with *chronic*? I'm just not sure what to think here. Elena's pediatrician disagreed with the diagnosis of anorexia. He told me he didn't think she had it at all."

"He isn't an expert, is he?" the middle psychiatrist pointed out. And the two psychiatrists who flanked him nodded in perfect agreement. I waited for him to enlarge upon this point and explain why he thought the pediatrician was wrong. But he fell silent again, watching me gravely.

Oh, well. Maybe the medical tests would turn up something to explain the weight loss. In the meantime, I had other questions.

"Do you know why she circles like she does?" I asked. "These weird blackouts she's been having?" And *this* question the psychiatrist actually answered.

"It's a pseudoseizure," he said. "It's nothing to worry about."

"But why? What does it mean? *Pseudo*: Does that mean she's faking it? Because I think I saw her jabbed with a needle."

"It's dissociation. It's like a form of wishful thinking. She's retreating from an unpleasant reality. She controls the blackout, but she doesn't control it consciously."

I could understand this on one level. I had even guessed it myself. Elena was retreating from the brutal threats of Dr. Petras. She was refusing to allow them to come true in her world.

But at the same time, I couldn't understand it at all.

Elena was a girl who, at the insecure age of twelve, had gone almost alone into a foreign school. She hadn't had a single hysterical attack there. In fact, she had thrived. She had loved the challenge. She had quickly become a leader.

Something was wrong here. I knew it was wrong. The Elena who could wait out that barrage of blustering threats and then calmly sit up and dictate a packing list shouldn't have needed to shut down like this, not so disastrously or so long.

I was missing a piece of this puzzle, a piece that would bring it all together.

"But *why*?" I asked the assemblage of psychiatrists again. "How did this happen? Never in her entire life has Elena done this, or anything even remotely like it. She's never passed out, never had fainting spells. This is a child who doesn't stay in bed even when she's sick!"

Once again, the psychiatrists didn't answer. They just gazed at me impassively. If they had any idea, they were keeping it to themselves.

"We're putting your daughter on an anorexia protocol," the middle psychiatrist said next. "Your daughter will have her meals brought here, and she'll eat them under supervision. Her output will be measured, and at night, the feeding pump will feed her while she sleeps. A sitter will be staying in the room to watch her."

"Oh, now that's good news!" I said.

I wasn't at all convinced that Elena had anorexia nervosa. But this I did know: Elena certainly had a problem with eating meals in a hospital. Now she could finally put on the weight she had lost, and in the meantime, the medical doctors could run their tests and find out if something serious was wrong.

We've hit bottom, I thought hopefully as the set of three psychiatrists walked away. *Maybe we'll have to be here for only a week or so.*

As that first day passed, Elena began to spend more time awake. She still fainted and circled from time to time, and she gave the nurses several more shocks, but overall, as I lounged on my foldout bed and caught up on my own rest, nothing disturbed my drowsy optimism. I reminded myself: *We're the lucky ones—except, there's no such thing as luck.* And I fell asleep to the soothing rhythm of the feeding pump.

The next morning, Elena was awake before I was, flipping channels on the television. That cheered me up immensely. Dr. Costello reported that she had been doing very well eating her meals and that none of the medical tests had turned up anything serious. That, too, was a huge relief.

"So, about that anorexia diagnosis," I said cautiously after the doctor left.

"Bullshit!" Elena said in such a firm tone of voice that I didn't ask further questions.

She has so many different teams of doctors and students coming by to question and poke and prod, I thought. *There's a sitter in the room while she sleeps, and techs are watching her eat every bite. The least I can do is show her a little respect and give her a little space. There's little enough privacy here.*

By the following morning, the staff and I had formed a routine. As soon as I saw the techs show up with Elena's meal, I would grab my book and my purse and leave the room. I would go eat in the cafeteria, send a couple of emails at the library, and walk the halls and stairwells for exercise. By the time I got back, Elena would be in bed again and ready to tell me the latest gossip she'd learned. Then she flipped channels while I sat at the desk by the window and updated web pages on my laptop. All in all, it made for a pretty satisfying day.

I love routines. It's an important part of who I am. I love patterns of all sorts. I love learning foreign languages because each sentence is like a little puzzle, and only certain patterns can unlock it. I love art and architecture because their composition follows certain rules; I once read an entire book devoted to stairs. I love poetry because most poems are about comparing things that seem to have nothing in common and showing how they match in some unexpected way. I love metaphor and simile and certain beautiful shapes of English sentences, as well as flowers and the leaves on trees.

The house I grew up in was chaotic and disorganized. For years when I was young, my own bedroom was a jumbled heap of treasure and trash mixed together. Everywhere I went were toppling piles of books and papers, and if I needed something specific—say, a pair of scissors— I might have to search for a good quarter of an hour.

During the long summer days, I would complain to my mother: "There's nothing to do."

"Go clean your room," she would always answer. But that was only a joke. None of us ever cleaned our rooms in that house. My oldest brother had dismantled so many computers at his desk that his floor was thick with springs, nuts, and tiny snippets of copper wire. The shag carpet in his room actually crunched.

But one particularly boring day when I was about eleven, I took my mother's advice. And I did it. I cleaned my room.

The experience I went through compares to what gets shown on those programs about hoarding. My room was so packed, I had to have trails through the sloping mounds of rubble, and even those trails didn't reach bare carpet. Over three days, I cleaned my way down through layers of trash, going further back in time as I worked. I felt like an archaeologist uncovering a hidden city.

By the time I was through, I had stuffed six construction-size trash bags full to bursting with the trash from a ten-by-twelve-foot room.

That three-day cleaning orgy is one of the most empowering experiences I have ever lived through. It brought me, as pure discovery, the blinding realization that clutter had never made me happy. I realized that I'd much rather have a few possessions in their proper places than lots of things jumbled in a pile. I cherished this new understanding of myself, and I've never looked back.

I love knowing that my belongings are where they belong. I love the patterns I've built into the rooms of my house and the sections of my day. No matter where I go, I immediately unpack and start looking for new structures and new routines. They center me. They bring me their own kind of comfort.

By Day Three in the children's hospital, my routines were firmly in place, and the terror of the ICU experiences was starting to fade. The results of the various medical tests were reassuringly normal, and Elena was acting reassuringly normal as well. Thinking too much about the past or the future still brought more pain than I could handle, so I focused on keeping myself in the moment and letting my injured soul heal.

When the techs showed up for lunchtime, I said good-bye to Elena and hurried off to "my" table in the hospital cafeteria, the one where two glass walls met and displayed the widest view of sky and lawn. It was the closest I came to the outdoors during my days there. The hospital was like a biosphere.

As I ate, I let myself get caught up in an interesting science fiction short story I was reading. Venice had drowned, and the main character took tourists on dives through the buildings resting beneath the shallow sea. I thought about the glorious churches I had seen in Venice. Then I imagined them sunk in an indigo-gray twilight, with underwater weeds wrapping the marble funeral figures, while schools of fish swam over the mosaic floors.

Short stories are a wonderful gift. Each one creates a perfect little world, like a scene inside a snow globe. Then my imagination can fill it out and play with it to my heart's content.

When I got back to the room, Elena was watching a talk show on television. All the panelists seemed to be crying and yelling at the same time.

"How was lunch?" I asked her.

"Great!" she said. "Did you know that they had a possessed girl in this ward a couple of years ago? Things would fly around the room, even though the girl was tied down to the bed. The parents insisted that it had to be some kind of medical condition, but the doctor sent her home after a couple of days. He said, 'Look, I think you need a priest.'"

"Lordy!"

"I know, right? And there was another girl who was here for several weeks, so the art-therapy people paid her a visit—you know, do-a-little-coloring-to-cheer-you-up kind of thing. The picture she made was so beautiful they framed it, and now it's hanging by the nurses' station."

"Oh, hey, I think I've seen that," I said. "The torn-paper portrait of a lion?"

"Yeah, that's it."

"I thought it was donated artwork," I said. "She's really talented. But hey, when I asked how lunch was, I really meant to ask, how was lunch food-wise?"

"Meh," Elena said with a shrug. "Sandwich and a salad."

I tried to apply my newfound knowledge about anorexics to Elena as she said this. If she was an anorexic, shouldn't she be stressed and angry about having been forced to eat? I looked for some tremble of her lips or irritation in her voice, some sign that the meal had disturbed or upset her.

But Elena didn't look stressed. She just looked disinterested.

She doesn't seem like an anorexic to me, I thought. And my imagination played for me again the memory of that old-horse woman, with the rough skin sagging across her collarbones and bagging at her knees and the sharp bones poking out everywhere.

Elena didn't look like that. But it *was* true that Elena was thin these days. I studied her. In fact, she was terribly thin.

"So, *do* you have trouble eating?" I asked.

Elena shrugged. "Ask the doctor."

"No, I don't mean *are* you eating, I mean are you able to *enjoy* it?"

"Not the crap they serve me here, no."

"But . . . overall? If you could eat what you wanted? Remember, your school counselor was worried last year."

"Yeah, about my stress level because my sister was a moron. Look, you know Dr. Petras is an idiot. You don't need me to tell you that."

This was true. She didn't.

"I had chicken-fried steak," I said as I walked to the desk to put down my book and purse. "Also chocolate pudding for dessert. With Oreos."

"Lucky!" Elena said. "They don't give me dessert."

"Not even pudding? Doesn't that break some kind of law? I thought hospitals had to serve pudding with every meal."

"I wish!"

The note of envy in her voice convinced me: this anorexia diagnosis was nonsense. Elena didn't hate food at all. She just hated bullies trying to force her to do things. Probably if Dr. Petras had locked her up to get some rest, she would have stood in a corner of the room until she fell to the floor from exhaustion. And she never, ever would have come near the bed.

Dr. Eichbaum was right, I thought in relief. *She's completely normal. And why shouldn't Dr. Eichbaum be right? He was the only psychiatrist who actually took the time to run her through panels of tests. He tested Elena for hours. Dr. Petras just spent a few minutes talking to her, and that's what the psychiatrists here have done, too.*

The conversation reminded me, though, how much Elena liked pudding. When she was little, she used to ask for the stove-top kind. So, the next time I went to the cafeteria, I looked in the refrigerator case for chocolate pudding. There was plenty of vanilla, and there was a rainbow assortment of little plastic bowls of Jell-O. But there was a gap where the chocolate had been.

"Will you be getting more chocolate pudding today?" I asked one of the cooks. "It's for my daughter. She's on full bed rest, and I'd like to cheer her up."

"We'll make your daughter some pudding," he told me. "We can make her as much as you want." And sure enough, while I was eating my dinner at my table by the two glass walls, he tapped on my elbow and handed me a plastic takeaway bowl. Inside was a generous scoop of chocolate pudding, complete with Oreos crumbled across the top.

"How much do I owe you?" I asked, reaching for my purse. But he only smiled.

"No charge, ma'am. You just tell that daughter of yours I hope she enjoys it."

When I got upstairs, Elena was still finishing her dinner. I could hardly wait for the tech to leave.

"Check this out!" Elena said when the tech left. "They brought me my own video player!"

"And check this out!" I said, triumphantly producing the pudding. "It's not on the menu, but you've got your dessert."

Elena smiled. "All right, Oreos! Let's share it. Here, I'll scooch over to make room. You should watch this video with me."

So we lay side by side on her hospital bed and watched cartoons and passed the pudding back and forth. After the dark days and sad nights in the ICU, it felt amazing and wonderful to be able to share that pudding with my daughter.

I brought Elena a pudding every day after that, and we always ate it together. It became a symbol to me of everything the psychiatrists weren't bothering to learn about my daughter. I considered telling them about it, but I could just imagine their look of polite disbelief. If they were keeping secrets from me, then I was going to keep secrets from them.

They think she hates food, I thought, *but she's so happy to have her dessert! This is nonsense—there's nothing wrong with my daughter. Elena's going to put this ghastly time behind her, and we'll never look back. It's just one more obstacle she'll overcome.*

It was love—pure, devoted love—that led me to these conclusions. Given the circumstances, I know I would come to the same conclusions again. And I don't regret that. I can't regret giving Elena my wholehearted trust and support.

I'm not sorry.

But that doesn't mean I was right.

CHAPTER SIXTEEN

Dr. Costello told me that the EEG test of Elena's brain was normal. The heart echo confirmed the damage but also suggested improvement. Her blood values seemed to be fine as well. No big issues had cropped up.

"So there's nothing serious," I said in relief. "Elena just needs to gain the weight back, and then we can go home."

Dr. Costello hesitated. "Well, actually," he said with an apologetic look in his eyes, "she's supposed to go to an anorexia treatment center."

"I'm glad you brought that up," I said. "I've got my doubts about the anorexia." And I explained to him my problem with Dr. Petras, who hadn't taken the time to fully assess Elena, and the weight loss during one month, from normal to underweight, that seemed to form the entire basis for his diagnosis.

"Her pediatrician there didn't believe him," I said. "And I've been waiting myself to see if more evidence would turn up. For instance, aren't anorexics terrified to eat? But you say Elena's eating with no problem, and every time I come back after her meal is over, she's energetic and happy and full of interesting new stories she and the techs have talked about. So where is it? Where's that new evidence of obsessive terror around food? Is there any? Or are we still basing the entire anorexia nervosa diagnosis on one low weight on a scale?"

"Anorexia isn't my area of specialty," Dr. Costello said. "I have to rely on what the psychiatrists tell me. But I do see your point. We'll keep looking and see what we find."

Elena spent that whole week on full bed rest, with a different tech sitting by the door every night, staying awake to watch over her. The feeding? pump hummed me to sleep every evening, and each day, Elena ate her meals without complaint.

But when Dr. Costello had a scale brought into the room at the end of that week, and Elena climbed out of bed and stood on it, I could see—we *all* could see—that she was *still* losing weight.

I felt almost frantic!

"Why?" I demanded afterward as Dr. Costello and I stood in the hallway together. "Why is her weight still dropping?"

"I don't know," he confessed. "I thought it would be turning around by now."

"Just two months ago, her weight was normal!" I said. "All last year, her weight was stable. And ever since she's been confined to hospitals and fed these special meals, she's practically wasted away!"

"I'm not finding any answers," Dr. Costello said. "Nothing has turned up. A few blood values are slightly off, but it's nothing that the anorexia can't explain."

"Anorexia! How can this be anorexia? That's voluntary fasting, right? But you said she's eaten everything, and the feeding pump goes all night, and she's doing nothing but sitting in bed, and the weight is still melting right off her! I called Drew Center, that eating disorder treatment place the psychiatrists recommended, and they say they won't even take her as a patient. She's not in the anorexic range. *Not* in the anorexic range! Those were their exact words!"

"But the psychiatrists told me—"

"What, *more* psychiatrists who ignore their own diagnostic guidelines? Do you know that those psychiatrists have only been to see Elena twice? How are *they* supposed to know what's going on? What are they—*psychic?*"

"Believe me, believe me," Dr. Costello said hurriedly, "I'm just as frustrated as you are. But I can't explain it, and if they can . . . Well, I think she needs to get to the experts."

This sounded ominous. It sounded like a place we had been before. About a week and a half before, to be specific.

"*You're* the expert," I reminded him, and I couldn't keep the bitterness out of my voice. "That's why Elena's pediatrician sent her to you: to get to the experts, he said."

"I mean, the experts in eating disorders," Dr. Costello amended. "The psychiatrists at Drew Center do nothing but work with eating disorder patients. They'll be able to rule out once and for all whether your daughter has anorexia."

I could see the logic of this.

"Well, Drew Center won't take her," I pointed out.

"I'll call," he said. "I think I can persuade them to take her. And there are some more tests I'm going to look into."

As Dr. Costello walked away, I tried to talk myself out of my bad mood. I reminded myself that this time a week ago, I was afraid Elena would never open her eyes again. But the news that Elena's weight was continuing to drop frightened and baffled me. What if she had some strange metabolic disorder Dr. Costello just wasn't catching? Was she just going to waste away?

"So, it looks like we'll be here for a while longer," I told Elena as I walked back to my desk.

"Mmmph," she said without interest. "This is bullshit." And she went back to watching her DVD.

I sighed and opened my laptop. Elena and I didn't have much space in that little hospital room, and I had long ago exhausted the fun of exploring the different public spaces in the building. I was homesick for Joe and my pets and our house in Germany.

But at least I could go stretch my imagination in my various fantasy worlds. I had put together a complicated web project to occupy my time. I was moving the most interesting questions readers had asked me onto pages on my website. Thinking about those questions took me to new places. They were helping me stay calm and optimistic.

I brought up my email and rummaged through stored messages, looking for interesting questions.

"Why does Paul carve Maddie as a tree?" one reader had written. "That seems like a weird thing to do."

Paul and Maddie were characters in my Scottish werewolf book. It was such a sad, sweet love story that my heart melted as I read the question, and my bad mood vanished at once. I loved Maddie for her frank, open nature, and I loved my poor woodcarver, Paul, for the suffering he had lived through. Together, they were my favorite story couple.

"Maddie doesn't care for it any more than you would," I wrote. "She's down-to-earth and has a very different view of herself than Paul has of her." And as I wrote, my imagination played for me a scene in the small, windowless sod house full of peat smoke.

> The wooden figure was different. It still had a tree's crown of leaves and apples, but the trunk had turned into a pale, slim girl. Leaves grew out of her hair, and her two arms stretched out to become branches. Maddie walked toward the doorway and turned the carving in the light, studying it with wonder.
>
> "It's you," said a voice from the doorway, and she looked up to find Paul there. "At least, it looks like you," he added awkwardly. "Do you like it? I had just finished it that first morning when I looked up and saw you talking to Ned, and then I looked down and saw you in the wood."
>
> Maddie examined it. The tree girl was slender and sweet, poised and graceful. Maddie could see that she was happy by the lift of her arms and her chin. Happy to be an apple tree, happy to grow where she was planted. The tip of one toe-root just showed beneath her long skirt.
>
> "After I saw you," he went on, "every block of wood I saw had you inside it."
>
> "But why would you carve me? Who would want to see me?" Maddie held out the tree girl. "Just me, I'm not fancy like this."

Paul took the carving to look at it and then at her. She could tell that somehow he still saw the resemblance.

"You're beautiful, Madeleine," he said.

As I watched my two young characters, I felt again the love they shared—that magical first love that has such wonder in it. *I'm glad I wrote their story*, I thought. *I'm glad I brought them to life. Maddie has such a generous heart, and Paul makes such a fascinating monster.*

"Oh, hey," I said to Elena over my shoulder, "I forgot to tell you, but your sister says she hopes you get well soon."

"I don't want *anything* from her!"

The tone was so vehement that it stopped me cold. My hands froze on the keyboard. Elena had been calm and philosophical for so long now that I had forgotten she could still sound like this.

"But . . . ," I said.

"I don't know why you write to her!" Elena continued furiously. "I don't want you to tell her another word about me! She's the reason I'm stuck here. I'm *sick* because of her!"

After all the time and all the hard words that had already gone by, I ought to be prepared for this sort of thing. But to run into such violent hostility between two of the people I loved best in the world . . .

Without a word, I went back to my questions and answers. But the color had drained out of my day.

"How old are Paul and Maddie in the book?" wrote another reader.

Who cares? I thought. *Paul and Maddie aren't real. They aren't real, and they don't exist.*

Hopelessness welled up inside me.

My family is broken, I thought. *My family is irretrievably broken. I'm the mother, and I've let my children become damaged and ill. Two children in the hospital—not one, but two! Hatred and bitterness—how did it happen? What kind of mother would let that happen?*

"Hey, come watch this," Elena said.

"No, thanks."

There was a pause.

"Don't blame me," Elena said, "for what my shit sister did."

"No, I know," I answered quickly. "I'm not blaming you. I'm not blaming anybody."

Not quite true.

Sadness welled up around me like an invisible flood. It closed over my head without a ripple.

What kind of mother has a child who cuts and burns herself? What kind of mother watches her child disconnect from reality and jerk around on her back in a fit?

"You know, there's a social worker on this floor," Elena said. "She came by to see me yesterday. I think you ought to go talk to her, Mom. I think it would be good for you."

That's just like Elena, I thought. *She's the one lying in the hospital bed, but she's worried about me.* And that brought a little flicker of cheer into my heart, even at the bottom of that pool of sadness.

Elena had so little control over her life now. She wasn't even allowed out of bed. At least I could let her be a good influence on me. She could have a little control that way.

Besides, talking to a social worker would be a pleasant diversion. Wasn't a therapist like having a clever friend you paid to have coffee with? None of this *So, how's* your *day going?* stuff—you could monopolize the entire conversation.

"Sure, why not?" I said. "You're probably right."

So I set up an appointment, and I went.

The social worker was an ordinary-looking woman about my age who inhabited a tiny office absolutely crammed to bursting with paper. If it hadn't been for the large sections of glass in the walls, opening onto views of the hallway, I don't think I could have stood the place.

She waved me to a chair. "So, tell me what's wrong."

Over the next hour, it all came pouring out. Valerie's scars. Elena's heart. My fears about what my daughters' illnesses meant for our family and what our family might mean for them. Before, I had always seen our family as a circle of love and safety in a possibly dangerous, possibly unfriendly world. Now I had become very much afraid that it wasn't the world that was dangerous and unfriendly.

"I feel so old these days," I said. "Old and dried up. Ancient. It's as if all the pain and stress have attacked me physically. Some days—the bad days—I can almost feel the cells shriveling and dying off."

"Have you cried about this?" she asked. "About your daughter in the hospital, about her blackouts and her heart? About your other daughter? Have you given yourself permission to cry?"

I felt taken aback. I tried to be reasonable and evaluate the questions fairly, but then again—they just didn't make sense.

"You mean, since we got here, to the States? Well—no."

Obviously not, I thought to myself.

"And why is that?" she asked.

Why was that? Ask the small child sitting quietly in a corner of the room, working on her dot-to-dot puzzles. Ask Heathcliff. Ask Sara Crewe. Ask Florence Nightingale.

Laughter is always appropriate. A wry comment and a quiet chuckle are welcome even beside the grave. But crying is a special dispensation extended to widows and babies. Me, I needed to be doing and planning—not crying.

"Elena doesn't need that," I said finally. "She's going through enough. And besides—well, we're in *public* here!" And I tried to imagine myself breaking down in a busy waiting room. Nope. My imagination could picture monsters, but it couldn't see this.

"It happens here all the time," the social worker said calmly. "No one would judge you or bother you."

I didn't answer. Inwardly, I thought, *Why would that matter? This is my code of conduct, not someone else's.*

"Why are you doing this to yourself?" she persisted. "Why haven't you let yourself cry?"

"Because . . ."

But how could I explain it? Why did I even need to explain it?

Why couldn't this woman just leave it alone?

"Because it's too much," I said at last. "I can't even let myself touch it. All I can do is kind of stand back and look at it for a while. Think about it: think about seeing your daughter, out of her mind. Think of your baby, whose little body you cradled and protected from birth, and now you're seeing dozens of burns . . ."

I had to pause for a minute. But I found my stiff upper lip.

"So, you see," I continued, perfectly calmly and reasonably, "there aren't enough tears for that. If I start crying, you might as well lock me up in a padded room because I'm never going to stop."

The social worker frowned. "You need to be able to cry," she said.

What happened to not judging me or bothering me?

"I need to be able to cope," I countered. "I could scream for the rest of my life, but how is that going to get the bills paid and the insurance arrangements taken care of? I was on the phone just this morning with our insurance company—again. I had to sort out charges from the military hospital for them. Who's going to do that if I'm bawling in a rubber room?"

And the thought of the insurance company acted on my torn and injured feelings like a cool menthol lozenge on a sore throat. It helped me breathe. It laid soothing coats of logic and procedure over the burning pain inside me.

The social worker seemed to sense my change in mood. At my growing calm, she grew sterner than ever.

"So you turn to your writing," she said. "To your books."

"Well, yes," I admitted, and the thought of my characters completed the job of helping me re-center.

It's not fair to Paul and Maddie to say that they're not real, I thought. *They're as real as anything else about me. Their love is certainly just as real, that true adolescent first love that makes the whole humdrum world we grew up in somehow look different overnight.* And at the thought of those two shy, serious lovers, a little glow of happiness warmed me.

"But don't you see," the social worker said, "that you're doing the same thing as your daughter? You're both dissociating! Elena is dissociating by escaping into her blackouts, and you're dissociating into your books."

What?!

How dare shc!

How dare she!

Did this woman have the foggiest idea what dissociation really looked like? Had she ever wandered, lonely and miserable, through a chaotic, paper-piled house while every single person in the world found other things to do? Had she ever lain in the dark, racked with terrible pain, while doctors shrugged and smiled and the adults who should have helped stood back and snapped out insults? Had she ever sat next to the phone, hour after hour, single-mindedly willing it to ring, while the adults who had been closer than family—closer than *family!*—stepped away and closed off? Just stopped caring?

That was dissociation: it was pulling away from risk to safety— just flipping off the switch that says *I care*. And me, I had actually *lived* through the hell that happens when adults do that to a child. Is *that* what this woman actually thought my books were—just a spa where I hid to escape my obligations? Is *that* what she actually thought fiction was— nothing but a pretty little *playground*?

God, how I despise those people who put on their long "I'm a grown-up now" faces and sit in judgment of the value of fiction! They keep themselves safe inside their rigid little closed minds and live out their rigid little lives. And if anything they don't understand comes along, they shrill out their little judgments, and they attack it.

Dissociating into my *books*! . . .

I took a deep breath. Logic and reason—I needed *logic*, and I needed *reason*! I needed to think this through. Why would she attack me? Here was a thought: maybe it had been a bold gambit to try to shock me into tears.

Well, it was going to take a whole lot more than *that*.

"Dissociation." I echoed the insult in my stiffest, most unemotional voice. "So that's what you think my books are. Well, *I* like to think that there's a difference between me and my daughter. I get *paid* to do what I do—pretty well, in fact. *My* dissociative states are going to put *her* dissociative states through college."

And that was the end of my talk with the social worker.

As I stalked back to Elena's hospital room, Dr. Costello waved me over. I could see by his face that he had news.

"The endocrine tests I ordered have come back," he said. "Elena is at the beginning stage of Hashimoto's thyroiditis. That's nothing to worry about. We're going to start her on a low-dose thyroid replacement. She'll take it every day."

"Is that what caused her weight loss?"

"No. Her thyroid levels are mildly deficient. If anything, that might make her weight go up."

I tried to think of everything I'd ever learned about the thyroid gland. All I could remember was that it was shaped like a butterfly and needed iodized salt.

"Isn't thyroid trouble another old person's problem, like Elena's heart?" I asked. "What happened to her thyroid?"

"Hashimoto's is an autoimmune disorder," Dr. Costello said. "It's fairly common," he added reassuringly.

I didn't feel reassured.

"So, her thyroid," I said. "First her heart, which the cardiologist didn't understand at her weight; then the blackouts; and now the thyroid. What's the link? Could anorexia nervosa cause the thyroid damage?"

"I don't think so. I think they're unrelated."

"Three different chronic health issues in one month, and they're unrelated?"

"I don't *think* they're related."

"So now Elena will have to be on thyroid medication for life. And what about her heart? What did the cardiology team say we should do about her heart?"

"They don't think it's a grave concern. They say that when her anorexia nervosa improves, her heart will heal."

"And did anybody ask them how her anorexia nervosa managed to cause this when she was at a normal weight in June? And how her anorexia nervosa is *failing* to improve even though she's now consuming several thousand calories a day?"

Dr. Costello sighed.

"Mrs. Dunkle, I'm sorry," he said. "I wish I had better answers, but the fact is, I just don't know. The good news is that the Hashimoto's is very mild. It's probably only turned up by accident. And concerning the anorexia, we'll just have to wait and see. Drew Center says they're ready to take her. We'll transfer her there in a couple of days. They'll be the best ones to examine her for anorexia."

He hurried off, and I continued my angry march to Elena's room.

Dr. Costello was a good man and a fine doctor, but in the end, this hospital had let me down. I had come here to find answers, and all I had gotten were more questions. It had all gone on long enough now—three whole weeks since Dr. Petras had forced Elena into the hospital and her pediatrician had failed to back him up. It was time for us to get this anorexia issue sorted out once and for all.

The sooner we could get to Drew Center, the better.

CHAPTER SEVENTEEN

Two days later, I once again followed Elena's gurney out into the sunlight. This time, the EMTs were loading her up to drive her to Drew Center.

As I waited my turn to climb into the ambulance, I thought about the day ahead. We would arrive at the eating disorder treatment center, where the experts would be waiting. There would doubtless be some sort of initial consultation and probably an evaluation as well. Then would come the point at which Elena and I would sit down with them, and they would go over their findings. I would ask about the things that had baffled me, and they would give educated answers. They would sketch out an appropriate treatment plan, and we would have a way forward.

After three weeks of questions and professional disagreements, we would have a way forward at last!

The young EMT reached down a hand to help me up, and I took a seat in the back of the ambulance next to Elena. This was my first time riding in the back of an ambulance. It combined the ugliest, most utilitarian features of an enclosed truck bed and an emergency room. It wasn't exactly an attractive place.

Traveling with Elena was Elena's medical file. At this point, it was about three-quarters of an inch thick, housed in an impressively oversize interoffice mailer. This seemed to me to be a pretty hefty document to deliver the message *WE DON'T KNOW*. As the ambulance bumped along, the EMT skimmed it and gave a snort. The first set of pages, he said, was nothing but one long rant.

That would be Dr. Petras, I thought. And yes, a rant sounded about right.

After an hour-long drive through stop-and-start city traffic, we arrived at Drew Center. I had gotten a little spoiled by the welcome at the children's hospital and expected us to be ushered right in to wherever Elena belonged—the privilege of the ambulance-driven. But this place wasn't going for that, so while the EMTs loitered in the lobby behind me, I sat at an intake desk and signed dozens of forms.

That was all right. Hospitals run on paperwork. I understood that.

When the forms were out of the way, Elena's EMTs put her into a wheelchair, and a tech wheeled her out the door and under big shade trees, across what looked like a college campus. At one of the redbrick buildings, we got buzzed through a locked door into an empty waiting room. The tech took the wheelchair away and left us there alone.

Elena and I didn't speak. We fidgeted in our chairs. I didn't know what she was thinking, and I didn't want to ask. She had chosen not to discuss anything about her medical care, and I hadn't pressed her to. I wanted to respect her autonomy and privacy as much as I could. And, at the back of my mind, I still feared another blackout and seizure.

But as for me, I couldn't have been happier or more excited as we sat in the little waiting room. I kept thinking: *This is it!*

Any minute now—the consultation. The chance to ask questions. The chance to hear real answers!

The inside door opened, and a young woman leaned out.

"Elena Dunkle?"

Elena left the room. It was an initial consultation, the young woman explained, and even though my daughter was a minor, I wasn't supposed to attend. But that was fine. I had already gotten used to being excluded. If it weren't for the puddings I'd been bringing her every day, I wouldn't even have seen her eat for the last week and a half.

But soon we would sit down together, and then we would find things out. Soon, we would have our answers.

Over and over, while I waited, I ran through my list of questions for the experts:

- What are the diagnostic factors that determine anorexia nervosa? Can you explain them to me, and can you explain whether or not Elena's history indicates that she meets them?

- What do Elena's blackouts have to do with the anorexia diagnosis?

- The endocrinologist says that her Hashimoto's thyroiditis is mild and appears to be recent. Could the hyperthyroidism phase of Hashimoto's be responsible for her weight loss and dissociations?

- How did her heart get so badly damaged if her weight was so recently normal?

- If restricting caused her weight loss, why haven't the feeding tube and supervised meals turned that weight loss around?

And, most important of all:

- Even after all the weight that Elena's lost in the last two hospitals, she doesn't meet the established criteria for anorexic inpatient care. So, if you had seen her at the weight she was when Dr. Petras first put her in the hospital—a higher weight by several pounds than her weight now—would you have agreed with his diagnosis?

I had my questions in order. I was ready for this. I was ready for answers.

The young woman returned and waved me into a small office. I was surprised to see that Elena wasn't there. On the desk was one of Elena's suitcases.

"These are the things your daughter wasn't allowed to keep in the facility," she said, opening it and exhibiting items as she spoke. "We don't allow hoodies, jackets, or oversize clothing, only simple cardigans. It's cold here, so she asked if you can buy her a sweater. And her razors weren't allowed, either. She's asked if you can please bring her an electric razor."

I closed up the suitcase, feeling odd. In my head, the questions were still running:

. . . *factors that determine anorexia?*

That's what was wrong. We were off script.

"So, I'll be meeting Elena's care team, right?" I asked.

. . . her heart be so badly damaged if her weight loss . . .

"I'm not sure which therapist she'll have," the young woman answered. "If you like, I can set up an appointment with Dr. Moore."

. . . Heart damage . . . Recent thyroiditis . . . What are the factors . . . ?

"Then—you mean, there isn't an appointment?"

The young woman was already on the phone, conferring with a secretary.

"Okay," she told me, "that'll be tomorrow at nine o'clock."

"Tomorrow," I said stupidly. "Tomorrow?"

Initial findings . . . my brain kept playing. *Consultation, questions, diagnosis. Treatment plan. Way forward . . .*

"But . . . ," I said. "But what about today?"

"You can come back at seven o'clock and see Elena," the young woman said brightly. "Visiting hour is from seven to eight in the evening."

That's when it finally got through to me: the meeting I had been looking forward to with such eagerness wasn't going to happen. I could feel myself deflating, shoulders slumping, excitement draining out. The buzz of questions in my head stuttered to silence.

"Then do you mind if I borrow that phone for a minute? I need to call my hotel."

As I climbed into the hotel shuttle, my disappointment was practically choking me, but the shuttle ride through peaceful green neighborhoods cheered me up. The hospital had been like a walled city. I had barely stepped outside. And ambulances aren't known for their picture windows.

Now, I was out in the sunshine, and I was seeing simple things I hadn't had the chance to see in weeks: mailbox planters and swing sets, owners jogging with their dogs, squirrels making suicide dashes across the road. And look, here was a shopping mall just a couple of blocks away from my hotel.

The front desk staff raised my spirits further. They joked with me and made me a cappuccino to order. And I opened my hotel room door to discover that, without being asked, they had upgraded me to a suite.

The views out my windows weren't boring roof gravel this time, either. They were those same nice neighborhoods and cute little shops I had passed on the drive in. Now I was looking down at them through a rustling green canopy of trees.

Trees! The children's hospital had had lawns and bushes, but no trees.

So I pushed open the curtains as wide as they would go and let myself relax. Hopefully, Elena was getting good care. At least she was out of bed and free of IVs. That had to count for something. And for the first time in weeks, my day didn't have to revolve around hers.

I had my own room. I had my own bathroom! I didn't have to stay cooped up in a building full of the sick and injured and dying. I could walk down the street on this gorgeous summer day and go anywhere my feet wanted to take me.

So I did.

First, I walked to the mall and bought Elena the electric razor she had asked for. But the mall felt too much like the hospital. I didn't want to stay indoors. So I wandered back to my hotel, basking in the hazy afternoon light. It warmed me through and through, until I felt as relaxed and sleepy as a cat.

Should I go to visiting hour? I thought as I entered the lobby. *The shuttle driver was nice about it, but I don't want to wear out my welcome.*

I entered the elevator and punched the button for my floor.

No need to decide yet, I thought. *I have several hours to kill first. Maybe a nap.*

I walked down the long hall and swiped my room key.

A nap in my own bed! After sleeping for days on pullout furniture, I have my own king-size bed!

The door clicked open.

The first thing I saw was the blinking red light on the phone.

The message didn't make sense. Or maybe it made too much sense. Dropping my bags, I dialed the number it gave me.

"Hello, Drew Center? This is Elena Dunkle's mother. You say she fell? Is she all right?"

The voice on the other end of the line was crisp. "Mrs. Dunkle, do you have your daughter's glasses?"

"Of course not!" But that came out sounding a little rude. "What I mean is, I couldn't have them. Elena wears them constantly. She's practically blind without them. Can you tell me, please—what's this about?"

"Elena fainted at our facility, and we called an ambulance when we couldn't bring her around. She's at the emergency room right now, so don't come to visiting hour. I don't expect her back until tonight. But I got a call from the staff member with her that she doesn't have her glasses. That's why I'm checking with you."

"But—my God!—is she all right? When did this happen? Where is she?"

And my brain began whirling again:

Insurance. Medical tests. Preferred provider hospitals. Is it her heart? Her brain? Oh, my God!—a stroke?

A steely edge crept into the crisp voice on the phone. "I'm sure your daughter's fine, ma'am. You don't need to concern yourself with where she is. She's our responsibility, and we'll see to it that she gets the care she needs. I'll let the staff person know that you don't have her glasses. Thank you for calling back. Good-bye."

And the click of the receiver left me alone with a swirling cloud of worries.

Another emergency room! Would Elena end up in the ICU again? Was her heart weaker than Dr. Costello had thought? Would we end up spending more weeks stuck in a hospital room while her condition remained unsolved, or even got worse? Her first day out of bed, and she had fallen again! Why did she keep blacking out?

It's dissociation. It's not anything to worry about, the middle psychiatrist said in my mind, while the two psychiatrists beside him nodded their approval. Then the serene expressions on their faces got mixed up with Dr. McKinney's broad smile. *It's hypochondria. It's nothing to worry about. Some children just want a little attention.*

Seventeen years without a single fainting episode—and now this!

I sat down on the edge of my king-size bed, stress pulling my muscles into stiff bundles. My legs bounced, my heels drummed against the floor, and my shoulders twitched and clenched. I couldn't even remember that just moments before, those same muscles, warmed by sun and exercise, had been as soft as taffy and ready for a catnap.

Where were those glasses? Oh, poor Elena! If she had to live without her glasses now, in a new place, possibly for days . . . We both have very bad eyes, the kind of eyes that can't see the giant *E* on the wall chart, so I knew exactly how demoralizing such an awful possibility would be.

Would I need to order new glasses for her? This was no easy process. Elena didn't have a simple prescription. She had three different conditions that complicated her vision in unusual ways and kept her from being able to walk into the typical places in a mall or shopping center. Getting her fitted with new glasses was both time-consuming and expensive. Those glasses that had gotten lost had cost about eight hundred dollars, and her German optician had checked her vision three different times on two different days—altogether, several hours of testing—before he had felt that he had enough data to order them.

I felt these worries snatching at me now, pushing me toward panic. What should I do? What could I *do*?

Calm down. Logic and reason!

I made myself go out for another walk and find a fast-food restaurant, and I made myself sit down there and eat dinner. An hour passed before I got back to the hotel room. No blinking red light this time.

But—were those glasses really gone? And how would we go about replacing them? I consulted my scribbled note and dialed the number again.

"Hello, this is Mrs. Dunkle. I'm just wondering if you've found Elena's glasses. Have they turned up?"

A different voice was on the phone now. It sounded a little harried but no less stern. "Mrs. Dunkle, I'm sorry, but could you call back later? We're dealing with mealtime here."

"When should I call back? In half an hour?"

"No, we'll be prepping for visitors then. Why don't you call after lights-out? That's when the staff has time for special requests."

"But—this isn't really a special request. You're the ones who called me, looking for her glasses. I just wanted to know, have you found them yet?"

The voice was firm. "I have to go. We're dealing with mealtime here. The night nurses will be happy to help you with that."

I tried to turn my mind to other things. I picked through one of the novels Elena had brought. Then, after the sun went down, I went to the phone and tried again.

"Hello, this is Mrs. Dunkle. I'm calling to see if you've found my daughter Elena's glasses."

"Elena Dunkle isn't here right now. She was taken to the hospital."

Panic fluttered around my ribs. "She's still there? Is she all right?"

The voice at the other end of the line sounded maddeningly unconcerned. "I'm sure she's fine, ma'am. We expect her back this evening. Is there something I can help you with?"

"Oh. Yes, there is. Did you find her glasses?"

"Ma'am, she isn't here."

"Yes, but are her glasses there?"

"Ma'am, I'm sure she has her glasses with her."

"Well, but that's just it," I said. "Your staff called me several hours ago because she *didn't* have her glasses with her. You were wanting to know if I had them. And I'm wondering, have you found them there after all? Have they turned up?"

"I'm sure they have, ma'am. We haven't been told that anything's missing." And something in the tone of voice sounded like *good-bye*.

"Yes, but if you could please just check," I said quickly. "Those glasses mean a lot to my daughter. She has very bad vision. She can't even see faces without them." And I remembered following her gurney down vague gray hospital hallways.

Imagine going through new routines in a psychiatric hospital like that!

"We'll need to get to work right away on replacing them if they're gone," I continued. "She has a complicated prescription, so the ordering process will take several days—even the testing process can take more than a day. Could you please check? Maybe we should call the ambulance service. Is there a record of which ambulance service drove her?"

The voice remained precisely as uninterested as before—which is to say, completely uninterested. "Ma'am, I'm sure she has her glasses with her."

And I found myself thinking wildly: *What a touchingly profound and irrational faith!*

"Well—if she doesn't, could you *please* give me a call? It's important because we don't live here, you see. Elena's eye doctor is in Germany. If those glasses are gone, I should make arrangements to get her prescription sent over right away. They aren't open on American time, they open six hours earlier. That means they close six hours earlier"—and I thought of our German optician's office, a little kingdom unto itself—"well, even earlier than that, maybe." Now I was babbling. "So, if they're there—or if they're not there—*please* just let me know. I can give you my number so you don't have to take the time to look it up . . ."

"Ma'am, we have your number," the voice on the phone informed me. *Drama queen!* the tone of voice added. "I'm sure your daughter has everything she needs. If we need to get in touch with you, we will. Good night."

And with that sadly ironic wish, the call ended.

I tried to have a good night. I took a long shower and went to bed. A king-size bed—a veritable helicopter landing pad of a bed after the narrow little pull-out foam chair I had been using!

But the physical comfort didn't help. Between stress dreams and sudden awakenings, the night was like a long bumpy road. Around five in the morning, I gave up on sleep. The optician's office back home in Germany was about to close for its leisurely German lunch. And was this one of the days when it wouldn't reopen in the afternoon? I couldn't remember.

Joe was coming over to visit us in two days. He had volunteered to attend a meeting at a nearby Air Force base so that he could take some vacation days and spend time with us afterward. Maybe the German optician's office could do a rush order, and Joe could bring the new glasses with him. I could call them to see if it was possible. But was this all moot anyway because her glasses had already been found? I didn't want to badger people on the other side of the Atlantic for nothing. So I picked up the phone, and I tried again.

"Hello, this is Mrs. Dunkle—Elena's mother. Is she all right?"

The voice on the phone was different. It was friendlier this time. "Good morning, Mrs. Dunkle. Yes, she's fine. She got back several hours ago."

"And do you know if they found her glasses?"

"Does she wear glasses? I don't remember if she had them on."

"Yes, she does, and here's the thing: they were missing yesterday, and I've been trying to find out if they turned up. Is there any way you can check?"

"I'm sorry to hear they were missing," the friendly voice said, and I was surprised to discover that I was almost in tears over the kind thought. "But your daughter and her roommate are sleeping right now, and she had a short night as it is. I hate to disturb them both by turning on the light to look for them. I think it would be best to wait until she gets up, don't you?"

And when she put it that way, I did, too.

"Why don't you give a call back after breakfast is out of the way?" the friendly voice continued. "I think this is something the day nurses can help you with."

At nine o'clock, the hotel shuttle drove me back to Drew Center for my meeting with Dr. Moore, Elena's new psychiatrist. After my bad night, I felt achy and sluggish, and my feelings about Elena's stay in this institution were considerably less rosy than they had been the day before.

Finally, some answers! I thought as I sat in the little waiting room once again. But the mood that went with that thought now was grim.

Elena met me at the door of Dr. Moore's office.

"You've got your glasses!" I blurted out.

"They were on my nightstand last night when I got back," she said.

Now, why couldn't someone have told me that?

Elena looked awful. Her forehead had a big white knot on it, and a wide purple bruise. "I don't remember it," she said dully, probing the bruise with her fingers. "The first thing I knew about it is when I woke up in the ER."

I knew that Elena had fallen, of course. But, no matter how reasonable I tried to be about it, I felt very upset to see her so badly injured.

I left her with them, I found myself thinking. *I trusted them! Why didn't they keep her safe?* But I knew this wasn't really fair. After all, Valerie had been under *my* care when her hands had erupted in third-degree burns.

Dr. Moore came into the room and shook hands with us. He seemed pleasant enough, although not particularly warm. But that didn't matter. What I needed was intellect and experience, not sympathy.

I held back at first, expecting Dr. Moore to do some explaining or educating, to sketch out what the plan was for Elena. When he didn't do that, but instead asked me what I had wanted to talk about, I started in on my list of questions.

But the answers Dr. Moore gave me were the same nonanswers I had already heard. No, he couldn't really say why Elena might be having blackouts, but he didn't see it as a cause for concern. No, he didn't see how the recent autoimmune attacks on her thyroid could have much to do with her anorexia. And why did he think she had anorexia nervosa at all? Well, because the hospital had sent her here.

"Okay, this keeps happening," I said. "Her first care team, at the military hospital, didn't agree that she had anorexia nervosa, so they sent her to the children's hospital for further tests. The military doctors told us she needed to get to the experts to be properly diagnosed. Then the children's hospital doctor said he wasn't sure one way or the other, that anorexia isn't his area. He thought that we should get her to you because you would be the experts who could properly diagnose her. Everywhere she goes, she gets treated for anorexia, even though no one's willing to say she actually has it, except for the original psychiatrist, whose opinion I don't trust."

Dr. Moore steepled his fingers. "And why don't you trust this psychiatrist?"

"Because his rationale wasn't very convincing." I said. "He seemed to base the entire diagnosis on one weigh-in. And then the other medical issues came along: the thyroiditis, the cardiomyopathy . . ."

"We see cardiomyopathy in anorexia patients," Dr. Moore pointed out.

"Yes, *but,*" I answered. "The cardiologist who found that condition in Elena was surprised and concerned about it. She told me she didn't expect to see it in a patient at Elena's weight. In fact, she told me she had tested numerous anorexics, and none of them had a heart like Elena's."

"It sounds like what you're telling me is that you don't want your daughter treated for anorexia."

I hung on to my temper.

"I want my daughter treated for whatever is wrong with her," I said. "I just need to know what that is. And the question is, does she have anorexia nervosa or not?"

"Well, we haven't had much time with her, but I would say that yes, she appears to fit the profile."

A profile! My heart gave a leap. At last, we were getting to some diagnostic parameters, some evidence that might help clear this question up. What linked my daughter to this dangerous disorder? Was there more than one odd weight on a scale? I needed to know! I needed to hear specifics.

"What profile is that?" I asked eagerly. "What factors into it?"

Dr. Moore shrugged. "Naturally, it's complicated."

I waited.

But—inexplicably—so did he.

"But there *are* quantifiable factors, aren't there?" I said, almost desperate by this time. "I need to know what they are. I need to know how they apply to her. I need . . ." I struggled for words. "I need to understand! Two months ago, my daughter's weight was normal." *And our life was normal, too*, I thought. "Her weight had been in the normal range for at least two months straight. Then she had a month with a significant weight drop. One month, one value. Is that what this whole diagnosis rests on?"

"Well, that's the most important factor, of course."

"But how? How is that factor being applied? *That's* what I need to understand! This whole question of anorexia nervosa is like a fog. I can't find out anything definite about it. The weight—okay, the most important factor. Well, her weight doesn't fall into any of the ranges I can find on the Internet. Your own institution didn't want to take her as a patient. Her weight wasn't low enough, you said."

"That's true. But she's here now, getting the treatment she needs." And Dr. Moore favored me with a benign smile.

Mentally, I dug in. Logic and reason. Facts! There *had* to be facts here, even if no one seemed to care about them but me.

"If Elena's weight isn't in the range that defines an anorexic," I said, "then I don't see how you can safely assume that she's getting the treatment she needs. What are the other factors that support her being here? I *have* to know these things. She's a minor. Her father and I are responsible for getting her the care she needs. We have to be able to make the right decision on her behalf. So, again, I ask, does my daughter have anorexia nervosa or not?"

Dr. Moore smiled and spread his hands in a conciliating gesture.

"Well, we'll have to watch her for a while before we'll know that," he said. "Your daughter has only just arrived. I haven't had a chance yet to look at her file."

I stared at him in stunned disbelief.

Days after they knew she was coming. Twenty-four hours after locking her up. One emergency visit and a head bump later. And still, no one knew a thing!

Poof! went the facts. My expert hadn't bothered to check them. I wouldn't be finding any answers here.

"So . . . ," I said slowly. "So . . ." And my brain dug back through its list of questions—the ones I'd been asking for weeks now, through three different hospital stays.

But what could I ask, because what could Dr. Moore answer? He hadn't even bothered to look at her chart!

I couldn't just give up like this. I began groping through the fog to a plan B.

"So," I asked, "what time will you need to get around to diagnosing her? When will your analysis be complete?"

Dr. Moore continued to smile. A consummate professional, he took no notice of my sarcasm. There would be no angry bullying from this psychiatrist.

"I think after a week, we'll know more," he said. "That will give us time to do our own observation."

"A *week*?" I said. "A *week* before you even decide whether or not she needs to be here at all? Elena's already been in hospitals for almost three weeks. Her whole summer break is going to hospitals!"

"Of course," Dr. Moore murmured. "Because your daughter's health is much more important than vacation plans." *Isn't it?* his eyes challenged. *You bad mother!*

And that was the end of our consultation.

After Dr. Moore left the room, Elena burst into tears.

"Please don't make me stay here!" she sobbed. "It's worse than a prison. They yell at you for no reason. They look into the toilets! I can't stay here!"

I took a long, hard look at my normally high-spirited daughter. I had never seen her looking so thin. The last few weeks had left her cheeks hollow and gaunt, and her arms were covered in needle pricks. Her eyes were dull and bloodshot, and her skin was pale, with the exception of the deep lilac bruise.

"I'm sorry, honey," I said. "I hate it, too. But if you need it, he's right, it's important."

"I *don't* need it!" she sobbed as a smiling nurse showed up at the door and beckoned. "I'm not like the people here. They scream and throw things. They're crazy! I'm not *crazy*! I want to go *home*!"

And the smiling nurse led her away.

That afternoon, I did a lot of walking. First, I walked to the mall and found Elena a regulation sweater because the young woman yesterday wasn't kidding: it was so cold in that place that even I was chilled to the bone. Then I walked through the pretty neighborhoods to Drew Center to drop the sweater off.

It took a while to get there, but I didn't mind. The walk gave me time to think. And I needed that time. I *had* to think what to do.

I arrived at the cluster of handsome brick buildings housing the psychiatric hospital and made my way by guess and signage to the one that housed Drew Center. Once again, I was struck by how much the place resembled a college campus. Stately trees shaded the sidewalks. Birds and squirrels bounced through the grass. I might be walking to class or to the library.

Since my mother was a professor, I grew up on a campus like this. Academic campuses felt like home. Except that this wasn't an academic campus after all, but a massive multibuilding hospital for the mentally ill. That made its resemblance to home feel distinctly eerie.

I rang the doorbell at Drew Center and got buzzed into the waiting room. No one else was there, so I crossed to the intercom and checked in.

"The reason for your visit?" the voice on the intercom asked.

"I'm bringing a sweater for my daughter."

"Oh. All right." And in another few seconds, the door opened, and a white-coated staff member took it from me.

I walked back across the empty waiting room and pushed on the outer door, but it had locked automatically behind me. *Not a problem*, I thought. *The staff member will know to let me out.* I waited by the door.

Nothing happened.

After a minute, I realized: *She's forgotten about me.* So I crossed back to the intercom.

"The reason for your visit?" the intercom wanted to know again.

"I've already given you the sweater," I said. "I need to be buzzed out."

"Just a minute, please."

So I crossed back to the door.

Nothing.

I waited.

Nope, still nothing.

After a couple of minutes, I went back to the intercom. "Can you please let me out?" I said.

This time, the voice on the intercom was new. It also had a distinct edge. "We're very busy with mealtime," it told me. "Can you please be patient?"

Did I have any choice?

I sat down and tried to be patient, but the silent waiting room unnerved me. I couldn't recall a single time in my life when I had been locked in somewhere against my will. What if there was a fire? Would they evacuate through here? Or would they use a different exit? Would they remember that I was stuck in here?

Instantly, my overactive imagination produced a picture for me of thick black and white smoke pouring underneath the door by the intercom, filling the room with a gray haze. I saw myself frantically waving to firemen passing outside through the thick glass of the undoubtedly high-security shatterproof windows that lined one side of the waiting room.

Now I saw myself coughing uncontrollably. I was falling to my knees as axes thudded on the heavy wooden door . . .

How silly! Of course there wasn't going to be a fire. I wasn't some hysterical child, to give way to an attack of nerves like that. I was a reasonable, responsible adult, and there was a reasonable explanation for all this. The staff were reasonable people. I had let them know what I needed. They had asked me to be patient in return, and that was what I was going to be.

So I made myself choose a magazine. And I waited.

I waited for fifteen minutes!

Okay, this wasn't reasonable. This was downright insane! I crossed to the intercom again.

"Hello?" asked yet another voice. It sounded surprised. "The reason for your visit?"

"I'd like to leave the waiting room now," I said with some force.

"Of course!" replied the voice, sounding even more surprised. *Why didn't you tell us sooner? You crazy woman!*

And the outer door buzzed open at last.

I was halfway back to the hotel, walking very fast and out of breath, before I could calm myself down enough to think straight.

Drew Center was failing to impress me—that's exactly what it was doing. Yes, there had been a friendly and normal interaction every now and then, but from the psychiatrist who hadn't bothered to look at Elena's file to the staff who couldn't bother to open the front door, the majority seemed disinterested and unprofessional.

Not only that, but I couldn't help comparing my fifteen-minute ordeal with what my poor daughter must be going through.

Elena had been locked in against her will for weeks now, labeled with a disorder that might be nothing more than the figment of a brutal quack's imagination. In her entire life, I had never seen her looking less healthy or more stressed, and she was back to having those mysterious blackouts again. Without anybody justifying such a serious step or even taking a position one way or the other, she had become an inmate in a psychiatric institution where she might not even belong.

It was horrifying, that's what it was. It was horrifying!

Your daughter is completely normal, Dr. Eichbaum had told me. But what happened when a normal person got locked up in an institution and treated as if she weren't normal? It added up to nothing less than serious psychological trauma. No wonder Elena kept blacking out!

When I got back to the hotel room, I called the only psychiatrist in the entire United States with whom I had ever felt a connection. That was Dr. Harris, the Texas doctor who had worked with Valerie before she had run away. Not only was he an expert in adolescent and young adult psychiatry, but he specialized in eating disorders, too. I was pretty sure that I remembered him telling me that he even ran an eating disorder center for a while.

I wasn't expecting very much when I placed the call. It was more of a shot in the dark than anything. But amazingly enough, Dr. Harris took the time to talk to me. I found myself babbling out the whole story, and Dr. Harris didn't hurry me or cut me off. His voice on the phone, patient and engaged, helped me to get through the painful details without breaking down or leaving out anything important.

"I can see why you're worried," he said when I came to the end of my tale. "It sounds like each doctor is just passing her on. It may be that no one has taken the time to do the proper tests to see if she really does have anorexia nervosa."

Relief washed over me. "So there *are* proper tests!"

"Oh, yes. Patient history, physical condition, lists of questions, medical tests. It can take several hours to do a full assessment. And have they done a twenty-four-hour EEG on her yet?"

"No. I know they did a CT scan, and I think they did a short EEG one afternoon."

"It would be a good idea to do a brain MRI and a twenty-four-hour EEG," he said, "just to rule out the possibility of anything neurological causing the blackouts. And a full psychiatric assessment to find out if your daughter does have anorexia nervosa, and also whether there are other psychological conditions comorbid—that is, present along with it."

Outside my hotel room, dusk was settling in, but I felt as if the clouds had just rolled back to reveal the sun and a chorus of angels was singing Hallelujah. "If I bring her to Texas, will you see her?" I asked. "Will you arrange for those tests?"

"You're a long way away," he pointed out.

"I'll rent a car," I said. "We can be there in two days. We *have* to get a handle on this!"

"Two days. Friday. Let me check with the secretary and see what my schedule looks like." There was a pause. "Yes, I can see her on Friday afternoon."

Full of excitement, I called Drew Center and told Elena the plan. Then I asked to speak to Dr. Moore. This time, when I spoke to him, he didn't sound so complacent.

"She was transferred into *my* care," he said. "We had to clear a bed for her, and you agreed to it."

"That was before she had another one of these fainting episodes and wound up in the emergency room again," I countered. *And before you couldn't get around to diagnosing her for a whole week*, I thought.

"We are *working* with your daughter, Mrs. Dunkle," he said. "We have her best interests in mind."

"I understand that," I said. "I never doubted it. But the fact is that Drew Center turned her down in the beginning because she probably shouldn't even be there. I want to get her the neurological tests and the psychiatric evaluation she should have had before she even came to you."

"That's *our* job," he said, and now he sounded even more annoyed. "If Elena needs evaluation, we'll evaluate her. By law, I can hold her for seventy-two hours. She's in my care, and that's what I'm doing."

This caught me completely off guard. It wasn't as if I were trying to take Elena out of Drew Center in order to deny her proper care. It had never even occurred to me that I might be refused the right to choose the medical care for my own child.

Very upset, I called Dr. Harris again. But he soon calmed me down.

"I'm sure the Drew Center psychiatrist is just concerned that you may be removing Elena from treatment altogether," he said. "But I've worked with Drew Center on several occasions. They've seen several of my clients. I'll call and explain that they'll be releasing Elena into my care. That should clear it up."

Thank God for one rational psychiatrist, at least!

I hung up the phone and started looking at maps on the Internet. Once again, my mind was churning with plans. *Motels . . . Routes . . . Rental cars . . . Aren't there websites that will let me compare all the rental car companies at once?*

The phone rang and pulled me away from my plans and searches. Dr. Harris was on the other end of the line again. This time, he sounded puzzled, and even a little sheepish.

He said, "They won't release Elena to me, either."

CHAPTER EIGHTEEN

When I heard him say that—when I realized that my daughter had to stay locked up in a mental institution where she very likely didn't belong—what I felt was beyond horror. To know that my beloved child, who trusted me, was being held prisoner and that it was my signature on a form that had put her there . . .

My imagination immediately dredged up all the most ghastly images that anxiety and guilt could conjure and played them all for me in one long, gruesome ordeal. Outside was a honey-colored sunset and the long, inconspicuous process of twilight, but none of the mundane things I saw around me seemed to match what I was going through in my head. It was as if I were watching a movie about my hotel room while actually being somewhere else, somewhere very dark and scary that I couldn't escape. And in that dark, scary place was this movie of a lit-up hotel room, playing on a little computer monitor in the corner.

Gray dusk congealed into black night. All the lights were on in that little hotel room on the monitor. But they couldn't light up the dark, scary place I was in.

It isn't that I stopped thinking. If anything, my thoughts spun too quickly. I was worrying, and I was regretting, but strangely enough, I wasn't thinking about Elena. All I could think of was Kate, my Jane Austen girl from Marak's goblin kingdom. She ended up locked in the caves underground, and for a very long time, she hated it there. She would go to the doors and argue and beg to be let out.

Now, as I staggered around in that dark, scary place, I could hardly bear to think of what I had made Kate suffer. *How could I have done that?*

I thought. *How could I have been so cruel?* And I found myself obsessing over how I could reach her—how I could apologize to my character for what I had put her through.

"What?" asked a voice. "They won't do what?"

I was crying on the phone to someone. It was Joe. I could hear his voice. It sounded very far away, as if I had set the phone down somewhere. But at the same time, another part of me couldn't absorb that I was talking to a person at all. It was if I were bawling away to the phone itself, and nobody was listening.

Nobody was there with me. I was alone. I was all alone, next to the phone, and I had the most horrible headache of my life.

People say, *She's got a gear loose.* When my family was together, I was the central gear. My husband came to me for things, and my daughters came to me for things. I paid bills, I made calls, I filled out forms and permission slips, I bought clothes, I cooked meals, I planned birthdays, and I booked vacations. The other members thought about themselves and each other, but I'm the one who thought about the whole family.

Then trouble came. We went into the bad years. The harder it got for my family, the more they counted on me to keep everything going. The more trouble the other gears in my family had, the more I pushed against them to keep us all on track. I was turning, turning with all my might, turning for all of us, because when Joe was working twelve-hour days and Valerie was covered in burns and Elena was thrashing around, out of her mind, I couldn't be out of my mind, too, could I?

So I turned. I struggled to turn. It took all I had to turn: to ask the right questions, to pack the suitcases, to stay by the hospital bed, to be the advocate for my family. And then, just when it had reached the point that I was pushing with all my strength—*poof!* No more gears were meshed with mine.

In that hotel room, I was one lone gear, whipping around like crazy. I was staggering around in a dark, lonely place that wasn't the real world anymore, while little images of physical life played out on a tiny computer screen nearby. And dear *God*—how my head hurt! It hurt like *crazy*!

Then there was a click at the door, and there stood Joe.

I had known once upon a time that he was coming, but when I saw him, it was as if I'd had no idea. Joe walked through the door like a flesh-and-blood miracle, and with him came normal life, and minutes and hours, and the hotel room around me again, with afternoon sunlight pouring through all the windows.

I collapsed into his arms and bawled my headache away. Within five minutes, I was myself again.

Joe had rented a car. He was hungry, so he drove us out to find a burger place. He ordered for us, and the miserable little burger he handed me, with one pickle and a teaspoon of chopped onions on it, tasted absolutely amazing.

While we ate, I told him everything that had happened. I told him about the matched set of psychiatrists at the children's hospital who had politely ignored all my questions. I told him about Dr. Harris's calm, interested approach and Dr. Moore's inexplicably hostile one.

"Maybe you got on his bad side somehow," Joe said.

"Maybe I did," I said. "I'm certainly not on his *good* side."

"I'll see if he'll meet with me," Joe said. "If he feels so strongly that Elena needs to stay at Drew Center, maybe I can get him to talk to me about it. I'd like to hear what he has to say."

When we got back to the room, Joe tried to follow through on this. He got on the phone and asked for an appointment with Dr. Moore. But no, that would be impossible, he was told. Dr. Moore didn't have time to meet with him.

"Okay," Joe said. "Well, could you please ask him to call me back, then?"

No, came the answer: Dr. Moore didn't have time to do that, either.

"Oh," said Joe. "Well . . . thank you for trying."

He hung up and looked at me.

"I'm going to hope," he said, "that Dr. Moore is really, *really* busy. Let's just assume that. And while we're assuming that, let's go get some coffee, too."

So Joe and I walked to the nearby shopping mall, sat in the food court, and talked about our plans. Dr. Harris in Texas had moved Elena's appointments to the next week. Tomorrow, we would pick her up from Drew Center and start driving.

Dr. Harris's office was over fifteen hundred miles away. That should have seemed daunting. Actually, I couldn't wait.

"Should we book a hotel room?" Joe asked.

"Nope, let's just drive till we get tired. I'm ready to have a little less structure in my life."

At six forty-five that evening, we headed to Drew Center for visiting hour, ready to see our captive daughter. Joe hadn't seen Elena in over two weeks. Fifteen or so relatives and friends of patients had gathered in the little waiting room with us. At least this time, I didn't have to be locked in by myself.

At seven o'clock, the door to the center buzzed open, and a staff member appeared with a clipboard.

"Edgerton," she read out loud. "Towney. Dunkle. Your family member is not allowed to have visitors. The rest of you, proceed past me to bag check." And the other visitors filed inside.

One of the mothers whose name she had read started to cry. I wondered if she, too, hadn't seen her child in weeks. I wondered if she had traveled a long way to see her child, and if Dr. Moore was keeping that patient by force, too.

"Why can't we see Elena?" Joe asked the nurse. "What did she do?"

"She didn't gain weight today."

"What rule did she break?" Joe asked.

"She didn't break any rules."

"Then she didn't eat everything?" he wanted to know.

"No, she was fully compliant."

I didn't know how Joe felt about this, but I started shaking. I was literally shaking with rage.

"So, let me get this straight," I said. "Our daughter did everything you asked her to do. You're punishing her for something that's out of her control."

The nurse set her jaw. "Weight matters."

Now I could see that Joe, too, was barely hanging on to his temper. "Then why didn't you feed her more?" he demanded. "You're punishing her for doing everything you asked, and I'm not going to stand for it. I am *going* to see my daughter!"

The mother who had been crying was still standing next to us. She said, "And *we're* going to see our daughter, too!"

The nurse gave an exasperated sigh, and I could feel it again: that sense of hostility and distrust. It had crackled through Dr. Petras's stern voice and angry threats, and it had hummed behind the bland comments of Dr. Moore. It had even been present when I was talking to the set of three psychiatrists, hidden though it was under polite serenity.

Hostility breeds hostility. Now it was mutual.

"I have to check," the nurse muttered. A minute later, she came back. "Oh, come on, then," she grumbled. And we joined the rest of the visitors.

Next morning, Joe and I packed the trunk of our tiny hatchback rental car and drove over to pick up Elena. We spent a tense twenty minutes parked under the big shade trees of the college campus that wasn't a college campus at all—the stately redbrick University of the Mentally Ill. Then Elena burst out the front door, lugging her suitcase.

"So, did Dr. Moore tell you good luck?" I asked.

"It was kind of weird," she said. "It wasn't him. It was another guy, an older guy who looked nice. He asked me where I was going, and I told him we were going to see Dr. Harris in Texas, and he said we'll like Dr. Harris, he's a great psychiatrist.

"So I said Dr. Moore didn't seem to think so, because he wouldn't let me leave, and the old guy snorted and said, 'I bet he threatened that you'd be leaving against medical advice, too, didn't he?' And he left that box unchecked. See?"

Elena produced her discharge paper. Sure enough, the *Against Medical Advice* box was unchecked.

That put the crowning touch on my happiness. After all the frustration and hostility I'd faced, those friendly words about Dr. Harris and the scornful ones about Dr. Moore seemed like a vote in my favor. I had made the right decision. We were doing the right thing.

Joe took the on-ramp to the highway, and our car picked up speed, and my spirits soared as they hadn't soared in months.

My family was with me, gathered together again despite almost insurmountable obstacles. Valerie wasn't here physically, but she'd been writing me more and more often, and I felt that she was safe and content and connected, too. The dark time was over—the dark, imprisoned time. I had rescued my daughter. I had rescued us all.

Outside my window was bright sunshine, and inside my mind was bright sunshine, and between the inside and the outside, I felt like a flake of transparent crystal. I felt as if the clean, fresh light was shining straight into my soul and striking rainbows that stretched to the horizon.

"That doctor was really nice," Elena said in a low voice, almost to herself. "I kind of wish . . . I wish maybe I'd stayed."

CHAPTER NINETEEN

This odd comment puzzled me for a while. Elena couldn't seem to explain it, and I couldn't work it out into anything that made sense. But I was so grateful to have my family together again that nothing could bring me down for long. I sang along to the new CDs I'd bought at the shopping mall, and the heartfelt smiles I saw on the faces of gas station employees and convenience store cashiers that afternoon must have been a reflection of my own.

We stopped whenever and wherever we wanted to stop, and when we pulled off the highway for the night, the little countryside motel seemed particularly charming. We all crowded onto one bed to sit and watch the old-fashioned boxy television, and the six channels it pulled in seemed to be loaded with hilarious shows designed especially for our amusement. I listened to Joe and Elena laugh together, and my heart brimmed with happiness.

But by the next morning, I was already feeling anxious again.

Something was different about Elena. She could still laugh, but her laughter no longer felt spontaneous. A part of her was shut off, and she was watching over it. I knew Elena could be careful with people outside the family, even with the ones she considered friends. But I hadn't felt this kind of reserve toward Joe and me before.

And when we stopped for food, the change was even more pronounced.

"Where would you like to eat lunch?" I asked her.

"Nowhere yet," she answered. "I'm still full from breakfast."

I didn't see how this could be true since she'd eaten only a couple of bites of pancake before announcing that it was soggy.

"Breakfast was four hours and two states ago," I said. "It's time to sample the charms of another roadside diner."

Elena groaned. "They're all so fatty!"

"We could stop at a grocery store then," Joe suggested, "and put together sandwiches."

"Hmm. Nah, too much trouble."

"Snack foods," I suggested. "Nuts. Dried fruit." And when Elena gave a disgusted mutter, I circled back around to the beginning. "Well, where *would* you like to eat, then?"

"I don't care. Look, Taco Bell's coming up. Dad likes Taco Bell."

At Taco Bell, Elena suddenly turned on the chatter. She told us story after story from Drew Center with barely a break to catch her breath in between, as if it were her assignment to entertain and educate a supper club of two. Finally, Joe looked at his watch and said he'd better visit the restroom.

"Me, too," Elena announced, jumping up.

"Hey, what are you doing with your tray?" I demanded as she swept its contents into a pile. "There's a taco and a half there still."

"I don't want it," she said.

"Well . . . You could save it for later."

"A cold taco? *Please!*" And into the trash went Elena's lunch. Once again, she'd eaten about two bites.

Elena might pass up food when she was stressed, but I hadn't seen her reject or ration it when she was just relaxing with her family. She was a nervous, picky eater—but she did eat.

I worried over this as we drove. *It must be because it was so upsetting being ordered to eat,* I thought. *Thanks to Dr. Petras, she associates eating with being bullied now.*

So I changed my tactic. I decided not to comment if I saw her throwing away meals. The next time we stopped, I ransacked the gas station store for snacks I knew she enjoyed.

"Hey, a pecan roll!" she exclaimed in delight, looking into the bag I handed her. "I haven't had a pecan roll in years!"

But when I was cleaning out the car that evening at the hotel, I saw that the pecan roll hadn't been touched.

After two days, we arrived in our city, but we didn't have a place to stay. It was strange being back in our own hometown and being homeless. Before, whenever we had come home, we had stayed with good friends. But we didn't call anybody this time to tell them we were coming.

Joe drove down the highway access road, pulling into one hotel parking lot after another, and I hopped out of the car and checked rates. I wanted to find a weekly rate without having to go to the weekly hotels, which didn't seem very nice. But one front desk clerk after another quoted me the regular room rate.

"It's fixed in the system," a clerk told me. "I'd like to give you a better rate, but there's nothing I can do."

Here's what I didn't know then: many hotels offer a special medical rate, and that medical rate can be substantially lower than the regular room rate. Unfortunately, I didn't think to mention the reason we were in town.

The sixth or seventh time we stopped, I walked into a midrange motel, not fancy but not bottom-of-the-barrel either, and the man behind the counter asked what he could do for me. He had a strong accent, and his English was fluent but ungrammatical, like my German.

I explained that I was looking for a weekly deal but that we had been unable to find one. "It's fixed in the system," I said.

"*I* can make you a deal," the man told me with pride. "This is my motel. I own it." And he named a very reasonable price for the week— more reasonable than I had hoped for.

Uh-oh, I thought. *Maybe the furniture is old and shabby. Maybe none of the appliances work.*

But no, the room he showed me was neat and cheerful, with red curtains and red patterned carpet on the floor. I saw no stains, and I saw no scuffs on the furniture. The room was immaculate.

"My family does the cleaning," he said. "I oversee the breakfast." Again, I heard the pride in his voice. And I realized: This wasn't a motel. This was a home. It was this man's home!

My damaged, traumatized family wasn't going to have to stay in an artificial box. We were going to stay in a home—the home of this man and his family. It didn't matter that we were paying him money. He loved this place, and he took pride in it. In his eyes, we were his guests.

It had been weeks since I'd been home, and when I realized this, I almost burst into tears. And throughout that week, as I saw his family at work around the place—as I saw him up on a ladder, changing light bulbs, or his wife sweeping up leaves while their children played nearby—I felt again that warm swell of emotion.

It did me good to have that connection to a home again. As fragile as I was, I felt it healing me.

Dr. Harris, the psychiatrist we had come to see, also made me feel at home. He had that gentle courtesy and natural discretion that used to distinguish a certain kind of well-educated Texan when I was a girl. He was the sort of person I had met many times, and the sort of person my old Texas family had raised me to be: the one who smiles at strangers and says *sir* and *ma'am* and opens doors and picks up things people drop without being asked to. Those old-fashioned Texas manners aren't so much a set of rules as a philosophy I've tried my best to live by, and I suspected that Dr. Harris lived by it, too.

We left Elena at Dr. Harris's office to meet with him for several hours, and Joe and I went to a nearby coffee shop. Joe said, "So, do you want to take the phone card and call anybody while we're here?"

I did want to call our friends. But at the same time, I didn't know how to. The trauma of the last three weeks was still too fresh. I couldn't talk about it yet. I didn't even want to have to say, "I don't want to talk about it," because that would still be talking about it.

The only friends I'd seen since coming to the States on that medevac flight were a husband and wife whom we had known well in Germany. Phil had been Joe's boss, and I had become Jackie's partner in crime, as she put it. Phil and Jackie had left Germany while the girls were still at the boarding school.

When Jackie had learned through the grapevine that I was staying at the children's hospital, she had taken matters into her own hands. A nurse herself, she knew better than to wait for me to reach out. Jackie had called Elena's hospital room, and when I had answered, she'd said, "I'm coming by to pick you up for lunch." And her tone of voice informed me that she would listen to no excuses.

That had done me so much good I couldn't even measure it. Worlds of good. Entire worlds.

Jackie had swept by several times over the next week and dragged me out shopping with her. She had even taken me away for a "slumber party" at her house. It had been so wonderful to see her. She and Phil had been nothing short of a godsend. It would be wonderful to see our other friends, too.

But—

"Maybe not today," I said. "What do you think?"

"No," Joe said. "Not today."

Elena's MRI was already scheduled. We picked her up from Dr. Harris's office, drove her to the imaging center, and waited in the waiting room while she went back to have the MRI. *I hope she doesn't have a blackout due to the stress of the machine*, I thought, and that thought grew and grew, like a huge black balloon, until it became the subject of all-consuming dread. Each time the nurse popped open the waiting room door, I jumped and flinched, afraid of what she was coming to tell me.

But after half an hour, Elena came back out, holding a massive envelope of printouts. "*That* was boring," she announced.

Then we drove to the hospital to meet Dr. Knox, the neurologist Dr. Harris liked to use. And Dr. Knox started the twenty-four-hour EEG.

Since Elena would be staying overnight, this meant admission to yet another hospital. Once again, I sat at an intake desk and signed handfuls of forms. It was one of the largest hospitals in town, but the place felt shabby and ugly to me. Or maybe I just wasn't comfortable in hospitals anymore.

Then the nurse called us back to Elena's small hospital room.

I paused by the door and struggled to control my expression of dismay. My daughter had metal probes wired all over her head, like a victim in a cheap horror movie. Dr. Knox was busy setting up a camera on a tall tripod at the end of the hospital bed, and Joe and I peered over his shoulder at the little monitor. Sure enough, there was a tiny Elena, head wired with tiny probes, sitting on her tiny hospital bed.

This is kind of awful, I thought, looking at the miniature horror-movie Elena. Then I looked around the gray, featureless room, with its television set hanging on a bracket in the corner. *All of this is awful*, I thought. The ugly room, the unfamiliar wires, the single camera like an alien eye, the knowledge that we were there to examine the possibly faulty insides of my daughter's skull: it all felt dreary and upsetting.

"How do you think we can trigger one of these attacks?" Dr. Knox asked.

"I know how you can do it," Joe said. "Clare and I need to leave. Elena doesn't have them when we're around."

He was right. Although Elena had had several attacks during her days at Drew Center, she hadn't had a single one on our drive across the country.

"Then I think it would be best if you leave now," Dr. Knox said. "Is that okay with you?" he asked Elena.

"Sure," she said.

I was impressed at how matter-of-fact she was being. Maybe that was because she was the only person in the room who couldn't see how scary she looked.

So Joe and I left and drove to a big shopping center nearby. Real stateside shopping—that would be fun! But once we got there, we discovered that it wasn't. We couldn't seem to think of anything to shop for. We ended up spending most of our time sitting in a restaurant, nursing glasses of iced tea.

"Want to call any of our friends," Joe asked, "and see if they can get together for dinner?"

"I don't know," I said. "Who were you thinking of?"

"I don't know."

I looked out toward the loose arrangement of skyscrapers that marked our city's downtown, and I thought about the inevitable questions.

Not that our friends would pry. Not that they wouldn't understand. They loved us. They would be thrilled to see us, and we would be just as thrilled to see them.

"Maybe tomorrow," I said. "I don't feel ready for it today."

"Me neither," Joe said. "Not today."

In the morning, Joe and I drove back to the hospital to meet up with Dr. Knox and see how Elena's scan had gone. The sight of our daughter was even more shocking now. Elena looked awful! Her face was pasty, and her hospital gown was loose at the neck. White dressing pads, taped together, covered her whole upper chest and her collarbones.

"What happened?" Joe and I exclaimed.

"I don't know," Elena said. "It *really* hurts."

"What do you mean you don't know?" Joe asked. "How can you not know?"

"I just don't know," she said. "I wasn't awake."

Dr. Knox came in and stopped the camera. Then he connected a laptop to it and studied the footage. "Take a look," he said to us after a few minutes.

The three of us crowded around him and peered at the tiny Elena on the screen. Sure enough, without us there, she had had one of her blackouts. The small screen showed her hands rotating, then her feet, and then her head. Since she was alone in the room, nothing intervened to stop her.

Around and around, Elena's circling hands swept by her chest. She wasn't doing it on purpose. She was doing nothing on purpose. The hands moved mechanically, mindlessly, swiping by her breastbone again and again. Each time they came around, her fingernails took away strips of skin.

Helpless, I watched scratches appearing on the white skin of that small mindless figure, and I felt almost overwhelming nausea. Around and around went the hands with their scraping fingernails, and there was nothing I could do to stop them. The scratches widened and spread, and I had to swallow again and again. I was afraid I might have to run out of the room.

Over time, the doll-like figure on the monitor grew more and more violent. It wasn't a question of violent emotion. It was a case of less control from the brain. Minute by minute, the body seemed freer to carry out its own mechanical actions. Not only were the hands circling, but also the arms were circling from the elbows, and the legs began to bend at the knees. Gradually, this series of movements evolved, until the whole tiny body was jerking in a methodical series of circles, folding and unfolding at the middle like a Swiss army knife.

Suddenly, during one of those pocketknife folds, the figure flipped over the bars of the hospital bed. The camera kept filming the rumpled sheet.

Dr. Knox stopped the video. He said, "It goes on for another twenty minutes."

Throughout the slow, mechanical fit, which had lasted forty full minutes, Elena's nails had raked all the skin off her chest. What was left under the gauze pads was a wide expanse of weeping, gooey dermal tissue that blazed with pain like a gigantic burn. "I think I banged my head when I fell, too," Elena told us. "It really hurts. The nurse found me on the floor."

She couldn't tell us why the fit had started.

"I had a headache, and it got very bad," she said. "Then the television got really loud. The sound comes out through a speaker on the remote, and the last thing I remember is trying to wrap the remote with my blanket to muffle the sound."

Joe looked shaken, and his face was pale. Even though Dr. Knox had stopped the distressing video, I still wasn't sure I would be able to hold down my breakfast.

What was going on inside our daughter's brain? Was there damage? Had the hunger strike at the military hospital caused some sort of stroke?

A certain amount of matter-of-fact callousness may be expected from a doctor who deals with seizures every day. Dr. Knox ignored Joe's and my pale, perspiring faces and led us straight down the hall to examine Elena's MRI. One by one, he took the big blue plastic sheets out of their envelope and set them up in front of a light box.

On the plastic sheets were slices of my daughter's brain.

When I was seven months pregnant with Elena, I was carrying Valerie through the house, and I tripped on the living room carpet. I couldn't let myself fall onto my face because I would have fallen on both of my children, so I threw out a knee instead. I managed to stop myself, but the whole weight of the three of us came down on that one knee. Instantly, I felt something crack in my pelvis, and searing pain shot down my legs. I crawled to the phone and called for help, and a friend drove me to the hospital.

In the ER, the nurses bundled me into a bed, and a doctor hurried in to assess me. But almost immediately, he had good news.

"I don't think bones are broken," he said. "I think you've torn a pelvic ligament. But we're going to have to do an X-ray to be sure. I know you've heard that X-rays can be dangerous for a fetus, but don't worry: your baby is far enough along that everything will be fine. We'll go for one exposure and be as quick as we can."

I rode a gurney up to the X-ray department. When it was over, two techs moved me back to my ER cubbyhole and pulled the curtains around me again. Joe was at work, over forty minutes away, and I didn't want to call him and worry him until I had some answers. My friend had taken Valerie home to babysit her, so I lay there, alone and in pain.

After a few minutes, a man I didn't know pulled the curtain aside. "Excuse me—Mrs. Dunkle?" he said. "I thought you might like to see this." He looked shy and out of place, an introvert caught out in public, but there was a light in his eyes that spoke of Christmas.

It was my X-ray. He held it up against the light for me, and I forgot all about my pain.

There, against the slick dark gray background that signifies secrets, were the big white bones of my spine and ribs and pelvis. And nestled inside those big bones was another set of tiny, perfect bones. My unborn baby lay sideways, with her hands folded against her chest and her delicate spine and ribs curved like a seashell. Her little head leaned trustingly on my lap.

No wonder the shy radiologist had left his office and come to find me. That X-ray was one of the most beautiful things I had ever seen.

But on this day, almost two decades later, as I looked at the inside of my daughter's skull, I thought, *This is not Christmas, and this is not beautiful.* The blue plastic sheets reminded me of crime scene forensics, of viciousness, blame, and guilt. The two round eyeballs, protruding into the sequence of images, looked monstrous and alien, and the odd shadings and folds of brain evoked lichen and fungus growth. The images jarred my fragile spirit and upset my queasy stomach, and my imagination flashed again to the hideous, unforgettable sight of my doll of a daughter, twitching and folding in half like a pocketknife.

I thought, *Everything I am having to learn now is grotesque.*

"Your daughter doesn't have epilepsy," Dr. Knox concluded. "Her MRI is normal. I believe these seizures are psychological in nature."

That should have been reassuring. Shouldn't I feel relief?

But when Elena's mind could do such things to her body, what relief could there really be?

Before we left Texas, we all had a long meeting with Dr. Harris. First, Elena met with him one last time, and then she stayed in the waiting room while Joe and I met with him. Dr. Harris was the only psychiatrist I had met all summer who didn't treat Joe and me with coldness. He was warm, wise, and personable, and he did his best to answer our questions.

"Your daughter does have an eating disorder," he said. "I can't go so far as to say that she has anorexia nervosa. She may, but then again, she may not."

"So it's a difference of degree?" I asked. "The eating disorder diagnosis isn't as severe as a diagnosis of anorexia?"

"There are certain physical characteristics to the anorexia diagnosis," Dr. Harris said. "The number of months without a period, a weight below a certain BMI percentage . . . And the fact is, the parameters don't do all that good a job of guiding us here. Anorexia nervosa, bulimia nervosa, they were established back before psychiatrists realized that many eating disorders aren't that clear-cut. Let's say you have a patient who primarily restricts, but also purges. And what about bulimics who also spend weeks fasting? Ultimately, I think we'll see the diagnostic guidelines reworked to do a better job here."

"I see," I said. But I wasn't entirely sure that I did.

"It's all tied in to body image, too," he went on. "How the patient sees himself or herself—most of my patients are female. Do you know, I had three different anorexic patients who decided to go to work as strippers in order to tackle their negative body image. I thought that was a fascinating approach to the problem! It seemed to help them, too."

I puzzled over this. It hadn't occurred to me before that Elena might have body-image issues. Why should she? Everywhere she went, she got compliments. It just didn't compute.

"And then there's the overlap between obsessive-compulsive disorder and eating disorder," Dr. Harris went on. "Elena has OCD. It's not unusual to find them together."

"Oh. She does?"

This was something else I hadn't thought about before, much less learned anything about. I tried to recall the tiny bit I knew about OCD, and my imagination presented me with a hypothetical Elena, stuck washing her hands for hours.

"Yes," confirmed Dr. Harris. "You could say that, in a lot of ways, eating disorder is very much the condition of obsessive-compulsive disorder centered on food. When anxiety increases, the compulsions increase. In this case, they're compulsions to restrict and diet."

"I guess . . . I can understand that," I said. "Yes, Elena does have trouble eating when she's upset." I paused. "But what about her seizures?"

"I'm sure they were brought on by the forced hospitalization," Dr. Harris said.

Now, here was something definite and also, finally, something that I could understand. It seemed to be something that clicked with Joe, too. He said, "Then, since Elena's not in the hospital anymore, will the seizures go away?"

"It all depends," Dr. Harris said. "It depends on whatever stress she may be under later."

Joe and I exchanged glances, uncertain again. "Does that mean they're deliberate?" I asked. "Does she do them on purpose to control stress?"

"Well, define *on purpose.*" And Dr. Harris smiled, the wistful smile of a gentle soul. "I have one patient who had dissociation seizures all the time. Right in the supermarket, down she'd fall. She goes to my church, and there she'd be, on the floor right down in the middle of service. There didn't seem to be anything she could do about them; they came on completely without warning. So I said to her, 'You're having these seizures so frequently, I'm afraid we're going to have to talk about taking your driver's license away.'" Dr. Harris's gentle smile grew broader. "And, do you know, her seizures got a *lot* better."

He lapsed into silence, but I could think of nothing to say. My horrified imagination had locked onto the image of Elena, tumbling over in a produce department and mindlessly circling right next to the stands of apples and pears.

There was a pause.

"Where do we go from here?" Joe asked.

"I'd go home, if I were you," Dr. Harris said. "It seems as if you all could use a rest. And the Germans are doing excellent work in the area of eating disorder. I see no reason why Elena can't get fine treatment right where you live."

"So, no need for six months in a psychiatric institution," I said bitterly, remembering Dr. Petras and his threats.

"I do think some time in an eating disorder treatment center would probably be good for Elena," Dr. Harris said. "Six months, that's probably too long, and anyway, I'm sure your insurance wouldn't cover it. They're very bad about covering eating disorder stays. I'll give you a piece of advice: never let them hang up the phone."

"I—what?"

My mind was still grappling with the statement *Some time in a treatment center would probably be good.* That statement wouldn't fit into place for me. I had such feelings of pain and hostility against Drew Center that my brain was refusing to consider it.

"Never let them hang up," he repeated. "An insurance company gets monitored for that. They're not allowed to hang up on clients. So, you get on the phone with them, and you *stay* there. You keep going up the line, one supervisor after another, until you can make someone listen."

Elena came back in from the waiting room, and the three of us shook Dr. Harris's hand good-bye. My respect for him had done nothing but grow during the week Elena had worked with him, and I made a mental note to steer her toward college in our home city so she could continue to work with him when we came home next year.

Then we went back to the motel, collected our luggage and our various medical statements, test results, and receipts, said good-bye to our motel family for the last time, and crammed ourselves into the tiny car to drive back across the country.

My mood was no longer euphoric.

"Mom, it's *my* business!" Elena snapped at dinner that night.

"I know. I'm just saying that Dr. Harris said a food diary is very important."

"So fine, I'll do one! You know, just because you had one little meeting about me doesn't mean you're an expert on me now."

It didn't make sense, that anger. It wasn't part of the pattern of Elena. Was this hostile, closed-off person really the same girl who had snuggled down next to me and shared her chocolate pudding?

"Of course not," I said. "All I wanted to say is: Why wait? Why not start it now? We could stop by Walmart and get a—"

"*Leave* it, Mom! Just *drop* it!"

And the fury in Elena's voice left me stunned.

By the time we flew back home to Germany, it was late August, and Elena's senior year was set to start in little over a week. The Summer from Hell had eaten almost every bit of her vacation. And the Summer from Hell was still gobbling up my time.

Insurance forms had poured in during the weeks I was gone. More were showing up every day: benefits statements for each doctor, each psychiatrist, each blood test, and each lab, not to mention the lengthy statements concerning the four different hospital stays. Even though by this time I was a veteran of insurance billing problems, this batch of forms still brought surprises.

I was sitting at the desk in the office one afternoon that week, talking on the phone and working through the stack of problems. "On the claim dated August third," I said, "the visit to the ER, I need to know why you kicked it back as not a preferred provider. That hospital was on your preferred provider list."

"Yes," said a polite female voice in my ear. "But the doctor your daughter saw there is not."

"Wait—You're telling me that you told us to use that hospital, but then we're not supposed to use the doctor who works there?"

"He isn't in our network, ma'am."

"But he *works* for the hospital. He works in the emergency room! So far as I know, he was the only doctor there."

"Yes, but we don't have him listed on our list of preferred providers—"

"The same list where you have the *hospital* listed."

"Yes, ma'am."

I gave up this particular fight with good grace. I knew when I was beaten, and I knew better than to take my problems out on the phone representative. *Oh, well,* I thought as I thanked her for her time, *this isn't so tragic.*

It certainly wasn't the worst problem I'd faced that day.

"What are you having for breakfast?" I had asked Elena that morning.

"Chill out, Mom."

"I can make you something. Eggs and toast, biscuits . . . I can heat up last night's spaghetti . . ."

"Chill *out*, Mom!"

Now, as I hung up the phone and wrote a note on the insurance form, I thought again about that baffling hostility. Elena wasn't a nervous eater anymore, I admitted to myself. No, she was a downright hostile eater.

Elena heard me put down the phone and came to the doorway.

"So, we're going to base after I shower, right?" she said. "I haven't finished my school shopping."

"I need to have lunch first," I said. "Did you have lunch?"

"Yeah . . ."

But her face didn't convince me.

These days, whenever Elena and I were together, she always seemed to wear the same expression: eyes slightly narrowed, mouth in a line, as if she were constantly bored. No longer did I get to watch that vivid parade of feelings I had loved since her earliest childhood.

It was just one more loss to grieve.

Now, as I watched her remote expression settle into place, I debated what to do. No, Elena hadn't had lunch, and she hadn't had breakfast, either. And now she wanted to get out of the house and run errands. Would she eat at the food court? Not anymore. Too much noise. Too many eyes.

Whether Elena and I liked it or not, we were inseparable at that point. Without a stateside license, Elena couldn't drive in Europe. It was a bargaining chip I couldn't resist.

"Okay. I'll take you," I said. "*If* you eat lunch with me."

"*Mom!*"

After Elena stalked away to take her shower, I sat there and argued with myself. Did I really want to do this? Should I really bargain and bribe? Elena was an independent, almost-grown woman. This wasn't appropriate parenting.

But what was I supposed to do—just watch my daughter starve?

She still hasn't put back on the weight she lost in those hospitals, I reminded myself. *Her weight is still lower than it was at the beginning of July—not to mention what it was in June.*

And at the thought of early summer, I felt a rush of fond nostalgia.

Just imagine! Only two months ago, we were all relaxed and content. Elena was telling me about her summer reading. She and Barbara were working on their tans . . .

June—so recent, but already softly blurred, like the memories of vacations long past. And was I only imagining the sparkling sunlight that lit those memories, as if I were seeing the scenes through a glass of champagne?

June—happy, golden June. The brief, bright pause before the Summer from Hell.

It felt like a lifetime ago.

CHAPTER TWENTY

The next day, I took Elena to the big military hospital for her first medical appointment since we had reached home. The lanky young doctor was new to us both, of course. The pediatrician who had worked with her in July was already gone, cycled downrange or cycled back to his home in the States. But this new doctor seemed thoughtful, friendly, and interested.

I had brought with us all the test results and discharge forms from the various hospitals so that he could review them, and he spent quite a bit of time familiarizing himself with their contents. Elena's discharge form from the children's hospital showed that she needed a follow-up cardiac echo exam and an endocrine consult, as well as more blood work to check on her new thyroid medication.

"I'll get these referrals into the system this afternoon," he said. "It'll take a day or two before they're picked up, though, so I'd wait until Monday to call for the appointment and lab times. And I'll see you back here with the results of the blood work next Wednesday."

That afternoon, I drove Elena to the high school so she could attend senior-class orientation. I was supposed to be working on a sequel to the book about Martin and his computerized dog, but for weeks, I'd done no writing because of all the hospital time. Now I was playing soccer mom.

Poor Martin! I thought while I sat in the car, and in my mind, I could see him standing there, waiting for me to join him on an adventure. His scowl was a good match for Elena's hostile expression. Thirteen-year-old boys don't like to wait.

I'm coming, Martin! I promised in a rush of guilt. *Next week, I promise!* I could have spent a few minutes working with him while I was waiting for Elena's meeting to finish, but the car got hot, so I left it and wandered inside.

Mr. Temple, the school psychologist, spotted me in the main hall-way and came over. "Mrs. Dunkle!" he said, sounding surprised to see me. "How's Elena?"

"She's fine, more or less," I said.

Mr. Temple was a very nice man. He looked more like a professor than a therapist. It took me a minute to remember that he was the person who had referred Elena to Dr. Petras last spring in order to help deal with Valerie's running away. That was where all this had started: with Valerie.

"I don't think that grief therapy worked out the way we all thought it would," I added bitterly.

"Why don't you come into the office and tell me about it?"

In Mr. Temple's office, I poured out the story of Elena's enforced hospitalization and the bullying behavior I had seen from Dr. Petras.

"I've lost all respect for the man," I said. "The final verdict from an eating disorder specialist is that, yes, Elena does have an eating disorder, but calling it anorexia nervosa goes too far. What's more, he concluded that it was Dr. Petras's heavy-handed treatment that caused Elena to go into that cycle of blackouts."

"I'm sorry to hear this," Mr. Temple said. "Dr. Petras's specialty is child psychiatry. He has the degree as well as experience. I had no reason to believe he wouldn't do her good."

"I'm not blaming you," I said. "How could anyone know what he was going to do? But I know what I saw, and it wasn't professional behavior. He forced Elena into a hospital that wasn't set up to treat her, and he triggered a dangerous drop in her weight. She still hasn't regained the weight he made her lose." *And I'm beginning to worry now whether she ever will*, I thought. But I didn't say that out loud.

Mr. Temple looked upset.

"I hardly know what to say," he said. "It's shocking. Really shocking."

"Yes," I said grimly. "It was."

The week passed in a rush of back-to-school shopping and reunions with friends. By the time Elena had her next appointment with the lanky young doctor at the military hospital, classes had already begun. I drove to the school and signed Elena out, and we headed to the hospital— that one-stop-shopping medical center away from home for thousands of Americans overseas.

"This time, we need to tell him about the episode of chest tightness you had," I said as I parked the car. "That pain you're having in your chest now—he needs to hear about it. I've never heard you mention chest pain before."

"Mm-hmm," Elena said. She had that expression on her face again— cool, distant, and wary.

The lanky young doctor came into his office and greeted Elena first, which I liked. In fact, I liked a lot of things about this doctor.

"Your blood work looked good," he told her. "Of course, I didn't run the thyroid tests. So," he continued to me, "did you get her appointment set up with Endocrinology?"

"I tried," I said. "But your referrals didn't seem to be in the system. I couldn't make the appointment with Cardiology, either. Something must have gone wrong with the paperwork."

"Well, strictly speaking, it isn't paperwork," he said, smiling. "It all stays right here in the computer system. Hold on a minute while I take a look, and we'll get it straightened out."

He sat down at his messy desk and tapped on the keyboard for a minute. Then his brow furrowed, and he cocked his head sideways.

"Oka-a-ay," he said slowly. "This is odd."

The thing about axes falling again and again is that you get to be good at detecting them. I heard him say this, and I held my breath. I told myself that this was going to be a good kind of odd, but that old familiar tension climbed up my spine and knotted the muscles in my shoulders.

The doctor did some more tapping. Then he stopped and rubbed his chin for a minute.

"There's a note in here," he said. "It says that you're to be denied care. That's why my referrals got kicked out of the system."

I could feel my head swivel sideways, too, just like the doctor's had done. Elena was staring, baffled. We must have looked like a roomful of golden retrievers listening to a dog whistle.

"I—excuse me, what?" I said. "Denied care? Is there some kind of insurance problem?" And my mind flashed to the stacks of forms still waiting to be straightened out. No, I couldn't recall a problem that would affect us receiving care.

The doctor answered my question with a question of his own:

"Do you know a Dr. Petras?"

Elena started to laugh.

I didn't.

"What does Dr. Petras have to do with Elena's care?" I asked. "He's a doctor who hasn't seen her in months."

"Well, he put a note in the system that tells every department to deny this patient care. He put it in . . . last Thursday."

Last Thursday. The day of the school orientation. The same day I had told Mr. Temple how unprofessional he had been.

Elena asked, "What does the note say?"

"It's . . . confidential," the young doctor said. But his tone wasn't formal. It was amazed.

Anger is a furnace. I could feel myself heating up. I could feel boiling blood mount into my face and course down my arms into my hands. I clenched those hands together and tried to stay calm. Logic and reason. Against a world gone crazy, that was all I had.

"Are you telling me," I said, "that some doctor Elena hasn't seen in months has put a *secret* note into her file?"

"Yes," the doctor said, with the air of someone having a pleasantly interesting adventure. Clearly, his work didn't bring him this kind of diversion every day. "Yes, in fact, that's exactly what's happened."

"Well? What *does* it say?"

For the first time, he grew serious. "Technically, it's just for staff to read. I could get into trouble."

I counted to ten, and then to twenty. Silence fell while he pondered what to do. He clicked back and forth between different screens on his computer, and the puzzled look on his face continued to deepen.

"I've never seen anything like it," he said. "I've never seen *anything* like it! And honestly, I don't see why he should get away with it."

Then he read out the secret note:

> *Do not treat this patient. She was sent to the States to*
> *receive care for anorexia nervosa. She should not be at*
> *this hospital. She should not be in Germany. She and*
> *her mother . . .*

That was all I heard.

She and *her mother*?! What had *I* ever done besides exactly what this man had wanted? When had I opposed his demands? He hadn't consulted with us, and he hadn't educated us. He had gotten his hospitalization just as he had wanted, and he had gotten his medical evacuation, too.

What was *wrong* with this man? Was he *insane*?

"I'll put the referrals back into the system," the doctor told us. "But I don't think they'll do any good. I think it's just going to keep kicking them out. I'm sorry. I don't know what to do."

I was still boiling with rage as we walked out to the parking lot. But rage wasn't a luxury I could afford, so I turned my back on it and went into planning mode.

"We'll fight it, of course," I said to Elena. "I'll find out the complaint procedure as soon as we get home." And my mind started making a list: *ombudsman, commander, insurance company appeals process.* "Not that it will help right now since the hospital is on a full-scale war footing. We civilians are an afterthought these days."

Elena didn't speak. She was still smiling. She looked as if she were thinking about a funny joke.

"So he thinks he's got us, doesn't he?" I said. "He thinks we're typical Americans, tied to the military hospital over here for all our medical care. Well, what he doesn't realize is how good our German is and how good the German doctors are. We're civilians. He didn't think of that. Civilians don't have to use this hospital. I'll schedule you an appointment with my German doctor, the Doctor with the Three First Names. He's thoughtful and very conscientious. I like him better than any of the American doctors I've seen here."

"Also, he's sexy as hell," Elena pointed out—which was true. All the little old German ladies dressed up and put on lipstick when they got sick and had an appointment with the Doctor with the Three First Names.

"Now, it's a little tricky dealing with his appointment system," I continued. "But we can go in next Thursday during his extended consulting hours. And then, he can put in consults for you to local specialists. Germans need cardiac care, too."

When the phone rang the next day, I didn't even feel stressed about it. The ax had already fallen, and I was actively dealing with the aftermath. I felt ready for anything.

"Mrs. Dunkle? This is Dr. White." The voice was pleasant. "I'd like to set up an appointment with you and your husband, if that's convenient."

"Of course, we'll be happy to see you," I said. "Am I correct that you work in the ombudsman's office at the hospital? Is this about our complaint?"

"No, I work for the commander at your husband's base. And this appointment . . . well, it's just a discussion, really." The voice continued to sound warm, and also amused and slightly apologetic, as if Dr. White and I had been caught in the rain together and he needed to share my taxi. "It's really just a chance to get to know you and Mr. Dunkle."

A chance to get to know us?

"Dr. White, exactly what is this about?"

"There's been an allegation made," Dr. White explained. "An allegation of child abuse."

This time, I was the one who laughed. I couldn't help it; the whole thing was just so over the top. After having accompanied Elena through weeks of stays at four different hospitals, after having allowed her to undergo every single medical or psychological test more than a dozen different experts could dream up—after lavishing our savings on doctor bills and driving her over *thirty-two hundred miles* to receive the very best care we could find—Joe and I had been accused of child abuse.

I didn't feel angry. I had felt angry yesterday because the note denying Elena hospital treatment had actually threatened her welfare. But this,
now—this was just stupid.

"The meeting is purely informal," Dr. White told me cordially. "I
investigate this sort of thing all the time. In fact, it's all I do. And I want
to assure you, I don't let anybody influence me. I'm on your side here. I keep
an open mind."

"Am I right," I asked, equally cordially, "in assuming that this allegation comes from the hospital?"

"No," he said. "It comes from your daughter's school."

The school, was it? We'd deal with them. Yes, indeed, we would.

"Dr. White," I said, "we'd like to see you as soon as possible."

So, once again, Joe and I packed up our paperwork, lab results,
discharge papers, and big blue plastic MRI sheets—even the DVD of
Elena having her blackout. And the next day, we went to see Dr. White.
He was as pleasant and engaging as he had seemed on the phone, and his
office was pleasant, too. It had a large, comfy couch with a big coffee table
in front of it, which was good because we needed that room to spread out
all our forms.

"Thank you very much for coming in," he said, shaking our hands.
"I want you to know that you are not obligated to talk to me. But it will
help me get a handle on what this is all about, so I'd very much appreciate
it if you would."

"We're happy to talk to you," Joe said. "We're glad to have a chance
to be heard." Joe had been as practical as I had been about this meeting,
but I could tell that he was much more angry.

I still didn't feel all that upset. I saw the whole thing as just one more
attempt on Dr. Petras's part to bully our family. As attempts went, it was
nasty, but it was considerably less dangerous and stressful than locking
Elena up and yelling at her—and I'd watched him do both of those already.
This particular method of bullying was so extreme that it just felt silly to
me. It felt about as destructive and serious as peeing in somebody's Jell-O.
It was juvenile, that's what it was—juvenile.

Besides, this time, as Joe pointed out, we had a chance to tell our side.

One by one, we handed Dr. White Elena's records from the summer. First, we showed him the treatment letter Dr. Harris had written for us to take to her future psychiatrists, the one that said he was sending her back to Germany. Then we went through every piece of paper we had been given, from the lab sheets and the doctors' summaries to the four hospital discharge forms. And we pointed out that nowhere, not on a single one of all those papers, had Joe and I denied Elena the recommended care. Nowhere had we gone "Against Medical Advice."

As I watched Dr. White read through the paperwork from Drew Center, I felt grateful once again to that nice older doctor who didn't like Dr. Moore. *I wonder who he was,* I thought. *Maybe if he had been there to talk to me instead of Dr. Moore, I wouldn't have had to go all the way to Texas to get answers.*

"So, it says here that Elena needs follow-up cardiac treatment," Dr. White noted. "Have you already set that up?"

Joe and I exchanged glances.

"Here's where it gets a little surreal," I said. "We *tried* to get that arranged. But Dr. Petras put a note into Elena's hospital file that says she's to be denied care."

"In other words," Joe said, "the same people who don't think Elena is getting enough medical care are *preventing* her from getting medical care. And then they're coming back and *blaming* us for not getting that medical care. Although, that's just my assumption," he added bitterly. "Since no one has reached out to discuss this with us directly, we have no *idea* what they're actually blaming us for."

"You don't need to take our word for this," I added. "You probably have access to the hospital computer system, so you can look up that note for yourself. That note . . . this accusation . . . it all feels like a vendetta at this point. God knows why."

And that phrase, *she and her mother,* pricked at my nerves again.

Dr. White nodded. He didn't seem at all surprised to hear about the note in Elena's file. He must already know about it. And he was so warm and engaged that he really *did* feel like a person on our side. He must be very good at his job.

Or—had he already had run-ins with Dr. Petras?

"If you can't get her care at the hospital, what have you decided to do?" he asked. "Of course, with your language skills . . ." And he looked at us expectantly.

"Exactly," I said. "We don't need the American doctors. Elena already has an appointment with our local German doctor. He's fantastic; he used to be a hospital surgeon before he decided to return to his hometown and do family practice. He'll be sure Elena gets the care she needs."

Dr. White nodded.

"Thank you for coming to see me," he said. "I feel completely satisfied with your answers, and I'm closing this child-abuse inquiry. It stops right here, with me."

Then he paused and sighed, and he seemed to be searching for the right thing to say.

"It's a byword in our business," he mused, apropos of nothing. "The social workers: they're just about saints. A lot of times, I'd swear there are no better people on this earth. And we psychologists: most of us have our heads screwed on straight. But the psychiatrists! I tell you, they're either great—or they're just God-awful!"

Yes, I was right. This nice man *was* on our side. This was not the first time he'd heard of Dr. Petras.

Dr. White might be finished with his work, but Joe and I weren't. We drove straight from his office to Elena's high school. We had been put through enough pain that summer. It was time to spread some of the pain around.

"We need to see Mr. Temple and the principal," Joe told the office secretary. "We need to see them right now."

"Of course," she said. "I'll see if they're both free."

The principal came out and shook our hands. I hadn't spoken to him before that day. He was a short man with a comfortable, boyish face and eyes that were asking questions.

Mr. Temple trailed along behind the principal. His eyes asked no questions. In fact, he looked distinctly unhappy to see us.

The four of us went into an empty conference room. "Now, what can we do for you?" asked the principal.

"We just came from a child-abuse investigation," Joe said. "It was initiated by a staff member here at this school."

The principal looked grave. "Of course, you know I can't divulge anything about that," he said. "These sorts of matters are confidential."

"We know that," Joe said impatiently. "We're not here to ask things. We're here to say things."

Then, one after another, Joe and I laid out all the forms and papers that we had just showed to Dr. White. Step by step, we walked both school officials through Elena's care that summer. We even showed them Dr. Harris's four-page curriculum vitae, which detailed his extensive experience with eating disorder clients.

"Now," Joe said when we were finished. "Your staff member"—and here, he glared at Mr. Temple—"alleged that we were negligent in bringing our daughter back to Germany. You've seen the whole picture for yourselves. What do you think we should have done? Should we have kept Elena in the States, where she would have had to go through the stress of changing schools for her senior year and make a whole new circle of friends? Or should we have taken the advice of Dr. Harris, an eating disorder expert, and brought Elena back here, where she could take the courses she's already signed up for, in an environment she knows and loves?"

The principal nodded. "I see what you're saying," he said. "I support your decision to bring her back. Nothing I see here warrants uprooting her like that."

"Well, you'll be happy to hear," Joe said caustically, "that the child-abuse investigator agrees with you. He's closed our case, with no further action warranted."

"Very good," said the principal, in the voice of one summing up a discussion. He, too, seemed to feel that no further action was warranted.

"We're not done here," Joe told him. "You brought up confidentiality. Okay, let's talk about confidentiality."

"That's right," I said. "Let's talk about the confidentiality laws your staff have to follow."

The principal looked puzzled. "I'm not sure I understand you."

But I didn't speak to him. I turned to Mr. Temple, and the unhappy look on his face told me everything I needed to know.

"I spoke to you the other day," I said, "about confidential matters. I had every right to assume that you would protect my daughter's privacy. But I happen to *know* that you shared my daughter's medical information with a man whom you knew was not her doctor."

"He has training I lack," Mr. Temple said. "I defer to his training."

"You *knew* that man wasn't her doctor," I repeated, staring him down.

But Joe looked as if he could hardly believe what he was hearing. "So you admit it!" Joe said. "You *admit* that you broke patient and student confidentiality laws."

Mr. Temple didn't look as if that's what he had intended to admit at all, but he couldn't very well take it back now. "He's a specialist, an expert," he explained stiffly. "I often consult with him."

"So, you picked up the phone," Joe ground out, "and you discussed details of my daughter's *psychiatric* and *medical care* with—what? With a *buddy* of yours? You weren't consulting about hypothetical cases here. *You used her name!*"

Mr. Temple opened his mouth. But then he shut it again.

"You *knew* that man wasn't her doctor," I reminded him. "You *knew* that we wouldn't agree to that man knowing *anything* about her care. *And* you know perfectly well why!"

Mr. Temple looked away from us, and from the keen stare his boss was giving him, too. "Yes," he said. "Yes, I knew that. I did know that."

Joe drew himself up. Not for nothing had my husband spent years in management. He looked formidable, and he knew it. "You violated every rule that exists," he said, "concerning patient and student confidentiality!"

Mr. Temple started to speak, but Joe wasn't done.

"You turned us in for child abuse!" Joe said. "You instigated a completely unfounded investigation. We would have been *happy* to meet with you to answer any concerns you might have had. We would have been down here the minute you said the word! But you *didn't* ask. You *didn't* let us know you were concerned. Instead, you discussed the details of our daughter's care with that *quack*, and *you broke the law!*"

Mr. Temple started to speak again. Again, he changed his mind. He looked as uncomfortable and upset as a grown man can look.

As uncomfortable as we *were supposed to look*, I thought, *if that child-abuse case had gone differently.*

But that brought me out of my anger. I found my good mood again, and I began to feel sorry for Mr. Temple. He wasn't the enemy here. He was just another victim of Dr. Petras's lunacy. I had no doubt that Dr. Petras had managed to convince him that Joe and I were dangerously obstructive. He had probably whipped the whole situation into a frenzy.

Mr. Temple wasn't a bad man. I felt sure of that. He'd made a terrible mistake, and he shouldn't have done it, but he hadn't meant to cause our daughter harm.

"You did what you did because you were concerned for Elena," I said. "I'm sure you had her best interests in mind. But if you had concerns, you could have brought them to us."

Joe swept all of Elena's records into a pile and stood up with them under his arm.

"We are *done* here," he said in clipped and distinct tones. "If you have *any* further concerns about my daughter—for *any* reason—you had *better* bring them up to me. And if you ever—*ever!*—violate confidentiality laws again, *I* will know what to do about it!"

Joe and I walked out of the room, and that was the end of the Summer from Hell.

But it wasn't the end. That's what I came to realize. It couldn't end—not anymore.

We couldn't repair what the Summer from Hell had broken.

CHAPTER TWENTY-ONE

Elena's eighteenth birthday fell on a weekday just a few weeks after the start of school. She had invited over a few good friends to help her celebrate. But fifteen minutes before they were supposed to arrive, I found her in bed, sound asleep. I hated to wake her up. She got so little rest these days.

"Elena," I whispered.

She didn't stir. She hardly seemed to be breathing.

My daughter was running herself ragged, wedging into her busy schedule as many committee meetings, study sessions, and volunteering opportunities as she possibly could. She didn't allow herself to rest. She seemed to be saying, *No senior year? I'll show you a senior year!*

It was a battle, and I wasn't sure who was winning.

"Elena," I said again. "They're almost here."

She opened her eyes and blinked at me without recognition. Then she closed her eyes again.

I hesitated. Could I call off the get-together? No, by the time I could find the right phone numbers, it would be too late. And besides, what would Elena think if I did that? Wouldn't she just think I was interfering?

These days, that's all she thought I did.

"The party," I said, prodding her. "It's in fifteen minutes. Your friends will be here soon."

This time, Elena's eyes stayed open.

"*Why?*" she wailed. "Why do you have to bother me when I'm sleeping? I hurt so much, I couldn't get to sleep all night long last night! You woke me up. I was finally asleep!"

These days, everything on Elena seemed to hurt: her chest, her head, and her bones. Scoliosis had started curving her spine several years ago, but it seemed to be getting rapidly worse.

"You're right," I said. "I can tell your friends that you're sick. They can come over some other time."

That got Elena scrambling out of bed. With quick, angry movements, she straightened the sheets and the pillows. I helped her from my side.

"You'd like that, wouldn't you?" she snapped. "You don't think I can do anything!"

"I think you're exhausted," I said. "In fact, I know you're exhausted."

Elena arranged the throw pillows at the head of the bed. Her room was charmingly girly and impeccably neat. Nonetheless, she stalked around the room, dissatisfied with everything. She moved a Korean doll half an inch this way and a glass cat sculpture half an inch that way. Her face was as grim as if she were scrubbing toilets.

"So what if I'm exhausted!" she hissed. "Like that makes any difference! You don't think I can get anything done. You think I'm a complete failure!"

"That's ridiculous!" I said, following her into the bathroom. "I just want you to get some rest."

Elena's bathroom was a jewel box of shiny, pretty things: nail polish jars in every pastel shade, sequined photo frames around smiling faces, and a rose-pink Tiffany-style lamp shaped like a dress. Taped to the big mirror were pages of bright crayon artwork from the children she babysat.

Elena leaned toward the mirror as she fixed her makeup. "I'm an officer in the Future Business Leaders of America. I'm making As in every single class. Major Meadows says he would *hire* me to work in the ER because I'm such a valuable member of the team. But does that mean anything to *you*? No!"

This was familiar ground.

"Of course it does," I said doggedly. "I'm proud of you. I am! I just wish you could slow down and enjoy it."

"You always criticize me!"

"I don't . . ."

"You *do*! Nothing I *ever* do is good enough for you!" Elena was shouting now. "No matter what I do, you're always back there with that look on your face. Just once, I wish you could *actually* be proud of me!"

Now I was shouting, too. "Elena, I'm proud all the time! I just *said* I'm proud of you!"

The doorbell rang. Elena dropped the lipstick she had just finished applying into the silk-covered box that held its mates. She slipped past me and disappeared down the stairs. "Barbara!" I heard her exclaim, her voice honey-sweet—a tone of voice she didn't use with me.

I trudged downstairs after her to play host to her friends, feeling like I'd been hit by a truck.

The next morning, Elena announced over breakfast, "You may as well cancel the appointment you made for me with that German psychologist. I'm not going. I'm eighteen. You can't force me to go."

Joe and I exchanged worried glances.

"But you know Dr. Harris said you need to work with a therapist," Joe said.

"I don't care," she said. "Doctors held me against my will—twice! They didn't even try to work with me. I walked in the door for a one-hour counseling session, and I didn't get home till over a month later. Nobody is ever going to do that to me again."

It was obvious that Elena had been thinking about this for weeks. In fact, it seemed to be the biggest lesson she had taken away from the Summer from Hell.

"Dr. Harris worked with you, though," I reminded her. "He didn't lock you up."

"I like Dr. Harris," she admitted. "But I'm not going to risk it. Some psychiatrists and psychologists might not do that kind of thing, but there's no way to know until it's too late. Cancel the appointment. I'm not going."

As the months rolled by, our days fell into a very unhealthy pattern. Dead tired, Elena dragged herself out of bed and outlined a day with far too many commitments. If I tried to persuade her to slow down or skip something, she chewed me out. For everyone else, she had a smile or a laugh—even for her father. Only to me did she show her constant exhaustion, misery, and bitterness.

I am the stepping-stone she pushes off to keep from getting stuck in the mud, I thought. *Her anger toward me keeps her going.*

But it brought me almost to a standstill.

Martin's new story wasn't going well. I didn't know why. I was fond of him and his bright, affectionate dog, and I liked the colorful, dangerous world he lived in. But I couldn't keep up with Martin on his adventures anymore. He would take off to go do something, and I would be left behind, asking myself, *Why did he do that? Where did he go? Do I even know Martin anymore?*

But this story was already sold. We already had the money in savings. I couldn't back out on it now.

Guilt and worry started to needle me. I began to set word counts. Never before had I needed to force myself to write. But the next day, when I read what I had written, half of it would turn out to be garbage. I could tell that I'd written it only to fill up the word count.

So I began to set a timer: twenty minutes to start with. Any more than that, and I couldn't stay focused.

Maybe it's Alzheimer's, I thought. *Maybe it's incipient dementia. Martin's world is hazy now, and I can't figure out what he's doing. I can barely even spell anymore!*

As the weeks passed, I developed elaborate writing rituals. First, I had to brew the perfect cup of tea. Then, I had to check my email. Then, I had to check three news sites, always in the same order. Then, I had to set my timer. Then, I had to play a game of FreeCell. (And the longer I took on my FreeCell game, the less time I would have to write.)

Finished with my game, I would check the tea temperature. Was it too cold? I would get up and warm it in the microwave. Then I would have to check my email again. Then the news sites, one—two—three.

Sometimes, this ritual ate up the whole twenty minutes.

Even when I did manage to get some pages done, it didn't seem to matter. "Do you want to read what I wrote today?" I asked at dinner. But, as it turned out, nobody did.

"You know I don't have time," Elena said. "I have an essay plus thirty study questions to get through by Friday, and I promised Jason I'd help him with his college application."

"Sure," Joe said absently. "Why don't you email it to me? I'll read it at lunch."

But I didn't want Joe to read it at lunch. I wanted him to read it *here*, right in front of me, the way he used to do, while I peeked over his shoulder and read it along with him.

I didn't want to send my story off in an email. I wanted to *share* it.

"Never mind," I said. "It doesn't matter."

But it did matter. It mattered a great deal. The next time I sat down and opened my laptop, poor Martin wouldn't get anything done. *Why go on a journey,* he would tell me, *if nobody cares what I do?*

They'll kill you if they catch you, I would remind him.

I'm dead anyway. Who cares?

At which point, I would notice that my tea had gotten cold. I would get up and reheat it. And then I would check my email. And the news sites.

And repeat.

One sunny winter afternoon, I picked up my laptop and brewed myself a fresh, hot cup of tea. The cats were stretched out in the garden room, and I carried my tea and computer into the sunlight to join them. I curled up in one of the big brown chairs, brought up Martin's Word file, set the timer ticking, and—*Ring!*

It was Elena's phone number.

"Hello?" I said, wincing.

"I need a ride to the hospital," she said.

"But I'm working right now. Can't you just take the bus home, and I'll take you in an hour?"

"This is important!" she said. "This is my college career on the line. What are you doing? Just writing stories!"

"I'm doing my best to earn your college tuition."

Elena's voice rose. "So am I! You want me to get scholarships, don't you? Do you think I *want* to go volunteer? Do you think I wouldn't *like* to come home and sit around? You had all day to get that done! Why do you have to do it now?"

I would have argued, but I recognized that exhausted teenager. Decades ago, I had seen her in my mirror. And I had heard that exhausted, bitter girl yell at her mother, too:

Unload the dishwasher? Do you realize I'm trying to write my college essay? Do you realize I'm trying to earn scholarships with this? Why don't you unload the dishwasher? You're not doing anything important!

And I had seen my mother turn away, defeated.

So now, in penance, I set aside my laptop. I ran a brush through my hair and found my car keys.

It wasn't supposed to be this way, I thought as I stepped into my shoes. *Or maybe it was—maybe, no matter what we mothers try to do, we can't escape the curse of the bad karma we earned as children. But—my children were supposed to be different! They were supposed to be happy!* And I remembered my two girls, dashing through the house, shouting and shrieking with laughter.

Where had it gone? How had we lost that happiness?

Anyway, this is the last year, I reminded myself as I trudged out to the car. *Next year, she'll be away at college. She hates being dependent on me, and besides, she has a point. I could have written more during the day. I should have.*

While Elena did an hour of volunteering, I bought groceries and ran errands to kill time. It wasn't worth going all the way home and back again. Then I swung back by to pick her up. And this—this was the time that made it all worthwhile, that made up for my stress and Elena's exhausted hostility.

This was the time when Elena told me stories.

The things Elena was seeing in that wartime hospital awed and inspired her. Even if she had wanted to keep them to herself, I don't think she could have done it. She was a born storyteller, and these were stories that cried out to be told.

Today, Elena had been working in the little building where wounded soldiers could stop by and receive free clothing and toiletries. Since they arrived straight from the battlefield, they usually had nothing of their own.

"One of last week's new arrivals came down in his pajamas and robe today," she said. "He just wanted to get out of his room. He's not badly injured; he'll be going back downrange soon. He sat at the table while the volunteer coordinator and I set out the new clothes, and he talked—just talked, the whole time. He's been married for two years now, and he's only been home once. He got married to his high school sweetheart right before he deployed, and a month later, he was gone. He has a baby boy— he showed us photos—and he hasn't even gotten to hold him.

"First, he was deployed for a year. Then he and his wife were so excited, they thought he would be home for a while. But the Army came out and said he needed to go downrange again because he should have been gone for eighteen months—that's what the new terms are. So he was home for less than half a year, and then gone again, and this time, it's for eighteen months. Just think, the first three years you're married, and you're only home for maybe six months."

"I can't even imagine how hard that would be," I murmured.

"So his wife back home—he's practically frantic, he's so worried about his wife back home. She's young, she's pretty, all her friends are still single, or their husbands are right there, and here she is, she has no help with the baby, she might as well be divorced. And she tells him, 'I don't know if I can keep doing this.' And he's so torn up, he can't stop talking about it. 'I don't think she'll wait for me,' he says. He shows us her picture, she's just a girl like me, cute blond hair, nice makeup, she's smiling like she just wants to go have some fun, and he says, 'What do I do? I don't think she's going to wait.'"

Elena fell silent, brow furrowed, watching the twists and turns of the little two-lane road as it took us through a town. I was dodging around parked cars, weaving and do-si-do-ing with oncoming traffic in a polite German automotive dance. *You first*, we signaled with our hands and headlights. *No, please, you go right ahead.*

It would never work in America. We'd smash right into each other.

My heart ached for the poor young soldier. It was what Elena did so well, I thought. She found people to care about, and she told me their stories, and they came to life for me. With just a few words, she could break my heart.

And maybe Elena was thinking about that, too.

"I want to write a memoir," she said. "About my time in the hospital. An eating disorder memoir for girls like me."

"I think that's a great idea!" I said. "You have a special gift for memoir, I think. You see the stories going on all around you."

"The thing is, I don't know how to start."

Several years of visits to writers' clubs and creative-writing classes had left me with dozens of minilectures stored away in my head. I found the memoir minilecture and started it rolling.

"Well, I wouldn't worry so much about how to start or where you're going to end up. I'd start first by capturing vignettes: little scenes, the details you remember, character sketches, the small stories you observed. That way, you won't lose them. Then worry later about how to string them together. That's the least of your problems right now."

Elena was silent for a minute.

"You could help me," she finally said.

It was a generous offer. Sharing anything with me seemed hard for Elena these days. But—did I hold it against my daughter that my own writing was going so badly? If I did, I disguised it well, even from myself. But I didn't consider the idea—not for a second.

"You know I'm not a memoir person," I pointed out. "That's your gift, not mine. My writing mind works best when it's escaping to a world I can make up." And I thought of what a writer friend of mine said whenever someone hit him up with a book idea at a party: *Thanks, but there's another book I'd rather write.*

"This is your book," I reminded Elena. "I think you'll do a great job with it."

"But I don't have any time," she pointed out.

I thought of Martin's Word file, waiting at home. *Neither do I!* I thought. *In spite of what you seem to think, neither do I.*

But I didn't say that out loud.

"I know senior year is crazy," I said. "That's another reason to record the little stories. Just fit in those vignettes where you have time so you don't lose the details."

"Yeah," she said. "That's a good idea."

That night, as I lay in bed, I thought again about Elena and her memoir. It was touching that she thought of my writing skills with such faith. It had made me happy to be asked. But—write about the Summer from Hell? Me?

There's another book I'd rather write!

Martin's sullen face intruded into this reverie. *Or maybe not,* he pointed out, *considering how little writing you're actually doing.*

Poor Martin! I told him in an agony of guilt. *Don't give up on me!*

As I lay there, guilty and unhappy, a vision floated up in my memory of a glorious day back from the time when the girls were still at boarding school. Back then, I had a bad cold that had deepened into a sinus infection. I was feverish and thoroughly miserable. But the scene I had been working on the night before was boiling away in my brain.

Eventually, on that glorious day, I couldn't contain myself any longer. I had to get out of bed. I pulled on my bathrobe, made some tea to soothe my aching throat, and shuffled upstairs to the garret room and my computer.

Marak's goblins were meeting a traditional band of elves for the very first time—which meant that I, too, was meeting them for the first time. What did they look like? How were they dressed? What did my goblins think of them? What were these newcomers thinking of the goblins?

That day, I was nowhere, and I was everywhere. I hid behind trees, and I looked into the minds of strangers. I didn't feel aches and pains. I didn't even exist.

Not a sound or a worry interrupted my concentration. The girls were still happy at school. Joe was working late. Our old dog and cat were sleeping like the dead.

After a while, an annoying little problem began to tug at me. Misspellings were starting to appear on the computer screen. My fingers weren't finding the right spot on the keyboard. And why couldn't I see my hands?

I pushed my chair back and looked around. Night had fallen while I'd been working.

I had been with my goblins and elves for *ten straight hours!*

I didn't feel like an author that day—not at all. I wasn't published yet, and I couldn't have cared less about genres or markets. All that mattered was that I had gone somewhere amazing and had seen things no one else in the world had seen. My house was a mess, and dinner came out of a box, but I was wildly, exuberantly happy.

And that night, the night after that glorious day, as I went shuffling off to find the cough syrup, I couldn't wait to wake up and do it all over again.

Now, as I lay in bed and agonized over Martin's stalled story, I recalled that day with wistful disbelief. My house was tidy, but my imagination was a total wreck. I was extremely lucky if I could forget my nagging fears and worries for as long as twenty minutes. And even when I did manage to forget for a little while, I seemed to interrupt myself on purpose. It was as if falling into my other world had become a dangerous pastime. I would get close to it, just close enough to feel the gravitational pull, close enough to find myself start to light up with interest . . .

And then I would jump up and run away from the keyboard to go iron a shirt or defrost a chicken.

Maybe if I were just writing something different.

If I can't bring myself to care about you, I told Martin sternly, *then the reader won't care about you, either.*

You always criticize me! Martin said. *Nothing I ever do is good enough for you.*

Meanwhile, Valerie, far away in Georgia, was making a happy life for herself among people I had never met. She'd found a job as a waitress, and she and Clint had been dating for a year. Clint's mother sent me an email with photos of the two of them.

"Why aren't you proud of your daughter?" she wrote to me. "I'd be proud if I had a daughter like Valerie."

This comment made me very sad. I knew Clint's mother adored Valerie. I knew that she wasn't being mean. She was only trying to reach out—to build a connection with that stern, disapproving woman who had driven Valerie away. It wasn't Clint's mother's fault that that woman didn't exist . . .

. . . Because she *didn't* exist, did she?—that stern, unhappy woman?

"I am proud of Valerie," I wrote back to her. "And I'm so glad she has you there to help her while we're far away."

Valerie and I were emailing back and forth very often by this time, but we still rarely spoke on the phone. I could tell that this hurt Valerie. She was missing me.

"When you call, it's only for five minutes," she said one evening. "I'm not much for writing letters. Why can't we really talk? I said I was sorry for leaving. Are you still mad at me?"

"No," I said. "It's hard to explain. Each time I hear your voice, you sound better than the time before. When you left home, there was no color in your voice. It was flat and disinterested. But, little by little, the life's coming back. You're getting better. I can hear it. And I'm afraid, if we get close to you—"

"—that I'll screw up again?"

"No, that we'll make you worse. Because maybe it was *us*, Valerie— our fault. Maybe we're the reason you didn't get better here. What if our family is toxic?"

Valerie's voice on the phone was small and sad, as it used to be sometimes when she was a little girl. "You're not toxic, Momma," she said.

"You don't know that, honey," I said. "You don't know what made you sick. I miss you, too, but I want you to have the chance to keep getting better."

Because your sister is sick now, I thought but didn't say. *And she surely seems to think that I'm the one to blame.*

My relationship with Elena had never been worse. Not in my wildest dreams had I imagined that it could be this bad. Day after day, she berated me, exhausted and angry. But if Elena had transformed into the evil witch of my world, I had become the evil witch of hers.

With the best will in the world, day after day, I nagged and scolded her. I could hear the whining edge in my voice these days, but I couldn't stop. It was because I watched every single bite that went into Elena's mouth now. And it wasn't enough. It was *never* enough.

So I had to speak up. I had to say *something*.

Day after day, I stood in the kitchen and wondered and worried and agonized. What should I cook? What would Elena eat? I tried out meals she had liked last year, but that didn't work anymore. I tried the food she'd liked when she was younger, but she seemed to hate it now.

No matter what I cooked, Elena hated it.

"What would you like to eat tonight?" I would ask her on the drive home.

Elena would shrug. "I don't care."

But she did care. She cared deeply. And not in a good way, either. Never—never in a good way.

As I carried a platter of chicken to the table, she wrinkled her nose and said, "I don't eat meat. The way chickens are raised is horrible, they can't even stand up properly. Besides, that's a baby. The poor thing is only eight weeks old."

The day I made pork chops, she said, "Did you know that pigs actually cry?"

But vegetables were no better. Broccoli tasted gross. Peas had a horrible texture. Yogurt was runny. Eating eggs was like eating rubber. Mushrooms were slimy. Carrots were boring and hard to chew.

"Potatoes?" she said as I was working at the counter with a potato masher. "They're so gloppy, they're like glue. *Salmon?* Did it have to be salmon? You *know* I don't like fish!"

So I bought more boxes and bottles to make our meals. I heated up more and more frozen things. At least this way, the bad cooking could be somebody else's fault.

"There's rocky road ice cream in the fridge," I reminded her as she hauled her school books into the house.

"Mom! You know I don't like cold food."

"I made cookies," I said on another day. "Chocolate chip."

"Dad will be happy," she said.

"What about you?"

"Mom! When have you ever known me to like chocolate?"

"But don't you want to try one? They're right out of the oven. The chocolate's still all melty."

"Maybe later," she said, disappearing up the stairs. And I knew what *later* meant.

Later was her word for *never*.

So I would eat the cookies or the ice cream or the cake. And *I* started putting on weight. My clothes got tight, and then lots of them hung useless in my closet. I picked up the nervous habit of pressing my hand to my side to feel the roll of fat there. But I couldn't stop bringing home high-fat food. It was the payoff that made it worthwhile.

One piece of pizza, I thought, *will give her the calories she'd get in an entire plate of healthy food. Then she'll fill out and look happy again. She's starting to look so . . . grim.*

Elena's face wasn't girlish and pretty anymore—not like I remembered it. These days, it was sharp and angular, and it had developed—not wrinkles, exactly—but lines. Lines banded the bridge of Elena's nose, rimming the hollows under her eyes. Lines carved the surface of her concave cheeks, running down in sets to pull her thin lips into a smile. Her cheekbones stood out now, distinct knobs above dramatic hollows that stretched into the knifelike line of her jaw.

Elena still looked striking, but she didn't look happy—not even when she was laughing.

So the dinner table turned into a battleground. I was the aggressor, dogged and relentless, while Joe, worn out from work, kept quiet or tried to negotiate a truce.

He should be backing me up, I thought. *He knows I'm right about this!*

But Joe didn't stand shoulder to shoulder with me on this, and when I brought it up, he didn't explain. Maybe he simply thought I was doing more harm than good, or maybe he just didn't like to upset his daughter. Elena went out of her way to cater to him these days—the opposite of the way she treated me. Their mutual-admiration society left me feeling resentful.

On a typical night, as I heated up a pepperoni pizza, I was determined to keep dinner pleasant. Tonight I would stay relaxed, I vowed, and I would enjoy myself. I wouldn't let Elena get to me with her comments.

"Pizza?" she said when I called her to the table. "Really, Mom?"

"You like pizza," I said.

"Not this kind."

"So, what kind *do* you like?"

"I hate pepperoni!" she said—which wasn't what I had asked.

Nevertheless, the meal started off well. Elena was full of news. She talked fast, telling us a dozen different funny stories about her classmates. She brought each friend to clear and sympathetic life. I wondered sometimes if her friends had any idea that I knew so much about them.

Part of me enjoyed these mealtime stories, but another part of me was on guard. Over the months, I'd discovered a secret: Elena used storytelling as a shield against food.

After the Summer from Hell, I had never seen Elena eat naturally again. She never forgot herself and just ate. She planned, she rationed, and she distracted. Storytelling was an important part of that distraction.

Sure enough, Joe finished his slices of pizza while she was still deep in the middle of one of her tales. He was ready to leave the table, and she had eaten only two or three bites. I took a third slice to hold them both there and tried to interrupt her with stories of my own. I wanted to buy time for her to finish her first slice, but Elena was too smart for that.

For every bite she took, I ended up taking four or five.

Eventually, Joe got tired of listening to our story swapping. He stood up. And so did Elena.

"Big exam tomorrow," she announced casually. "Gotta get to my study group. Eight chapters of sociology to get through."

But I wasn't going to be put off so easily.

"Elena, you didn't even finish your slice of pizza."

"That's the crust. I never eat the crust."

"That's the top third of your slice. See that cheese? That's not part of the crust. Don't eat the crust if you don't want to, but if you don't, then eat another slice."

Cue Elena going ballistic.

"You always do this!" she stormed.

That's true, I thought. *I always do.*

"It's creepy! You spy on everything I eat!"

Damn straight I do.

"This stuff kills! It sticks in the arteries! It's not good for my heart! Why do we have to eat such crappy food?"

Because if I serve you tofu, you'll still only eat seven bites. I'm maximizing calories here.

"I'm *full*!"

That's a lie.

But actually, it probably wasn't.

Joe gave a sigh, and I saw that look in his eyes again, the look of an old dog who just wants to go lie down. *He should be supporting me,* I thought, and I felt real anger with him for leaving me to deal with this alone. *He knows how important this is. He can't just be a buddy. He has to be a parent, too.*

But the cavalry wasn't coming. Time to open up a can of evil witch.

"If you eat a second slice," I said, "I'll drive you to Barbara's tonight. If you don't, I'm not going anywhere."

Cue the expected rise in volume.

"This isn't a party, Mom! This is a study session! Do you want me to do well on this exam or not?"

I am stone. I am solid rock. I will not give an inch.

"You always do this! You always mind my business! You ruin every single meal. Well, if you won't drive me to Barbara's, I'll *fail*. Is that what you want, Mom—do you want me to *fail*?"

The waves break over me, but they only push me further into the ground. I am not moving. I will not budge.

At this point, Joe finally intervened.

"Elena, you know it's important to get enough food in your system," he said. "You have to think of your heart. Just eat one more piece. Please."

And Elena did it—not for me, but for her father. She ate standing, glaring at me, taking four or five swift, angry bites, and then dropped the second piece of pizza half eaten beside the first.

"There!" she snapped, and she stormed out of the room.

I don't care, I thought as I listened to her clatter up the stairs. *I don't care that my heart's pounding and my dinner's ruined and I've got no help now* with the kitchen. *All that matters is that Elena has more food in her stomach. That's the important thing. I made Elena eat. That's what counts. It doesn't matter how I did it.*

But later, when I tried to write, I was too worn out. Stepping into that fantasy world meant making myself feel sorrow, joy, excitement, fear—all the emotions my characters were feeling. But I couldn't do that. I was too exhausted to feel. All I could do was worry.

So Martin did nothing. He did absolutely nothing. He simply stood and stared at me while his computerized German shepherd shifted from foot to foot and let out anxious little whimpers.

Do something! I told him. *I'm here for you now. I need help. I need a distraction! Distract me!*

And perhaps it surprised my editor, but it did not surprise me when Martin embarked on a death-defying quest to rescue his mother.

CHAPTER TWENTY-TWO

Helicopter parents," the counselor said. "It's one of our biggest challenges."

I was sitting in an auditorium-style classroom, in a comfortable padded chair. That was new. College classrooms didn't have padded chairs in my day. Around me sat people of my same age and situation: the men with thinning hair and the occasional streak of silver; the women with short, discreetly dyed, practical styles.

This group of steady grown-up types had come together for our children's college orientation weekend. Our youngsters were off somewhere on a campus tour while the counselors sat us oldsters down and talked to us about parenting—

Specifically, about the need to stop.

"Helicopter parents," the counselor said, "are the moms and dads who pop by campus all the time. They show up at class. They want to know things we're not allowed to tell them—things about attendance or grades. We call them helicopter parents because they hover. They can't let go of their children."

My imagination presented me with the image of a college student. He had longish hair and a bored expression, and he was walking across campus to class. Meanwhile, his two anxious parents hovered along after him. They hung in the air a few feet above and a few feet behind him, their helicopter blades gently humming.

The image caught my fancy, and I smiled. I glanced around at the nearby faces to see if anyone else was smiling, but the other parents looked grave.

As a group, we were soberly dressed, but with a few well-chosen bright touches—chunky silver jewelry, perhaps, or a kelly-green cardigan over a linen shirt. *I still know how to have fun!* these touches said. *I'm not old yet!* But in fact, our definition of fun had changed considerably since our own college days, along with many other things about us. The close attention we were all paying to the lecture, for instance: that was something I didn't remember from the old days.

"It's important for you to step back now," the counselor said. "You've done your job. You got your children here. And that's great! But now it's time for *them* to take over." He paused while we all pondered that extraordinary thought. "You've given them roots," he said. "It's time to give them wings."

Roots? Wings? My imagination spun for a second or two. Then it coughed up an image of an eagle whose claws had grown into the ground. He was flapping his wings, trying to fly, but the root-claws wouldn't let him.

Roots *and* wings? That made for one very unhappy bird!

And once again, I smiled.

But once again, as I glanced around, I found that no one else was smiling. The other parents were nodding solemnly.

Maybe I have been hovering too much, I thought, a little abashed. *I do mind Elena's business. I need to back off and let her take care of things. She's right: she's done amazingly well this year.*

And my imagination found another image to show me, a thrilling, joyful memory. Elena stood at the podium in her black cap and gown, with the bright yellow honors ribbon draped around her shoulders. She was standing in front of two thousand family members and students. And she was delivering a high school graduation address—in German.

My heart swelled at the thought. I was so proud of her!

The counselor continued to mix his metaphors, but I was lost in my own reverie. Summer had come, and once again, it was a summer of changes. I was one year out from sitting by Elena's bed in the ICU. I was two years out from sitting by Valerie's in the ER. But this time, the changes the summer was bringing were happy ones.

After seven years in Germany, Joe and Elena and I were back in Texas again. We were back in our old house, back in our old neighborhood and church—back among old friends.

Elena was finally getting that independence she had wanted. She had her driver's license, a little used car, and a dorm apartment at our local state university. What a cute place she and her roommate were putting together, too—orderly and soothing, aqua blue and sage green, with a spa-like Zen feel and a bowl of woven rattan balls on the coffee table.

The counselor is right, I thought as we parents stood up to leave the auditorium. *Elena's fine now. It's time for me to let go.*

A few weeks later, I was standing on my front porch, surrounded by towers of cardboard boxes, while moving men wrestled a king-size mattress through the front door. The dining table and chairs, swaddled in massive sheets of white paper, sat on the driveway next to the moving truck.

My cell phone rang.

"Hey, Mamacita!" said Valerie's easygoing voice. "Have the movers gotten there yet?"

My runaway daughter hadn't been able to call me when I was in Germany. Her cell phone plan wouldn't let her make international calls. But now that I had a regular Texas phone number again, she was taking the lead in our relationship. She called me several times a day.

It made me happy that she wanted to include me in her life like that.

"Yes, they're here," I said. "It's pretty much chaos. And you know, it doesn't matter how nice your furniture is, when you stick it out on the front lawn, it still looks like Walmart burped out a clearance sale."

"That's why I don't have furniture," Valerie said cheerfully.

Poor she might be, but Valerie had achieved quite a bit in her year and a half of independence. She was still living with the fundamentalist family, and she and Clint had been dating the whole time. At first, she had supported herself with a job as a waitress, and now she had an almost-full-time job in a department store—steady friendships, a steady relationship, and steady employment.

Pre-runaway Valerie had been anything but steady.

While Valerie and I talked, the movers came hustling through the door again, and Joe followed them out. "I'm going to pick up lunch," he said. "What do you want?"

"Hang on," I told Valerie. "You'll need my keys," I told Joe. "You're parked in by the movers."

Joe's new BMW was in the garage. I used to joke that every American left Germany with a BMW and a cuckoo clock. Sure enough, although we had resisted the clocks, we'd brought home the BMW.

"But it's a great deal," Joe had pointed out at the time. "I could sell it tomorrow for what I paid for it." And I had supported him in that. After all the hard work he'd put in, I was happy to go along with the idea that this purchase made practical sense.

Now the BMW was in the garage, its luxury-car interior protected from the vicious Texas sun. Joe doted on that car. He kept leather wipes on the passenger seat so he could wipe it down while he waited at stoplights.

My car wasn't a luxury model, but I didn't feel deprived. I had discovered the Hyundai Elantra during months of premove research. Earlier models had had an iffy reputation, but the last two models had been winners, safer and more reliable than most small cars. Consumers hadn't noticed this yet, so the Elantra was still a well-kept secret. It was thousands of dollars below the other used cars in its class.

I'd arranged to buy an inexpensive used Elantra for Elena to use as her college car. We'd gone straight from the airport to pick it up. It was tawny tan, like a desert cat, and the minute I got into it, I was in love. It was graceful and modest, simple but not cheap—everything I needed, and even a few things I wanted, without feeling the least bit hedonistic.

So I had bought another Elantra for myself—a white one this time. Joe could have his beautiful, powerful BMW. I loved neat, orderly, thrifty things.

The movers left a couple of hours later, and Joe and I spent an obsessively busy afternoon trying to locate and unpack enough of our possessions to allow us to resume normal life. Then, the next morning, Joe and his BMW left for work while I cracked open the towers of cardboard boxes, and Tor and Simon, terribly excited, pounced and hid amid welters of white packing paper.

My phone rang again. This time, it was Elena.

"Hey, Mom, guess *what*! There was a dorm mixer last night, and Meghan and I went—you remember Meghan, the one from the orientation with the dad who made a fortune selling unpainted furniture."

"Yep," I said. I did remember Meghan. Thanks to Elena's stories, I was already getting to know her new college friends.

"So, there was a raffle," Elena continued, "and we won! A full-day pass for four to that big amusement park. We're going today."

"Fantastic!" I held the phone with my shoulder while I unwrapped a vase with both hands. "So, who are you thinking of going with?"

"We're thinking those two cute guys in the apartment next door."

"I thought three cute guys lived there."

"Yeah, but Harley is a douche. Did you know, he saw us taking the trash out of our apartment, so he put a bag of *his* trash on our doorstep. Like we're going to haul his trash for him! His bedroom is next to mine, and the walls are so thin, I could hear him on the phone, calling up prostitutes in Austin. *Then* he came over and wanted to go on a date. Ha!"

"Coed dorms are supposed to help you learn about the opposite sex," I observed. "With walls like that, you'll learn more than you ever wanted to know."

"You've got that right," she said. "I already have!"

Our relationship had improved the second Elena had moved into the dorms. It wasn't just that we were apart now. Elena was happier with me because she was happier with life. Elena had always had a sense of boundless curiosity, and now that she was on the campus of a large university, she was learning dozens of interesting new things every day. And when she learned them, she wanted to share them. That's when my phone rang: "Guess *what*!"

I could never guess. Elena might be about to tell me about an eighteenth-century poem she'd found or an odd bit of trivia about spiders. She might be about to share some sizzling-hot celebrity gossip or a gruesome medical fact. Whatever it was, she could hold me spell-bound. Day after day, she brought me the chance to learn new things effortlessly, without even having to look them up.

Over the next several weeks, I finished unpacking and settled into being the opposite of a helicopter mom. Valerie was doing well in Georgia, and Elena was doing well at school. Even though some of Elena's classes had hundreds of students in them, all her professors knew her and loved her.

"The secret," she told me, "is to sit in the front row and ask tons of questions."

Indeed it is, I thought.

Joe's new Air Force job took him to Asia and the Pacific on regular multiweek trips. To me, it sounded horribly stressful, but Joe seemed to be thriving. He Skyped me from the hotel one day that fall. "Did you see the photos?" he asked. "The ones from the orchid garden? You can't believe the colors!" Then he paused, trying to find in his tidy engineer's brain the words to describe that kind of extravagant beauty.

But he didn't need to find them. I could hear the awe in his voice.

On a cool day in November, Joe was away on one of his trips. Once again, my cats lounged beside the big brown armchair while I typed on my laptop, black words against white. But I wasn't seeing black and white. Martin and Chip, his computerized German shepherd, were standing in a parking lot full of derelict cars.

What does a parking lot look like, I wondered, *when it hasn't been used for fifty years?*

Not like a parking lot anymore. The rust-colored cars weren't on asphalt. Weeds had sprouted and sprung up. No, not weeds, summer wild-flowers. The cars were almost buried in big dense groups of yellow Maxi-milian sunflowers.

I smiled. I remembered playing in Maximilian sunflowers when I was little. I started to type.

> Chip cavorted through the yellow flowers, then pounced. Seconds later, he came prancing up with a stick. He sidled into Martin, knocking him off

balance, and whipped his bushy tail back and forth.

Yellow petals went flying like confetti.

Then Martin looked up and saw the ruined skyscrapers of the abandoned downtown ahead of them. When he saw them, I could see them, too.

About a mile away, a cluster of thin buildings reached improbable heights, as if some giant hand had come down from the sky and pulled them toward the heavens. Some were faced with polished stone, still stylish and dignified. Others were faced with panels of mirrored glass. These had shattered and left dark squares here and there, so that their sides looked like surreal chessboards. Flocks of birds swooped in and out and gave their solid lines the illusion of movement.

I thought about that for a quiet minute—that ruined city.

The phone rang, and my view resolved once again into two unconscious cats and my green backyard. But I didn't wince as I answered it. My life contained plenty of peace nowadays.

"Hey, Mamacita!" said Valerie's voice. "I've got something to ask you. Do you think Clint and I are too comfortable?"

"Hello, honey," I said. "I guess I don't know. What do you mean by 'too comfortable'? *Comfortable* sounds like a good thing, doesn't it?"

"Yeah, but we've been dating for almost two years," Valerie said. "That whole time, we haven't gone out with anybody else. We don't even argue. It's like we're an old married couple already. Don't you think we're too young to be that settled?"

My black sheep daughter, too settled. That idea felt so good that, mentally, I took off my shoes and ran barefoot through it. Valerie, settled and comfortable, like part of an old married couple. Yellow petals whirled into the air around me.

Ruins, yes. The ruins of old structures, old habits, and old ways of being. But from the ruins, new flowers were springing up. Life and growth were all around.

"I don't know about being too young to be settled," I said aloud. "Isn't dating just a way of finding the person you love? If you've already found the person you love, why change?"

"I just think maybe we'll regret it later," Valerie said. "You know, making up our minds so soon." So I set aside the laptop and its flower-filled ruins and spent a while listening to her talk out the pros and cons. I'm a lot like Valerie that way. I like to talk out my plans and decisions, too.

Several hours later, Valerie called me again. Her voice was excited and purposeful. "I've broken up with Clint," she said. "He's pretty upset, but I think it's best for both of us. He really doesn't get the whole too-young thing, but I just don't want us to feel sorry about it later. And hey, we can always get back together again if that's what we decide we want."

"Sure," I said. "It's your decision. It's not as if there's a right or a wrong here."

Over the course of the next day, I didn't have time to feel lonely for Joe, who was now in Japan. I didn't even have time to play in the sunflowers with Martin. Valerie called me every couple of hours, and she agonized for hours. Not only was she missing Clint, but she was also starting to rethink her decision.

"I hope I did the right thing," she said. "No, I *know* I did the right thing. It's best. It's best for both of us. Right?"

"You and Clint are the only ones who can decide that," I said. "This is about what you want for your life."

"Well, I just want us to be *sure*."

The next morning, as I was putting down food for the cats, Valerie called me again. This time, she was in tears.

"Roll over, Simon," I said. "Hold on, honey. Simon! Roll *over. Over.* Good kitty! Valerie, you'll have to say that again. I can barely understand you."

"I said he's *flirting*!" Valerie cried. "He's flirting with another girl! He doesn't love me!"

"Tor, roll over . . . *That's* my good kitty! But, honey, aren't you two broken up?"

"Yes, but I wouldn't flirt with another guy. I care too much!"

"But . . . Okay, let me get this straight," I said as I stepped over the cats to rinse out their water bowl. "You broke up so you'd be able to flirt with other people, right? You didn't want to make up your mind too soon. It was your decision. And you broke Clint's heart, didn't you?"

"Apparently not!" Valerie exclaimed with stormy bitterness. "If he really had his heart broken, he'd be too upset to flirt!"

There was a lull, filled only by the sounds of sharp teeth crunching dry food pellets, while I pondered the highly personal etiquette of the breakup. As I was considering and rejecting different comments, I heard someone else speak in the background of the phone call. Valerie moved the phone away and raised her voice to respond.

"Hey, wait a minute," I interrupted. "Is that Clint?"

"Yes."

I sat down to watch the cats finish their meal.

"Okay, I don't get this," I said. "If you're broken up, what's Clint doing there?"

"I have to get to work, Momma." Valerie's tone of voice implied that this should be perfectly obvious. "You know Clint drives me to work."

"But"—and I found myself waving a hand in the air, even though she couldn't see it—"Valerie, you just broke up with him!"

"But how else would I get to work?" Valerie asked, a little indignant. "Clint *knows* I don't have another ride in."

"In all fairness," I said, "I don't think a lot of guys who'd had their hearts broken would care how you got to work."

"That would be mean," Valerie declared. "Got to go now. Love you, Mom." And she hung up to continue her argument.

Meanwhile, I was thinking, *I* like *this guy!*

An hour later, Valerie called back, over the moon with happiness. She and Clint had gotten back together.

While I was washing the dishes, the phone rang again. I expected it to be Valerie, but it was Elena this time. "Guess *what!*" she said. "I've got a job! I'm working at the mall. It's only five minutes from campus. Meghan and I were walking through the mall together, and this guy came up to us and said, 'We're looking for people like you. If you want work, you've got a job.' I thought he was some kind of creeper, but it turned out that he works for a local clothing store. They've already accepted my application, and I already worked my first day."

"That's great, hon!" I said. "I hope you have a good time working there."

"A big part of the job seems to be spraying everything with their 'signature scent,'" Elena said. "After about ten minutes of spritzing jeans, my hand cramped up."

"I'd hate that!" I said. "I don't want to buy clothes drenched in cheap perfume."

"Technically, it's not cheap," she pointed out. "And no offense, Mom, but I don't exactly think you're our target shopper."

"Maybe I'll surprise you," I said. "Did Meghan get a job, too?"

"Meghan already has a job. She waits tables."

"She seems like a good friend," I said. "Fun things always seem to happen when you're around her. She's such a bright girl—really funny, too."

Elena grew unexpectedly somber.

"It's really sad," she said. "Meghan has this great mom—sweet, great sense of humor—I know you two would bond. But when she's around, Meghan clams up. They don't talk like we do."

Like we do. Once again, I ran barefoot through that idea, back and forth, while yellow flowers bloomed.

As an early Christmas present to all of us, Joe and I flew Valerie and Clint out to visit for a couple of days. Valerie was her old self again, with that easy laugh and laid-back temperament that had won friends on two continents. It was almost impossible to picture her as the haunted, depressed girl who had burned and cut herself. Clint was earnest and even-tempered, with a dry sense of humor that fit in perfectly with our family.

The four of us drove to a Chinese buffet. Valerie was playing songs off her playlist when a Sum 41 song came on.

"Oh, hey," Clint said mildly, "I used to listen to these guys a lot back in my 'angry young man' phase."

"Um . . . Clint?" Joe said, grinning. "You're not even old enough to order a beer. When did you squeeze in that 'angry young man' phase?"

Throughout the weekend they stayed with us, Elena was absent from our lives. But on the morning of their last day in Texas, she called.

"Put Valerie on the phone," she said.

A few minutes later, Elena walked through the door, and within five minutes, she and Valerie were chatting away on the back porch, just as if they'd never been apart.

It was a sight that brought tears to my eyes.

As winter gave way to spring, I felt comfortable enough with our new life to start doing some things for myself. Joe and I were empty nesters now. It was time to embrace that change. So I began taking piano lessons from a dear friend whom I'd known for years. It was interesting work for me because it was entirely nonverbal—it was about sounds, but it wasn't about words. But that didn't stop me from trying to use words to describe it.

"Okay," I said to myself as I practiced, "I need to hit that hop in the middle, where the song goes from slow to bright. More rabbit—I need more rabbit."

I also started jogging in the neighborhood to try to lose the extra weight I'd put on cooking for Elena. But that didn't result in a subtraction. It resulted in an addition.

I was jogging a few blocks from home one morning when I saw a small dirty-brown dog sitting on a front porch. She appeared to be part terrier and part bird's nest. I always greet animals when I'm out and about, including (sometimes) very large bugs—the kind of bugs that seem to demand respect. So I greeted the little dog:

"Hi, baby."

She raced across the yard to me and threw herself down at my feet, hiding her face in her little paws. *Help me!* she said without saying a word.

I took a closer look at this small terrier-nest cross. She was horribly underweight, and her face was covered with scabs. So I took her home with me, *just until her owners come home from work,* I thought. *And I'll give her a bath, too. She's filthy.*

Four hours later, I was still soaping her with medicated shampoos. The little thing was crawling with the largest fleas I'd ever seen, and she was anemic from blood loss. But, even though the treatments stung and hurt, the sweet little thing didn't object. She danced around me while I dried her off, thrilled to have the attention.

Okay, that's it! I thought angrily. *Those morons aren't getting her back!* Not, apparently, that they wanted her back—I watched for days, but no signs went up around the neighborhood. So I kept her, and I named her Genny, after the stray dog in the Madeline books.

Love and care took Genny from being a skinny, scrawny, ratty-looking dog to being a round, plump, ratty-looking dog. She was already old when she found me, and the closest I ever came to discovering her "breed" was a warning picture on a Norfolk terrier website: *If you purchase your Norfolk off the Internet, you could end up with a dog that looks like THIS!* When Genny was at rest, she looked like a blond wig that had accidentally gone through the washer, and when she was in motion, she looked like a chicken nugget on sticks. But she danced and played and bounded around me as I worked. She still had the heart of a puppy.

One day, Elena came over to do laundry. Genny bounced up to greet her while I made myself a cup of tea and prepared for the exciting and highly enjoyable ride that is a catch-up conversation with Elena. What would it be today? Multiple-personality disorders? A foreign movie plot? Japanese host club boys? Just lately, she had been telling me all about porphyria and vampires.

"What's new?" I asked with interest.

Elena was measuring out laundry soap. "So, I went to see somebody," she said.

"You mean a doctor?" I asked with a flutter of worry.

Elena was starting to get sick a lot. She was overdoing it at school again—involved in too many activities. Just recently, she had had another sore throat she couldn't shake.

"I mean a shrink," Elena said.

When we had returned to Texas, I had encouraged Elena to see Dr. Harris again. But she hadn't wanted to, and in the first flush of excitement over college, she hadn't seemed as if she needed to, either. She had started out the fall semester taking better care of herself than I'd seen her do in a year. Her college friends ate, so she did, too.

At first.

But now, I assessed her over my teacup. She was starting to look nervous and jumpy, the way she had looked during her senior year of high school. And now she was going to see a psychiatrist on her own.

This could be good—or it could be very bad. I waited to see which it was.

"The counselor on campus thought it would be a good idea for me to see somebody after my blackout last October," Elena said. "She thought I should go see an eating disorder specialist, you know, to make sure I'm over that whole thing—since I had trouble with it when I was in high school."

I recalled the incident in October with another unpleasant prickle of worry. Elena had ended up in the ER for a few hours. But she'd been drinking pretty heavily, the doctor told us. He thought she'd just passed out.

At the time, I had said to her, "It sounds like you had one of your blackouts from the Summer from Hell." But Elena had laughed it off and told us she'd been partying too hard. I had remembered my own freshman-year parties and put it out of my mind.

But now here she was, calling it a blackout.

"Turns out," Elena continued, "there's a place in town that works with eating disorder patients. Sandalwood, it's called. I met with their director."

She found a Coke can in the fridge and took a few seconds to open it. I watched her in silence. Elena always opened her Cokes just a little bit, so that almost nothing could come out. I couldn't remember how long it had been since I'd seen her finish a Coke.

Elena said, "She told me that I *do* have anorexia nervosa."

"I know," I said sadly.

This wasn't something I thought about every day. It was something I tried not to worry about anymore. Elena was an adult now. I wasn't supposed to hover. There was nothing I could do about it. God knows, I had tried.

But the mother who had lived through Elena's senior year—the mother who had watched her measure out every single bite and avoid more than the tiniest ration of calories—that mother had learned a long time ago: *Yes, my daughter* does *have anorexia nervosa.* Maybe she hadn't had it before the Summer from Hell. Maybe her eating disorder had been less severe. But, after the trauma of being forced into hospitals and psychiatric facilities—

And, once again, my mind locked on to the image of Dr. Petras, blustering and issuing his threats.

"The director said my anorexia isn't the family's fault," Elena continued. "She told me, when it's caused by the parents, it starts really young. Mine didn't start till I was a teenager. That means it was caused by something else."

"Oh. That's interesting," I said.

But I didn't get it.

I didn't think to ask, *So, why did this question come up? Does that mean you* thought *your anorexia was our fault? What gave you that idea? Was it something we did? Was it something somebody else did?*

Or, even better:

What do you *think caused your anorexia?*

I didn't ask these questions. I just didn't think. My imagination was still playing me the tape of Dr. Petras having his meltdown. It was so stuck on what it *did* know that it didn't notice what it *didn't.*

"So," I said, "how does the director think you're doing now?"

"Okay," she said vaguely. "We talked about me joining a support group."

"How often does it meet?"

"Doesn't matter. She didn't think it would help."

She didn't think it would help? That sounded odd. "Really?" I said, trying to keep my tone light. "I thought those people love support groups!"

But Elena declined to elaborate.

"Anyway, you'll see a bill," she said. "They copied our insurance card."

I did see a bill. It got tangled up in our insurance system, and I wound up having to call both the insurance company and Sandalwood before payment came through. But I didn't bring it up again to Elena.

My daughter was an adult now. I needed not to hover. She had told me to let her deal with her business. I was ready to let her deal.

I had an adoring, ratty little dog to pet and jogging to do. I had piano to practice and books to write. Whenever my daughters wanted to reach out, I was right there to cheer them on. But I was through minding their business and running their lives.

I was done with being Elena's evil witch.

CHAPTER TWENTY-THREE

But over the next few weeks, I began to realize that this conversation had marked a turning point. Whether that was due to Elena or to me, I couldn't quite figure out. For my part, I found that it had reawakened old fears. Against my will, I began to worry again.

Elena seemed to have gone through a change as well. The fun and excitement of her freshman year had drained away. Now, everything she talked about involved more achievement—and more stress.

Like the morning she called me during my jog to tell me about the ROTC scholarship.

"The major says, with my grades, I'm a sure thing," she told me on the phone. "Then the Air Force can pay for my nursing school."

"Genny, no! Don't eat that. Dogs are so gross," I said, dragging the little terrier away from something awful in the gutter. "But, honey, you don't have to get a scholarship. We can help with nursing school."

"Mom, I don't want to use all of your and Dad's money! I thought you'd be happy that I'm trying to be independent."

"No, I am, I am. It's just . . ."

"It's just what?" she wanted to know.

It's just that you get sick a lot, I thought. *Your immune system isn't robust, and I should know; you inherited it from me. It's like that doctor told me when I was your age, "Some people can stay up partying all night, and then there's you." No way could my body have handled a military life, and I don't think your body can, either.*

But I knew just how furious Elena would be if I were to say that out loud, so I hunted for a more acceptable response.

"It's just that I don't want you to feel like you have to."

I could hear it in the dogged tone in her voice, however: Elena felt like she had to. Once again, she was driving herself to meet Herculean goals. She was doing exceptional work in her classes, and she had even won a rare departmental award. I was proud of her, but I could see that it was taking a toll.

Sitting in one of the brown chairs a few days later, with my laptop open on my lap, I listened to her voice on the phone detailing her final exam schedule. Eight prenursing classes' worth of final exams. The workload was absolutely crushing.

Oh, well. At least she'll be able to rest up this summer, I thought.

But no.

"Guess *what!*" Elena said on the phone a couple of hours later. "I've been selected as a summer RA!"

"Hey, that's fantastic!" I said. The resident assistants (RAs) had their meals and dorm room paid for and brought in a salary, as well. It was hard work to become an RA, and I knew Elena had worked at it for months. It would finally give her that financial independence she had pushed herself to achieve. Finally, she could say, "I'm taking care of myself."

"So," I said, "you'll be quitting the mall job now?"

"I don't need to quit the mall job," she said. "It's not like the RA job will take that much time."

Worry plucked at me.

"Yes," I said, "but you promised when you took all those classes this spring that you'd take some time to recharge this summer."

"Yeah, but the mall job doesn't stress me out."

"Elena, you're often there until one or two in the morning, and then you're up before seven the next day. Maybe you don't see that as stress, but your body does. It deserves a little rest."

"Yeah, maybe . . . I'll see how it goes."

I was still working at my laptop a little while later when a call came in from a number I didn't know.

"This is Clint. From Georgia," the voice said.

Worry plucked at me again. Clint sounded upset. Had something happened to Valerie?

"Oh, hey!" I said. "Is everything okay?"

"Yeah," he said.

There was a pause on the line, and then came a sudden rush of speech, the verbal equivalent of a barrel ride over Niagara Falls.

"It's just ... I want to marry Valerie. I mean, I don't just want to, I'm going to ask her to marry me; I've got the ring and everything. But before I do—before I ask her to marry me—I wanted to ask you and Mr. Dunkle first. If it would be okay with you. Okay if I married your daughter."

My heart melted completely. How adorable was *that*!

Valerie asked Elena to be her maid of honor, which was lovely in light of their old feud. But it also brought tension to the surface.

"You need to talk to Valerie!" Elena told me on the phone a couple of weeks later. "Aside from wanting to be barefoot at the beach, she hasn't made any decisions at all about this wedding. She's got to pin down a date. Maybe she can take off anytime she wants from her department store job, but I have to plan ahead. I've got two jobs to work and a full semester coming up."

More than the words, I picked up on the ragged edge in Elena's voice. That brought out the worrier in me again.

"Oh! Two jobs?" I said. "I thought you were quitting your mall job to do the RA thing."

"There's no need," Elena said. "I can make more money this way. You want me to be independent, don't you?"

"Well, you know I want you to get a little rest this summer. You keep getting sick!"

And I couldn't keep the flutter of anxiety and reproach out of my voice, even though I knew she hated it.

"Chill *out*, Mom! I can handle it!"

Sure enough, she had heard that flutter.

Why couldn't I leave my daughter alone and quit badgering her about her choices? Was I really one of those dreaded helicopter parents?

By the end of June, Elena was busy enough that we rarely got to see her anymore, so Joe and I met her for lunch one day at a restaurant near her dorm. As I hugged her hello, panic shivered through me. I could feel ribs. I could feel spine. And Elena was pale again—sickly pale. She had a washed-out, anemic look.

The place was busy. Old-time advertising signs on the walls and waitresses in baseball caps—it was supposed to look homey. Actually, it was a massive chain, and the dining room held a couple of hundred people. That saddened me. I missed the little European restaurants, the ones with about ten tables. They actually *were* homey.

While we waited on long wooden benches for our name to be called, Elena dazzled us with stories of RA work. She enjoyed it, and she was good at it. She was pretty sure she was becoming a favorite of the RA managers, too—a set of young people who each controlled several of the dorms.

"We got a complaint about this one room," Elena said. "The roommates said it smelled so bad they couldn't stand to live there. It wasn't my floor, but the RA in charge of it doesn't like confrontation, so she talked me into going in with her. We were walking down the hall, and you could smell it already. Something strange—like garbage, but worse.

"'What *is* that?' my friend asks.

"Then the guy opens the door, and this *wall* of stink hits us. It was so bad, it was like the air looked dirty. It felt as if we were looking through a haze, but it was probably just our eyeballs saying, *No, please! Don't open me in here! It's not safe!*

"This guy had a hot plate set up in the kitchenette, and he had these jars everywhere—*everywhere!* Jars of fish oil, jars of sauces, sitting out, sitting right in sunlight, oily brown, with these weird blobs floating in them—it straight up *stank* in the whole place like rotting fish. The other RA couldn't stand it! She had to run out. I thought she was going to throw up in the hall."

My imagination pulled up the whole scene for me: beige dorm walls coated with that dirty, oily stink, the jars, the blobs, the light green face of the RA as she ran from the room . . .

I loved that! I loved Elena's stories.

But once we got to our table, Elena switched to an activity I found more worrisome these days: sketching out plans for her nursing school future. Planning was good, but Elena, like her father, tended to be a bit of a pessimist. She saw the future through gloom-colored glasses. It wasn't open doors and opportunities; to her, it was an obstacle course. And nursing school was an obstacle course with forty-foot-high walls.

The waitress took our drink orders and brought us a hunk of bread on a cutting board. Elena pushed it aside.

"Here's my grades so far in the prenursing classes," she said, writing out numbers on her paper napkin. "Composition, Intro to Psych, Developmental Psych, Nutrition, Anatomy. I haven't taken Physiology yet; that's a blank." She drew a line and wrote *Physiology*. "Now, the nursing school liaison says that five years ago, these grades would have been good enough to get me in. But not now. They're getting more applicants than they used to."

"They're all As and Bs," I pointed out.

"They should have been all As!"

Joe and I were hearing more and more about this lately. Elena had begun fretting constantly about whether or not she would get into nursing school. In her mind, she was already grappling with that letter of rejection. Sometimes, it seemed as if she were already living through the shame and disgrace of it.

"I'm sure you'll be fine," I said as I sawed off slices of bread. This didn't seem like a good topic for us to be talking about right before a meal, and I could see already that Elena was struggling to eat again. I handed her a piece of bread, and she dropped it on her plate as if it had burned her. "So, what else is going on?" I asked.

"I got a new job," Elena said proudly.

"Congratulations!" was Joe's response.

"Oh! *Another* job?" was mine.

I could hear the flutter of worry in my voice again, and I tried to steady and brighten it. But Elena was working two jobs already!

"It's just that—when do you have time for more work?"

"It's no trouble," Elena said. "It fits in the schedule because it's at night." And she named a posh gym across town. "It's not hard," she said. "It's a lot easier working there at night than during the day. Not very many people come in after one in the morning."

Joe looked interested. "That place is supposed to be beautiful," he said.

"Tell me about it! We have five pools. It looks nicer than a bank!"

The waiter brought our entrées. Chicken-fried steak for Joe, chicken with mixed vegetables for me, and spaghetti for Elena. No matter where we went, she ordered spaghetti. She'd done that since she was a little girl.

I used the interruption to try to figure out how to react. *You're supposed to be recharging!* is what I wanted to say, but I knew what would happen if I said it.

"The thing is . . . ," I began.

"Oh, here it comes," Elena commented to her father. "I knew Mom would find something to gripe about."

My heart sank. I was back to being the evil witch again. Why? I didn't want to be! But I held on to my poker face and didn't show my hurt. I tried to put together a persuasive argument—not that I had *ever* managed to persuade Elena to do anything.

"It's just that staying up all night is hard on the body," I said. "You have trouble sleeping already, and you just said you don't feel hungry. Well, keeping the body awake at night throws it off in all kinds of ways. It affects appetite, number of hours of sleep, everything."

The argument certainly convinced me. It made me worry even more. I knew that others of us might listen to our bodies and make up for that lost sleep. But Elena? When it came to taking cues from her body, that girl was completely tone-deaf.

"I eat just fine," Elena said emphatically. But she didn't look it. She was eating her spaghetti, but not the sauce. All the meat was falling off to the sides.

If I was already the evil witch, I might as well say it.

"You're doing too much, Elena. You promised when you took all those classes in the spring that you'd take a break in summer and rest up."

"I *am* resting up," she said. "I'm not taking summer school."

"Three jobs isn't resting!"

I could hear it in my voice: that whiny, nagging edge. I hated to hear it, too, but I couldn't help it. She drove me to it! All the frustration I'd felt during Elena's senior year resurfaced. *Why* was she doing this to herself? *Why* was she doing this to *me*?

"You know," Elena said, "most people would be happy if their children got a job. No matter what I do, you're never satisfied!"

The same old song, I thought. But I kept quiet.

"It's only a summer job, Mom. It's just for a few weeks. I think I can handle staying awake nights for a few weeks!"

We finished our meals—or at least, Joe and I finished our meals. Then we hugged Elena good-bye, and she drove off in her dusty tan Elantra. I went back home to my adoring little dog and my piano and my writing. But worry—the same old worry—followed me home.

It followed me from room to room. It got between Martin and me when I tried to revise his manuscript. It floated in the air in front of the keys when I sat down to play the piano.

But I didn't do anything about it. I just kept it to myself. *I need to quit hovering*, I thought.

A couple of weeks later, Valerie called up. "Hey, I've got some news," she said in her abrupt, practical way. "Clint and I are having a baby."

"Oh!"

Valerie knew better than most young women what sort of reaction this comment would get. She knew she wouldn't face a lecture. She knew I would be too busy remembering a similar phone call—a call I myself had had to make.

I remembered that call. I remembered the disbelief. I remembered the disappointment. But more than anything, what I remembered was my own fierce determination. I had been scared—no, I had been more than scared, I had been petrified! But I had made a promise to this scary new ghost who had just joined me in my graduate school apartment.

You will not be the one to suffer, I had said. *This was my mistake, not yours. No matter what we decide we need to do, you will come* first. *You will have a family, and you will have a loving home.*

That scary new nameless person haunting my life, that morning nausea and surprising result on the pregnancy test—that baby who, no matter what, was going to come *first*—

That baby had been Valerie.

"Oh!" I said, caught up in past fears and present worries. "What . . . what are you going to do?" And my mind immediately started running down the list: *High school diplomas, low-paying jobs, fleabag apartment . . .*

I didn't have to say it. Valerie knew what I was thinking about.

"We're not worried about money," she assured me. "Don't worry, we don't need money. Clint and I know how to get by on nothing."

"But babies cost a lot more than nothing," I said. *No insurance, no employee benefits . . .*

My imagination showed me snapshots of Valerie's own tiny nursery, with its handmade mobile and big paper animals that I had found in a teacher's store somewhere. It all seemed so dingy and dreary in those memories, with only baby Valerie herself to brighten the room.

Joe and I had had so little!

And that was with two college diplomas, an engineer's salary, and health insurance!

"I know, I know, it's not the greatest time," Valerie said. "But we're halfway there. Clint's only got three more college classes to go before the Air Force lets him in. And you know Clint. He'll get through them."

"That's true," I said with a feeling of relief. Clint was the sort of man who *would* get through them.

"Clint and I are used to being poor," Valerie reminded me. "When we didn't have a car, we used to catch a ride into town and go to the dollar movies. When we didn't have two dollars, which was a lot of the time, we'd go to the bookstore and read. Compared to back then, we're rolling in it. And hey, now we don't have to plan a big wedding!"

Valerie's voice was jaunty, but I could hear the edge of strain in it.

"How are you feeling?" I asked.

"Oh, *you* know," she answered. "I've had better days. I'm starting to feel pretty sick. And I haven't smoked a cigarette in three hours now, so I kind of want to punch somebody in the face."

Valerie without cigarettes was not a pretty picture. I'd seen that picture before.

"How's Clint?" I asked next.

"Clint's pretty thrilled about the baby," Valerie said. "Which, right now, kind of makes me want to punch *him* in the face."

"Well, I think you'll want to resist that urge," I said. "It'll get better in a couple of days, when the withdrawal symptoms ebb." And the two of us said good-bye.

A few minutes later, my phone rang again. This time, it was Elena.

"Did you hear about Valerie?" she demanded, and her voice was genuinely angry. "Oh my God! I can't believe it. You know Valerie's not ready to handle this."

"It's going to be hard on them," I agreed. "They'll need support to get through it. Fortunately, Clint's mom and stepfather are nearby. I know they'll help all they can."

"I can't believe it!" Elena said again. "Really. I can't believe it!"

I was worried for Valerie and Clint, but Elena was sounding much more upset than I was. Her exemplary work as a resident assistant had impressed the managers, and she had earned an RA job slot in the fall. She had a tidy sum in savings from her jobs at the mall and the gym. She would have free room and board all next year. But I could hear for myself how high a price she had paid. She sounded sick, stressed, miserable, and exhausted.

The three jobs, the being awake day and night—Elena had overdone it again. This summer that was supposed to recharge her had run her completely ragged. And in another week, she would be back in the classroom, stressing over grades. She was taking another crushing course load.

Why is she doing this? my mind wailed. But I kept my voice steady and my worries to myself. One little flutter, and Elena would go off like a Roman candle. As worn out as she was, she was one raw nerve.

"Your cold is still sounding pretty bad," I said as casually as I could. "Did you make it to the doctor yet?"

"This morning," Elena said. "I saw the doctor's assistant. He says it's sinusitis again. He gave me drugs."

"Oh, good!" I said, and I really meant it. Good for my bear-pain-in-silence daughter for seeing the doctor. This was a win! "Did you fill that prescription yet?"

"On the way home."

My worries rushed back. That was unusually prompt. Elena must be feeling horrible.

"So, you're not going to your other jobs anymore, right?" I couldn't resist saying. "Not the gym one, at least. Especially not with that infection." *Please!* I added silently. *Please get some rest!*

"I quit the mall job last week. I go one more time to the gym, on Saturday. I'm not going right now because I'm in the middle of moving. RA Orientation starts tomorrow, and I got my new room and my floor assignment this morning. Why don't you meet me at the pet store by the house? I want to get a fish for my dorm room."

A fish? I felt myself tense up further. By now, both girls had stressed me out enough that I was starting to feel jumpy about everything. And a fish—such a sad little life.

But I felt like a total idiot when I heard myself say, "I don't know . . . Fish don't do well . . ."

And I deserved it when Elena said, "Mom, it's a fish! Will you *please* chill out?"

"But you should get some rest," I reminded her. "You should be in bed with that infection. You sound awful!"

"Mom, you know I'm not going to bed."

This was true. Elena had never stayed in bed when she was ill, not even back in the days when she and Valerie had filled the house with their laughter. When she was sick, I had put her to bed over and over, only to have her drift into the room ten or twenty minutes later, all wrapped up in a sheet, pale, like a very small ghost.

Little Elena had wanted to be wherever I was. That was her comfort when she was sick. She had stayed put only when I went to bed with her and we read books and told stories to one another.

"Come on," Elena said to me now. "It'll be like resting to poke around in a pet store. It'll be better than all the other work I have to do. And I'd like your opinion about the fish."

What mother doesn't want to be part of her daughter's comfort routine? So I met Elena at the pet store, and I prepared to enjoy myself.

But fish . . .

For a few brief days in childhood, I had owned a grocery-store gold-fish. My mother had been quite upset over its rapid decline. The memory of her unhappiness, combined with my own unhappiness, had left me with an impression of improbability, fragility, and loss.

Poor fish! Such sad little lives.

"What about one of these?" Elena said, pausing at the collection of bettas.

Of all the sights in a pet store, the collection of plastic drinking cups holding motionless betta fish has to be the most depressing one of all. I stepped closer to the poor prisoners. Most of them looked as if they were already dead. But Elena appeared to be immune to the aura of misery rising from the transparent prison cells.

"Oh, look!" she said. "A red one!"

But I didn't look. I was already reaching out my hand. "How about this one?" I said.

A blue fish rested on the bottom of my cup. But calling him blue doesn't begin to do him justice. He didn't look like a living thing so much as an elaborate piece of enameled jewelry. His body shone like metal tinted deep aquamarine, and in his fins, I could see hints of teal and emerald.

I noticed a sticker on the top of the cup. His price was a mere fifteen dollars. It is absolutely wrong that such an impressive little animal should feed our collective American appetite for cheap toys.

"How about this one?" I said again, and once I had picked him up, I found that I couldn't put him back down. He rested gently against the clear bottom of the cup, looking out at the world. His body was broader and more muscular than the other bettas.

"I don't know," Elena said. "There might be a better one."

"There isn't a better one," I said.

While Elena looked through the other sad little captives, I studied this betta fish. As he swirled to the surface, his fins rippled and flowed like a ballroom dancer's skirt. Yes, there *was* emerald in those fins. He was beautiful—absolutely beautiful.

"Okay," Elena said. "You're right. He's the best one."

We put the betta plus his habitat into Elena's car—bowl, gravel, water drops, test strips, and of course a pagoda. Elena said, "What do you think I should call him?"

"You could give him a Welsh name," I said. "Dylan was the son of Arianrhod. As soon as he was born, he jumped into the water."

"Dylan," Elena said in a pleased voice, and I knew she was thinking of Dylan Thomas, the poet. "I like that. I'll call him Dylan."

It made me happy to hear her sounding happy, and I was glad we'd saved Dylan from his hideous cup. But when I looked at Elena out in the sunlight, worry gnawed at me again. She looked terrible. She looked really sick. Her skin wasn't just pale, it was sallow. The healthy pink flush to her cheeks that I had seen last fall was gone, ground down by her relentless demands on herself.

Why was Elena even out of bed?

But I knew the answer to that. Elena was out of bed because she had forced herself out of bed. She allowed herself no rest. Somehow, the very idea of rest brought this girl no rest. I thought of her driven, type A father as a young man, before the Zoloft had calmed his anxiety.

"Don't forget to take your medicine!" I begged as she climbed into her car. "And *sleep* tonight—please!"

"Sure, sure," she said as she waved her fingertips good-bye.

A couple of days later, the phone by the bed jangled its shrill tone at four thirty in the morning. I was so deep asleep that, at first, I tried to turn off an alarm.

"Room! My room!" Elena was babbling. Or sobbing. Or shrieking. Or all three.

I sat bolt upright. Every nerve in my body tingled. "Slow down! Calm down! I can't understand you!"

It's true that I couldn't understand the words, but the message got through anyway. The hair stood up on the back of my neck, and gooseflesh enveloped me. On a purely physical level, my body knew what my mind was still puzzling out. My body knew: Elena was in fear for her life.

"My room!" she sobbed. "She's here! She's in my room!"

Joe woke up with a grunt, and I tossed him the phone. My hands were already shaking so badly that I could hardly pull on my clothes. I grabbed my keys and drove through the dark streets. The steering wheel was slippery with sweat.

On a very ordinary day decades ago, my mother and I stood in line in a bank lobby. Suddenly, from the offices, a piercing scream rang out:

"No, no, no, no, no!"

It was a sound I had never heard before, but I knew what it was. We all knew what it was. It was the sound of the banshee wail. I've heard thousands of screams in hundreds of movies, and some of those movies won Oscars. But I have never, before or since, heard a scream like that.

Instantly, I knew, just as every person in the silent lobby knew: somebody somewhere was dead.

When I asked about it later, I learned that one of the employees had just lost her son in a car wreck. But I didn't need to ask. There could be no doubt. The woman herself had told us.

Communication is older than language. Anguish and heartbreak are much, much older than the words we use to describe them. And terror . . .

Elena was in fear for her life.

Dawn was breaking when I got to her. She was sitting outside on the stairwell that led to her dorm room, still talking on the phone to her father. By this time, she was calm, but the tears were still running down her cheeks.

"She was in my room," Elena told me after she hung up. "I saw her out of the corner of my eye. She put a hand on me. She pressed against me; she leaned into my back, and I saw her raise a knife over my head! And then, she wasn't there. She just wasn't there!"

I felt relief so intense that I thought I might burst into tears myself. This was what my brain had been telling me had happened, even while my body was undergoing the terror Elena had transmitted to it so well.

Joe suffers from night frights: *pavor nocturnus*. His father had them, too. He rouses out of sleep in complete terror, thrashing around and striking out violently, yelling about the bugs or rats that only he can see.

Night frights are the reason Joe and I don't have guns in the house. When I tell people this, they think I'm joking. I'm not. The intensity of the experience far exceeds normal nightmare, and night terror victims have an impressive ability to carry out complicated tasks while still asleep. Some have driven cars, and some have killed their family members while trying to save themselves from the monsters they see.

But fortunately, Joe's unconscious mind usually recognizes me. All I have to do is put a hand on him and say, "It's all right." Then he goes limp, drops straight back into deep sleep. The next morning, he may not remember anything about it.

Elena, too, has suffered from night frights since she was barely older than a toddler. In one of them, she came running down the hall to me, screaming, chased by a cat-size spider. Both Elena and her father have gone years at a time without a single night fright, but stress, poor sleep, and unfamiliar surroundings bring them on.

It all fit. Elena had just moved into a new dorm room, and I had seen for myself how exhausted and stressed she was. As for poor sleep, with three or four nights a week awake until five in the morning on gym nights, and two or three nights a week awake until one or two in the morning on mall nights, it's a wonder Elena's body had relaxed long enough to get any sleep at all.

"You know you have night frights," I reminded her, "just like your dad does. His night frights get worse with stress, too."

"She was *there!*"

I felt puzzled by Elena's vehement response. Why wouldn't she want to take comfort in this simple explanation? What made this episode different from the other times she had woken up in terror?

"Your dad always thinks his bugs are there, too," I said. "Remember the time he started yelling in the middle of the night, and he scared me so badly, we were both jumping up and down on the bed before I could figure out what was going on?"

"I know about night frights, Mom. I wasn't asleep. I was awake! I'm telling you, she was *there.*" And Elena stood up and went indoors. I could see her shutting down, turning away from this uncomfortable topic.

"Did anybody else come by?" I asked. "Did they hear you yell and come check on you?"

"No," Elena said. "The RAs around me haven't moved in yet. That reminds me, I have RA Orientation in an hour," she added, and I could see the relief on her face, the relief of being able to go back to work.

Poor girl, her cold still sounded so bad, but even when she tried to sleep, she got no rest.

"How about staying while I take my shower?" she said, and I knew she still wasn't feeling safe.

"Sure," I said. Anything to provide her nerves a little relief—to let this driven, ambitious, exhausted young woman relax on some level, even if she couldn't get any more sleep.

While Elena took her shower, I wandered through the apartment, willing myself to calm down, too. My hands were still shaking from the jolt of adrenaline I'd received. I turned my mind to more soothing subjects. Elena's new place was starting to look nice. She had her favorite mermaid picture up in the tiny living room, and I paused to study it.

This was no cartoon. It was real art. It was the signed print of a photograph done by an award-winning underwater photographer. The mermaid was slightly blurry, as if she were a real underwater creature the photographer had spotted and captured in only one quick shot. The photograph was full of those gentle blue and sea-green tints that Elena had matched in her decorations throughout the room.

Underneath, on the brown couch that came with the furnished dorm apartment, were her Zen pillows, steel blue with chocolate stitching. And here was Dylan in his bowl on the coffee table, the perfect counterpoint to the mermaid swimming on the wall. I greeted him: "Hey there, little fishy!" And he rewarded me with a couple of nervous azure-blue circles of his pagoda.

What a remarkable little creature!

On the counter in Elena's kitchenette were several bottles of pills: Advil, Tums, and two brown prescription bottles. I picked up one. It was her antibiotic. The other was an antianxiety medication.

"I didn't know you were taking this," I called through the closed bathroom door. "This drug for anxiety, I mean."

"Yeah, the doctor gave it to me a few weeks ago," her muffled voice came back. "I've been getting a little stressed out."

Tell me about it! I thought. Hopefully, the medication would bring her some relief.

The white bag the antibiotic had come in was still lying on the counter, and its information sheet was poking out. I opened it up. For a simple antibiotic, it had an impressive list of side effects.

Including hallucinations!

"Hey, Elena," I said, coming to the door of the bathroom again. "Your antibiotic can cause hallucinations!"

Elena popped the door open. She was putting the finishing touches on her makeup. She had her mask in place again, too: calm, competent, and disinterested.

"And?" she said.

I had the information sheet in my hand. "See? Hallucinations," I said, pointing to the word. "It also says you're not supposed to take it with the other type of drug you're on. They interact. They intensify the side effects." I thought angrily of Elena's already high stress level and her loss, once again, of a good night's sleep. "The doctor should have been more careful! She shouldn't have given you both these drugs together."

Elena leaned toward the mirror and made a moue with her mouth, smoothing out her lipstick.

"The doctor didn't," she said. "The PA gave me that one."

I felt upset that she was taking the news so calmly. She was always so hard on herself but so easy on everybody else.

"I'll bet this antianxiety drug can cause dream problems, too," I said. "It's a double whammy that you took them together. No wonder you had such an intense night fright!"

"Mom! She was *there*," Elena said.

She picked up her sweater and purse and slipped on her shoes, and we headed out the door together. She took the turn to walk across campus to RA Orientation, and I walked back to the parking lot.

By the time I had driven home and brewed a cup of coffee, the horror of the predawn ordeal was starting to fade. I told Joe about the drug interactions while he was getting ready for work.

"And you know she just moved in there," I said. "That makes night frights so much worse. Remember the first night we spent in Germany, and you and Elena *both* had night frights? You yelled, and she screamed! I was a nervous wreck—I thought surely someone in the hotel would call the police."

"Dad told me he was napping once," Joe said, "and this hideous face grinned at him through the window. It was peeking in at the bottom, where the shade wasn't pulled all the way down. He figured he had just had a bad dream, so he got up and walked over to the window. He bent down to look outside, and there it was, still there—nose to nose with him."

"Oh, my God! Then did he wake up?"

"Nope," Joe said. "I told you, he was awake. He was on his feet, standing by the window."

"What did he do?"

"He yelled, and it vanished."

With this vision in my head and adrenaline still coursing through my system, I gave a jump when my phone rang. Worry fluttered up at me when I saw that it was Elena again. But I calmed down when I heard her hello. She sounded normal. Her voice was measured and even.

Then I registered what she was saying:

"I have to move out of the dorms. I just got fired."

CHAPTER TWENTY-FOUR

Joe took the morning off, and we met Elena at a pancake place to talk it over. I felt so stressed and jittery that I almost wanted to wring my hands and cry, "What do we do? What do we *do*?" like a mother in a Victorian melodrama. But Elena, in spite of her horrible morning, was matter-of-fact. Her good sense calmed me down.

"Your manager fired you?" Joe asked. "The same one who just hired you?"

"No, it was the dorm managers who hired me, but it's their new boss who did the firing," Elena said. "She just got here on the first day of RA Orientation."

"Did she give you a reason?"

"No. She said that by law, she didn't have to give a reason."

I couldn't help thinking back to the hysterical call we'd received. "Maybe somebody saw you having your night fright after all."

"No, that didn't happen," Elena said. "I didn't see anybody. And even if somebody heard me, they'd ask first what was wrong."

We ordered pancakes, and Elena filled us in on her theory. The boss was new, so she didn't know Elena personally, and Elena had reported yesterday evening that another RA had been planning a suicide attempt.

"That RA's got a vindictive streak," Elena said. "None of the other RAs will have anything to do with him. I've only been nice to him because I've felt sorry for him, so he's got to know it's me who told. If the boss talked to him, I'll bet he told her a bunch of lies."

"Wouldn't she talk to the dorm managers and learn the truth?" Joe asked.

"I don't know about that," Elena said. "This woman looks pretty insecure to me. She might not have wanted to ask for anyone's opinion. I'm not sure she's into the whole power-sharing thing."

While I drank my coffee, I tried to take heart from Joe and Elena. They were both being reasonable. But my nerves were shot. They were just shot. I couldn't think of anything to say.

"The weird thing," Elena said, "is that the boss didn't just fire me, she also threw me out of the dorms. Ordered out of the dorms—that never happens! Even students who break laws are given a second chance. I've known underage RAs who were caught with alcohol in their rooms, and they got a second chance. I've seen RAs falling-down drunk, right in front of their manager, and they got counseled, but they kept their job. I don't know of a single RA who got denied permission to live on campus. That's really strange."

The coffee and calm conversation worked on my shattered nerves. A plan. We needed a plan.

"Is there an appeals process?" I asked.

"I'm way ahead of you, Mom," Elena said. "I've already looked it up."

So Joe went to work while Elena and I went to the library, and I helped Elena write an appeal letter. It was sober and tactful, and it apologized for any offense Elena might have caused inadvertently.

"That's in case you're right about the insecurity problem," I said. "Maybe you hit one of her trip wires."

"And will you come with me to the appeal meeting?" Elena asked. "It might be a good idea for me to have a witness."

The appeal meeting took place a couple of days later with the head of Housing. He was a grandfatherly gentleman. He seemed very nice, and I couldn't imagine, after Elena's excellent work for them, that he wouldn't give her another chance.

But that isn't what happened. "Elena, we're denying your appeal," he said sadly.

I felt stunned.

What could Elena have done? Granted, she had gotten run-down and been sick, and granted, she had had that night fright. But no one had even known about it. And RAs were student employees. They *were* given second chances. The idea was that this was part of their education, learning how to prepare for the business world.

Elena wasn't a risk taker. She prided herself on obeying rules, and she had worked hard to get this job for three solid months. Right before this, the managers had loved her. What could have happened?

If my daughter felt as stunned as I did, she didn't show it. She simply said in a courteous tone, "I'd like to know what this is all about." And then, just as she had done for Joe and me, she went on to relate all the different examples she knew of RAs who had gotten second chances.

But the head of Housing wouldn't elaborate. He didn't say, "It's because you were caught with alcohol in your room," or some other concrete rule violation. Instead, he launched into vague advice. Elena should take time to smell the roses. Losing this RA position would give her a chance to relax. She shouldn't be working so hard.

I felt even more stunned. Yes, Elena was tired, but what did that have to do with being competent at her job?

Elena just smiled and pointed out that she liked the work and was good at it. While she appreciated his concern, she felt—with no disrespect—that *she* should be the judge of what she could handle.

At this, the head of Housing put on a grave face. And then he said something so incredible that I could hardly believe I was hearing it:

"Resident assistants have to be role models to the students under their care. That's an unwritten contract I have with their parents. And in good conscience, Elena, I cannot put you forward as a role model for new students."

A high-GPA dean's list member for two semesters running.

An involved and outgoing volunteer on campus.

The winner of a rare departmental award.

And this girl wasn't a good role model?!

I fought down my fury. Excess emotion is a weakness. Logic and reason. Logic and reason!

What did I know that told badly against my daughter? Yes, she could be prickly to family, and yes, she tried to do too much. She was looking a little thin and stressed, but she wasn't excessively thin—not as thin as she'd been during the Summer from Hell, for instance. Yes, she saw a hallucination the other morning, but the mix of medicines almost certainly brought that on, and besides, who would have known, and why would anyone hold that against her? And I handled her finances, so I knew she hadn't had tickets or fines for bad behavior. Her paychecks were getting deposited straight into her account. There weren't odd withdrawals that might be drugs or alcohol.

Meanwhile, Elena kept her composure. She smiled and pointed out her dean's list status, her long record of volunteering, and her complete lack of disciplinary issues.

"I was the first RA chosen for this year's batch of fall hires," she said. "The managers watched my work all summer, and then the senior dorm manager said, 'We aren't sure about everybody we're keeping yet, but we knew we wanted you.' The university ambassadors asked me to join their group. They represent the best this school has to offer. But you're telling me that I'm not a good role model. Can you tell me why?"

The head of Housing looked distinctly uncomfortable. He also looked surprised. I got the feeling that this wasn't the result he had expected. I got the feeling that here again was a man who had hoped for tears and drama. They certainly would have strengthened his case.

"I'm sorry, Elena," he said. "But I'm not going to discuss this any further."

And that was the end of the meeting.

We left the office without speaking, got into my car, and started to drive. Elena still looked unruffled, but I knew she was seething. As for me, I felt as if I'd been punched in the gut.

"I don't get this!" I said. "I just don't get it!"

"I think I do," Elena said.

It had happened during their RA Orientation. "It was a sensitivity session," she said. "We were supposed to share our experiences with disabilities, and even share our own disabilities. So I stood up and told them about the people I'd met at Drew Center. It was to raise their awareness about eating disorders."

"That can't be all there is to it," I said. "Not to get you fired."

"When I was leaving the session, I walked by that new boss," Elena said, "the one who fired me but told me she didn't have to state a reason. She's a personal friend of the head of Housing, and he brought her in here to run the dorms over all his managers who applied for the job. She's never even worked at a university before, so she's got to be feeling insecure. She's a little pudgy, and she was wearing this short tight skirt, like she wants to project that no-nonsense businesswoman persona—I can tell that body image matters to her. And she was *glaring* at me. Just *glaring*."

No—it was incredible! It *couldn't* be true that a woman would fire another woman just for having an eating disorder—just for being thin! Besides, anorexia nervosa was a disability, wasn't it? And weren't we in the days of ADA now, where everyone on a college campus was supposed to help disabled students meet their potential?

Disabilities weren't supposed to matter anymore. They weren't supposed to hold anyone back.

"That boss is a new hire," I said. "Maybe she was just trying to look tough. I can't imagine that she was deliberately holding your eating disorder against you."

But on the other hand, the unimaginable had happened. My mind was still reeling, trying to take it all in.

I cannot put you forward as a role model. For God's sake! What did that even *mean*?

"Yeah, but that doesn't explain what she did next," Elena said. "She had my manager call me up that evening and ask me to come to the Counseling Center before Orientation the next morning. I thought it was to help that RA who was suicidal, but it wasn't. It was just me! That same new boss was there to walk me to the Counseling Center, and when I got out of the session they'd set up, the boss was *still* there, waiting around for me to get out of the session, like she had nothing else to do. And then she made me take the day off. She made me go back to my dorm room and miss a day of Orientation."

"I thought you said Orientation is mandatory."

"It is!" Elena said. "That's what I told her! But she wouldn't listen. And then, halfway through the day, two of the RA managers came by my door to 'check on me.' I was bitchy, sure. I told them they knew perfectly well I was off duty and that they had no business knocking on my door. They left after a couple of minutes. But right after they left, the police came."

"The police!"

"Yeah. They said they'd gotten a wellness-check call. And it came from one of the managers who'd just been there."

"Wellness check?"

"Suicide or drugs," Elena explained. "It's supposed to be when your life's in danger. If you don't open the door, they unlock it."

My brain was reeling even more now. I could barely drive. I focused for a few seconds on the street, the cars around me, the stores we were passing. There was the office-plants rental place that held a sale on used palms and bromeliads every couple of months. I'd always meant to stop by . . .

It didn't help. My brain kept on reeling. *Wellness check?* I said.

"That's what I said!" Elena told me. "And the police were pretty confused about it, too. They kept looking around, like they thought I was hiding the person they were supposed to check on."

"Were you maybe confused or disoriented when you talked to the managers?" I asked. "You were on that antibiotic medication by then, and sometimes you can have trouble waking up."

"Nope, I remember exactly what I said. I wasn't friendly about it, and I let them know that it was bullshit—they can't check up on off-duty RAs like that. But I didn't give them any reason to call the police."

"So . . . ," I said. "A Counseling Center visit, a special rest day, a room check, and then the police get called. It all adds up to you being unable to do your job—because you have a mental illness."

"It was a setup," Elena agreed. "That crap with the head of Housing about being a good role model—they don't want to turn me loose with students because I'm anorexic. And everybody knows that anorexics recruit other anorexics, right? People say that about us, that we get newbies hooked on our diets, we teach them our tricks . . . A lot of idiots treat anorexics like we've got a contagious disease."

That tone of voice, grandfatherly and sorrowful: *I cannot put you forward as a role model.*

"No—that's crazy!" I said. "I can hardly believe it."

But then again, the whole morning had been crazy. Overnight, our world had become crazy.

Again!

The plan. I clung to the plan. I didn't think beyond it. We had a deadline of midnight to move Elena's belongings out of her room. She was coming back home to live with us. The head of Housing had graciously removed the restriction against her living in the dorms, but Elena wouldn't do it.

We scrounged boxes and packed up Elena's pretty dorm room that she had just finished unpacking. My nerves were jangling like so many plucked guitar strings, and I just wanted to stand on Elena's balcony and scream. But she was strong and calm through it all. She had such dignity.

The Little Princess would have understood Elena that day. So would Heathcliff. So would a certain fiercely proud little freak in Goodwill clothes, sitting and reading next to the fence at the far corner of the playground.

It matters how you hold up your head in retreat. It matters how they look away when you look them in the eye.

We drove home and dismantled my tidy guest room, and Elena piled her boxes in the middle of its floor. She put Dylan's bowl on the counter of the hall bathroom. He was a bright blue spark of defiance in the red haze of the day.

The plan. I needed a plan. We had come to the end of this plan, so I started working on another one. "You can fight this," I told Elena as we sat down with cups of tea. "I'll help you if you want."

"Oh, yeah," Elena said. "Let's do this."

First, we went to the Counseling Center to check up on that odd morning appointment. The counselor who had spoken to Elena that day turned out to be surprisingly candid. Yes, she said, the new dorm boss had come in to speak to her as soon as Elena had left.

"She wanted to know if, in my opinion, you were competent to do your job," the counselor said. "I told her we don't make those sorts of judgments."

Competent to do her job! I felt the shock of that run through me. This girl who had assisted at surgeries, who had smiled and helped soldiers with bloodstained bandages on, with chunks of shrapnel still sticking out of them . . .

I felt the shock, and I felt fury. But I smiled, just as Elena was smiling. The plan. Stick to the plan.

"Would you be willing to write a letter to that effect," I asked, "to help us in a wrongful-termination case?"

"Oh, absolutely," the counselor said. "I'll be happy to do that. And to state this to a board of inquiry as well, if that comes up."

There: That was some good news for a change.

Then we went to the campus police station and talked to the police chief. We needed a copy of the police report filed after the wellness check. The police chief invited us into his office. He heard Elena out without interrupting, and he was thoughtful and sympathetic.

"That man who runs Housing is an idiot!" he said. "But they train us to keep an eye out for self-harm when we talk to our students. And I have to say," he said, taking Elena gently by the wrist, "that this looks like it might be self-harm to me."

He pointed to a pink scar that spiraled down Elena's forearm. And he didn't ask the question, but his eyes did.

I leaned forward in my chair. I knew when the cut had occurred: it dated from the day last October when Elena had ended up in the ER with her blackout. I knew what Elena had told me about it afterward: it was an accident that had occurred while she was unconscious. I had seen how her arms circled during her dissociation blackouts, so I had assumed that that's how it had happened.

But what did I know about this scar—really?

Elena smiled at the police chief. She seemed completely at ease. "That," she said, pointing at the scar, "was an accident. But I'll be honest: I was pretty drunk at the time."

The police chief checked his department's records and discovered that his officers didn't even write up a report after the wellness check because they hadn't seen anything worth reporting. In fact, they could see no reason why they had been called to Elena's room. So the police chief supplied us with evidence of the nonreport, as well as a statement that Elena had a completely clean record at the school.

"It certainly looks suspicious to me," he told us.

That was more good news. The plan was going well.

That was all we could do for one day. We drove home and tried to busy ourselves with normal things. But I couldn't manage to do this. I was in complete turmoil. The more it seemed that Elena had been fired unfairly, the more upset I got. My brain couldn't stop scheming, making plans, making lists of questions and bullet points: meetings to set up, advice to gather, calls to make . . .

Nighttime came. Midnight came. I lay in bed and tried to relax, but it was completely out of the question. The minutes crawled by while I lay there, perfectly still, silently battling what felt like a kind of hysteria.

The ax had fallen.

Again.

Our normal, reasonable, safe world had blown apart.

Again!

Why? I almost screamed out loud. *Why did this happen* again?

Joe wasn't there. He had left for a dream vacation with my brother, hiking in the mountains of Wyoming. The two of them had planned the vacation for years. Now, poor Joe felt terrible. He couldn't help me at all. He couldn't even call to hear the latest developments unless he walked to a hill several hundred yards from their campsite.

"It's okay," I tried to tell him. I didn't want to ruin his precious free time. I wanted him to know that I had everything under control. But each time we talked, I ended up crying on the phone. I could hold it together for everybody else, but I couldn't when I talked to Joe.

I tried my best to be normal. I cooked Elena and me fine meals, and I did everything I always did. But for the entire week after Elena's firing, I lost a pound a day.

It wasn't because Elena was home. That was no hardship. I loved her company, and I knew all too well that I would have plenty of years away from her. It was a blessing to share as much time with my daughter as I could.

But somehow, this shock had triggered PTSD for me. It was if time had telescoped, and it was the Summer from Hell all over again. It was as if the dorm boss and Dr. Petras had gotten together to attack Elena, and Valerie was walking into the room again, covered in burns.

The ax had fallen.

Again.

The ax had fallen *again*!

By day, I joked with Elena and petted my dog. But each night, I lay awake, hyperventilating, while the hours crawled slowly by, and I thought, *It's happened again! It's happened again! This cannot be happening* again*!*

So we fought it this time. We didn't just sit there and suffer. We collected our statements and our reports. Our last stop, after we had everything put together, was the university's Equal Employment Opportunity (EEO) office.

The lawyer we talked to looked over our material and admitted that the sequence of events looked suspicious. He wasn't sure he could treat the case as an EEO violation, but he promised to look into it as carefully as he could. He told us he'd get back to us in two or three weeks.

Then we left campus. We had done all we could do.

"Can I get a manicure?" Elena begged. "I'm tired of thinking about this. I just want a nice distraction."

So I drove her to the mall and sat beside her while she got French nails. There were small bamboos in clear glass vases all around us, and the floor and the counters were gray slate. The young Asian lady who worked on Elena's hands applied the French nails with lightning speed. Meanwhile, she carried on an equally rapid and entirely indecipherable conversation with the nail salon worker next to her.

Their language fascinated me. It was like the liquid music of songbirds.

Meanwhile, Elena delivered an engrossing lecture on the purposes of all the mysterious tools and potions on the nail salon tray. Then she ventured on a brief but highly entertaining roundup of nail-salon scenes in recent movies. She ended with a description of favorite manicures and explained why she liked French nails best. The variations are more interesting, she said, and if they're done well, they're the most natural-looking nail.

I paid for Elena's new French nails, and she walked out, smiling.

But the next morning, as I passed the hall bathroom, I caught her peeling them all off.

I didn't know then, but I know now: Elena had gotten the manicure to distract herself from engaging in the kind of behavior that fed her eating disorder. And maybe it had worked for one day. But not for two.

Elena's world had blown apart—again. And whether she liked it or not, her mind was reaching for the only defense it knew. Against the bullies, all Elena had was starvation. It was the only force strong enough to stop the monsters and silence the humiliation and fury.

Or, as Elena would put it later: "Ah, yes . . . the vomit hand."

My daughter's anorexia nervosa was back.

With a vengeance.

CHAPTER TWENTY-FIVE

School didn't start for another week, so Joe and I sent Elena out to Georgia to Valerie's apartment, to have a vacation with her sister. Unsettled, I wandered through the house, finding new places for things. Elena had taken down my decorations from the guest room and left them in a neat stack on the bed. She wanted to put up her mermaid picture when she got back.

I stood in the guest room—now, her room—and remembered when this had been Valerie's and Elena's room. Their bunk beds had been right over there.

While I was lost in wistful memories, Genny trotted past me and jumped up onto Elena's bed.

"No, come out of here," I told the old terrier. "I have to shut this door."

From the depths of Elena's pillow, the little dog eyed me sadly.

"Genny, come on!" I said. "I have to shut this before . . ."

And, sure enough, Simon strolled in.

"Okay, now, both of you," I said, picking up the black cat. He wasn't fat, but he was so big that he overflowed my arms. "Now, Genny. Come on!"

But Genny just continued to gaze at me, so I put down Simon and went to pick up Genny instead. I pitched her through the door and gave the double-clap that meant *exit*. Simon ran out of the room. He might be a cat, but he was better trained than the dog was . . .

. . . in some ways.

The reason all the bedroom doors were closed was that Simon had taken to spraying again. He was an indoor cat, and he was upset that the dog got to go outside. He longed to get at the birds and—even more—at the other cats, who came and taunted him through the window. Simon was neutered in body but most certainly not neutered in mind.

Before Genny had come along, Simon had been heading into sleepy old age. But the sight of the terrier cavorting in the Saint Augustine grass outside every day had fired up his cat spirit. Now, he sang battle songs through the window at the feral cats, and when they sprayed the back door, he sprayed back—in my house.

Everybody wants things I can't give them, I thought with a sigh as I gathered up the pictures. *Where to put these? This place needs more storage.*

My quest for storage options took me into the hall bathroom, where Dylan was circling around and around his little stone pagoda. I stopped to admire his shiny blue beauty, and he puffed out his fins for me. The pleated fins fell in soft waves around his blue body like the cascades of hair on a pampered show dog.

"It's easy to take care of him," Elena had told me before she left. "Here's his food. Here's his chemical drops. Change twenty-five percent of his water one time while I'm gone."

But as I watched Dylan sail grandly past in a parade of one, I worried. Fish are fragile. Such sad little lives . . .

My overactive imagination immediately started supplying me unwanted snippets of film: Simon, with his long black arm stretched into the bowl, raking open Dylan's gorgeous blue skin. Tor, bumping his tabby face against the glass and rolling the round goldfish bowl off the counter.

How improbable is it, anyway, I thought, *that fish need to take their entire habitat into our world? What if dogs and cats had to do that?*

And my imagination promptly supplied me an image of a cat in a space suit, hooked up to a portable breathing machine.

Besides, I worried, *isn't that bowl too small? And what about the temperature? The air conditioner is blowing right on him. And won't he go crazy, swimming around and around? He doesn't have anything to* do*!*

By the time Elena got home at the end of the week, Dylan was living in a five-gallon tank with its own heater, light, filter, and locking lid. He loved threading his way through his new silk plants. I even found him sleeping on the leaves.

"I think he likes the background I printed out for him," I told her. "I catch him studying it sometimes. The book says you should move his plants around each time you change the water so he'll have a little variety. And look, I got him ping-pong balls to float on the top. I read that some bettas like to play with them. And I'm teaching him to bite my finger for his food. I practice with him four times a day."

"Mom," Elena said, "I *seriously* think you're overthinking this."

She was right. But as I watched Dylan drift majestically through his watery realm, I felt happy. "*Such* a beauty you are!" I crooned to him. "You're *such* a blingy boy!"

Three weeks after our earlier visit, the campus lawyer called us back, and Elena and I went to his office for a meeting.

"Here's the thing: I can't pursue this under EEO," he said. "There's precedent right now that's not allowing it. But I called in the manager who fired you and questioned her anyway, and I'm positive she was telling me lies. She told me she fired you because you had failed to report a suicide attempt."

"That's not true," Elena said. "I told them about a suicidal RA *before* he made an attempt."

"That's what I told her you had reported to me, and then I asked her if that RA was still working for her. She couldn't explain to me why she had fired *you* for not reporting an attempt but hadn't fired *him* for making an attempt. She was very uncomfortable during the interview," he added.

This brought a smile to Elena's face. It wasn't a pleasant smile, but at least it was there. And it probably matched the one on my own.

"I'm sure you can win if you take this to the university employment office," he said. "If she's going to use that rationale, then there's no excuse for her firing one of you but not both of you. I hope you *do* pursue it," he concluded as he gave us a copy of his written report.

Good, I thought as we walked back to the car. *The plan is working. It's going well.*

"So," I said, "we can call the employment office when we get home." And my mind was already filling up with lists: *phone call to the employment office; best times for a face-to-face meeting; where did I put those copies of the reports and letters we collected?*

"No, Mom," Elena said. "I don't want to do it."

This stopped my list-making cold.

"Why not?" I said. "You heard him say you'll probably win."

"Win what?" she said. "My job is already gone. They put somebody else in my place. So what are they going to do if we pin them to the wall? They'll get rid of the RA who has my floor now, or they'll fire that other RA. Mom, he's a pathetic loser. Without that job, he can't finish school."

"That pathetic loser probably did all he could to get *you* fired."

"So?" Elena's voice was sad. "He's fat, and he's ugly, and his parents control his whole life. I was his only friend. I know he's evil, but his world is very small—I knew that when I spent time with him. I don't want to be what he is—I don't want to be the kind of person who works to get somebody else fired. Honestly, Mom, I just want to forget about it."

I fell silent. I had encouraged Elena to pursue this appeal because I had hoped to force the university into giving her the job back. But it hadn't occurred to me that some other enterprising RA now had her floor. And it hadn't occurred to me to think about how the bottom would drop out for that other student if he or she suddenly lost the income and the free room and board.

It had occurred to Elena, though. In the middle of her own pain, she could feel compassion for that unknown RA. She could even feel compassion for the scummy RA who had probably contributed to getting her fired—and who undoubtedly would pay the price if her appeal succeeded.

My daughter is a better person than I am, I thought. *She's better in so many ways.*

But stopping the appeal didn't just mean taking the high road. It also meant accepting defeat. It meant reliving the pain and rejection of that hard, bitter day.

As we reached the parking lot, Elena pulled out a pack of cigarettes and lit one. I looked away. Filth and dirt and slow destruction, all the worst aspects of self-indulgence and self-contempt . . . And now, after having fought it in Valerie's life, I was having to watch it sink its teeth into Elena.

For the sake of her unborn baby, Valerie had immediately stopped smoking cigarettes. I'd had exactly one week to celebrate. Then Elena had told me that she had taken up the habit. She'd started it during the stress of the summer, as a way to handle the pressure of three jobs.

The weeks passed. Joe and Elena and I settled into a pleasant rhythm together in the house. Once again, we had her lively company to brighten our days and make us laugh. And I certainly didn't get lonely now when Joe needed to go on long business trips.

But Elena lived on a different schedule than Joe and I did. Thanks to the gym job, she had gotten used to staying up at night, so she went to bed when she got home from class. Then, late at night, when Joe and I were heading to bed, she got up to study or go out with friends.

This should have been good for me. It meant that I had all afternoon to do quiet things, like writing and updating web pages. But I quickly figured out that it also meant Elena was skipping lunch *and* dinner. And that started up the worries again.

"I eat when I get up, after you're in bed," she told me. I wanted to believe her, but I couldn't. I was the one who bought groceries and cleaned the kitchen, and I didn't see any food disappearing. So I started developing strategies to keep Elena awake in the afternoon long enough to get her to eat.

"Hey, do you want to watch *Gilmore Girls* with me?" I said when she got home from school. "I'm working my way through the series."

"Sure thing," Elena answered, and she curled up in her fuzzy blanket on the media room floor while I put in the DVD.

"I'm getting some ice cream," I added casually. "You want some? Rocky road . . ."

"Sure! I'll take a scoop," Elena answered.

Day after day, I filled two cups with rocky road ice cream, or butter pecan, or chocolate fudge, and we ate it while we watched old movies and television shows. It was the perfect plan. While they were on, Elena couldn't use talking to block the food.

Elena and I had a great time together. After the show, we would sit and talk for hours sometimes. I started to put on a few more pounds from the rich snacks, but I could always lose them later. And it was good to see Elena having a good time and eating a little ice cream, even if she never seemed to finish her cup.

After a couple of hours, Elena would get up, blinking sleepily, wrap the fuzzy blanket around her middle, and shamble off to smoke a prenap cigarette on the patio.

"Mom!" she would call about half the time. "Simon and Tor got out *again!*"

At first, I chased them down and brought them back inside. But then I gave up.

Would the cats be okay? It was just one more thing to worry about, but I couldn't fight on every front at once. Joe, Martin, Elena, Simon and Tor, Valerie and Clint and the grandbaby . . . I was starting to have to pick my priorities, and Martin and the cats were losing.

Oh, well. At least the cats loved it outside. And Martin—

Martin was having to grow up.

Last year had been the most successful writing year I'd had. I had brought in almost as much money as Joe did. But this year had been completely miserable. Martin's first adventure had come out, but the publishing house had shoved it down a hole. They had done no marketing at all. Almost no one knew that his first book even existed.

I didn't feel it as a blow to me personally. I had never felt like a real author. But the thought of Martin and his dog, Chip, out there on their own, having the adventure of a lifetime . . . They should have had reader friends to go with them on that journey.

First, I had failed to help Elena. Now I'd failed Martin, too, and my sadness over these failures soaked into his world. They didn't change who Martin was, but they changed what happened to him.

One afternoon, I sat at the kitchen table and sipped my coffee. My laptop was open, and I was rereading a marked-up Word file, working on some last-minute revisions. But I wasn't seeing words. I was seeing what Martin was seeing. He was face-to-face with heartbreak and loss.

> Martin couldn't make up his mind about the skeleton
> slumped over the table. One second, it seemed small
> and pitiful. The next, it seemed uncanny and horribly

inhuman, and he wanted to smash it with the nearest heavy object he could find.

Rudy had told him that the people who hadn't gotten picked for the domed suburbs had lined up to be given euthanasia shots.

"I guess I'd want to die at home too," Martin murmured to Chip. "You know, have a little peace and quiet."

Because skeletons were only people, after all—people who had faced the ultimate rejection and experienced the ultimate failure.

Martin plucked up the courage to come closer. Dry brown skin encased the bony hand in a glove of its own making. It lay in that flattish nest of fur that was piled up in the basket. A pet basket to match the little paw print bowls in the kitchen. A cat bed. The pale fur belonged to a cat.

A vision wove itself together in Martin's mind of the house before the dust, when the neat row of potted plants in the kitchen had been green and flourishing. The world was ending, and people were forming long lines to get their shot. But this man with the paw print bowls couldn't do that. What would happen to his cat? He couldn't just put her outside and not come back. He loved her too much. So he gave his cat poison and stroked her until she lay still, and then he took poison himself. And the soft fur of his cat was the last thing he felt as he drifted away into death.

Martin's throat ached. He knelt down and buried his face in his dog's shaggy fur. "I wouldn't leave you, either, Chip," he said. "Not ever."

The door banged open, and I turned away from the laptop screen with relief. Thank goodness! An interruption.

"Oh. My. God!" Elena said as she dropped her purse and books on the piano bench. "I've *got* to play you this song. It's a-*maz*-ing! Here, let me see your laptop."

"Wait! I have to save my file. How'd you do on your statistics test?"

"Kicked *ass*! Best grade in the class."

I was in no hurry to get back to Martin and his skeleton. Sadness and worry seemed to be all around me these days. "Which song is it?" I asked as I pulled up YouTube.

Elena and I sat and chatted and swapped favorite songs and YouTube videos for a happy half hour or so. Then she gave a yawn. "I'm going to go lie down," she said. "I've been up since four, studying."

"How about letting me fix you a little lunch," I offered. But I already knew what the answer would be.

"Nah, not right now. Later."

Later . . .

That meant *never*.

"I could do with a break," I said, following her across the living room. "How about a *Sherlock Holmes*?"

Elena and I both adored Jeremy Brett as Sherlock Holmes. As far as we were concerned, he had been genetically engineered to play that role.

"Okay," she said. "But I get to pick which one."

"Caramel corn?" I offered, turning back to the kitchen.

"Hells yeah!" she answered.

Yes! I thought. *A win!* And I sprinkled the caramel corn into two bowls with a generous hand—even though I knew I would be the only one to finish mine.

Sometime later, my daughter finally headed off to bed, and I returned with the stacked bowls to the kitchen. I snacked on the rest of her caramel corn while I opened up my laptop again. Martin's story was going through final edits, under deadline. I *had* to do my writing!

I opened up the file again, stared at the black letters against white, and waited for my imagination to bring me the right film. I waited while it flitted through scenes of YouTube kittens and the *Sherlock Holmes* episode. He was brilliant! That nervous twitch, the sudden turn of the head away from the villain . . .

Now I was seeing the interior of the pantry. Was there anything in there that maybe Elena would eat later tonight?

I closed my eyes and took a long, calming breath.

Finally, the turbulent rush of images stilled, and I could focus on the text again. I was in a dusty room. Martin had a lump in his throat. He was hugging his dog . . .

"Mom!" Elena yelled from her bedroom. "The cat peed in here again, all over my pillows!"

And *poof*! Martin was gone.

"You've *got* to keep your door shut!" I called back.

"I *do* keep my door shut! They sneak in!" Which was certainly true. And they *were* my cats, after all.

I set aside my laptop to go retrieve the pillows and wash them. *That's a good use of time, too*, I thought, perking up. *I'll separate the laundry. It's starting to pile up. I'll wait to work on this file until the house quiets down tonight.*

Anything to put it off. Anything to keep from living through Martin's sadness as well as my own.

"Close the door," Elena murmured as I carried the offending pillows out of her room.

My phone buzzed as I was loading the washer. Valerie had sent me an ultrasound. And there she was, in black and white: my granddaughter.

I felt joy. And I felt pain. The two were mixed together so that they couldn't possibly be separated. Joyful pain. Painful joy. The gift of every child to every mother.

That new life opens up a door—a door to feelings so wonderful and so agonizing that we can't imagine them ahead of time. No matter what happens, that door can't be closed again.

Valerie didn't know this yet. She was still invincible. But I already knew what waited for her. As happy as I was over this precious new life, I felt worry and pain for my daughter.

"How are you feeling?" I asked her when she called a few minutes later.

"Not bad," Valerie said. "Still kind of a nervous wreck, though. Everybody's so thrilled, and I'm so stressed. And my back *hurts*! Yesterday I had to lie down in one of the fitting rooms for half an hour before I could go back to work."

"Everything loosens up when you're pregnant," I said. "It's got to be rough that you're on your feet seven hours a day."

"Yeah, that reminds me," she said. "My feet hurt, too."

Lately, Joe and I had been discussing a plan with our Georgia kids. Clint was scheduled to go into Air Force basic training in the spring. Valerie's lease would be up in March. We'd offered to bring Valerie out here to live with us while Clint was going through his training. Then the Air Force would start moving the three of them around as a family.

But this thought awakened a new swarm of worries in my mind. So much needed to get done—

Specifically, Martin's book needed to get done.

Joe knew this, too. At dinner, he asked, "So, how much writing did you get done?"

"Not too much," I said, thinking with guilty misery about the neglected file. "I don't know where the time went."

Where *had* my time gone today? What *had* I accomplished? A few pages of edits, a bowl and a half of caramel corn, and three loads of laundry.

Joe didn't comment, but I could see the disappointment on his face, and that disappointment hurt. I just wasn't very good at balancing my priorities, I thought. I didn't have the knack of pleasing everybody at once.

Joe and I washed the dinner dishes. Okay, no more interruptions now. I would get to that file—very soon. But first, I would practice piano, just for a few minutes, just to clear my head. That would take my mind off my worries.

Or would it?

Lately, even the piano made me feel guilty and unhappy. Week after week now, I didn't seem to get any practicing done. Each time I saw the piano teacher, my old friend, I felt her patience with my lack of progress. But it hurt. I was failing even at my hobby.

Now, I ran through last week's song over and over. My hands were so clumsy! They never seemed to be where my brain told them to be. But slowly, the plaintive melody formed under my fingers. It was a little piece in D minor. It sounded like a Russian folk tune.

As I played, my mind filled with scenes of snow. Then a city floated up among the snow drifts, all gray columns and gray stone, with a white, frozen river threading through it.

"Mom?"

There was a broad window with light shining out, golden light that sparkled like champagne. Tall men in black evening dress floated past the golden window, clasping pale women in flowing ball gowns.

"Mom."

A peasant clumped by beneath the window, out on the icy street. His long brown beard was snowy, and his feet were wrapped in rags.

"Mom!"

Elena was at my elbow.

"Can't you do that later?" she begged. "I was up all night studying for my exam."

In my mind, I reached for the snow-filled city again. "But I can't keep putting it off," I said. "I never practice anymore!"

"You can practice while I'm at school."

"But I don't. That's when I write." *Try to write*, I corrected myself.

"You can write while I'm asleep."

"But I don't! It's too late in the day by then!"

"Mom, *please*."

The city was gone. Elena's face was all I could see now. It was exhausted. No, not just exhausted—drawn and pale.

Remorse and worry shot through me. *She's sick again*, I thought. *She just got over being sick, and now she's sick again!*

"Please?" Elena said again.

So I stopped.

I need to drop these piano lessons anyway, I thought. *We'll have a baby in the house soon. And I've got deadlines. I need to save up my time for writing. And speaking of writing, I need to get back to Martin.*

The edits weren't going to go well, I realized with gloomy certainty. They were going to be . . .

Gloomy.

But they had to get done. They *had* to get done!

Anyway, it was good that Martin was facing these kinds of scenes. He needed to learn that life wasn't going to be all that I had hoped for him. I had wanted him to have reader friends, but that wasn't going to happen now. He would have to get used to loneliness and neglect.

Even my characters wanted things I couldn't give them.

CHAPTER TWENTY-SIX

The next week, my oldest and dearest friend came to town to pay me a visit, the one who, once upon a time, had held deep philosophical conversations on the playground with a certain ugly little freak. "Why do we even need feelings?" she had asked me back then as our classmates had run and played and balls had bounced around us. "What do feelings add to our lives besides trouble and pain?"

It hadn't occurred to us back then that we should have been letting ourselves be children.

Throughout our whole lives, this dear friend and I had never stayed out of touch for more than a couple of months at a time. But we had the chance to see each other only every half year or so, when one or the other of us made the trek up or down six hours of highway. This time, she had made that long drive. She had come to stay with me for three precious days—a chance for us both to catch up, cheer up, and reconnect with what mattered in ourselves.

The day after my friend arrived, the two of us were in the living room, chatting, when Elena threw open her bedroom door:

"You didn't wake me up!"

I remembered as soon as Elena said it. When she had come dragging home from school that day, she had asked me to wake her up for a meeting she needed to attend. Elena had been going to set her alarm, too, but she almost never woke up for her alarm anymore. It was all I could do some days to get her to wake up for me.

She was starting to sleep like the dead.

"You promised you'd wake me up!" Elena cried. "I counted on you!" And, across the coffee table, I saw my old friend asking questions with her eyebrows.

Those were questions I didn't want to answer.

The presence of a visitor made me take in the details more keenly. Elena's voice, for instance: I registered with a shock that it was a shrill, exhausted monotone again.

It sounded as it had during her senior year.

"Honey, I'm sorry," I said. "Really, I am. I just forgot." And Elena, worn out by the unusual effort, turned around and crept back to bed.

"She's sick right now," I said by way of explanation, and my friend nodded and let the subject drop. But once again, worries seized and shook me. Elena was sick more than she was well these days.

Around ten thirty that night, as my friend and I were sharing some after-dinner chocolate, Elena passed through the room again. This time, she was wearing makeup and strappy heels. She picked up her purse and her car keys off the piano bench.

And my friend's eyebrows started to ask questions again.

"Where are you going?" I asked Elena.

"Study session for statistics. I don't know when I'll be back."

"But you're not feeling well," I pointed out.

She certainly wasn't *looking* well. Again, I seemed to see my daughter with fresh eyes.

Elena's extra-small double-zero skinny jeans were baggy at the rear. There was no rear to hold them up anymore. Her arms and legs were so long and spindly that she looked like a colt trying to stand for the first time. I half expected to see those legs fold up and drop her to the ground.

Panic gripped me. When had this happened? How had I missed seeing how thin she was getting? I had known that she was back to not eating, of course. I tried every single day to get her to eat. But I hadn't realized how bad it was now. I had let myself not notice.

"You've missed dinner again," I said, trying to control my panic. "Take a minute to grab a sandwich."

"We're ordering pizza," Elena said. "I'll eat there."

For the sake of my friend, I didn't cross-examine Elena. But I was pretty sure this wasn't true.

Elena wasn't back the next morning before my friend left. Both of us studiously avoided mentioning her. But I could see the look in my old friend's eyes: the worry and concern.

Why do *we have to have feelings?* I wanted to ask her. *Did either one of us ever figure that out?* But instead, I hugged her tightly as we said good-bye. It wasn't as if her life was a picnic, either.

Elena didn't get home that day until almost noon. I tried calling, but she didn't pick up her phone. Was she safe? Was she sick? Mornings like this left me feeling completely helpless. I felt old. I was starting to feel so old.

"So, how was the study session?" I asked as she dragged herself through the front door.

Elena looked horrible. She looked more ill than before. "Study session?" she muttered, baffled.

"The one you're just coming home from."

"Oh. We got a lot done."

"And class?"

"Class got canceled."

"Canceled? Really?"

"The professor's sick," she muttered as she dropped her purse and car keys on the piano bench. And before I could ask any more questions, her bedroom door banged shut.

Helicopter parent or not, I dug in, and I started fighting. I went back to nagging full-time. It had gotten Elena through her senior year, I told myself. Maybe it would get her through the last few weeks of the fall semester to the Christmas break.

"Come out here and eat some breakfast!" I called.

"I'm not hungry," she called back.

"Come out here and eat some breakfast anyway!" I called.

"Stay out of my business!" she yelled.

"You don't *let* me stay out of your business," I answered. "You've made me your alarm clock *and* your taxi service!" Because, more and more often, Elena seemed to find ways to rely on me for rides.

Why did I do it? Why did I haul her around? Because at least I knew it would get her safely to class. I was holding my breath now over each final project and each exam. I wasn't sure she'd manage to pull it all off.

Once again, I was lying in bed at night, unable to sleep, while I turned over options. Everything I came up with was sadly inadequate. Elena was an adult. I had no authority to order her to treatment. Besides, given how badly she responded to shows of force, I couldn't imagine that forcing her into care would work.

But persuasion—that never worked either.

Please, dear Lord, I prayed. *Please help Elena get through this! She needs your help. She needs all our help! She's like a racehorse running on a broken leg.*

Anorexia came and went in cycles, I reminded myself with more optimism than evidence. When Elena was under stress, it got worse. When she did well at her goals, it got better. The firing from her RA job at the start of the semester had made this episode very bad. But maybe a successful finals week would change that.

So I rousted Elena out of bed to study. I drove her to class. And each day, as I watched her struggle off through the crowd, with her skinny spine bent beneath the almost unsupportable weight of her backpack, I begged: *Please, Lord,* please *just get my poor sick daughter to the winter break so she can recharge.*

But I recognized the sad irony of that prayer: *Lord, didn't I ask you for the same thing last summer?*

On the drive home one afternoon during finals week, Elena's cell phone rang. "Can't they just leave me alone?" she said out loud, and her voice held more genuine emotion than I had heard from her in weeks. Then she answered the phone, and I expected to hear that honey-sweet voice kick in, the one she saved for friends but not for me.

"Oh, yeah?" she said, smiling at the phone. "Yeah, I wish I could, too."

But it wasn't that honey-sweet voice. It was a gruff parody of it, as if Elena were making that voice in her mind, but her vocal cords couldn't pull it off. What came out was a gravelly, colorless voice. An old voice.

Elena's face looked old now, too, I realized with a jolt. She'd always had a striking face, but now, in the bright Texas sunlight pouring through the windshield, that face was a little bit shocking.

Her skin was sallow and rough. Her forehead was bony. And was her hairline actually receding? It seemed higher on her forehead now, so thin, so brittle and dull. She fussed over it all the time and applied countless treatments to it, but none of them made any difference.

It was as if my daughter was gone, and in her place was a skinny little refugee from some famine country, looking very old and very young at the same time, impossible to match to an age. I could see wrinkles under her sunken eyes. I could see the cords at the corners of her mouth that pulled her dry lips into a parody of a flirtatious smile.

"Yeah, I can't. I'm in Austin right now," she was saying. "No, it's a concert. I'm here overnight. Maybe tomorrow." And she hung up the phone.

"Is that Ryan?" I asked.

"Yeah."

"Didn't you tell him you had a party to go to when he called a couple of hours ago?"

"Dunno."

"You tell these wild stories to your friends," I pointed out. *And to me,* I added in my mind. "There's no way they can believe you. You don't keep the stories straight."

Elena was gazing blankly at the cars going by. After a minute she said, "So?"

I felt panic. I couldn't reach her. She was slipping away again—slipping away from health and curiosity and life.

When had she last told me a story?

We pulled up to the house. "You parked your car against traffic again," I said, and the panic inside me made me raise my voice. "You did it *again*! You know it drives Dad crazy. You're going to get a ticket!"

How many times had we fought over this? How many times had she raised her voice and told me to mind my own business? But now she said simply, "I'll move it." Her voice was a ghost, a thing almost without breath.

"And while you're at it," I snapped, "get it closer to the curb!"

This was completely unfair. The car wasn't that far from the curb. I said it just to hear her tell me that—to yell at me, to fight back.

Push up! I begged her in my mind. *Push back on your stepping-stone—push up into life!*

But she didn't.

"Yeah, I'll fix it," she muttered as she slid out of the car and left me alone with my worries.

Winter break came a few frantic days later. Against all odds, Elena closed out the semester with excellent grades. Now the pressure was off. Yes! The pressure was off! Maybe she would start to eat again!

I dragged her to the grocery store and put anything into the cart that she so much as glanced at.

Christmas came. Joe and I went out of town to visit family. Last year, Elena had stayed in town because she was too busy to slow down. This year . . .

What about this year?

"I'm going to be busy," she told me in the barest of whispers from underneath the covers. "You go have fun. You deserve it. And shut the door, please. You and Dad are so loud."

So we left her there, with Pop-Tarts in the kitchen—anything I thought she might eat. Maybe it was good that I would be gone for a while, I thought. Maybe my nagging made things worse.

The little vacation eased my worries for a few days. The year was ending—the bad year. *Another* bad year! But this next year was going to be a good year. My granddaughter was about to be born, and three months later, she would be living with Joe and Elena and me.

"I can't wait to get this over with," Valerie said on the phone as Joe and I drove home across Texas. "The baby's bouncing around in there like a basketball!"

"Pregnancy," I said. "It's the only thing bad enough to make life with a newborn seem like a dream come true."

"I believe it," Valerie said. "I believe it."

Her practical good sense steadied me.

Valerie hung up, and I daydreamed the miles away. Yes, this year would be different. This was going to be a better year. We reached the house, and I opened the door full of good resolutions: plans to make, talks to have, meals to try.

But Elena hadn't had a good vacation in our absence. She seemed to have had a falling-out with friends. I heard her yelling into the phone, with a frantic edge to her voice—a wounded sound. I stopped by her room to check on her, but she waved me out.

And on top of it all, Elena was down with the flu, she said. The flu—after everything else! How was this fragile girl ever going to finish college?

All that week, Elena lay in bed. And then another week. I prowled in and out of her bedroom. I brought her plates of snacks. Then I took them away again, untouched.

"Can I make you some soup?" I asked one evening.

Elena lay motionless in the darkened room. Her shade was down, and the light was off. "I'm having pizza with friends later," she muttered.

But Elena stayed in her room all night, and no friends came by with pizza.

I didn't really think they would.

Next week will be better, I thought. *Sometimes the flu lasts two weeks, but not three. Anyway, Elena's got school soon, and that'll get her out of bed. Maybe she's finally recharging. This could be good, right? After all, I'm the one who begged her to rest.*

The days continued to creep by.

Elena stayed in bed.

"When do your classes start?" I asked, standing at the door of her bedroom.

"Next week," whispered the mound beneath the covers.

"No, they started last week," I told her. "I looked it up."

"The ethics professor sent out a note. She had an accident. We're starting late."

"Okay . . . Well, what about your other classes?"

"The Tuesday-Thursday classes start this Thursday."

I pondered these statements. Could they really be true?

No, they couldn't possibly be true.

But then again, if they weren't true, that meant Elena had missed the first day of school.

Could *that* possibly be true?

This was the girl who, from first grade on, couldn't wait to get home each day to start on her schoolwork. This was the girl who read ahead in her textbooks for *fun*. This was the girl who rewrote her notes in five different colors of ink. I still had a tin box with thousands of her handmade flash cards in it, Latin flash cards with German on the back.

Elena, missing the first day of *school*? How could that even happen?

Shocked, I pondered new strategies. A plan. I needed a plan. "Do you want to go to the mall?" I asked. "Maybe get a manicure? Some clothes for the new semester?"

This was the best gambit I had. Elena was a die-hard shopper. During high school, she had wheedled me out of more money for clothes than was good for either one of us.

"No, you go ahead," the mound of blankets answered from within the darkened room. "Find something nice for yourself."

"Really?" I asked, lingering. "You don't want anything? No new clothes?"

And the hollow voice drifted out from the lump under the covers:

"I've already got everything I need."

That night, I lay awake in bed, almost frantic with worry. The semester break hadn't helped. Elena hadn't recharged. She was getting weaker and thinner by the day. When was the last time I had seen her eat? I couldn't even remember.

Like a cold weight settling on my chest, reality sank in. Elena hadn't gotten up for the first week of class. That meant she wasn't going to get up. She didn't intend to get up again. Ever.

I lay there in the dark, and I prayed, and I pondered, and I forced myself to face the facts:

Elena was dying.

Elena was killing herself.

And there was nothing I could do to make her stop.

CHAPTER TWENTY-SEVEN

Once I realized this—once I felt that knowledge all the way through to my bones—I couldn't just lie there anymore. I had to get out of bed. I wanted to go shake Elena and wake her up. I wanted to tell her about the cliff I saw, about how close she was to going over . . .

But I knew what would happen. Elena wouldn't wake up well.

She'd raise her voice. Then I'd raise my voice. We'd end up yelling about something completely different, like why she always answered her phone when I was talking to her but never answered when I was the one calling.

Or maybe not. Maybe she'd lie there and whisper agreements: *Sure, Mom. I know, Mom.* That would mean she wasn't even listening at all.

I talk, I thought, *but the two of us don't talk. It's just me, talking at her. Whenever I say something good, it breaks against my daughter like a wave. I can see my words flow away and get lost. But the bad things I say—they crawl inside my child, and they stay inside her forever.*

As I thought about these things, I wandered from place to place in my dim house, trying to find the comfort that would help me resurrect my sense of hope. I find hope easily—too easily. It's almost a failing of mine. A cat settles down into a soft circle on the sofa, and I decide that I'm worrying too much. A cup of tea makes all things right again.

But now, I found no comfort, and I found no hope. My fear and helplessness were so intense that they seemed to be toxic drugs flooding through my body. Poison seemed to be spreading inside me, weakening me, attacking healthy cells. Meanwhile, the night crept on outside my windows, and the darkness smothered me.

Maybe daylight was only an illusion. Maybe the night would never end.

I didn't know what I would say as I began the letter. I just needed so desperately to reach my daughter, sick and sleeping her life away in the next room. The things I needed to tell her were bursting through my skin.

> Dear Elena,
>> I'm so sorry for how you're feeling these days . . .

I wrote, and I wasn't even sure what I wrote. The act of writing seemed more important than the words.

> Of all the people I know, you are the most outward-seeking, the most inquisitive. That makes you naturally active. You find your happiness in observing others—and, after observing, in helping—in celebrating—others.
>> But you've found a way to change that. It's called starvation.

My sentences were stumbling over one another, shadowed by worry and lack of sleep. Probably they weren't saying anything very helpful.

> Food doesn't help us be. It helps us do. It enables us to volunteer, to see the world, to accomplish our goals. It gives us the power to change lives. Your future patients need you. Little children who haven't been born yet need you. Your real friends—the ones like you, who have compassion and who want to help the world—need you. Your busy days need you to be able to meet them, complete them, get out there and get things done.

My sentences filled one page, and then another. As they stretched out across the whiteness, I felt the frantic worry inside me start to calm down.

> Please make yourself eat. I know it's not fun. But life is a marathon, and right now, you're sitting on the sidelines. Eat to do. You'll burn those calories the minute they come in. Don't look at yourself in the mirror. How you look will change over the years, but what you do makes

you who you really are. And nobody can take that away
from you.
        Love, Mom

Shortly before dawn, I printed the letter out, one crisp sheet after another. I lined the sheets of paper up and folded them in half, a good sharp bend. Then I turned them lengthwise and folded them in half again, another good sharp bend.

I wrote my daughter's name on the outside of the folded square: *Elena*, a name I had loved before I even got to meet her, a name of ancient queens, perfumed with frankincense and spices. Then I tiptoed into Elena's room and laid the letter next to her cheek.

Anyway, those sentences are there, I thought as I went back to my room and laid my heavy head down on my pillow. *They're solid. They'll stay put. They aren't like spoken words that are only a little air and drama, that can twist this way or that or be made to disappear. I've done all I can.*

And I drifted away into sleep.

In the full light of morning, I woke up. Instantly, I remembered my fears from the night before. But now I was feeling hopeful again.

Maybe I had been exaggerating. Maybe things weren't so bad.

Always, daylight could do this to me. It made me doubt the doubts of the night. There was the Elena by daylight, a bright, gifted student with a brilliant future ahead of her, who maybe stumbled and struggled sometimes and who was rendered a little fragile by stress. And there was the Elena by night, a deeply damaged, devious invalid whom I could not trust and who was bent on self-destruction.

No matter how long I spent on this problem, I couldn't tell which Elena was the right one. I could add up facts to make each one turn out right.

So I went to her room to see which one I would find.

Even though I'd slept for hours, Elena hadn't stirred since the last time I was there. The folded letter still lay next to her cheek, opening a little like an awkwardly made fan and spreading its sharp corners of pages in the air. Elena heard me push her door open, and she blinked for a few seconds at the ceiling. Then she reached for her glasses, and the letter crackled under her hand.

"What's this?" she muttered.

I didn't answer. My words were all there, folded next to her cheek. I had nothing more to say.

Elena propped herself up on an elbow and read the letter through, first one page and then another. And then she began to cry.

Suddenly, for the first time in weeks, words were pouring out of her, a torrent of words: regrets, fears, lost opportunities, missed deadlines. Revelations came floating out in this gush of words that astounded me—but somehow confirmed what I'd somehow already known. The ROTC scholarship she'd talked about so longingly that had suddenly disappeared from conversation? The ROTC major had asked her to gain weight. Those odd meetings up at school before or after class? They were counseling sessions she'd arranged.

But they hadn't helped. Nothing had helped, and nothing was helping. She was running down a path that kept getting steeper all the time—so steep that she couldn't stop anymore.

At the bottom of that path was a cliff.

"I wish I'd stayed at Drew Center," she sobbed, and the honesty of those words cut me through and through like razor blades. I was the one who had taken her out of the treatment center, over Dr. Moore's advice. The day she'd left was one of the happiest days of my life.

"I wish I had taken the advice of Sandalwood's director last year," she sobbed. "I wish I'd gone into treatment."

"How about now?" I said.

The question surprised Elena so much that she stopped crying. She stared at me as if she'd just been dropped down onto the moon. But before she could think up an argument against it, I was ready with arguments of my own.

"You need to get out of your classes now anyway," I said. "You've missed too much work to make it up, but it's early enough that you don't have to withdraw with a pass or fail and damage your transcript. You don't have your jobs anymore. It's perfect, really. This is the perfect time."

"Well—where would I go?" she wondered. "I don't think there's any-where nearby. Sandalwood is just for day patients, not for twenty-four-hour care. That's what she said I needed."

"Where did Sandalwood's director tell you to go?"

"To Clove House," she said. "It's an eating disorder treatment center for residential patients. You get care twenty-four hours a day."

Elena named the location of Clove House, and we looked at each other a little blankly. It was several states away. I had driven through that city once on the highway a long time ago, and my imagination pulled up a memory of wide, smooth freeway lanes. It played me scenes of an impres-sive downtown, of swooping green hills, crummy little apartment houses, and then forest.

"Let's look it up," I said, and I fetched my laptop. I sat next to Elena on her bed, and we paged through Clove House's website together. The images we found there looked friendly. They didn't scare Elena off.

"The map says it's by a park," I pointed out, and for some reason, that seemed encouraging. "I'm going to go call them," I said before she could protest. But she didn't seem able to protest anymore.

Maybe it was good that she was so weak.

The admissions lady at Clove House was encouraging, too. "Yes, we're on your insurance plan," she said. "We don't have a vacancy at the moment, but we expect to have one in a couple of days. If you like, we can do an intake interview with your daughter at one o'clock this afternoon."

This sounded very promising. I could barely believe our good luck—except, there's no such thing as luck.

Please help us, dear Lord. Please please please . . .

One o'clock came, and Elena sat up in bed to take the call, and I could hear her from the other room, answering the interview questions in her clear, high "company" voice. The answers were confidential, so I wasn't lis-tening to what she said, but her voice sounded stronger than it had in weeks.

The admissions lady told me that the interview went well, and they would expect to see Elena on Thursday morning. I searched for my purse and read out our insurance information to her and asked if there was anything I should do.

"Should I call our insurance company?" I asked.

"No, we'll get that arranged," she said. "But there are tests we need from her medical doctor there in Texas."

I found a pen and started a list on a Post-it note: *Patient files. Standard blood work. EKG.*

A plan. We had a plan!

"Here's our fax number for those test results," she said, and I jotted it down below the list. "Till Thursday morning, then. Oh, and if you'll just call and tell us which flight she'll be on, then we'll know when to expect her."

I drew a line on my Post-it and added: *plane ticket.*

"Do you send a shuttle to pick her up?"

"No. She'll need to take a taxi. But it's only a fifteen-minute trip."

So I jotted down *taxi* as well. Then I called Joe at work and told him what was happening.

"Thank God!" he said quietly.

As I was on the phone to Joe, I heard the bathroom door shut. A few seconds later, the shower came on. Such a simple thing, but it reduced me to tears. It was all I could do to keep control of my voice.

Elena was up and in the shower—without me nagging her!

I hung up the phone, and now I was racing to get ready, racing to beat her out of the shower. By the time she opened the bathroom door, I had my keys in my hand, and I drove her to school so she could sign herself out of classes.

On the way, we didn't speak. Elena stared out the window. It was her first day out of the house in weeks.

Can it be possible? I thought. *Is this really going to happen?*

Together, we stood in lines and filled out papers. While we waited at the registrar's office, Elena reached into her purse, pulled out a little notebook, and began to make a long list.

I peeked over her shoulder. The list was titled *What to Pack.*

The title swam. I was blinking away tears again. *This is real!* I thought. *This is going to happen!*

A couple of days began to seem like barely enough time for everything that needed to get done. Elena said she needed toiletries. Oh, and she needed new pajamas. We scoured the bookshelves for interesting books to take. I needed to find her a flight. She needed her blood work done.

She was still up at midnight, kneeling next to her half-full suitcase.

"I need to go to Walgreens to pick up photos," she said. "And a new hair straightener. Mine doesn't work right anymore."

"Tomorrow," I said, yawning. "I'm going to bed."

But an hour later, Elena came into the bedroom and woke me up.

"I think Valerie's having the baby!"

I tiptoed out into the living room and took the phone.

"How are you doing?" I asked.

"Oh, *you* know," Valerie said. Her voice sounded as jaunty as ever. But sure enough, her contractions were starting.

"I wish I could be there," I said, feeling sudden sharp guilt that my daughter was having to go through her big day without me.

"It's all good," Valerie said. "Kinda glad you're not. It's not like you'd see me at my best."

"Are you going to the hospital now?"

"Nah. There's plenty of time. I'm going back to bed. The hospital's only five minutes away."

In the morning, Valerie called again to say that they were on their way to the hospital. She sounded amazingly relaxed. Then Elena and I talked to Clint. He sounded like he was being mugged.

"I hope Clint doesn't drive," Elena confided to me. "He's so nervous, he might pass out behind the wheel."

Off and on, Elena and I got updates. Then came the first photo of Gemma, Valerie and Clint's new baby girl.

I sat down on the bed, and I looked at her, and I cried.

What is it about a new baby that makes life seem like such a miracle? Is it the thought of the danger along that first lonely journey? Is it the fact that so many things have gone right when they could have gone so terribly wrong?

A brand-new person has entered the world. Something completely unique has been added. Our lives—the entire planet!—will never be the same.

Valerie's baby. Clint's baby. Their voices brimmed with excitement and wonder. The most ordinary sentences vibrated with hidden awe. As the photos came in, I could see it on their faces: *This is an event greater than each of us and greater than all of us. History and Fate have paid us a visit.*

The air of the hospital room was thick with angels.

I remembered that very first day, when Joe drove home from the hospital at twenty miles an hour, cursing out the window at any motorist reckless enough to drive within fifty feet of the car because our precious newborn baby was in the backseat. I remembered carrying her up the apartment stairs—oh so carefully! We put her down on our bed and the two of us sat and looked at her . . . just looked. "Our baby is beautiful," Joe had said softly, and I could hear the awe in his voice.

Now, I was a grandmother, and Joe was a grandfather. The wheel had turned, and we took our rightful places.

The birth of this new family member wrapped a spell of peace and happiness around the whole house. Elena finished her packing. Very early the next morning, Joe and I drove her to the airport and hugged her good-bye. We watched her walk away through security. Then we went to a nearby pancake house and ordered breakfast—just the two of us again.

The last few months had been chaos. The next few months would be crazy. But right now, I stirred my coffee in its chunky mug and felt contentedly old and ordinary. The relief I saw on Joe's face mirrored my own relief.

One daughter was a real adult, with a husband and a family. The other daughter was getting the help we couldn't give her. Joe and I were well on our way to fading into rest and retirement, and we were more than ready to play that part.

"Do we get the senior discount?" Joe asked the waitress. "We're grandparents now. Look!" And he showed her Gemma's picture on his cell phone.

Joe dropped me off at the house and went on to work, where he would no doubt field complaints from colonels and generals as far away as Korea and the Indian Ocean. I crawled back into bed and slept like I hadn't slept in months.

Elena woke me up to tell me that her plane had landed and that she needed help finding Clove House. Then she called again to tell me that she'd gotten there and they were processing her in. She had to put away her cell phone now, she said. She wasn't allowed to keep it with her.

She sounded nervous, but I felt perfectly calm.

I had heard of people feeling lighthearted. Right then, every single part of me felt light. I could feel the enormous weight of Elena's life-or-death struggle lifting off my shoulders. I got up to feed Dylan dinner, and he puffed his blue-green fins out like sails and swam into the palm of my hand. I fixed food bowls for Genny and the cats and watched them roll over, one after another. Then Genny went scampering around the yard on her ridiculously thin legs, and the cats bolted after her and raced up and down the tree, while I stood in the bright, clear sunshine and laughed.

Later, when I cleaned the kitchen, I turned my favorite music up loud. Elena wasn't there to creep out of her room, sick and exhausted, and beg me to let her sleep. Elena was where she needed to be. This was her decision, and it was the right one. The professionals would help her rediscover her passion for life.

It was going to be okay.

My poor damaged daughter was going to be okay.

Late in the afternoon, the phone rang. It was a staff member from Clove House. "We need you to book another airline ticket," she said. "Your insurance company won't pay for treatment. They say it's not medically necessary. Your daughter is going to have to go home."

CHAPTER TWENTY-EIGHT

The refusal of insurance companies to pay for care that is "not medically necessary" is supposed to prevent frivolous or fraudulent treatment. Until Elena's diagnosis, I had never even heard the term. But psychological care is much less precise than medical care, and it can also be a great deal more expensive—particularly the long months of around-the-clock care for anorexia nervosa.

I'm not the only family member of an anorexic who has had to hear this unhappy news. More anorexia patients than could possibly be numbered have gotten kicked out of treatment because their insurance won't pay up. In most cases, the insurance company has stepped in and cut off treatment as "not medically necessary." And many of those patients have gone on to die from their illness—some within a matter of weeks.

Anorexia nervosa isn't just a deadly mental illness. It is the deadliest mental illness of all. This isn't just me being dramatic, either. It's a medical statistic anyone can look up. Anorexia nervosa is orders of magnitude more deadly than other mental illnesses. It kills three times as many victims as bipolar disorder and twice as many victims as schizophrenia.

One out of every five anorexics will die early because of this disorder. One out of every five!

And the "not medically necessary" snafu doesn't help.

When I got this devastating phone call, it was too late in the day to do anything about it. Offices around the country were already closing. So I found out what I could from the Clove House staff, and I asked them to give me one more day. And then, all evening long, I made my plans.

My insurance company had ruled that Elena's care at the treatment center wasn't medically necessary. They were refusing to pay the bill. And if they didn't pay for it, nobody else could, either. The charge for residential care at Clove House was eleven hundred dollars a day.

But if Elena came home . . .

I knew what would happen if Elena came home. This disappointment would only speed things up. She would disappear into her room, and she wouldn't come out again.

Not alive, at least.

That made my plan simple. It was childishly simple. There was only one thing I could do. Somehow, I had to make the insurance company pay.

The lightness I had felt that afternoon was gone, nothing now but the dimmest of memories. Once more, my overwrought brain churned and schemed. The Clove House staff had told me that a psychiatrist at our insurance company had reviewed Elena's case and made the "not medically necessary" decision. Fine, then I would ask for another psychiatrist to review this psychiatrist's decision. And because I could argue that an insurance company employee couldn't be impartial, I wanted this second psychiatrist to come from outside the insurance company.

That's what I would do: I would demand an outside review of my daughter's case.

I knew how important these plans were. I knew that it wasn't enough to call and complain. In any bargaining situation, before going in, it's vital to know what you want. Only then can you work toward that goal.

Now I knew what I wanted, and I also knew I would have to back up my demand with facts. So I started digging through my files. I dragged out all the paperwork from the Summer from Hell. I pulled out old lab results and new lab results. I compared blood values and EKG findings, and I put together my arguments:

- The last time this patient had to go into the hospital, she was at a higher weight. She had a damaged heart at that higher weight—maybe she does again.

- You paid those claims, so at that higher weight, you judged that the identical eating disorder treatment you're denying now was medically necessary.

- That means this is a borderline case.

- That means it deserves an outside review.

The plan kept me busy for several hours. But once it was complete, there was nothing to do until the following morning, when the insurance company phone lines would be open. I should rest up. I would need to be sharp. I should get some sleep.

But of course, I didn't sleep.

If Elena came home . . . If Elena had to come home . . . I knew what would happen.

So I had to stop it. It was up to me to make sure it didn't happen.

In the morning, while Joe was eating breakfast, I started dialing the phone. While he got ready for work, I dialed the phone. In between washing my face and brushing my teeth, I dialed the phone. And before changing out of my pajamas, I dialed the phone again.

This time, I got an answer.

First, there was the menu, of course. There is always the menu. And the menu has always changed, of course, so I had to pay attention. Then the customer-service representative came on the line. I answered her questions. I bided my time.

Because I knew: You can't rush this. They have to fill in their blanks. Until they've got their blanks filled in, nothing is going to get done.

Then the representative asked, "And how can I help you?"

Now—the moment was now.

"I don't think you can help me," I said politely. "I think I'll need to speak to your supervisor."

Because I knew this, too: as upset as I was over this situation, rudeness wouldn't help. Rudeness just keeps a representative from doing her best work. The representative I was talking to didn't mess up this situation. She only wanted to do a good job.

I already understood what she could do. I knew that what I needed was over her head. But I also knew that she had to realize that as well. She wouldn't transfer me until she knew what *I* knew.

This representative wasn't just a pair of hands and eyes responding (too slowly and clumsily) to commands that would come from my brain. This representative was a living human being with her own skill set and a very tough job to do. I knew from bitter experience, from her side of the desk, that many people who called this woman every day treated her like dirt even when she did everything right. And I knew that if those people didn't like the answer they got, they treated her even worse.

Admiration and sympathy: those were my secret weapons. People help out when they can. Everybody wants to be a hero. Everyone likes being liked.

"Here's the situation," I told the representative. "My daughter just arrived at an eating disorder treatment center, under residential—that is, twenty-four-hour—care. Yesterday, a psychiatrist on your staff ruled that her care there isn't medically necessary. I need to reach someone who can order that psychiatrist's decision to be reviewed. I need an outside review of my daughter's case."

"Then you need to speak to the insurance specialist in charge of her case," the representative said. "Would you like me to give you that name and number?"

"No, I don't need it," I said. "I got that number yesterday, and I called it yesterday—several times. I didn't get past that person's voicemail, and I'm not going to wait for her to return my call. What's going on now is too important to wait. My daughter's covered care ends this afternoon."

"I'm sorry," the representative told me. "You'll have to wait for the specialist to call you back. I'm afraid there's nothing I can do."

"Yes, there is," I said, and I said it as warmly as possible, as if this woman were gifted with a secret magical power. "I'll be very grateful if you'll do me the favor of transferring me to your supervisor."

"Just a moment. May I put you on hold?"

"Of course."

Silence on the line.

"I'm afraid my supervisor is in a meeting," the representative said. "Can I put you through to his voicemail?"

"No, thank you," I replied. "I'll be happy to hold."

Because, as Dr. Harris had told me years ago: Never let them hang up the phone. As long as you're polite, an insurance company call center employee absolutely *must* not hang up on you. And the longer you stay on the line, the more your call skews their numbers for the day. They care about their numbers. They want to show the company that hired them that they're handling calls in a timely fashion. So, the longer you hold and the higher you go in their chain of supervisors, the more leverage you have to get what you need.

"All right," she said. "I'm just going to put you on hold, then."

Silence on the line again.

While I waited, I read over a few of the points I had written down. They were the advantages I had in this situation:

- Elena has had this insurance since birth—long history, know the system.

- Mental health claims are handled by a third party agency, hired by the insurance company—high expectations, play one agency off the other.

- Our policy comes through the federal government— very, very important client with a lot of clout.

All in all, I had a lot of advantages here. I was lucky—except, there's no such thing as luck.

The representative broke in on my thoughts. "Are you still there?" she said.

"Yes, I am."

"Then please hold while I transfer you."

We're getting somewhere! I thought as I waited through the clicks. Then I waited through the rings. Then I heard the line go live and opened my mouth to speak to the supervisor.

"Hello, this is George. I'm afraid I'm helping another customer right now. But if you'll leave your name and member number and the reason for your call . . ."

Now, why didn't I see this one coming?

I hung up the phone. Twenty-five minutes, gone. But—an important lesson learned.

Patiently, I dialed the number again. Patiently, I pressed buttons. Patiently and politely, I danced the dance with a new customer-service representative. Getting angry at this man wouldn't do either of us any good. I needed him to be doing his best work. It wasn't his fault that the system had let me down.

"I'm sorry," he said eventually. "I'm afraid my supervisor is in a meeting."

Of course he was. The supervisors are always in a meeting. I don't think it's a lie; they're always in meetings because they're spending their days with customers like me. They're meeting with the customers who need the things the regular representatives can't do for them. They can't meet with all of us at once.

"I'll be more than happy to hold," I said. And I meant it.

Silence again. Another ten minutes. While I waited, I read over my arguments:

- You're getting between the patient and her treatment team. They're the ones who need to determine her care.

- You designated this medical facility as a preferred provider. That means you encouraged us to trust their treatment decisions.

"Are you still there?"

"Of course I'm still here," I answered quickly—because I knew how quickly he would hang up if I didn't.

"Then please hold while I transfer you."

And have we learned our lesson yet?

"Just a minute," I said, "before you transfer me. I have your name noted down as James and your employee number as 657. Now, I need to tell you something, James 657. If you transfer me and this call goes to voicemail, I will count that as you hanging up on me, and I will duly record that hang-up, along with your name and employee number, in the complaint I file with the company that has hired *your* company to handle their phone support."

"Oh!" said James 657. And his tone of voice indicated that he was learning something, too.

"Now," I said, "if you'd like to check first to make sure there's a live person at the end of that line, I'll be happy to hold while you do that."

"Oh. Yes, please hold."

A much *longer* hold this time.

Then James's supervisor came on the line. A live supervisor! This was progress.

It had taken forty-five minutes. But it was progress.

Again, I explained the situation—to Stacy 112 this time. "You're getting between my daughter and the care her medical team recommends," I concluded. "So I'm going to stay on the line with you until you see to it that her case receives outside review."

"I can't do that," Stacy 112 said.

"Then I need to speak to your supervisor."

"She can't do that, either."

"Then I'll need to hear her explain that to me herself. And then she can transfer me to *her* supervisor."

"HIPAA privacy laws forbid me from discussing your daughter's case with you."

Ah! Well played, Supervisor Stacy 112.

"I'm not asking you to discuss her case with me," I replied calmly. "I'm discussing it with *you*, but I'm asking for no information in return. All I need is a guarantee that my daughter's case will receive an outside review. Since that review isn't medical, but insurance-related, telling me about it gives out no HIPAA-protected information. But I need that review, and I'm not going to hang up until I get it. I need a psychiatrist who *doesn't* work for you to decide whether her care team is right in recommending residential treatment."

"I can't do that. We can't do that."

"Then please transfer me to your supervisor. We'll see what she's able to do."

Very slowly, link by link, I worked my way up the chain. One of the supervisors tried to argue with me, but I declined to argue. Another one kept me on hold for an hour. I plugged the phone charger in, kept the phone to my ear, worked crossword puzzles, and answered promptly and cheerfully each time she broke in to see if I'd given up yet and hung up the phone.

Off and on, Clove House called me on my cell phone. They were working to try to get Elena's care extended, too. They weren't having much luck on their end, but they cheered me on.

"We can put together our best arguments," their staff member told me, "but nothing can replace the client calling. You're the one who pays their premiums. You're the one who can submit complaints to your employer and persuade your fellow employees to switch to another insurance plan. We don't have that kind of pull."

"I don't mind doing it," I said. "It's the least I can do. I have to admit, I get chills at the thought of Elena coming back home."

"It's extremely important that she stay here," the staff member said. "It took a lot of courage for your daughter to seek the help she needs. I'll be honest with you. Her physical health is very fragile. Her EKG and blood values are not normal. She could be days away from a heart attack. If she doesn't get this turned around, it's likely that she won't survive another month."

In a dream, I heard myself thank the woman and say good-bye. My hand shook as I set down the cell phone. So I had been right when I had roamed my dim house and it had seemed that dawn would never come. All my fears were coming true. This *was* a matter of life and death.

In my other ear, a voice broke in on the flowery hold music. "Are you still there?"

"Yes, I'm here."

"The supervisors are all in a strategic meeting. I don't know when they'll be out. Can I—*please*—have my supervisor call you back?"

"No," I said. "I'm very sorry, but no. I'll be happy to hold for as long as that meeting lasts."

"But this is keeping me from doing my work!" she said.

"My daughter *is* your work," I answered. "My daughter's survival is at stake. I'll hold on your line until this time tomorrow to get my daughter the care she needs."

One hour melted into another. The day crept slowly by, and still I was sitting on the floor in my pajamas with the phone held up to my ear. "My daughter's heart was damaged the last time her weight was this low," I told the next supervisor. "Her care team says that her heart rhythm is abnormal. Do you want to be the person whose name and employee number goes down in the letter I submit to Washington, DC, when I tell them that the insurance company they chose for their employees caused my daughter to die?"

"Her case was reviewed," the woman told me. "You have the name of the specialist in charge. There's nothing I or anybody else can do to change that decision."

"I don't know about anybody else," I said. "But I know what you can do. You can transfer me to your supervisor. Please."

"Well . . . Can you please hold?"

"Yes, I'll be happy to."

And flowery music played in my ear again.

A woman's voice came on the line. There was nothing new about that. But this voice sounded different. It sounded like it was used to giving orders.

"This is Clare Dunkle," I began, "calling for patient Elena Dunkle, insurance card number 509 . . ."

"Mrs. Dunkle," the voice interrupted, not unkindly. "I know who you are."

The woman proceeded to explain that she was authorizing Elena to stay at Clove House for seven full days, during which time the staff there could collect the data they needed to justify a longer stay. Then the insurance company would okay further residential care from week to week.

"Because your daughter went straight from no care to almost the highest, most expensive level of care," she said, "that put us in a predicament. No one had put together the paperwork to justify this level of care. No one had said, 'We tried to treat her with day therapy'—for example— 'and that treatment failed.'"

"That makes sense," I said. "But we couldn't persuade Elena to seek treatment until she hit bottom. And now that she's hit bottom, there's no time to lose on care that isn't going to work."

"Yes, I understand," the woman said. "In fact, it isn't all that unusual with this kind of illness. Now, I'm going to make arrangements to have your daughter's case flagged so that I can keep track of it personally, and we need to get in touch with her facility to give them the authorization codes they need. I have to let you go now, but I promise that someone will call you within half an hour and let you know when our work is completed."

Hang up? Now? After all this effort?

But—what if it was nothing but a trick?

"I . . . I would prefer to hold," I said.

"Yes, I know you would," the woman answered. "And I understand your concern. But I'm not talking to you from my line. I'm at the desk of one of my employees. Here is my full name." And she gave it to me. "Here is the number that rings at my desk." And she gave me that, too. "I am an associate director at this company, and I am in charge of patient relations. One of my employees will call you within half an hour. Mrs. Dunkle, I give you my word."

What could I do? I thanked her, and I hung up. My ear tingled from the cool rush of air and the sudden silence.

In an instant, panic overwhelmed me. Had I done the wrong thing? Was the number this woman gave me even real? Would I have to start all over again? Would they know my name now and keep me holding at the lowest level until the work day ended and everybody left for the weekend? Would my poor damaged daughter return home, bitter and frustrated, and disappear into her bedroom for good?

I couldn't think. I couldn't think what I should do. I couldn't calm myself down. So I stayed on the floor, staring at the phone as if all our lives depended on it—as if it were up to me not to break the spell.

After about fifteen minutes, the phone rang. I stabbed the talk button, and a motherly-sounding woman introduced herself.

"My name is Lynn," she said, "and I'll be Elena's assigned advocate in the insurance company. I used to be a behavioral-health nurse before I switched over to the dark side and started working insurance. Nowadays, I work with complicated cases like your daughter's to make sure nothing gets overlooked. Elena is all set up until this time next week, when we'll review her progress. But I don't foresee problems extending her stay beyond that. Your daughter's health is very fragile. It'll take weeks of residential treatment before she's ready to move to a lower level of care."

This was so exactly what I had been waiting to hear all day long that hearing it didn't feel real. All day, I'd been on high alert, rehearsing my arguments and keeping them ready. Now I couldn't think what to say.

"So, your daughter is in good hands," Lynn concluded. "Mom, you've done a good day's work. It's time to look after yourself."

At this unexpected thoughtfulness, a lump rose in my throat, and tears swam in my eyes. "Thank you," I said to Lynn. "Really. You don't know what this means."

Life and death, I thought. *Life and death.*

"Thank *you*, Mom," she answered with a nurse's brisk kindness. "Your daughter is lucky to have you. Now, here's my number. It's a direct line. If anything goes wrong again, I want you to call me *first*."

I scribbled Lynn's number down next to the number of the associate director. Then I thanked her once again and hung up. Slowly, I uncrossed my legs. Time to stand up. But I couldn't just yet. My leg had fallen asleep.

Time to call Joe and tell him the good news. And time to take that shower.

It was midafternoon. I'd been on the phone for almost six hours.

CHAPTER TWENTY-NINE

S o Elena stayed in treatment. She called us every few days to check in—brief, laconic calls. If they didn't tell us much, I got the impression that that was for our sakes. They were the sort of calls a soldier might make to loved ones during wartime.

A week later, Joe and I were standing in the garage, planning where to put things. Valerie, Clint, and Gemma would be out next month. It was time to turn my office into a bedroom.

"Let's keep one side of the garage free," Joe said. "I'd like to still be able to pull the Bimmer in at night." We went back to my office and started packing books into boxes.

"I took Tor to the vet this morning," I said as I cleared off a bookshelf. "He's got new food to help with the throwing up." Then I pulled the bookshelf out and set it aside, happy once again that we had had the foresight to go modular with our shelves.

Joe sighed. "Smart cat! Tor always knows when things are about to change."

This change might be stressful, but it was a change I was very much looking forward to. I couldn't wait to have my grandbaby in the house, and I couldn't wait to spend time with Valerie and Clint. I'd been delighted and impressed by how Valerie was taking to motherhood. She called me almost hourly with updates. Gemma had colic, and as far as I could tell, Valerie and Clint never seemed to put her down.

Joe smiled as I told him about this. "They'll figure it out," he said. "Sooner or later, you have to let them cry it out."

"Valerie told me, 'I love it when other people hold her, and she cries, and then, when she comes back to me, she stops crying.' She says, 'I know it's mean of me, but I can't help loving that.'"

Joe's eyes softened with memories. "I did my fair share of carrying *her* around."

"Remember playing airplane when Valerie was a month old?" I said. "Flying her around the room, making jet noises? Now you'll get to play airplane with your grandbaby." And I picked up a stack of shelves to take to the garage while Joe hauled out a box of books.

Genny trotted out to the garage to explore while we had the door open. She found something interesting next to the trash can, and I made her put it down. *At least the cats are outside now,* I thought as I shooed the old terrier into the house again. *Otherwise, Simon would probably be spraying in here.*

The phone rang, and I walked inside to pick it up. It was Elena, calling from Clove House.

"Oh, hey, hon," I said. "I was going to call you tonight to tell you I ordered those books you asked for. But I thought it was against the rules to call in the middle of the day."

"Screw them and their rules!" she shouted. "I'm done with this place!"

Okay, I thought. *This is different . . .*

Elena was talking now, very loud and very fast. It seemed that she had gone out for her lunchtime smoke break, and one of the staff said she didn't wait for a proper escort. Or maybe she had gone out for two smoke breaks instead of one—I couldn't quite make out the details.

"That *bitch!*" she said. And then, "Yes, that's right, I said you were a *bitch!*"

"Elena . . . ," I began.

"So get me a plane ticket, because I'm leaving!"

My orderly mind commenced boggling.

"You're—*what?*—You're leaving treatment because of a smoke break?"

But before I could finish my sentence, Elena had hung up the phone.

I called Clove House back and asked to speak to Elena's care team. Dr. Greene, her psychiatrist, was calm and upbeat. "Don't worry," she said. "Elena's just adjusting to some new medication."

Adjusting? I thought. *That's adjusting?*

I walked back out to the garage and told Joe about it. "It was crazy!" I said. "I'm really glad that's over."

But it wasn't over. It was just the beginning.

During the next couple of weeks, call after call came in. Each one highlighted a new clash between Elena and a staff member.

"This is bullshit!" she yelled one morning before I could say hello. "I've *had* it! I'm *done!*"

At least now I knew what to expect. I listened patiently through the rambling complaints.

"Elena, we are not buying you that ticket," I told her after she was done. "Not for something as minor as who oversees your breakfast."

"I knew you'd take their side!" she yelled, and the line went dead.

When I talked to Dr. Greene about the calls, she sounded unruffled. "Elena's on a lot of new medication," she said, and she rapidly reeled off a dizzying list of drugs. "It's a work in progress getting her stabilized. Over time, her mood swings should stop."

But Emily, Elena's therapist, was less optimistic and more blunt.

"I haven't encountered this level of hostility in a patient before," she said. "Elena just simmers with anger. And I'm not sure why, but most of it seems to be directed at me."

I remembered those long days during Elena's senior year, when I had been the stepping-stone Elena needed to stomp in order to make it through her exhausting days.

"She's done that to me when things got really bad for her," I said. "Maybe you're the new me."

Joe and I finished getting the house ready for our long-term guests. It had been hard work, and I was happy I could look forward to a little vacation. I'd gotten a call from a librarian in central Texas a few weeks before.

"We're holding a book festival at the end of February, and I hope you'll attend," she had said. "Can we book you for the week? We'd like to arrange to have you visit our middle schools."

I had quickly agreed to a reasonable price. The chance to pamper myself in a nice hotel and talk to teens about books all day—really, I should be paying *her*.

"Great!" she had said. "And I'm ordering copies right now to make sure all the libraries you visit will have your books, the Hollow Kingdom trilogy and *By These Ten Bones*."

"What about my new book, *The Sky Inside*?" I asked. "The one about a boy and his futuristic dog that came out last year?"

"Oh!" she said. "You have a new book out?"

Poor Martin!

As I was packing my suitcase the night before my trip, the phone rang again. I cringed when I saw that it was Elena.

"Hello?" I said cautiously.

But Elena wasn't yelling this time. In fact, she sounded only half awake. "They put me on a new medishin. Medi . . . cine," she amended.

A new medicine? *Another* one?

"How do you feel?" I asked cautiously. "Do you feel more relaxed?"

"I feel like shit," she muttered. "I'll talk to you later."

And the line went dead in my ear.

The next morning, I packed my car, loaded a CD holder with my favorite music, and drove a four-hour-long stretch of Texas interstate. The festival committee had put me up in a hotel suite for the week, and I'd brought *The Mystery of Edwin Drood* to help me pass the time. There was no one to clean up after and no one to cook for in the evenings. I could lie in bed and read to my heart's content:

> Not only is the day waning, but the year. The low sun is fiery and yet cold behind the monastery ruin, and the Virginia creeper on the cathedral wall has showered half its deep-red leaves down on the pavement. There has been rain this afternoon, and a wintry shudder goes among the little pools on the cracked, uneven flag-stones, and through the giant elm-trees as they shed a gust of tears. Their fallen leaves lie strewn thickly about. Some of these leaves, in a timid rush, seek sanctuary within the low arched Cathedral door; but two men, coming out resist them, and cast them forth again with their feet; this done, one of the two locks the door with a goodly key, and the other flits away with a folio music-book.

I could see it all: the great cathedral with its massive gray tower and the yellow and red leaves curling in an eddy at the feet of the black-robed men. I took another Hershey's Kiss from the bag at my elbow and gave a little shiver of happiness.

Now, *that* was writing!

The next morning, I tapped the first address into my GPS and drove through residential streets to the first school. The entire seventh grade was waiting for me in the library.

Seventh graders are my favorite audience because seventh grade was my least favorite year. When I talk to seventh-grade students, I feel as if I'm talking to my own ghost. *I respect you*, I try to tell that ghost, along with its living peers. *I know how hard this year can be. You're brave, and you're going to get through this. Life will get better, I promise you.*

A girl came up to me at the second library I visited. "I like Marak best," she said. Her manner was shy but also bold, as if the two of us shared a secret.

"He *is* amazing, isn't he?" I said. "Never without a plan!"

"Yeah," she said, relaxing into a smile.

This is the way I like to talk about my stories. I don't know what to say to the ones who come up and say, "I love your books!" It's so broad it's like telling God, "I really like your universe!" I can imagine Him thinking, *Which part? The nebulas? The anteaters? Wisdom teeth? What?*

But when a reader comes up and talks to me as if my characters are alive, well, that's how they are to me, too. Then it's as if we both know the same people. We have common ground. We have things to talk about.

"I wish you'd have them change the book cover, though," the girl continued. "Kate's eyes aren't dark there like they are in the books."

"I don't really . . . But wait a minute. Kate's eyes are pretty light. After all, they're blue."

"No, they're not," she said. "Kate's eyes are brown!"

Look, I'm her creator! I wanted to say. *I know perfectly well what color Kate's eyes are!* But then it dawned on me: *this* girl's eyes were brown.

"Well, you know how it is with book covers," I said. "It's what the publishing house wants. They don't let us authors have much power there."

"Too bad," she said, and she rewarded me by relaxing into another quick smile before her teacher came over to shoo her away.

After three days of library visits, I felt like royalty. Lovely long days of talk about books and reading. Lovely long evenings of chocolates and *Edwin Drood*. Such splendid, confident prose!

Dear Lord, I thought, *why didn't You let him* finish *this one?*

It was Wednesday night. Two more days of visits to go. I turned out the light and stretched out under the puffy down comforter, feeling very virtuous and sleepy.

My cell phone rang. It was Elena. Wincing, I hit the talk button.

"Hello?"

"So, there's something they want me to tell you," Elena said. And the nice, sleepy feelings streamed out of me as if there were a butcher's drain underneath my mattress.

"Okay," I said cautiously. "What is it?"

"I was raped when I was at the boarding school. Not at school. At a party. It was a free weekend, and Mona and I went to a party with a bunch of the boys at the boys' boarding school."

Raped? My girl? My little girl? *Raped?* And my imagination pulled up images of the young boarding-school Elena, of her awkward adolescent body and goofy grin.

Who was he? my brain howled. *WHO WAS HE?*

"Who was he?" my voice echoed.

"I don't know," Elena said. "I didn't see his face."

That idea dug its claws into me. Before I could stop it, my imagination started to work. Attacked, held so close to another person, an enemy! But still, a total stranger—an unknown.

"You don't know anything about who he was?"

"He was German, I think. At least, he yelled at me in German when I bit him."

And I could feel myself scrambling back from these details, trying to shut down my imagination, pushing away the images it started to feed me, no—no—no—

"Oh, dear God, Elena!" I said. "Why didn't you tell us?" And my mind was still locked on that question: *Who? WHO? WHO??*

"I thought Dad would kill him. I didn't want Dad to go to jail in a foreign country. I thought, *This is my fault.* I thought I was going to hell."

This shook me out of my feelings of revenge.

"But, Elena, you had to know that wasn't true," I said. "You had to know God would never punish you for another person's evil like that. It wasn't your fault . . ."

"It was my fault I was there."

"Okay, so you were a kid, and you sneaked out when you weren't supposed to. You were only fifteen . . ."

Elena's voice was like a whiplash. "Thirteen."

Thirteen? No. No, oh, God! And my brain got tangled up and tripped over itself, trying to fix dates to years, years to grades.

"Thirteen," I echoed, trying to keep my voice calm. "You sneaked out. That gets you grounded for two weeks. Not hell! Elena. It's not your fault!"

She just repeated in the same dull tone, "I felt like I was going to hell."

Here is the whole story as Elena told it to me later. Joe and I dropped our happy-go-lucky children off at boarding school and drove home to a house that still seemed to echo with their laughter. Then, three weeks later, Elena called me up and told me she wanted to go to her friend Mona's house for the free weekend. Meanwhile, Mona called and told her parents they both were coming to our house.

And then the two teenage girls took the train together and met their boyfriends from the boys' boarding school.

The boys' boarding school was over an hour away, but the two schools got together for special events. Many of the girls at the girls' school had brothers or cousins at the boys' boarding school. It was considered quite a coup if a girl had a boyfriend there, and Elena and Mona were doubly popular because their boyfriends were good-looking upperclassmen. Secretly, the two thirteen-year-old girls exchanged letters and took phone calls from these "older men." Other girls at the boarding school—even the senior girls—were green with envy over their good luck.

And now, the two of them actually had a date!

"It was almost my birthday, so they said we should celebrate," Elena told me later. "We thought they were taking us somewhere nice."

In a glow of happy anticipation, the two underage girls got all dressed up. They were beautiful! They were desirable! They were being treated like grown-ups at last! But they didn't go somewhere nice. Instead, their boyfriends took them to a party at the house of one of the boarding school boys. His parents were away on a holiday. And no other girls were there.

The two boyfriends, too, were showing off *their* good luck.

The party got loud and raucous: a bunch of high school boys with lots of beer around. It was a situation no thirteen-year-old would know how to handle.

"It was when I went upstairs to the bathroom," Elena told me much later. "One of the ones I didn't know attacked me. I tried to bite him because his hand was over my face, holding me down, but it was his palm, and I couldn't close my teeth on much. I thought he was going to put my eye out. His finger was in my eye, and I was afraid he would gouge it out. That's what I remember most."

When it was over, Elena stumbled downstairs and threw a fit and yelled at the two boyfriends, and then she and Mona left. "My boyfriend said, 'You're ruining our good time.'" And that was the end of the two girls' romantic date, and the end of Elena's exciting birthday celebration.

Elena didn't tell me all this on the night of the phone call, but I knew enough to guess some of it. *No wonder the laughter died in my house,* I thought. *No wonder that girl—that poor, lost, miserable girl—*

But Elena cut into my thoughts again that night, and her voice was flat and hard. "There's something else," she said.

Something else? Something worse—I could feel it. But how? What could be worse than that? And I felt my body tense up, as rigid as a board under the puffy comforter, bracing for whatever came next.

"This January," Elena said, "when I stayed in bed, I was pregnant. I lost the baby."

I grappled with this new catastrophe. "When?" I managed. "Who?"

"Doesn't matter," she said. "He was a loser."

Memories flooded me, and I was reliving my own miscarriage over twenty years before. I remembered the flood of grief. Again, I felt the sorrow nestle inside me, the emptiness—literal and emotional.

I am a grandmother, I thought. *I am a grandmother twice. I have my grandbaby Gemma. And the other baby.*

"That was my fault, too," Elena was saying. "Because of the eating disorder." And she said it matter-of-factly, completely without pity, as if she were passing judgment on someone she barely knew and didn't like.

I pushed past the sorrow. My thoughts dug in and found traction. Grief was a luxury I couldn't afford right now.

"But, honey," I said, "lots of miscarriages are normal, natural things. Many pregnancies can't progress—one in five, I think. There may not have been a baby there at all."

"There was. I heard the heartbeat," she said.

Once again, pain from the past caught me off guard and stabbed through me. The heartbeat. My baby's heartbeat, fast and light and perfect. The obstetrician's voice: "Mrs. Dunkle, don't worry. You're not going to lose this baby."

The joy. The relief!

And the very next day: The poker-hot bursts of agony. The blood. The loss. The grief.

Who would that baby have been, my child of the light, perfect heartbeat? What adventures would we have had together? No way to know . . .

There's no time for this! I told myself sternly. Because Elena was speaking into the silence again, and her voice, for the first time, carried emotion.

Which emotion? What was I hearing? Excitement? Anxiety? Eagerness?

"Maybe you don't believe me," she was saying.

"No," I heard myself answer. "No, I believe you. I lost . . . I heard my baby's heartbeat, too."

I am a grandmother, I thought again. *I was* a grandmother. *My grandchild died in my house.*

And somehow, this thought just destroyed me.

In my house.

In my own house . . .

"No, about the rape," Elena said quickly. "It happened years ago, and nobody knew."

I rallied once again. This was important.

"I don't have to believe you. I know," I said. "I could almost tell you when it happened."

"You *didn't* know," Elena said. "Nobody knew." And she sounded a little bit like my teen had sounded the other day, stubbornly insisting that Kate's eyes were brown.

"Elena, remember when you came home for the free weekend, and I started following you around, asking what was wrong? You had changed. You were like one raw nerve. You couldn't eat, and you couldn't sleep. I would wake up at one, two in the morning, and you would be wandering around the house."

And you turned mean, I thought. *Overnight, you became cynical and hard. You turned against your sister and pushed her away. Your hope, your idealism had been scorched right out of you. Your laugh . . . how long was it before I heard you laugh again? And it wasn't the same . . .*

"I always had trouble sleeping," Elena answered. "I always had nightmares. You didn't know."

"But this was different," I said. "Remember the child psychiatrist? Remember how he tested you for hours? That was because we were worried about you. We knew something was wrong."

"Oh, yeah. I remember him . . ."

"And he told me—" But my throat closed up unexpectedly, and I had to start again. "He told me nothing was wrong with you." I could hear the hurt in my voice. "He said—I remember exactly what he said—'She is very ambitious and a little dramatic, but what teenage girl isn't? You have nothing to worry about, Mrs. Dunkle. Your daughter is completely normal.'"

Silence. And in that silence, sadness began to well up inside and around me, a gentle, invisible force. The dark walls of the hotel room, illuminated by the tiny blue light on the front of my laptop, seemed to waver a little, like the sides of a marine trench deep below the surface of the ocean.

That poor little child, wounded and scared, shocked out of her high spirits and laughter and her trust in goodness and mercy. Yelled at, attacked. Cast off to crawl back to her life. Guarding her secrets, face-to-face with hell.

"Why did the doctor say that, Elena?" I asked. "Why did he tell me you were fine?"

"Because I lied my ass off," she said.

After Elena hung up, I didn't move. I just lay there, holding the phone. Sadness drowned me, weighed me down, crushed me flat under the heavy comforter. I didn't think. I didn't do anything. I just lay there, unable to move.

Sleep didn't find me for a very long time.

The next morning, I got up and went on with my school visits. That was just as good as anything else I might be doing. I seemed to stand next to myself and watch myself, as if I were an interesting stranger. I listened to my own voice lilting up and down, and I marveled at how natural it sounded.

Just as if I were an ordinary woman.

Just as if today were an ordinary day.

CHAPTER THIRTY

A week and a half passed, a week and a half of gray highway under fast-moving clouds and stormy spring rain. A week and a half of being on the move.

After the hard truths I had had to hear, it felt good to be on the move.

The time and the travel brought me to Valerie's living room in Georgia. They were waiting for me when I arrived. We were going to leave again within minutes.

"Here," Valerie said. "Take Gemma while Clint and I pack the cars." And she handed me my grandchild. I felt so much in that moment, it was as if my body weren't one creature but a committee of separate personalities.

My arms, especially. My arms had feelings all their own. *Ah, yes*, they were saying, *this is how a baby feels. We remember! We remember!*

And the rest of my body was clamoring for data: *Eyes, eyes! Tell us what you see!*

Gemma was a chunky little one-month-old, and she was staring straight at me, serious and slightly cross-eyed. She opened her mouth to cry, and the cry came out in even, expressionless wails. Then she closed her mouth and gave me another long, earnest gaze.

That's a newborn cry, my ears reported, feeling important and wise. *Yes, we remember. That's a newborn cry.*

My mind was on tiptoe with awe and respect. A new little person! A universe of potential. What would she grow up to be? A writer? A professor? A scientist? Because she would, of course, grow up to be brilliant.

Who would she grow up to look like?

Valerie already thought she might look like me.

It's a joke in our family that Valerie and Elena look exactly like Joe but not at all like me. They both have his dark eyes and dark brown hair. Put a pile of photos together, and anyone would sort them out to stand next to their Dunkle aunts. Elena also looks like my mother, girlish and arch, back when my mother was a popular young professor with bewitching long black hair. But, no matter who they look like, neither one looks a thing like me.

When we went to Italy, I was curious to see how my one-quarter-Italian girls would fit in. Up by Lake Como and Venice, Valerie was already blending in, with her warm brown eyes and creamy skin. But Elena, smaller and darker-eyed, didn't fit in until we moved south. Then, in Rome, she suddenly vanished. She could be standing right next to me at a crowded crosswalk, and I would have to scan the crowd twice before I could find her.

I didn't mind this, of course. I had fallen in love with Joe's dark Italian good looks. But what would it be like to have a person take after me? Might Gemma be that person?

So I studied my grandchild, and my whole body tingled with excitement and delight, except for my arms, which were entirely at peace. They felt the feel of baby again, as heavy and solid as a bag of flour, and they ignored everything but the holding.

Valerie broke in on my reverie. "Hey, Mamacita! Car keys. Clint and I have stuff for your backseat."

I was not meeting my grandchild under the best of circumstances. Valerie's apartment was small and dim, and it reeked of mildew and poverty. Valerie and Clint were hurrying by with what appeared to be random pieces of appliances and trash bags full of laundry and clothes hangers.

It was *The Grapes of Wrath*, twenty first century style.

"Okay, Momma," Valerie said, returning and whisking Gemma out of my hands, "let's start up the cars while I take the apartment key to the front office. Itty Bitty's coming with me, so Clint goes with you. Keep your phone on!"

And we pulled out of the parking lot for the long drive back to Texas.

Once we navigated to the highway, I had attention to spare for my traveling companion. Although Clint had a slight smile on his face, his blue-green eyes betrayed flashes of nervousness, like the uncertain look in a dog's eyes when it's afraid it might be going to the vet. I could imagine what he was thinking: *Four hours alone in a car with the mother-in-law!*

"So, how's life as a new dad?" I asked him.

"It's okay," he said. Then, after a pause, "Not much sleep, though."

Yes, announced the committee of my body. *Yes, we remember those days.* The eyelids remembered heaviness, and the brain remembered drowsiness, while the feet remembered small, quiet, monotonous steps, back and forth.

Meanwhile, the arms—the arms sang with happiness. *We remember!* they sang. *We remember!*

"Any idea what job the Air Force will train you for?" I asked.

Clint appeared to consider this new question carefully.

"You know," he said after a minute, "I don't really know."

A few more casual questions and a few more thoughtful but equally brief answers later, I thought, *I'm just torturing this poor sleep-deprived boy.* So I pushed *American Idiot* into the player, turned it up, and started singing along.

I have to sing along. And I have to think about the words. That's how my imagination finds things to look at while I'm traveling along a boring highway.

Out of the corner of my eye, I noticed Clint give me a couple of sidelong glances. I sing loudly but horribly. It's just something my family has to cope with.

Then Clint started singing along, too.

By the time another day was up and we were driving through Louisiana, Clint was talking to me. "Tell me a story," he would say from time to time.

What writer could resist such an appeal? I ransacked my ghostly lore for interesting hauntings to tell him. And in return, he related Stephen King stories he had read. Clint told ghost stories very well.

We reached home at last, after three days on the road. We drove up to the house and filled the driveway with small sedans: Valerie's avocado-green Elantra next to my white Elantra, with Elena's tan Elantra out at the curb. Three identical Hyundais in three different colors. It was the Korean invasion.

Joe opened the garage door, and we hauled in the contents of the cars: cracked plastic drawers full of random silverware and pots, trash bags stuffed with T-shirts and scuffed Converse sneakers, and electronics in cheap plastic silver-colored cases, sprouting black wires out the back. No household item looks good when it's not in a house, but Valerie and Clint's meager possessions looked particularly sad.

"These kids are worse off than we were!" Joe marveled as he surveyed the pile of trash bags and appliance parts. "At least when you and I got married, I had a ten-speed bike and a plastic desk."

Valerie and I set up Gemma's portable crib. Meanwhile, the men were supposed to move in the essential stuff. This turned out to be Clint's black nylon folder of PS3 games. By the time Gemma had settled down for a nap, Clint was blasting zombies with a shotgun while explaining to Joe the best use of the various weapons available. Joe seemed to favor an ax, which his avatar was wielding with untiring vigor. Perhaps he hadn't progressed far enough to get his hands on a gun yet.

"Valerie wants tacos," I announced from the doorway. "We're going to Taco Cabana. Who wants what?"

The next few days varied from this pleasant script in only a few particulars. Clint's avatar might be shooting a crossbow at dragons instead, or Valerie's avatar might be jumping from rooftop to rooftop, pursued by a gang of medieval knights. But the routine was the same: playing with baby Gemma when she was awake and playing games on the PS3 when she was asleep, occasionally varied by movies, some of which were based on games for the PS3. In the meantime, we ate lots of candy, and I cooked or baked all of Valerie's most fondly remembered meals and desserts.

It was like a family-wide slumber party.

"Oh, wow! Thanks!" Clint said one afternoon when a plate of hot chocolate-chip cookies appeared at his elbow. I paused to look at the screen:

a retro underwater world. I could see vividly colored art deco interior design, but fish were swimming by outside the windows.

"What's that?" I asked. "Oh! Watch out!" Because a creature, half human, half spider, had scuttled rapidly across the underwater ceiling.

Clint hurled a fireball and followed up with shotgun blasts as the creature flitted rapidly to and fro. Finally, it fell to the floor. It wasn't a spider, it was a thin man with hooks for hands. He was wearing an elaborate bunny-ear mask.

Bunny ears? That tickled my imagination. Which genius had thought of that?

"You don't know *BioShock*?" Clint asked as his avatar strode over and robbed the creature's corpse.

This was more interesting than zombies or dragons. This game's monsters reminded me of my goblins, and the setting was grimly beautiful: a kind of blood-spattered, poorly cleaned *Titanic*.

"What's it about?" I asked, sitting down and taking a chocolate-chip cookie.

"It's kind of complicated," Clint said. "Here, I'll start a new game."

Half an hour later, Joe was watching, too, and I was completely obsessed. "Does anybody want margaritas?" Joe offered as he polished off a cookie.

And the Dunkle slumber party rolled on.

Next afternoon, Valerie was changing Gemma on the floor while I picked up soda cans. Valerie never asked me to change a diaper. She was up with Gemma night after night for hours, and she never asked me to take a turn. I got to play with Gemma during the day, but I didn't have to do the hard work.

"Do you think Clint would like pizza?" I asked. "Yes? Then let's have pizza tonight."

Valerie laughed. "You're such a sucker, Mom. You spoil him. But hey, that's okay, I like pizza, too."

Valerie was right that I was catering to Clint. I couldn't help wanting to spoil him. Clint was very nice as well as smart and funny, and he and I liked the same kinds of monsters. Besides, he had worked hard to provide for his family. He had completed a year of college in his time off work, and in a few weeks, drill sergeants would be yelling in his face.

Clint's mother did everything she could to help Valerie, I thought as I dialed the phone for pizza. *I'm standing in for her right now. I owe her a debt I can never repay. She'd want to know that her boy is enjoying himself.*

But a few days later, as I was driving Valerie, Clint, and Gemma home from my parents' house through north Texas thunderstorms, a call came in on Valerie's cell phone.

"It's your recruiter," she said, handing the phone to Clint.

He talked for a minute, quiet *yes*es and *I understand*s. Then he handed the phone back to Valerie.

"They're not putting me in the April group," he said. "They're putting me through basic training in July."

This was a blow to Valerie and Clint. It meant another two and a half months added onto the time they would have to wait before they would be in a place of their own. I sneaked a glance at Valerie. She was in tears.

"You know it's fine with your father and me," I said. "You three are no trouble. You're the opposite of trouble." And I thought about how nice it would be to have my family around me for another two months. My granddaughter would be sitting up and learning to crawl.

"I'd better get a job," Clint said thoughtfully.

Valerie was silent for another minute. Then she gave a nod.

"Okay, here's what we do," she said. "Clint, you go back to Georgia and ask your old boss there if he can pick you up on the payroll again for another few weeks. You know it doesn't matter how many workers he's hired since, he'll take you back the minute he sees you."

"He never has enough guys he can count on," Clint agreed.

"Then I'll drive out to pick you up in the middle of June," Valerie said. "And your mom can visit with Gemma again."

Soberly, the two of them discussed the details while I changed lanes and watched through the watery windshield the parade of red taillights in front of me. *Valerie's stronger*, I thought with pride. *She really is a grown-up now.*

"Okay," Valerie concluded. "That's what we'll do. We've got a plan."

A plan. She sounds like me, I thought. *That's the first thing I do, too: set up a plan.*

But my own plans were about to change.

The next day, I got a call from Emily, Elena's therapist at Clove House. The last month had been quiet, and what little we had heard had felt like good news. But this new phone call shook me up considerably.

"Your insurance company wants to move Elena into day therapy," she said. "They won't continue to pay for residential care. Elena's finally putting on weight, but her negative feelings are intensifying. She's not ready for this. We're afraid she may try to harm herself."

Harm herself? What did that mean? What did they think she would do? And a horrible memory heaved itself up from the darkest, gloomiest corner of my mind: Valerie, coming down the stairs, humming softly, and her hands . . . What was wrong with her hands? . . .

"I . . . Okay," I stammered. "But what—what can *I* do?"

Emily's voice was carefully neutral. "We need to know if you'll pay the difference between day therapy and residential care."

"That's three hundred dollars a day!"

"Can you do it?"

My brain spun.

Three hundred times seven. Twenty-one hundred dollars. Over two thousand dollars a week!

"I don't know," I heard myself say out loud. "Maybe—but not for very long."

"Mrs. Dunkle, we need a definite answer. Her residential care stops today."

Today?!

Why do they always need these answers today? I thought frantically. *Can't they plan at* all?

"Okay," I said. "For . . . a week."

A week! Twenty-one hundred dollars!

I hung up and called Lynn, the brisk nurse who was Elena's liaison— the one who worked for the dark side now.

"Please understand, we do want what's best for your daughter," Lynn told me. "But she's been in residential care for a month and a half. She should be ready to move to full-day therapy now."

"Her care team says she's not ready," I said. "They're concerned that she'll hurt herself. Twelve unsupervised hours a day is a huge risk."

"We need to try it," Lynn said. "Six weeks in the hospital is a very long time. If your daughter isn't willing to make progress by now, there's not much anybody can do."

I felt the cold realism of this statement. It was practical. It made sense. And it sent panic coursing through me—panic so profound that it was all I could do to keep holding the phone. I felt as if I were sliding into a pit. I wanted to strike out, to claw the walls, to struggle free.

Because . . . what if the treatment didn't work?

I had never even *considered* that it might not work.

A plan. A plan! I would fight this decision. That steadied me and filled me with courage. It was good, in that moment, to have something to fight.

"Lynn, I have to go over your head," I said. "I'm calling Washington, DC. As long as the insurance company is standing between Elena's treatment team and the care they say she needs, I have to fight you any way I can."

"Of course you do!" Lynn said, and she meant that sincerely. "Mrs. Dunkle, I wish you the best of luck."

I spent hours on the phone that day and the next. Against the maze of bewildering phone lines in Washington, DC, I used every trick I had learned. I was pleasant. I was appealingly helpless. I let people rescue me. I used my storytelling skills to bring to life the tale of my tragic, desperately ill daughter.

"Please help me," I would beg each new person who came on the line. "I know I'm not calling the right number, but it's the only number I have. My daughter's doctors think her life is in danger."

Time after time, friendly voices reassured me, told me what they knew, and gave out phone numbers that weren't public. "When he asks, just tell him Leticia gave you this extension. I'm praying for you and your daughter."

For five anxious days, Joe and I had to pay the three hundred dollars a day that kept Elena safe in residential care. But by the time those five days were up, my phone calls had paid off. Another psychiatrist at the insurance company reviewed her case and okayed residential care yet again.

But the handwriting was on the wall. Day therapy was coming. It wouldn't mean two thousand dollars a week, but it did mean a fifty-dollar copay each day—probably for months. That meant fifteen hundred dollars a month. And then, there would be the cost of an overnight stay somewhere, and possibly a rental car, too.

Over coffee that weekend, Joe and I discussed strategies.

"You bought that pricey BMW because it was a great deal in Germany," I pointed out. "But it's a hassle to look after here in Texas, and you end up borrowing my car all the time because the Bimmer won't transport your bicycle. Maybe it's time to sell it."

Was it fair for me to suggest this? I'm not that sentimental about cars. But what did the BMW mean to Joe? Did he see it as a symbol of success? Was it a reward for his years of hard, steady work as an engineer? Did the sight of it in the garage give him a mental lift to tackle the daily grind?

I don't know. My husband is practical and straightforward. He doesn't tell me these sorts of things.

What I do know is that he didn't hesitate.

"You're right," he said. "See what you can get for it."

Three days later, I had exactly the deal I wanted, and it was a deal on—of course!—another Elantra. But it was the newest model, and it had leather seats. I owed my poor husband that much, at least.

Joe picked me up at the end of his workday, and we headed to the dealership to sign the final papers. Halfway there, my cell phone rang. I answered it through the Bluetooth connection in the dashboard, and Elena's angry voice reverberated through the car.

"I'm leaving today! There's nothing you can do to stop me!"

My heart sank.

"Hello?" I said. "Elena, what's going on?"

"Mrs. Dunkle," a smooth feminine voice answered, "this is Dr. Greene, Elena's psychiatrist."

"Yes, hello, Dr. Greene," I said. "I remember you."

"I've got Emily, your daughter's therapist, here with me," Dr. Greene continued, "and we're having a conference with Elena. She's very upset. She wants to talk to her parents."

"Yes, go ahead," Joe said. "We're both here."

"Your daughter wants a PEG tube," Dr. Greene said. "That's a tube that goes straight through the abdominal wall. We aren't sure it's a good idea, and your insurance won't pay for it. If we schedule it, will you pay for it yourselves?"

Joe and I exchanged startled glances. He was driving down a three-lane access road through rush-hour traffic. It wasn't the best place for absorbing fine details.

"Wait," Joe said. "You don't think an operation's a good idea. But you want us to pay for it?"

"We just need to know if you're willing."

A tube through the side of the abdominal wall. My imagination dredged up a photo I had seen in a science book of a man who was fed through a flap in his stomach. Doctors had experimented on him for years, putting things into his stomach and taking them out to look at them. My own stomach felt fluttery at the thought.

"I need that operation," Elena said. "They want me to eat five thousand calories a day. Five thousand *healthy* calories—that's plates and plates of food! My stomach can't process it all!"

"It is true," Dr. Greene agreed, "that the amount of food is hard on your daughter's system. But her metabolism is so high that unfortunately, it's necessary."

Joe took a right turn. Now he was on a five-lane feeder street: two lanes each way and a turn lane in the middle. Cars and people and big flashy signs were everywhere, crowding in and demanding attention. My stomach lurched and rolled from the motion and the mental images. I shaded my eyes with my hand and tried to be sensible.

"I'm still not getting this," I said. "Isn't the amount of calories going into the stomach the same?"

"It's different with a tube," Elena said. "With a tube, I won't notice. It can get spread out over twenty-four hours."

"When you were in the hospital before," Joe said, "you had a tube that ran down your nose for that."

My imagination found that image and showed it to me: my daughter lying absolutely still and silent in the ICU, the beeping of the machines, the chilly air . . .

"We've tried the nose tube," Elena's therapist said. She sounded harassed and unhappy. "A nose tube doesn't work for your daughter."

"How is that possible?" Joe asked. "Why wouldn't it work?"

For a few seconds, none of the three invisible parties spoke. Then Dr. Greene's smooth voice answered. "Elena's gag reflex is very sensitive. She's conditioned it with years of purging."

I blinked. A silver minivan came blasting out of a gas station and almost took my door off. Joe swerved.

"Years of—I'm sorry, we're on the road here," he said. "Years of doing what?"

Purging. Purging is vomiting, I thought. *But Elena doesn't do that.*

It was the one thing Dr. Costello had felt confident telling me during the Summer from Hell. Elena wasn't bulimic. She didn't purge. Over and over, I had heard her confident denial as one doctor after another had asked her about it. "Look at my teeth," she would say. And they would look at her white, undamaged teeth, and they would nod in agreement. No purging. My daughter didn't purge.

But Dr. Greene's voice was steady.

"Your daughter has been purging her meals for years, on a daily basis. Her gag reflex is so sensitive that it responds to the slightest pressure. We've tried it repeatedly, but she can't keep a nose tube down."

Can't keep a tube down. My imagination played with that—played with nerves in the back of my throat. My own gag reflex gave a heave in answer.

Joe pulled into a parking lot and stopped the car. It was that big chain toy store, a place with some of the most unnatural, grotesque childhood companions on the planet. In years past, I used to walk in there and feel as if I were trapped inside a can of soda. I used to joke that if I died in one of its aisles, no one would even bother to move my body.

A PEG tube. A hole in the side of the stomach. An unnatural, grotesque misuse of the body. Major surgery, against doctors' advice and on our nickel—just to keep from having to eat.

"No," I heard myself say. "We won't pay for a PEG tube."

Elena's voice filled the car again, bitter and furious. I could hear the loss of control in her voice that the medications had brought on, the loud tone and sloppy speech. Was this helping my daughter? Was she becoming more truly herself?

The further Elena went into treatment, the less I understood who she was. The tragic details of the rape and the miscarriage had made me feel closer to her. But in this moment, sick at heart and sick to my stomach, I had never felt so far away.

Who was this resentful stranger who hurled insults and vomited up food? How did my bright, nervous, imaginative child turn into this bony, bullying wraith?

Joe began speaking quiet sentences into the hectic torrent of words, stepping-stones to help us find our way. "I know this is hard," he said. "It's causing you great stress. But you can do this, Elena. I believe in you."

Little by little, Elena began to calm down. That allowed Emily to intervene. Over the course of the next few minutes, she and Dr. Greene talked Elena into trying again.

Shouldn't this make me happy? Shouldn't I be grateful to Joe for jumping in and being an effective, positive parent? Why should it leave me with such anger?

Oh, sure, she'll calm down for him! She always listens to her father. But who's been there for her? Who's lost sleep over her? And she treats me like I'm the enemy!

Joe and I said our good-byes to them, and he pulled out into traffic again. In silence, we drove to the dealership.

"I was beginning to worry!" the manager joked when we walked in.

I could feel the wrongness of my smile. It stretched my lips like rubber, but it didn't reach my eyes. Joe was the one who answered and reached out to shake the manager's hand.

As I watched my husband sign away his beautiful white BMW, my anger melted into guilt.

What's wrong with me? Don't I want my husband to be a good parent? Isn't it good that the two of them have a rapport?

We drove home in the new car. Its attractive interior appealed to me, and Joe seemed to enjoy it, too. Leather seats and a top-of-the-line trim package, for just the price I had wanted—I had practically stolen this car! And Gemma was awake when we got home. I hugged her warm, soft little body in my arms and walked up and down with her, singing the alphabet song.

I always sang Gemma the alphabet song. I wanted to condition her for life. My hope was that whenever she heard it, she would feel a little happier and a little more loved, even if she didn't know the reason why.

Meanwhile, Valerie was setting out plates and pouring drinks. Pizza again—I wasn't much of a cook these days.

"Let's have a salad, too," I said, feeling guilty. "We've got salad fixings, right?"

Valerie opened the fridge. "I think we've got a bag around here somewhere."

She scooped preshredded lettuce into bowls while I told her about the phone call. "Vomiting food!" I said. "It's like I don't even know her anymore."

"She's pretty crazy," Valerie agreed. "I think she's going to be okay, though. I don't have a reason for that, except that I'm okay now. I got through it—and yeah, I know it wasn't as bad as what she had to deal with. But still, I got through it, and I think she will, too."

As Valerie talked, I idly watched her hands, busy with the green salad leaves. The light played off those hands unevenly, in small flashes of pink and silver.

Valerie coming downstairs, humming. And her hands . . . the dark purple circles on her hands . . .

She was right. If those could heal up, anything was possible.

CHAPTER THIRTY-ONE

My phone rang. That meant something was wrong. Whenever something went wrong, my phone rang. I used to perk up when I heard the phone ring. Now, I simply hated it.

"Mrs. Dunkle, we have to talk to you." It was Emily again.

I waited with a sinking heart. This couldn't mean anything good.

It was the beginning of April, over two months since Elena had left to go to Clove House. She had recently stepped down from residential treatment to day treatment, which ran seven days a week for ten hours a day. During the off hours, Elena was staying in a halfway house that the Clove House management ran. A staff member stayed there with the patients and gave them their medicine, but they had breakfast on their own and less structure in the evenings. It was an extra charge, not covered by insurance, but it was the ideal solution for us.

So far, Elena's day treatment had been going well. And when I'd heard from Elena, she had sounded better—more like her old self. She'd even started to tell me entertaining little stories again about her days and about the other patients in treatment. But now, Emily was on the phone, and that meant only one thing:

Something had gone wrong.

"Elena cut herself," Emily said. "When she did that, she violated the contract we made with her. We can't keep her in our overnight house any longer."

Cut herself! I felt a shiver of disgust. *Isn't the not eating bad enough? Thrown out of the overnight program*—now *what are we supposed to do?*

But I fought down my feelings of frustration. My daughter was sick. She wasn't hurting herself just to complicate my days.

This wasn't about me.

"Well . . . Are there hotels nearby?" I asked. "Can we book her a hotel room and a rental car?"

"We can't allow that," Emily said. "We've discussed it, and it isn't safe. Elena can't stay overnight by herself. She needs someone there to monitor her. If no one can do that, we'll have to remove her from our program."

My frustration returned, tinged with pure out-and-out panic.

Where would Elena go if she couldn't stay there? What was this going to mean for her recovery? Because if there was one thing I *did* know about Elena at this point, it was that she was a very long way from recovery.

When Elena had first gone into full-time treatment, I'm not sure what I was expecting. The only thing I could really compare it to was classes I'd taken. I had expected a steady progress of some kind, a climb up the learning curve. By two weeks she would learn this; by a month she would know that.

What I hadn't expected was the kind of erratic, explosive non-progress we had observed from a distance. Elena zigzagged every few days from being fully compliant and gaining weight to calling me up in the middle of a medication-fueled fury, yelling over some real or imagined conflict at the treatment center. "Buy me a ticket!" she would angrily demand. "I'm done! We're done here!"

Just because I didn't understand what was going on didn't mean that the Clove House team was doing no good. On the contrary, Elena had made significant strides in their care. They had persuaded her to bring her trauma out into the open. This meant she could finally start to work through it.

But, for Elena, letting the rape come to the surface after all those years was like being raped all over again. Once more, she was living through enormous emotional storms of rage, hatred, and shame. This time, Elena didn't have the comfort of her eating disorder behaviors to calm those storms back down. She couldn't starve the feelings away. And the medications she was on didn't help her suppress those feelings, either. They were there to help keep her from slamming on the brakes and covering those feelings back up again.

I didn't understand much about the process, though, and it left me feeling anxious and mystified. When exactly was Elena going to get *better*?

Now, Emily suggested a course of action I hadn't expected at all. "Can you come out to stay with her, Mrs. Dunkle? You could bring her into treatment in the mornings."

This wasn't a welcome suggestion. I loved my daughter very much, but I absolutely hated minding her business. The times we had been happiest were the times when Elena had been well; she could share with me the parts of her life she wanted to share, and I could cheer her on. But the times when I had had to "manage" Elena—to wake her up in the morning and nag her through her days—those had not been happy times.

I had no desire to step back into that role. I didn't want to run my daughter's life.

"Oh! I—I don't know," I stammered. "I mean, you know I don't live there. I'm several states away. I can't just move into a hotel, I've got my family here to take care of." And in my head, I'm afraid I added, *It's your job to manage her. Not mine!*

"I'm not sure how long you would need to be here," Emily said, "but maybe only for a week or so. If Elena does well and stops self-harming—if she shows us that she's trying—then she can go back into our halfway house program. And it would give you two a chance to go through some family therapy sessions."

"Me? Why?" I said blankly. "Elena's an adult now."

Three years before, during the Summer from Hell, I would have jumped at the chance to do family therapy. But back then, one psychiatrist after another had blocked us from Elena's care. Now, Elena was an adult, and that was exactly how I saw her. She had lived on her own for a year, and even in our house, she had had her own independent existence. She had made it clear, in a thousand arguments, that that was how she wanted things to stay.

I was ready to let things stay that way, too.

"Elena's family has no say over her treatment," I pointed out. And, again, in my mind, I added, *This isn't my job! I'm not welcome in this part of Elena's life. This isn't my problem anymore, and that's fine with me. She tells me all the time to let* her *handle it.*

"We think family therapy would be helpful," Emily said.

"Well, sure, then," I said, and I let it drop. But I still didn't see the point.

Together, Emily and I worked out the details. Elena's care team would ask the insurance company for approval to put Elena back into twenty-four-hour care for a few more days. In the meantime, I would drive out, spend one night in a hotel alone while they assessed how well Elena and I did in some sample sessions together, and then, if all went well, Elena would spend the next week in the hotel with me. If she handled that week successfully, they would let her back into their halfway house program. Then I could go back home.

Waking up Elena, doling out medications, pushing her to get ready in the mornings and to eat dinner in the evenings—it all sounded very distressing. And then there was the purging. She had thrown up for years. What if she was vomiting, right there in the hotel room? Was I supposed to lock the bathroom door and do some sort of sick inspection routine?

And the cutting. What about the cutting?

Oh, this was going to be ghastly!

"You know I don't have any special training," I said. "Elena purged for years right here in the same house with me. So, if she decides to purge or hurt herself, I'm not exactly sure . . . I mean, what do you think *I* can do?"

"We're not looking for you to give her nursing care," Emily said. "It's just to keep her company, and to call nine-one-one if things go wrong. We'll see you soon, Mrs. Dunkle. Good-bye."

I replied automatically and hung up the phone.

Nine-one-one?

I got a shivery feeling in the pit of my stomach. I would have cried if I believed in doing that sort of thing.

Nine-one-one!

Some of my worst memories crawled out of the back of my brain, and my imagination served them up in my own private documentary movie. The crude slash of a razor cut healing on the inside of a forearm. "I wasn't trying to kill myself, Momma!" Valerie walking downstairs, humming, and her hands . . . What was wrong with her hands? . . .

I crept away from the memories like a kicked dog. I wanted to put my head under the blankets and howl. Of all the places I'd had to go with my daughters, this was the *one* place I had never wanted to come back to.

But I didn't howl. I reached for paper, and I wrote out a packing list. And then I walked out and had a matter-of-fact conversation with Valerie about it. "I just hope it goes okay" was all I would reveal of my anxiety.

"She's pretty crazy," Valerie agreed.

Joe and I talked it over that night as I packed. He was supportive and a little worried for Elena and me both.

"Tell her I love her," he said. "Give her a hug for me."

I remembered Elena's latest angry phone call. I wanted to give that hug, but would Elena accept it?

Would she even talk to me?

A long cross-country trip later, I arrived at the city that was home to Clove House and joined the traffic on its outer loop. The city was sprawling and impressive from the highway, full of modern glass office buildings and big hospitals. I drove further in, through gorgeous historic neighborhoods with wide lawns and quaint mansions. What a beautiful place!

And Clove House didn't look clinical, I was happy to see. It didn't look like Drew Center had, like a massive imposing University of the Mentally Ill. It looked comfortable. A busy Starbucks occupied a corner across the street from the office building that housed it.

With butterflies in my stomach, I introduced myself to the receptionist behind the glass. *At least this place has a receptionist,* I thought to myself, and I remembered getting trapped in the empty waiting room at Drew Center.

I'm so afraid, I thought while I waited. *I'm so afraid this is going to be ghastly!* And my imagination replayed for me snippets of that furious voice on the phone, of that stranger who seemed so full of rage.

After a couple of minutes, Elena came out to greet me, and all my worries melted away.

Elena didn't look like a stranger. She looked like my beautiful daughter. Her face wasn't gaunt and pale anymore. She looked better than she had in years. Even the color in her cheeks was different: a bright, healthy pink. I'd gotten used to the gray skin tone of anorexia.

A little shyly, Elena hugged me. So she felt shy, too! Maybe she, too, had been afraid.

"Do you want to eat lunch with me?" she asked.

"I'd love to!" I said.

Elena's meal arrived in courses: salad, soup, chicken tenders, and fruit for dessert. It was a lot of food, but she handled it like a pro. I hadn't seen my daughter eat with such matter-of-fact ease in years. While we had our meal, she told me stories about the girls she lived with. But she wasn't using the stories to keep the food away this time. That was an exciting change.

This new Elena was a little more subdued than I was used to, but hints of the old Elena surfaced from time to time: a wry smile, or a sudden sparkle in her eyes. It was obvious that she had made some important friendships. But what I couldn't get over was how much better she looked. Her whole body had filled out in a way I had never even known it could. She didn't look like a thin little old lady anymore or a child from a famine zone. Now she looked like a real young woman in her twenties.

"You look so healthy," I said. "You look fantastic!"

"Mom," Elena said a little apologetically, "it's better if we don't talk about appearances. That kind of talk can be triggering for eating disorder patients."

"Triggering?"

"It can make us obsess about negative thoughts." She sounded like she was reciting a rehearsed speech. "It can bring out our interior critic and increase the urge to engage in negative behaviors."

"Oh, I get it. Sorry."

"No, that's okay. Don't worry about it."

I watched Elena work her way through the plate of fruit salad in silence. I had said that I got it, but I didn't really. Why would a compliment release negative thoughts? I thought I understood insecurity pretty well, but compliments made me feel better.

"So, how's Valerie?" Elena wanted to know. "Is Clint nice? What's Gemma doing now?"

"She's smiling," I said. "And she's just started making a noise that's maybe a laugh—this robotic giggle that makes everybody in the room laugh. She's found her feet, too, so as soon as you put a pair of socks on her, she pulls them off. Valerie can't bear to put her down."

Elena smiled. "I wish I could see her."

"I watched her get her two-month shots," I said. "Clint wanted to come, too. Valerie was just like she always is, joking with the nurse, but you should have seen Clint's face! When the nurse gave Gemma her shot, he turned green. Really green! There he is, this big strong guy with biceps like tree trunks, but he couldn't bear to see them hurt his baby. He has more names for her than I can even remember: Angel, Itty Bitty, Precious, Princess . . . He just adores that child."

"I wish I could see her," Elena said again.

After lunch, I met Emily. Elena's therapist was very young. She hardly looked older than Elena herself.

"I'm going to arrange for you two to have a pass for the afternoon," she said. "Why don't you go take a walk together and get some fresh air? Just be back before the van leaves to take Elena to the overnight house."

Elena and I went downstairs in silence, and I waited while she smoked a cigarette. "I'm down to four a day," she told me, but her voice didn't hold much enthusiasm. I knew that the Clove House staff strongly discouraged her smoking.

"Do you know any good walks nearby?" I asked.

"I don't want to walk," she said. "I want to go to the hotel and rest."

"But Emily said we ought to walk," I said, feeling a little worried, as if I'd just been invited to cut class.

"This is the first break I've had in over two months," Elena pointed out. "They run their program seven days a week. I don't want to walk. I walk all the time. I just want to sit around and see what's on television."

This sounded so reasonable that I drove us both to the hotel.

I liked my hotel room. When the desk clerk heard I was in town to visit my daughter in the hospital, he booked me into a corner suite instead of a regular room. It was on the third floor, and it had wide clear windows on two sides, so I could see over the nearby buildings to distant gray clouds. The furniture and room colors, taupe and soft green, looked peaceful.

Elena turned on the television, curled up on the bed, and instantly fell asleep. I muted the television and unpacked my things into the dresser. It felt good to be moving in, even if it was just for a week. I lined up the books I'd brought with me on the kitchenette counter, and I set out my laptop on the writing desk.

After a couple of hours, I woke Elena up. She didn't yell at me in that exhausted monotone as she had a few months ago. She just blinked and stretched. Then we drove back to Clove House.

"Come back tomorrow afternoon," the receptionist told me. "After lunch."

The next afternoon, Elena had another free day, and this time, we did go for a walk. We wandered through the little shops nearby. Then we found a bookstore and vanished inside, vanished from ourselves and from each other like water drops soaked into a sponge.

When we returned to awareness forty-five minutes later, Elena had two books of short stories to read that night, and my imagination had the memory of dozens of old black-and-white photographs to play with: handsome young men standing by their covered wagons; earnest, unsmiling girls; grandmothers who had been born in the old country; and babies lying in their coffins. Bouquets of flowers had been tucked in next to those babies' little fists—flowers that had lived longer than they had.

I thought of Gemma and felt a pang. She was growing up every minute that I wasn't there. But at least I had the comfort of knowing I'd see her in a week or so. No wonder Elena felt so bad about missing out.

Emily came out of her office when we returned. "How did things go?" she asked. The question sounded artificially cheerful, like the greeting of a tour guide or a first-grade teacher.

"I had a lot of fun," I said.

Elena stayed quiet.

"That's great," Emily said. "Tomorrow morning, why don't we have a family therapy session. Say, nine o'clock?"

On my way out, Elena walked with me through the main room, where the other patients were resting. But this place wasn't what Drew Center had been, a sort of reform school dominated by locked doors. The whole place felt friendly and informal, like a small private school run by a principal with advanced views. The Clove House staff members weren't in white uniforms, either, and their greetings sounded warm and genuine.

But the patients—*they* were something else again.

The patients assembled in that warm, welcoming room looked very creepy. They were so abnormally, painfully thin—so ridiculously tall for their features—that they looked like grade school children who had been stretched on Willy Wonka's taffy puller. And even when they laughed, their eyes stayed tired and shadowed. They looked ready to give up on life.

Elena didn't look like that. She looked like Elena, a healthier and better-looking Elena than ever before. I couldn't see Elena as one of those skinny, towering little girls with abnormally long legs and knobby knees.

"I don't get it," I said to her. "What do they do about their schooling? Like that girl—is she working on homework over there?"

"Mom!" Elena said, and her tone carried an amused warning. "She's getting her master's degree."

I took another look, and a shiver caught me by surprise. That rail-thin Alice in Wonderland child—a woman in her twenties? It didn't seem possible!

In the morning, I climbed the stairs to Clove House again, feeling as nervous as I had on Day One. I'd been in only three therapy sessions in my entire life, and never in anybody else's. Except for the one disagreement with the social worker, I had enjoyed my sessions thoroughly. How could it not be fun to talk about yourself to an attentive audience?

But this time, things were different. This wasn't my session, it was Elena's, and I had never had a group session before. What would it be like? Would it be quiet and helpful? Or would it explode into some sort of horrible *Jerry Springer* episode, with nasty statements and sordid accusations?

Meanwhile, my imagination played me helpful scenes of counseling sessions from the movies: "Do you want to tell your sister how angry that made you feel?"

Was that really the kind of thing therapists said?

The receptionist directed me to Emily's office. She wasn't there yet, but Elena was sitting on the couch.

"Hey," she said as I sat down beside her. "I was thinking we might go to the mall. My clothes don't fit right anymore, and I'm not allowed to wear things that are tight. Do you think we could do some shopping?"

"I'd love to!" I said, and I meant it. The thought of Elena buying new and reasonable sizes put me over the moon. I didn't need to run any numbers in my head. This was exactly what money was for.

"Good!" Elena said. "So, maybe you could mention it to Emily. She's more likely to go for it if it's your idea."

"Really? But—I barely even know Emily. Why wouldn't she listen to you?"

I didn't get the chance to find out. At that moment, Emily walked into the room and closed the door.

And Elena became someone else entirely.

"So," the therapist began. "So . . ."

I gave Emily a puzzled smile. Elena didn't. She was staring at the closed door as if she were melting holes in it with her gaze. My daughter had become a concentrated ball of hate.

The moment stretched and stretched until the silence started screaming. I didn't want to break that silence. This was an ugly game of tug-of-war, and it had nothing to do with me.

Finally, Emily broke it herself.

"So," she began again. "Elena, would you like to talk to your mother about some of the progress you've made?"

"Nope," Elena said—the briefest of monosyllables, pushed out with the quickest, smallest breath of air.

"Well, then," Emily said, "how about if I do it?"

And Elena gave the briefest, most noncommittal shrug.

So Emily began to tell me about the work she and Elena had done together. She told me how Elena had brought her a favorite pair of jeans because they were her "measuring jeans": she had had a habit of putting them on to see how well they fit. When Elena had reached a certain weight, she and Emily had held a celebration and thrown the jeans away together. "Because you don't need them now, do you?" Emily said, giving her an encouraging look.

Elena just glared by way of answer.

I couldn't take it anymore. Combat is a very stressful spectator sport.

"That reminds me of something," I said quickly. "Elena talked about wanting to go clothes shopping while I'm here. She doesn't want to keep wearing the clothes that aren't a healthy size."

"That's a great idea!" Emily said. "Why don't you two go this morning? I'll write you a pass right now."

The instant we were out of the office, Elena became herself again. "You know, we go on an outing a week," she said as we walked to the car. "We went to the botanical gardens last time. And we've been to the zoo. One day, we went and got our nails done."

"So, why were you like that in there?" I asked.

"Like what?" she said. But her expression had become careful.

"Why were you mean like that to Emily?"

Elena curled her lip. "She deserves it!" And then she changed the subject.

In the car, Elena plugged her cell phone into the stereo. "Listen to this, Mom," she said. "It's my new favorite song."

I smiled to myself. How many times had I heard her say that?

Elena and her friends had had a number of outings to the mall, so she already knew where the best deals were. She led me into one of the clothes stores. "Not here, Mom," she said as I slowed down to look at a blouse on a mannequin. "They always put the pricy stuff out front. Just don't even look at it. You've got to walk straight through to the sale racks."

I had a lot of fun shopping with Elena that day. It was nice to see her buying clothes that weren't tight. She made some excellent choices, and thanks to her attention to the sale racks, we paid excellent prices, too.

"It's time for a snack," she told me after a couple of hours. "Let's go to the food court."

"Okay," I said. "What are you in the mood for?"

Elena ignored the question.

At the food court, she studied the menus like a student cramming for an exam. She decided on two scoops of ice cream.

"Will you order them for me?" she said. "I have a hard time asking for food."

"Well . . . What kind do you want?"

"It doesn't matter."

"It has to matter," I said. "There's ice cream you like, and there's ice cream you don't like."

"Okay. Pick some ice cream I like," she said, sitting down at a plastic table.

I chose two scoops of vanilla in a bowl because that's what she used to like when she was a little girl. "I hope that's what you wanted," I told her as I set down the bowl.

Elena stared at me in amazement, as if I had suddenly begun to speak French. Then, silent, grim, and focused, she ate her way through the scoops of ice cream. Everything about her body language spoke of the effort it was costing her. She might as well have been forcing down scoops of shortening.

I found myself choking on my own ice cream. I had known that Elena didn't eat much, but I had thought of that as a question of will-power. It had never occurred to me that eating, for Elena, might be just as difficult as not eating would be for me.

The next afternoon, Emily gave us a free pass again, and Elena and I escaped from Clove House like schoolchildren on a field trip. It was a sunny, sparkly day, and as we headed back to the mall, we passed an art fair in a public park. I stopped the car, and we spent a happy couple of hours looking around.

"Isn't this city great?" Elena said. "I like it better than Texas. I wouldn't mind living here."

"Better trees for sure," I said, looking up at the majestic trees shading the art fair tents. "Not like our shrimpy little post oaks."

"Maybe I could go to nursing school here," Elena said, and her face lit up with hope and longing. "There are several good nursing schools in this city. I've been asking around."

I hadn't heard Elena talk about nursing school in months.

Emily gave Elena a pass almost every day, and the two of us spent the whole time shopping. Then, in the evenings, we sat cross-legged on our hotel beds and told each other stories. Now that Elena had spent months in a treatment center, many of those stories were excruciating.

"One of my friends here got gang-raped on her way to school," she said. "She couldn't tell her parents. Each time she goes to Clove House, she gets better for a while, but when she goes home, she has to go to the same high school again, and the guys who raped her come up to her and laugh at her in the hall."

At the thought of that, my hands automatically balled into fists. There are times when a belief in hell can be a comfort.

"She needs to not have to go back to that school," I said. "She needs to tell her parents what's wrong."

"She can't. It would freak them out."

"It freaked us out, but you told us anyway."

"You aren't like them, Mom. Trust me on that."

Then Elena told me about a woman there who'd had parents who had joined a cult. The cult members would put on masks, and they would rape and torture the little girl. It went on for years, until the state took her away.

"My friend Stella told me that one of the little kids came in wearing a costume," Elena said. "He was so excited to show everybody what he was going to be for this movie premier that he wore his costume to Clove House. And that woman from the cult, she saw him, and she had a PTSD flashback. She couldn't stop screaming. They had to call an ambulance to take her away."

I thought about that: the little boy, happy and excited, trying on a new persona for the day. What had he been? Something monstrous, so he could be less afraid of the monsters in his world? Something strong and powerful, like a superhero? And then: the grown woman takes one look at him and starts screaming at the top of her lungs. She's locked in her hideous memories and can't get out.

What a horrible experience for them both!

"Another friend of mine was in a very serious car crash, and that's what started her eating disorder. Her family was badly injured, permanently injured, and she can't handle the guilt."

"Why? Was she driving?"

"No, she was too little to drive. But she was the one who had wanted to go out for ice cream."

"Oh, my God! That poor girl!"

Elena fell silent. She was staring out the window at the deepening twilight. I loved those big windows, too, with their view of miles of trees and outlines of city. But this time, I stared at Elena instead.

She was looking so much better, with rounded cheeks and shining eyes. With normal weight on, she looked so much more mature. She had always had a cute figure, but I used to laugh and say that she had the hips of a twelve-year-old boy.

Clove House had done medical testing. Elena's eating disorder had stunted her bones. She would never have the height or the full woman's figure she should have had. It hurt my heart to know that, to know this had happened on my watch. But we had trusted Dr. Eichbaum. We had trusted his diagnosis: ambitious, dramatic—but nothing to worry about.

So much to look back on. So much to regret. And maybe Elena was thinking the same thing.

"I've been working on my memoir," she began.

"Good for you!"

"We have lots of time to write in our journals," she said, "so I've been trying to write things down. But I can't. I just can't do it."

Immediately, I slipped into writing-workshop mode. "Maybe you're overthinking it," I said. "You don't have to hunt for big words or perfect explanations. It can be as simple as the stories you've told me tonight: just think how you would say them to me, and write them down like that."

Elena broke in on this well-worn advice. "No," she said. "It isn't that I can't *write* it. I just can't *do* it."

She turned back from the view of the window and glanced my way, and for a fraction of a second, the pain she was in shone out through her eyes. It seared its way into my soul.

Raped at thirteen, a goofy, silly girl, unable to defend herself or shed the shame. Locked up and bullied in one hospital after another, until her trust in authority figures was broken. Stressed out, pushed along through high school and college, forced to pretend that she was in complete control, that she *had* this, that she could get past it. Betrayed by her bosses at the university after all her hard work, belittled for the very condition she *couldn't* control—for the one part of her ambitious existence that she had carved out to belong to *her*, that was nobody's business but *hers*. And then, the baby, her own little butterfly baby, with its own light, perfect heartbeat . . .

Yes, I could understand why she couldn't do it.

"Well . . . Maybe it's just not time yet for your memoir," I said awkwardly. "It's something that can wait until you're ready."

Elena looked back at the view outside. Her brows were furrowed. She was chewing on her lip.

"I just wish," she said, "that you could help me."

And that pain seared through me again.

"I—I just think that it isn't my book," I said. "It's not what I'm good at, not at all, it's the way *you* think, it's what *you* do well. I'm right here, though. I'll read what *you* write. I can help *you* write it . . ."

Elena's expression didn't change. "Sure," she said, and she let the matter drop.

A few more days of stories and shopping brought us to the last full day of my visit. In the morning, I would take Elena back to Clove House, and I would start the long drive home. Elena had had no self-harming issues at the hotel with me, so Clove House was taking her back into their halfway house.

At the hotel that night, Elena sat on her bed and watched me pack.

"I want to go home with you," she said. "I want to see Valerie and hold my niece. I want to get to know Clint. I want to be part of Gemma's life."

And her eyes filled with tears.

Worry flooded through me. Yes, Elena was making real progress here—I could see that now. But I could also see how fragile that progress was.

"But you've got to get better first," I reminded her. "Remember, you came here to get better."

"I'm doing day treatment now. I can do that back home. Remember the director at Sandalwood that I talked to last year, the one who said I have anorexia? Sandalwood runs a day program just like the one I'm in here."

"But we don't know if they'll take you."

"Sure, they'll take me."

"We don't know if they're on our insurance program. I don't know if I could get you covered there."

"You can call them tomorrow and ask. But Dr. Greene already told me that our insurance company wants me back in Texas."

This was true. Lynn, the patient advocate, had recently told me the same thing.

But at the same time, those worries wouldn't stop fluttering around me. I hated myself for sounding so negative. Maybe the old, angry Elena had been right: I always seemed to have something bad to say.

"It's just that you're doing such important work here," I said, "and that work is very hard for you. At home, you'd have lots of distractions. You need to make sure nothing interferes with your recovery."

"I'm not doing anything here that I can't do somewhere else," she said. "Anyway, it's my decision."

It was true that I wanted Elena to be able to make her own decisions. She was an adult, and she needed to be able to feel like one. She had been the one who had decided to come to Clove House, and ultimately, that had been important in helping her push through some very painful times.

"But are you making that decision for the right reasons?" I asked.

"Yes, I am," she said. "I should be near family, and there's an eating disorder center near family, in our own city. It'll work just as well as this one."

The plan actually made a lot of sense. It would make the insurance company happy, and they had certainly bent over backward to make us happy. It would save us the cost of Elena's stay each night at the halfway house. And if family therapy really *was* important, well, we could certainly do that at home.

But still . . .

Was it my good sense talking? Or was it just my own anxiety? Was I becoming one of those faint, fearful mothers who hovered and fretted and never had anything nice to say? My imagination obligingly pictured an Edward Gorey mother for me, moping through endless passages of crosshatched stone, trailing a long handkerchief from one limp hand.

Maybe I didn't look like that, but it's how I sounded.

"We don't know anything about Sandalwood," I pointed out. "You may hate it."

"I hate Clove House. So what? That doesn't mean I can't get what I need there."

She certainly hates Emily, I thought. *Poor Emily! But she's right, they've still done good work together.*

In the morning, I dragged my suitcases to the car, and we drove through gray drizzle to Clove House. Elena went to talk to her care team about leaving while I stayed in the waiting room and made calls.

It surprised me how quickly everyone jumped on board with the plan. Sandalwood back in Texas had an opening. They booked an introductory appointment for the following Monday. Lynn at the insurance company thought it was a fantastic idea.

"You'll need a waiver, of course," she said. "Sandalwood isn't a preferred provider, but we don't have a preferred provider in the area that supplies that particular service. We'll have to arrange a single-case agreement with them. I'll start working on it right away."

Dr. Greene called me into her office within minutes and gave me an envelope full of paperwork to take with me.

And as Elena came walking out with her arms full of therapy art, was that relief I saw in Emily's eyes?

"Good-bye, Elena," Emily said. "I'm glad I got to work with you. Good luck!"

"Meh," Elena said, turning away.

In the parking lot outside, Elena was jubilant as she waved up at Clove House's windows. All the patients were standing there to watch her leave. Enthusiastically, they waved back.

We drove out onto the rainy highway, and Elena put her playlist on. "Oh, here it is, Mom," she said. "Listen to this. It's my favorite song."

"What happened to the other one?" I teased. "I thought that one was your favorite."

"This is better," Elena said. "That's my *old* favorite song. This is my *new* favorite song."

That made me laugh out loud, and I pushed aside the unwelcome image of the Edward Gorey mother.

We've gotten past the bad times, I thought. *Things are getting better now*. And I imagined the Dunkle slumber party with the addition of Elena's quick wit and ready laughter.

I can't wait, I thought. *The whole family will be under one roof again. How many families get that kind of second chance? How many mothers have that kind of luck? Except, there's no such thing as luck.*

And Elena and I sang all the way home.

CHAPTER THIRTY-TWO

Elena was the only thing the Dunkle slumber party had been missing. She couldn't get enough of her brand-new niece. She held baby Gemma and wouldn't put her down. And she and Clint fell into a fun and annoying brother-and-sister role that came naturally to both of them. They teased each other and tripped each other and punched each other on the arm.

"Oh my *God*, you two!" said Valerie.

The next morning, I came into the kitchen to discover my girls sitting in lawn chairs in the backyard, talking and smoking their cigarettes. Over my dead body, Valerie had started smoking again now that Gemma was born. I hated the habit—hated it with a passion.

But when I looked out the window and saw my girls that morning, I felt bittersweet nostalgia. They looked so much like Joe's own sisters had looked, years and years ago. I remembered watching those sisters and their mother sit outside and smoke and talk like that, years before Elena was even born.

Life isn't a line, I thought. *It's a circle.*

"Elena," I called, standing in the doorway as the cats weaved back and forth in figure eights and collided with me softly. "Did you remember to take your pills this morning?"

"Yep!" she called from the lawn chair.

"Did you eat breakfast?"

"Yep!"

"Liar!" Valerie said dispassionately between puffs. "You watched me eat, but you didn't eat."

"Oh, that's right. I wasn't hungry."

This didn't surprise me. Life at the treatment center had helped Elena gain weight, but she still had trouble listening to her body's cues. She didn't feel normal hunger yet.

"Well, why don't you come eat something now," I said.

"Sure. I will in a couple of minutes."

And I went back inside.

An hour later, the girls were watching a horror movie with Clint while Gemma dozed in Valerie's arms.

"Hey, Elena, did you have that breakfast?" I asked.

"Yeah," Elena said, distracted. "Mom, you ought to watch this. You'd like it."

"Nope," Valerie contradicted with calm enjoyment. She might be a wife and a mother, but tattling on one's sibling never gets old.

"Oh! That's right, I forgot."

"I reminded you," Valerie said.

This wasn't good. Missing a meal was one thing, but by this time, it was almost noon, and Elena had missed two. Back at Clove House, she would have eaten two thousand calories by now. Her high metabolism made it very difficult for her to hold on to weight.

"Elena!" I said. "You need to eat breakfast. And now you've missed snack, too!"

"Mom, you've got to chill out about this," Elena said kindly. "This is *my* problem. *I* have to manage it." And my imagination flashed to the image of a helicopter parent, humming along anxiously.

Why was she making me worry like this? Really, it was her fault that I hovered!

"Okay, it's your problem. So manage it!"

"I am. Tomorrow, I start at Sandalwood. I'll be eating five times a day there. It's not going to matter what I eat today. The real work of recovery starts there."

Did that make sense?

Not really. But sort of.

Did I like being a hovering, mopey mom?

Not at all.

"Now, come watch this," Elena said. "It's really good."

"It *is* really good," Clint echoed. "We can restart it."

"Well . . . Okay," I said, and I scooped my old terrier off the couch behind them and took her place. Then, at the look in her sad brown eyes, I scooped her back up and plopped her onto my lap.

So what if I should be doing laundry? The laundry could wait. My three children wouldn't always be together in one room like this, and they wouldn't always invite me to join them. How many mothers had that kind of luck? Treatment was starting tomorrow. This was a fight I could leave to the professionals.

That made me think of poor beaten-down Emily at Clove House. Emily had been the new me. Did I want to become the new Emily?

Not if I could help it.

The next morning, Elena got up early, wrapped herself in the darkest of emotional thunderclouds, and swept out the door to drive to Sandalwood.

"Have a good time!" Valerie called after her.

"Like hell!" Elena said.

At ten o'clock, my phone rang. My heart beat faster as I answered it. Phone calls never meant good news.

"Hello?" I faltered.

It was Dr. Leben, from Sandalwood.

Of course.

"Elena just walked out the door," she said apologetically. "I wanted you to know so you wouldn't be surprised."

I wasn't surprised. I was dismayed and upset, but I wasn't surprised.

"What happened?"

"Honestly?" Dr. Leben said. "I don't know. I think Elena was looking for reasons to make this not work."

That didn't surprise me either. And the Edward Gorey mother fluttered back into my imagination, wringing her hands and trailing her handkerchief.

I told you! she sobbed. *I told you!*

"So . . . What do we do now?"

What do we do? What do we do?

"Well, if I were you," Dr. Leben said, "I'd try to talk her into trying again. Let her know that we're right here for her. We're ready as soon as she is."

Almost as soon as I hung up the phone, the door slammed.

"Hey!" Valerie called. "Do I have to murder you? Gemma's asleep!"

"That place sucks!" Elena announced as she stomped into the room. "I'm never going back there again!"

"Why? ... ," I said. "What? ..."

I could hear the anxious whimper in my voice. I could feel the nervous thumping of my heart. And, oh, God! I could feel myself turning into *her*, that Edward Gorey mother, the silly Victorian melodrama mother whose shrill voice flutters around her children in a series of falsetto grace notes:

Oh, I don't think we should! Oh, I don't know about this! Darling, darling, wait! Can we please *talk about this?*

Meanwhile, Elena was ignoring me (such mothers are always ignored) to pour out an equally melodramatic tale of her own. According to her, Sandalwood was a terrible place where unqualified leaders used their work as a shallow excuse to hustle their closed-minded religious beliefs, where patients were either stooges or cheats, where the kitchen smelled horrid and the staff were uncaring; a place, in short, where no illness of any sort could possibly be healed and where Elena's only hope of survival lay in her rapid and headlong flight.

"It's bad for me to be around people as sick as those people are," she said. "I'm *much* closer to recovery than they are. All they would do is depress me and teach me new tricks. I'm better off here, with my family who loves me."

"But Elena!" I said. "Your family doesn't have the training to help you!"

"It doesn't matter," Elena said. "*I* have the training. I know what I need to do." And she went outside to smoke.

Valerie gave me an elaborate and meaningful shrug. And then she went out after her.

I wanted to burst into tears. I wanted to have a tantrum. Victorian melodrama mother that I was, I wanted to have hysterics.

How had I let Elena do this to me? *How* had I given her all the power? Hadn't I *known* she was too weak? Hadn't I *known* what she would do?

What are we going to do*?*

But I didn't have hysterics because Clint was standing there. Poor man, he was learning far more about our family's inner workings than I would have hoped. But then again, Clint *was* family.

"So . . . pizza tonight?" he asked mildly.

"I was thinking we'd change it up," I said. "Maybe spaghetti."

"Sweet!" Clint said. "I love spaghetti." And he followed the two girls out into the yard. From the kitchen window, I could see Valerie call him over to the chair next to her. Elena gave him a playful shove with her foot as he walked by.

The Dunkle slumber party continued over the course of the next week. Valerie and Clint sat on the floor and shot zombies while Elena cheered them on. I could hear their laughter as I worked on my web pages in the living room. The three of them were having a great time.

I wasn't. I was back to staring at the ceiling at night, almost sick with worry. Elena was surrounded by food, but she was eating almost nothing. She still had that vivacious personality and those pink, healthy cheeks. She could still get out of bed and go do things. But for how much longer?

Valerie asked me to watch Gemma for them while she, Elena, and Clint went out together to get very similar but slightly different tattoos. I wasn't a fan, but then again, it wasn't my money. While they were gone, I rocked my granddaughter and told her nursery rhymes. I sang her the alphabet song as I bounced her in time to its rhythm.

Gemma drank me in with solemn blue-gray eyes. She wrapped her tiny hands around my fingers and pulled them into her mouth to chew on them.

A universe of possibilities. What would she grow up to be?

The front door slammed. "Take a look, Mom!" They'd all gotten stars and their initials.

"They look like tattoos," I confirmed. "You know how I feel about tattoos. So, did you guys eat while you were out?"

"Nope," Valerie said as she walked to the fridge. She located the whipped-cream chocolate cake I'd made the day before and cut a piece for herself and one for Clint.

"Elena," I said, "what have you had to eat today?"

"Mom," Elena reminded me patiently, "*I* have to do this for myself. This isn't something you can do for me."

I held the lid on my anger.

"Sure, I know that," I said equally patiently. "I'm not trying to do anything for you. But: What have you had to eat?"

"I'm not sure," Elena said. "It's important not to count calories."

She wasn't sure? Of course she was sure! Food was all she thought about.

These days, it was all I thought about, too.

Elena had had one brown sugar Pop-Tart without the crusts. That was it, all day long. And what was that—maybe two hundred calories?

"How about the last piece of cake?" I suggested. It wasn't real food, but at least it was something.

"Nah," Elena said. "I'm not really a cake person. I'll get something later."

Later.

I knew what that meant.

And she didn't get something later, of course. I haunted the kitchen instead, consuming cookies out of a sense of desperation. It was a kind of primitive sympathetic magic, as if my own eating would somehow feed my child.

That evening, when Joe and Clint invaded the kitchen to whip up malts in the blender, Elena reached into the freezer for a frozen pickle. "It's the best thing in the world!" she gushed, gnawing on it while we ate our ice cream. "Pickles are great! I've been craving them all day."

Pickles! It was the last straw.

I didn't diet, but I knew an empty food when I saw one. A frozen pickle was nothing but an anorexic trick. Elena not only wasn't eating, she was working *hard* at not eating. She'd have hollows in her cheeks in no time.

"You need to work on your recovery," I told Elena after the others had left the kitchen. "Psychiatrist—therapist—something."

Elena put down her half-eaten pickle, and tears swam in her eyes.

"I miss Clove House," she said. "I miss my friends. You were right, Mom. I never should have left."

I told you! wailed the Victorian mother in my head, having hysterics on my behalf. *She never should have left—and* you *were the one who helped her leave.*

You helped her leave—again!

While the others went back to the PS3 and picked splicers off the ceilings of Rapture, I took myself off to bed and shut the door. Laughter and happy shouts came filtering in as I lay there in the dark.

I had done this. I had let Elena talk me into doing this. Three months ago, Elena had been dying in her room. The only thing three months of treatment had done was buy us a little time—and teach me just exactly how right I had been when I had realized that a little time was all we had left.

I pushed aside my anger and frustration. They were useless here. Elena had a horrible illness. She was the victim, not me. I had seen how painful it was for her to force herself to eat. Would I have the courage to face that kind of horror?

I pushed aside the terror and anxiety, too. They weren't helping, either. And I didn't cry. The quiet little child who had sat with her coloring books in the corner had learned what crying was for. It was for making other people solve your problems for you. Time after time, I had watched children break down and seen people sweep in to gather them up.

My adults hadn't done that. They had had more respect for me than that. They had known—as I had known—that I could solve my own problems. Yes, life had been hard sometimes, and yes, it had been lonely. But I had learned how to take care of myself.

So now, I looked inside my swirling cloud of emotions, and I found the guilt. I hugged it, and I let it help me.

Guilt has a bad reputation. People talk about it as if it's a dirty word. And it's true that undeserved guilt is as bad as any other false and unfair judgment. But it isn't bad because it's guilt. It's bad because it's a lie.

True, honest guilt is a reminder that once, we had the power to choose what to do—and the power to choose is what makes us human. Saying *I feel guilty* is the same as saying *I had options*. And where there were options once, there probably still are. I had made the wrong choice when I had let Elena talk me into bringing her home. Okay, then—what options did I have now?

And really, it was simple once I began to think about it. There was only one thing to do.

It was simple. But it wasn't going to be easy.

When Joe came to bed half an hour later, he found me sitting up in the dark, scribbling down notes on old receipts by the light of my laptop screen.

"What are you doing?" he asked as he passed me on his way to the closet.

"Elena has to go back to Clove House," I said.

"Yes," his voice agreed mournfully from the closet.

So he'd been noticing the lack of eating, too.

"And . . . I have to go with her."

I said it around a lump in my throat. I didn't want to leave my family—not now! We were finally all together again. Valerie, Clint, and baby Gemma: it was such a precious gift to have them with us. I loved the routine of my house. I loved my husband and my animals and my bright, happy blue fish.

But I blinked the tears away. Because I loved Elena, too.

I loved this funny, fragile young woman whose life had come from my life—loved her with a searing, shining passion. And right now, out of all the ones I loved, Elena was the one who needed me most.

Elena couldn't help herself. She didn't have a choice—not really. I was the one who had power here. I was the one who could solve this problem.

"I know Clove House won't take her back," I said, "unless she has someone to stay with her. She was already iffy at their halfway house. It wasn't working out, and I don't think they'll try it again. And the insurance company wanted her to come home because they want her interacting with family. It's supposed to be an important part of her recovery. So, if I promise to stay with her and go to family therapy with her, maybe I can get them all to sign up to it again."

Joe came back through the darkness and sat down on the bed beside me to look at the laptop screen. I'd been looking up hotels and running figures.

"How long will you be there?" he asked.

"There's no way to know," I said. "Only, the thing is—this time, I'm not coming home too soon. This is twice now that Elena's cried and said she wished she'd stayed in treatment. I'm not helping her get out of treatment again."

Joe didn't ask about the crying and wishing. He just sighed and picked up one of the scribbled pieces of paper. It was covered with columns of numbers.

He asked, "Can we afford it?"

I shut down the laptop and put it on the nightstand. "I don't know," I said. "I've got a few places to call tomorrow."

"Okay," he said. Then he lay down and pulled up the blanket.

"You're right," he said, and his voice sounded dull and empty in the darkness. "Since she won't go to the place in town, this is the only way." And when I brushed the notes off my side of the bed and lay down, too, he rolled over and put his arms around me.

I cried there in the dark, in Joe's arms.

I don't want to do this! I thought to myself, a little-child wail in my mind. *I don't want to leave my husband and family. I don't want to leave my grandchild!*

But it didn't matter what I wanted. It only mattered what I could do. And I knew, as clearly as I knew anything, that Joe and I were right.

This was the only way.

CHAPTER THIRTY-THREE

Once again, Elena and I were in the car, and once again, we were singing along to her music. But not for much longer. After hours of thick forests and little towns, the big city was reaching out to us again.

First, the hotel chains appeared, clustered on the outskirts. Then lane after lane added itself to our highway. Gas stations and fast-food restaurants popped up along the access roads, and wide avenues rolled off into new brick suburbs. One office building after another came into view. A green glass hospital sprawled on the crest of a hill.

"It's not far now," I said. "Let's see what thirty dollars a night can buy."

The city that houses Clove House is renowned for its medical care, and people come from hundreds of miles away to seek treatment. The Clove House staff had told me about a special charity in the city that offers cheap lodging and free food to patients and their families. That charity was going to put us up for thirty dollars a night.

As I thought about this, I felt distinctly sorry for myself. I had left behind my grandbaby and the Dunkle slumber party. I was missing the rest of my family. And waiting for us at the end of this drive wouldn't be our nice corner suite with the huge picture windows and the furniture in soft spa greens and browns.

No, Elena and I would be spending weeks—if not months!—at a charity house for thirty dollars a night.

I was grateful, yes. I was very grateful. Our bank account needed the break. But whenever I thought of this hypothetical lodging, my overactive imagination presented me with a youth hostel: bunk beds, shared shower facilities, trestle tables, and bare floors. It showed me a refrigerator full of moldy yogurt and other people's boxes of cold fried chicken. Uncomfortable folding chairs, and the smell of burnt toast. Children crying. Crumbs in the butter.

At least Elena could go to Clove House every day. Me, I'd have no escape from this place for weeks—if not months!

But the GPS hadn't gotten the memo. It didn't know it was supposed to take me to an ugly youth hostel. It led the car through a quiet neighborhood and up to a handsome brick building set back from the street in a green expanse of lawn.

"Welcome!" said the cheerful volunteer behind the counter.

It was a welcoming kind of place.

In the 1980s, she explained, the building had been designed to be an orphanage, and its halls swung out from the main building in an *X* pattern to allow as much light and fresh air as possible into the large rooms.

"Here's our cafeteria," she said, leading us through the clean, pretty space. Sunlight poured through French doors along two sides.

"Of course, we have a wireless network if you've brought your own computer. But here's our computer lab for the guests," and she opened a door to a carpeted room as quiet as a library. Ten or twelve desktop computers hummed softly on its long office tables, and the screens were as big as my monitor at home.

"You're welcome to use the exercise equipment," she said, walking us across a wood-floored gym to a line of treadmills and elliptical machines set up by tall windows at the back.

"And feel free to use any of the parlors," she added, pointing into cozy rooms filled with couches and easy chairs facing big-screen TVs.

I looked around in wonder. The place was . . . fantastic!

Thirty dollars a day—tax-free!

Elena's and my room was at the end of a long hall, with windows on two sides that looked out toward what had once been the playground: an acre or more of grass, and beyond that, a wooded suburb. Our room was plain but large, with white venetian blinds and simple furniture. Some kindly soul had decorated it with a couple of seagull prints and a small wooden lighthouse figurine. It held three twin beds, two desks, two nightstands, and a bookcase. The bookcase was particularly welcome.

Peace and hope flooded through my worried soul as I walked in. *Yes,* I decided as I sat down on one of the beds, *I will be happy in this room.*

That evening, Elena and I unpacked. Unpacking makes a place personal. I always do it as soon as I can. Elena quickly tired out and lay down to watch a video on her laptop, but I kept going. I needed my routines and my order. I needed everything to find its rightful place.

Last of all, I set up my printer on the desk. Then I pulled up the venetian blinds and looked outside.

A flock of Canada geese waddled by on the lawn, honking loudly and stabbing their big black beaks into the grass. They were massive. They were even a little bit scary. I'd never seen Canada geese up close before. And this part of the country had chipmunks. We don't have them in Texas. Several chipmunks were digging energetically in the flower beds outside our windows, showing off their bear-claw-striped backs.

Yes, I thought again, *I will be happy here.*

The next morning, the alarm on my phone woke me up at seven, and I woke up Elena. She smoked a cigarette out on the patio at the end of the hall, and we watched the geese parade by.

"What are they looking for in the grass?" Elena wondered. "Don't they need a pond?"

"No idea," I said. "Bugs maybe?"

I drove Elena to Clove House. It was about twenty-five minutes away, but the drive wasn't stressful. Big trees, handsome houses, and broad lawns: the Texan in me was thrilled to see so much green.

"The botanical garden here is really great," Elena said. "I mean it: it's world-class. You should go sometime while I'm in treatment."

I dropped her off and went home to do my writing work.

But when I got back to the orphanage, I didn't work. I slept. The last two weeks had been horribly stressful, as if I'd had the weight of all our futures on my shoulders. Now, Elena was back where she could be safe and get well. The professionals were taking care of her again. I could fade into the background and go back to a minor supporting role.

It felt blissful to have Elena back where she could get better.

I woke up at one and ate lunch in the sunny cafeteria. It was almost empty. The cook looked as if she were about forty, but she had to be in her sixties. She told me she had fed the "babies" twenty years ago, when the orphanage was still full of children. Her lasagna was amazing—*and* free. And she pointed out the pieces of cake she'd baked that day, waiting in the glass-doored refrigerators. Her black eyes were on me, patient but expectant. It would be impolite not to try a piece, now, wouldn't it?

Her cake was amazing, too. It was pure comfort food. I lingered over the sweet frosting and thought sadly about all the joy Elena was missing. Memories of every person who was important in my life came to me with happy memories of food: either the food we had fixed together or the food we had shared. From my grandmother's lemon pies to Joe's and my halved Cadbury chocolate bars, food was an important way I had been shown love.

I wondered: Was it the food that wasn't good enough for Elena? Was she simply blind to that love? Or was it Elena herself who wasn't good enough for the food and the love that came with it?

At six thirty, I drove back to Clove House and picked up Elena. She climbed into the car, excited and purposeful.

"Brenda's my new therapist," she said. "I actually kind of like her. She asked me to write down the things I want to accomplish while I'm here."

She opened her notebook and read out a very ambitious list. She wanted to be sure to pay attention this time because she knew now how strong the eating disorder was. She wanted to make the most of her time here. She didn't want to go home and repeat the same cycle again.

I almost sang as she read these sentences aloud. I felt over the moon to hear her putting together hopes and goals again. I felt as if I had wings, as if I were floating above my seat, as if the car were floating effortlessly down the highway.

"Oh, and this," Elena said, pulling out a handful of prescriptions. "They want me to start the new doses tonight."

The car and I thumped back down to earth.

"*More* pills?" I said in dismay. "They haven't seemed all that helpful." And I remembered Elena's wild rages from a couple of months ago.

"Six different kinds," she said, fanning them like a poker hand. "They're not all new, though; some are new doses. This one's morning and night now. This one's just morning. This one's three times a day. So's this. This one is just at night."

So many pills! But if Elena needed them . . .

"Are they sure this is necessary?" I said. "I didn't know anorexia needed so many different pills."

"Mood stabilizer," Elena explained, shuffling through them again and reading off the names. "SSRI. Anti-anxiety, anti-OCD, panic disorder . . ."

"Good Lord! Isn't *that* one for schizophrenia?"

"Yep, but for me, since I'm not schizophrenic, it's just supposed to make me sleep and help me gain weight."

"Well . . . That's good, I guess . . ."

But—an antipsychotic? *Really?*

Then again, it wasn't as if *I* knew what my daughter needed. She had made progress here before, and she was back here again because she needed help from the professionals. I sighed. Best to leave it to Elena's care team. They already had the insurance company second-guessing their every move.

Next door to our orphanage was a twenty-four-hour Walgreens. They were bound to have our pills. I parked in the orphanage's horseshoe drive next to today's crop of farm trucks and SUVs, and Elena and I hiked through the trees and the goose droppings to the Walgreens parking lot.

A Canada goose–size dropping is no joke.

At the pharmacy, we turned in her winning hand of prescriptions and then separated to waste time until they were ready. Elena found a horror title in the Redbox outside the door and came to fetch a credit card to coax it out. "It looks like it has awful special effects," she gloated. I found an air freshener for our room that smelled like warm cookies, then wandered into the candy aisle and discovered almond M&M's. Elena found me again with her hands full of beauty products that for some reason seemed to be named after vegetables. I hadn't thought about vegetables being beautiful before. I decided I'd better get a packet of thumbtacks.

We hauled Elena's pills home in a bulging white paper sack and retired to our separate beds to watch DVDs. Elena giggled over her horrible horror movie and called me over from time to time when things got particularly silly: "Mom, check this out!" Meanwhile I wasted an enjoyable hour watching *Lost*. Elena and I had both become severely addicted to that series. We compared notes off and on and shared thrilling plot twists or witty lines.

I loved the character of Ben best. He was such a magnificent monster.

Companionable quiet reigned as we watched our computers, each one turned down very low. Then, "I'm going to go smoke," Elena said. "Want to come with?"

I did. We sat in plastic chairs on the back steps while Elena breathed in her soothing poison and brought me up to date on the latest gossip.

"Sylvia unzipped one of the Foofs and crawled inside," she said, referring to Clove House's massive beanbag chairs. "She fell asleep in there, and the staff couldn't find her for hours. Someone even came and sat on her Foof, but she's so little, she had curled up beside the cushion, and even when you were sitting there, you couldn't tell.

"The staff were going out of their minds! They ransacked the entire place. They were going to have to call nine-one-one and report that they had lost a patient. That's very bad.

"Then, all of a sudden, there's Sylvia! She's sitting up, blinking, saying, 'What did I miss?'"

I laughed. "I'll bet they unzip every single Foof from now on."

"You've got that right!" Elena said.

We walked back to our neat, pleasant room. "So, where's my drugs?" Elena asked.

I picked out the two pastel circles that made up her nightly regimen and fetched her a glass of water. Then I put away the DVDs and her socks and lined my shoes up and went to change into pajamas.

By the time I got back a few minutes later, Elena was already out. Not asleep—out like a snuffed candle. Her laptop still spun and glowed with life, but she didn't. She looked like a fallen statue.

I watched my daughter for a minute, and the hold that the medications had on her felt so viscerally disturbing to me that the hair prickled up on my arms. She was barely even breathing! Once again, I wondered: did she *need* such powerful drugs?

But that was silly. She was asleep, and that was good, right? It was better than insomnia, anyway. She wouldn't be lying awake and fighting her compulsions.

I turned off her laptop and went to bed.

The next morning, when my alarm rang at seven, Elena didn't wake up well. She could barely follow what I was saying, and she certainly couldn't hold a conversation.

I doled out another round of pills: five pills this time. And then I packed up the medication she was supposed to take during the day.

The drive in was quiet, but that was okay. This wasn't the excitement of the first day, after all, but Elena had her hopes and goals to sustain her. She wanted to work hard. She would get through this.

"Do good work!" I urged as she got out of the car.

That evening, when I picked her up, I asked, "How was the day?"

"Slept through it," Elena muttered. And she fell asleep in the car on the way home.

The next morning was just as bad. And the next. And the next. Gone was Elena's enthusiasm and excitement. Gone were her lists of goals. My formerly lively daughter struggled just to keep her eyes open. She didn't tell me stories anymore. In fact, she could barely concentrate enough to speak.

"Have you told Brenda you can't stay awake?" I asked. "Have you told Dr. Greene?"

Elena grunted an affirmative.

"And what did they say?"

". . . Have to get used to it."

"But why? Why do you need these horse tranquilizers?"

No answer. Elena's eyes were closing again.

"Mrs. Dunkle, they're important," Brenda told me when I brought up the subject. Elena's new therapist was a pretty, dark-haired young woman with a no-nonsense attitude. "Elena needs significant help controlling her impulses."

"But why? She wasn't on this level of medication before."

"She had mood swings and anger issues then, too," Brenda noted. "Don't worry. We're monitoring this. If the doses need to change, they will."

But when they did change, they only increased.

Clove House's program ran seven days a week. Nothing broke our routine. Each morning I woke up, roused Elena, fed her pills, carted her to the center, and watched her shuffle off through the door. Each evening, I picked her up and tried to exchange a few words with her. She almost always fell asleep in the car, and any spark of life left in her got finished off by the evening round of pills.

I began to feel lonely and depressed. When Joe or Valerie called me, I couldn't think of any good news. But when I asked for their news, that wasn't all good, either.

"Simon's neck is torn up," Valerie told me. "We took him to the vet, and he's in a cone in the garage."

Guilt flooded through me. I had always taken such good care of my cats! I had never left them outside to fight. But with Elena's worrisome problems and the Dunkle slumber party, the cats had gone outside almost full-time. I just couldn't manage everything at once.

My poor black beast, locked up in the garage—he must absolutely hate it!

"How long will he have to be in the cone?" I asked.

"Until the stitches are out. At least ten days."

Poor Simon! It was my fault. I knew he was a fighter. Tor had the good sense to stay inside the screen porch and out of trouble. But not Simon. Now he was paying the price.

"Can't he be in the house?"

"Considering the fact that he promptly pissed in the living room," Valerie said, "no, he can't."

"It's the stress," I explained. "He does that when he's upset."

"Yeah, well," Valerie said, "I got the message."

That night, I tossed and turned. My head hurt, and I felt horrible. My peace of mind was gone, and so was my comfort.

"I don't feel good," I told Elena the next morning as she smoked and we watched the Canada geese. "I'm getting a cold. I couldn't sleep last night."

Elena flicked the ash away. There were big bags under her eyes, and her face looked puffy. "I feel like shit," she groaned, in agreement or in competition. "My head is killing me."

"It's going to rain again," I ventured after a minute. "More thunderstorms on the way. No wonder those great big peripatetic geese don't need a pond."

Elena rested her aching head on her hand as smoke dribbled out of her lips. She didn't bother to come up with a reply. And when she went to treatment, she didn't bother to change out of pajamas, either.

"Why get dressed," she muttered, "if I'm just going to sleep?"

The next day, or maybe a day three days later, or maybe a day a week later (they all felt the same), I dropped Elena off at Clove House and went back to the room to read manuscript printouts. The *Wuthering Heights* manuscript full of ghosts that I had written when Valerie ran away was back again, all grown-up like she was. It had reached the line-edit stage, the very last stage before my editor passed it along to the art department and it got made into a book. All I needed to do at this point was to make sure that every single word sounded perfect.

That was good because it distracted me from the fact that I had no other writing to do. Since bringing Elena to Clove House, I hadn't found the time or courage to start another new manuscript.

Now I carried the printout to the bed, picked up my red Sharpie fine-point pen, and got to work.

> I was not the first girl she saw, nor the second, and as to why she chose me, I know that now: it was because she did not like me. She sat like a magistrate on the horsehair sofa, examining me for failings.
>
> "I mustn't take a half-wit, though," she said reluctantly, as if she would like to do it. She seemed to consider idiocy the greatest point in my favor.
>
> "Oh, our Tabby's no half-wit," countered Ma Hutton. "She just has that look. You did say you wanted to see an ugly one, miss."

Miserable and sick, blowing my nose until tissues littered the bed, I lingered long and lovingly over this manuscript. The descriptions were so firm and decisive. The characters—even the dead ones—were so vivid.

Could it be true? Was this really my writing?

The supper bell rang. I brushed my hair and my teeth and my yellow tongue and dragged myself to the cafeteria. The old cook considered me gently as she filled up my plate with chicken casserole.

"Still got that cold!" she said, shaking her head.

Lonely for my family, I felt glad that she was worrying over me. She was the only person besides Elena and her therapists who noticed that I existed. Worried and dispirited, I hadn't tried to make friends with the other travelers there. They changed on a daily basis, and besides, they had worries of their own.

So now, I submitted meekly to the amount of food the old cook dished up. If I could have, I would have followed her around the kitchen at this point, like her "babies" from days gone by.

Only once, when I was newly arrived, did I attempt to assert to her my right to an adult existence. I had showed her a photo of baby Gemma. "I'm a grandmother," I had bragged.

And her black eyes, soft at the sight of the little one, had twinkled with amusement. "*Great*-grandmother," she'd said, jerking a thumb at her chest.

Time to pick up Elena. I shoveled in the last forkfuls of casserole because that great-grandmother, my only mother in this state, stood over the dirty-dishes trolley to take our plates from us. I didn't dare hand her my plate half empty. She wouldn't say a word, but her eyes would measure me.

The commute to pick up Elena was like a rubber band, sometimes short and sometimes long even though it was always the same. This evening, it was very long. The light came stabbing through my sunglasses. I felt feverish. My bones ached.

This is turning into sinusitis, I thought.

Elena climbed into the car and sat huddled like a lump of clay. She didn't return my greeting.

I couldn't help myself. I heard myself say brightly and downright idiotically, just like a mother with a grade-schooler, "So, did anything happen today?"

Not that I had ever needed to ask Elena that when she was in grade school. That Elena hadn't waited to be asked.

The middle school Elena wouldn't have waited, either. With her high spirits and merriment, she would have had me laughing over the way a therapist cleared her throat. Even the senior-year Elena would have told me. Hostility or not, she hadn't been able to resist telling me stories. She would have had me crying over the way a patient looked out the window.

If this were the freshman-year Elena, I would have known that twenty-five minutes' worth of commute meant twenty-five minutes of fascinating information on any subject under the sun. "Oh my God, guess *what!*" she would have challenged before she'd even gotten the car door closed. And the answer might have been anything from viper bites to death row confessions. I couldn't possibly begin to guess.

But this Elena, the new Elena, drooped against the window with her eyes closed.

"Nope," she said.

And then we drove in silence.

I couldn't stand it. I was so lonely! "Well, what did you do?" I prodded.

"Slept."

"You slept again. Did you talk to Brenda? Did you tell her that this medicine just makes you sleep?"

"Yep."

"And what did she say?"

"Keep taking it."

"That's it? That's all she could tell you? Just keep taking it?"

Elena opened her eyes and forced herself upright. She gazed out the windshield for the first time.

"This is shit," she said. "I'm not getting better. I want to go home."

Anxiety came fluttering at me, and I could feel it again: my transformation into that helpless Victorian mother who utters feeble protests in the background. The woman who is absurdly careful about drafts. The woman who never dares to wear her best jewelry.

I couldn't be weak like that. I had never been weak like that, not even when I was little. I couldn't turn into an invalid now and wring my hands and utter feeble cries. I needed to remember who I was. I needed to be strong.

But when I heard my voice, all I was really being was whiny.

"You wanted to come here," that whiny voice said. "No one made you do this."

"So? So now I want to go home."

And then later, I thought, *you'll cry and tell me how you should have stayed—and* I'll *be the one left with the guilt!*

"I'm not going to leave," I said. "I believe in your recovery. Your recovery is important."

"My recovery is bullshit. My recovery is a joke."

If only that didn't feel honest and true! If only I could point to all the progress she had made! But, since coming back here, what had Elena done besides sleep?

The Victorian mother in my head sobbed and waved her handkerchief. *This isn't working! It isn't doing any good!* And anger boiled up inside me—anger born of frustration.

It *had* to work! We had no other *choice!*

I pulled up in the horseshoe drive alongside a new crop of cars from out of town, and Elena actually summoned the energy to walk into the orphanage ahead of me. I followed her down the halls, arguing with myself.

I had to remember what was important here. No matter what, I had to hold on to what was important. This wasn't about me. It was about Elena's recovery. That was what mattered.

I couldn't whimper and fuss. I couldn't let myself give way to panic. That had never been who I was.

"Elena," I tried again when I caught up with her at our room. "I know this is very hard, but you committed to this, and your father and I have, too." But then the bitterness and loneliness overwhelmed me, and I couldn't keep the frustration out of my voice. "Do you have any idea how much we've invested in your recovery? Do you know how much this is costing us? You *have* to make progress. You *have* to make this work!"

"There you go," she snapped. "Drag money into it! That's all you ever think about is the money."

All I ever think about—!

A vision rose up in my mind to taunt me: a few of the plans we'd had for that year's money. There was the bathroom remodeling Joe and I had planned to do this summer, the one we had been promising ourselves for years, the one that would finally replace those nasty scratched sinks and smudgy mirrors and the garish '70s wallpaper. There were the cute outfits for Gemma that we hadn't purchased, and nice clothes to replace Valerie's threadbare ones. There were the movies I had wanted to watch with Clint. There was Joe's beautiful white BMW.

"Well, yes," I said, "if you really want to go there, I *do* think about the money, and maybe you could think about it, too. You could think about the hundred-plus dollars each day here is costing, and you could decide not to sleep through your therapy! Maybe then you'd make some progress and get a little better instead of thinking everything is just shit."

"All you do is see the negative!" Elena cried, throwing herself down on her bed. "That's all you've ever done. Well, screw you for your negativity, and your invalidating, and your undermining! Screw you for keeping me here!"

And now I was shouting, too.

"You know what? *I'm* not keeping you here! You go right ahead and leave. You're an adult: you can do anything you put your mind to. But don't think you're going to use *my* car or *my* gas to get yourself out of this, and don't think you're staying in a nice hotel on *my* credit card. Because *I'm* an adult, too, and *I'm* going to spend my money on the things that matter to *me*!"

"Bitch!" snapped Elena, hurling the word out through sagging lips, and even now, her eyes were still half closed. "You're a bitch, Mom! That's all you are is a bitch!"

"And you're a spoiled little plastic girl who's treating therapy like summer camp!" I yelled in return. "You're hanging out with your plastic friends and giggling together and having Spa Day and Nail Day and Pedicure Day. All you're doing, all of you, is sitting around, using up your parents' money! Well, you can all just go ahead and grow the hell up! You're an *adult*, damn it—an *adult*! Now, act like one!"

Elena jumped up, snatched her medicine bottles from my drawer, and stomped by me on her way to the bathroom. I watched through the open door as she ran a glass of water and gulped down her two nightly pills. Then she flopped onto her bed again and closed her eyes. She didn't move for the rest of the evening.

She had escaped and left me mired in a swamp of guilt.

Why had I done that? Why had I lost my temper? I had no idea what she was going through. She'd been through horror and hardship, and I was just making it worse. I felt as if I'd been wallowing in mud.

It wasn't Elena herself who had made me lose my temper. I felt sorry for that poor sallow-faced creature who couldn't stay awake for five minutes anymore. No, it was the fear of my own fear that drove me to it: my fear of that timid woman living in my mind, the one who fluttered and submitted and worried and did nothing.

I couldn't just sit there. I had to *do*! Or else . . .

Or else Elena disappeared into her room. Forever.

That thought skewered me and roasted me over hot coals. That thought ran itself under my fingernails, bit through my body, and crunched my bones. I found that I was walking, hurrying around the room, swinging my arms and cracking my hands together. My head hurt, but my heart hurt more. I could hear my pulse thumping in my ears, and my breaths were fast and shallow, as if I were running.

The white-hot agony of that thought made me want to grab Elena's unconscious body and shake her back and forth like a rag doll, shake her until she opened her eyes and smiled at me and said, "Hey, Mom, guess *what*?"—until she was normal, happy, lively Elena again.

Do something! Do something! I screamed in my head. *This* has *to work. Do* something*!*

But in the end, just what could I do?

The next morning, on the drive in to treatment, Elena managed to keep her eyes open, and she was deliberately even-tempered. We both talked about a few unimportant things, just to prove that we could. But we didn't say any of the things that mattered.

God, my head ached! I could feel the toxic slime of evil bugs gathering in my sinuses. My imagination presented me with a picture: green and yellow beasts, vaguely cow-like, pasturing in the open caverns of my cheekbones. Their manure was running into my nose, a poisonous fluorescent goo that choked me and made my breath stink.

I gave a little groan. Now my stomach was upset. People with imaginations shouldn't get sick.

I dropped off Elena, turned around in Clove House's parking lot, and made the twenty-five-minute trip back to the orphanage. I pulled into the horseshoe drive. Ample parking. The SUVs had scattered to hospitals and clinics for the day.

As I passed the offices in the main hall, the cheerful staff member popped out of a door. She didn't look so cheerful today.

"Mrs. Dunkle," she said, "I was touring guests through the building last night, and we couldn't help hearing the yelling and the four-letter words coming from your room. It was very embarrassing for this facility. I'm going to have to ask you to keep that from happening again."

So painful was this scolding—so unexpected, after the miniscule amount of social contact I'd had lately—that I almost burst into tears. I felt blindsided by it, completely unprotected. I didn't seem to have any emotional defense.

It was true. My daughter and I had been bad guests. We had failed to maintain the basics of good manners.

I hung my head and quickly scurried away.

In the safety of my room, I stood for a while and stared out the window. Thunderclouds massed behind the suburb and rolled in over the deserted playground. Rain hissed down on the gray sidewalk outside, and then hail tapped and rattled on the glass.

The chipmunks and the geese were gone.

If I were at home, Joe would be making special runs to the grocery store to bring home medicine and snacks for me. And Valerie wouldn't let me hold baby Gemma with this cold, but she would bring me cups of tea. She might even show up at my bedroom door and say, "Get dressed, woman! Dad called and got you an appointment. I'm driving you to the doctor."

But Valerie and Joe weren't here, and I didn't have the strength to go down the hall to the kitchenette and make that tea myself. So I huddled under the blankets and shivered and reached for my line-edit printouts.

Soon I was safe in familiar scenes I'd plotted three years ago, watching two little children play with their dolls by a crackling fire while ghosts crouched in the shadows nearby. I let myself get lost in the story, as if it weren't my work at all but an old book I'd found in a forgotten corner of a library.

Did I really write this? It sounded so confident—so unlike the person I'd become.

Would I ever have the nerve to write like this again?

Hour after quiet hour ticked by while drops of rain dribbled down the windows and I tried to do my work. Finally, the nausea and headache took a firm enough grip that I couldn't escape anymore. So I let the printouts slide to the floor, and I rolled over, aching, and the misery I felt flowed through and through me.

Elena was gaining weight, yes.

But she wasn't getting any better.

CHAPTER THIRTY-FOUR

On the morning of our weekly family-therapy appointment, the one day a week when I got to have a pleasant chat with a real living, breathing person who was looking me in the eye, Susan, the therapist, leaned toward me and remarked brightly:

"Elena says you think she's possessed by a devil."

Well, isn't that lovely! I thought.

Elena and I had been at Clove House for about a month. She was marginally more wakeful but still very subdued. To me, she seemed like a zombie, and our relationship had gotten so bad that neither one of us tried to converse anymore. Elena wanted to go home; I wouldn't take her. That was where things stood.

It was true that I hated Elena's eating disorder so much that I pictured it as a devil. My imagination showed it to me as a big, ugly, flabby demon with shiny, sweaty skin, crouching at the center of her soul. It opened its wide, froglike mouth and guzzled down great gulps of loneliness and isolation. It grew fat and sleek on her misery. Meanwhile, it let fall just a few crumbs of peace now and then—just enough shreds of satisfaction to keep Elena working hard to feed it that feast of hunger and pain.

Of course, Elena knew perfectly well that my imagination showed me *everything* in images like that. It pictured problems in metaphor and story. That's how I could write. But Elena must have known that Susan wouldn't get this, and she hadn't made any attempt to explain. She must have gotten a good laugh out of telling Susan about this devil and watching the therapist's shocked reaction.

Possessed by a devil—what a stupid thing to say!

"Well, I certainly don't think Elena needs to go through an exorcism with bell, book, and candle, if that's what you mean," I said.

Susan tilted her head, very professional and interested and coy.

"Can you tell us what you *do* mean?"

Us? There was no *us*, as Susan knew perfectly well. Elena was sitting beside me on the couch, but mentally, she was a world away. Her eyelids were drooping, and she had sunk into the cushions. Ten to one, she was already half asleep.

That left Susan, and Susan had brought this topic up with that slightly smug smile that says, *Until proven otherwise, I am going with the assumption that you are a superstitious, ignorant moron.*

Oh, yeah? I thought.

Time to open up a big ol' can of academia.

"You know I'm a writer," I said. "My writing is based on folklore—on myths. These are the oldest stories we have, and even today, we still can't stop telling them. They center on themes that are ancient and universal. Pluto drags Persephone off to the underworld; the Phantom of the Opera drags Christine off to the caverns below Paris."

In my mind, my goblin King brushed his striped hair out of his bony face and gave me a wry smile.

You, too! I told him, and he nodded.

"Stories like that exist in every country, in every language," I went on. "I think they explain how we deal with the psychological demands of our world. They may even have to do with how our brains are wired."

"I see," Susan said cautiously.

I could tell that Susan was disappointed. She'd probably been angling for emotional hot buttons between Elena and me. Maybe she'd hoped for a nice knock-down-drag-out fight over religion. But Elena was almost asleep. And I wasn't a professor's child for nothing.

"When it comes to anorexia nervosa," I said, "the first thing I think of is Ophelia. Did you know that Ophelia-style mermaid stories occur all over the world?"

Susan fidgeted. "Ophelia isn't a mermaid."

"The story repeats all over the world," I said again. "Ophelia is just the best example. Think about it: think about who Ophelia is. She's the girl who's been used and tossed aside. She more or less admits that she slept with Hamlet, and she may even be pregnant. Then Hamlet turns on her.

He tells her that he doesn't love her and won't marry her, and that she can't marry anybody else, either. Presumably, he's reminding her that she's no longer a virgin. He insults and humiliates her. He even kills her father.

"So Ophelia does what wronged girls and unwed pregnant girls have done since the oldest days of story. She finds some water nearby, and she drowns herself."

Susan glanced at Elena. "But to get back . . ."

"Compare that to the Little Mermaid," I continued, ignoring her. "And I mean the real Little Mermaid, not the Disney one. Andersen's mermaid gives up everything to win her prince—not unlike Ophelia. But her prince doesn't love her. She even has to dance for him and his bride on their wedding day. Her sisters try to persuade her to kill the prince, but she throws herself into the water instead."

As I spoke, I remembered the day when my mother first introduced me to that story, the story where the mermaid doesn't win her prince. So powerful was the spell it put me under that I could remember everything about where I was with the new book she had bought me: in my parents' room, sitting on the edge of their bed as the two of us turned the pages. My feet were swinging. They didn't touch the ground. That book was a board book, I was so little. It was designed so preschool children wouldn't spoil the pages.

A preschool board book about a woman, brokenhearted, unlucky in love, who can either commit murder or lose her own life. Wouldn't Susan have a field day with that!

Not that she would ever hear about it from me.

"So, I ask you," I went on in my blandest lecturing voice, "why has the legend of the Little Mermaid stayed with us? Why is Ophelia one of the most memorable teenage girls in literature? Why are there pools all over the world, watched over by the spirits of drowned girls who pull men down to their deaths?"

Susan's brow furrowed. "Pools?"

"You've never heard of a *rusalka*?" I countered. "That's either a drowned girl who was wronged and killed herself, like Ophelia, or a water nymph, like the Little Mermaid. Either way, the *rusalki* are predatory spirits that haunt sources of water, and they drown men without pity. Deadly female water spirits show up all over Europe and Asia. I know of a mythic water demon like that from Hawaii."

Susan leaned forward, intent again—but probably just intent on bringing this lecture to a close. She asked, "But how does this 'water demon' relate to you and Elena?"

That was a good question.

I didn't know.

"It's a pattern," I concluded. "An age-old human pattern, like Pluto kidnapping Persephone. But this particular age-old human pattern has a special meaning for Elena. She surrounds herself with images of mermaids."

And she didn't even grow up like I did, I thought, *with the tragic mermaid who loses her prince. In her generation, they've tampered with the story to make it work out to a happy ending.*

When was it? I mused. When did my daughter first start showing me pictures of mermaids and Ophelias? She would do Internet searches and scour library books to find them. Most important was Millais's famous Pre-Raphaelite Ophelia, so delicate, surrounded by flowers. *Her clothes spread wide, and mermaid-like, awhile they bore her up . . .*

Was it? Yes, it had to be. It must have been after the rape.

Would I be sharing that with Susan?

No.

"So, if you sum up the patterns," I concluded, "the mermaid/Ophelia embodies a history of sexual violence or mistreatment. She wanted a normal life, but it was a man who took that life away from her. Heartbreak drove her into the water—or back into the water. It was a step from life toward death, and the mermaid is happy to repay the favor. Think about this: the mermaid is the strong one when she meets a human man. He's the one who needs to fear for his life. Is that why mermaids bring mistreated girls such a sense of satisfaction? Is that why they seek out water? Because mermaids have transcended a man's mistreatment, and now they can kill?"

Susan declined to comment. *I brought up religion,* she was probably thinking. *I wanted indignation, vulnerability, and a reexamination in a new light of this family's most fundamental structures. I wanted to break something open, to get something started. This has nothing to do with what I wanted.*

Well, no. Because her approach had been idiotic.

The therapy session ended. I woke up Elena to say good-bye, and then I drove home to the orphanage. I walked quickly through the silent halls, temporarily buoyed up by the talk I'd had. It had been fun. For one hour, I had had fun.

At the turning to my hall, I bumped into a young woman with a black ponytail. Her toddler son was rolling a tricycle down the center of the hallway. I didn't want to interfere with his play, so I fell into step next to the woman. She gave me a wan smile and looked away.

He's sick, I thought with swift, instinctive recognition. *He's very sick. That's why she has that look in her eyes.*

The first night Elena and I had spent at the orphanage, I'd thought, *I'll bet I make lots of friends here.* But I hadn't. I had discovered that I didn't want to make friends. No one here wanted to make friends. We didn't wish one another ill, but our children, our parents, or our spouses were here for reasons that terrified us. We didn't want to have to ask or answer painful questions.

So, as I walked beside the young woman, neither of us spoke. We just smiled vaguely down at the busy little boy. At the end of the hall, he turned around and rolled back the way he had come, and I unlocked my door.

"Bye," I said—the first word I had spoken.

"Bye," the woman answered, turning away.

The minute I walked into the room, my happy mood popped like a bubble. Sad feelings and dreary memories detached themselves from the walls and rushed over to cling to me. Too many angry words and wretched silences . . .

This room was filling up with unhappiness.

It was too late in the day to get any work done now—or, at least, that's what I told myself. I shook a blanket out over my neatly made bed and curled up underneath it.

I could lecture Susan about myth and folklore to put off talking about the truth, but the fact was that I had begun to feel a deep alienation from the drab, silent person my daughter had become. She wasn't a thing like the Elena I had known. We felt so far apart now that I didn't know if we would ever manage to bridge the gulf between us.

Elena and I had done it before. I had looked inside my angry, dramatic teenager and felt a spark of kinship with that young person struggling toward adulthood—yes, and respect, too, because the birth of a grown-up is as messy and painful as the original birth was. And Elena had looked inside me and felt pity for the sad, anxious worrier her mother could be.

But this Elena wasn't like that. I couldn't find my way to her.

And this Elena couldn't find her way back to me.

So I slept. It felt like all I could do. I had nothing more useful to contribute. I woke up long enough to answer the phone and fend off Joe's concerned questions and Valerie's down-to-earth comments, and I made them tell me things so they wouldn't notice that I wasn't telling them anything anymore.

Day by day, Joe and Valerie had their own bad news to report. Simon was getting worse. His neck hadn't healed right, and the new treatments weren't helping. Dylan, my blue beauty, wasn't eating. Clint had left to go work in Georgia, and Gemma had colic again. She was waking Valerie up hour after hour every night.

If I were there, I could do something to help. But I was stuck where I was. And I wasn't in a position to help anybody.

I snuffled and sniffled with sinusitis so bad that it sent me to the emergency room twice. I took cold medicine day and night. I woke up to drive Elena in, and I came home and fell asleep, and I woke up to drive her home, and she fell asleep, and I fell asleep.

Seven days a week, nothing varied our routine.

But one morning, Elena called to me from the bathroom, and her voice had a new tone in it. There was a quickness there—perhaps a hint of excitement.

"Mom, can you come here?"

Elena, excited? Finally excited? Maybe today would be a different day—a better day.

"What's up?" I asked, coming over.

Elena was standing in front of the sink with her back to me. "I can't get it to stop," she said.

A swiftly flowing stream of dark-colored blood was sliding down her arm into the sink. Maybe it was the white porcelain and the stainless steel drain that made that stream of brownish blood look dirty. All I know is that I felt the ugliness of it like a physical blow.

The blood was slipping from a deep gash on Elena's forearm near the bend of her elbow. It was a razor cut—a deliberate cut. I grabbed a blue-checked hand towel off the top of the stack of clean towels on the shelf and clamped it over the wound.

"Lie down," I said. "Right here on the floor."

Elena lay down on the tile with her head on my lap, and I held her arm up in the air over her head. Simple first aid, learned out of boredom one summer in my lonely childhood, when I had devoted myself to the study of my brother's Boy Scout handbook.

A gash. An ugly, vicious cut. A deliberate mutilation. Damage, deliberate damage to the precious body I had cherished and nurtured—to the body I had guarded with my own life since before she was born!

I should understand. I had understood my character, Miranda, when she had cut herself to find relief from her mental anguish. I had even tried to understand the lost and wounded Valerie, with her patterns of burns. But now, I felt nothing but cold, hard anger. I was done with all this. I didn't want to understand.

It took more than ten minutes of pressure before the wound began to close, and the whole time, there was nothing to look at but the underside of the sink. *I should get that cobweb after we get up*, I thought. And then, unhappily, *This hand towel is probably ruined.*

"What did you use?" I asked.

"My razor."

"Why?"

"Because I had a panic attack."

"Elena, I was right here!" I said. "Why didn't you call me if you were in trouble?"

"It was last night. You were sleeping. I didn't want to bother you."

"And you thought *this* wasn't going to bother me?"

We both fell silent at that. Elena's logic was eluding me. As usual.

Elena herself was feeling not only excited but also upbeat. She looked happier than she had looked in days. Her high spirits disgusted me. I was done with understanding. There was nothing about this I wanted to understand.

This, Susan, is why the whole thing feels demonic, I thought with grim fury. *There's a hideous feeding off pain here, a hideous perversion of happiness.*

Elena's excitement only served to make me act deliberately, excessively sensible. "Here, hold this towel in place while I grab my purse," I told her. "And take a book. We'll probably be there a while."

"I'm not going to the ER," she said.

"What? Elena, we have to go! That cut needs six or seven stitches at least!"

"I won't go," Elena repeated. "I'm not waiting at an ER for hours. I need to get to treatment."

My sensible demeanor was gone. I was back to yelling again. "All you do is *sleep* through treatment!"

But Elena had already picked up her backpack and was walking through the door. "If you take me to the ER, I'll refuse care," she said over her shoulder. "When I get to treatment, Ms. Carter can tape it."

Steaming mad, I stalked after this awful stranger through the orphanage halls. Was Elena doing this just to upset me? For the sake of the cheerful volunteers, I kept my mouth shut until we got into the car, but once there, I couldn't contain myself.

"Okay, that's not just crazy," I said. "That's stupid!"

"*Crazy. Stupid.* Thanks, Mom," she said.

"Can you give me one good reason why you're refusing to be responsible about this?"

Elena stared out the window at the morning traffic. We were stopped at a light, with cars all around us. Traffic was heavy. Everywhere, commuters were heading to work. From outside our car, we must look like just another carpool.

"I don't want to have to wait," she said finally.

"Well, you should have thought of that before you sliced yourself up," I said. "That's too big not to stitch, and even so, it'll leave a scar."

Elena settled back and closed her eyes.

"I like scars," she murmured.

And there it was, like a slap across the face: more scars! More cuts, wounds, burns. Damage to my babies—my precious children!

I wanted to scream. I wanted to push my fist through the car horn. I wanted to floor the accelerator until the other cars became a blur, to punch us through to a world where things made sense. Because this cut—this Elena!—made no sense. I refused to allow it to make sense.

That's it! I thought. *I'm* done *with this! This person is a closed book to me. She is a riddle I have no more desire to solve.* I dropped her off at treatment and went home and went to sleep. I escaped from her and her problems entirely.

I know what the next day was. It was Saturday.

Ordinarily, Saturday would mean nothing to Elena and me. Treatment ran seven days a week. But this Saturday was Family Day. Once a month, staff and patients rallied around to help educate their friends and relations about their condition.

This Saturday was my first Family Day. I dropped Elena off at the door as usual, but this time, I parked the car and followed her inside.

The receptionist waved me down the hall toward a classroom-size conference room. About twenty parents, siblings, and friends of patients were sitting in a big circle there. They were talking together in low voices, making the kinds of jokes and comments people make before a tough training class to remind themselves that they're ready for anything.

I didn't have anybody to joke with, and I didn't feel ready at all. I didn't know anybody there, and even if Elena had been there, I wouldn't have felt that I knew her, either. But I took heart from the general atmosphere of nervousness in the room. Others were feeling what I was feeling, too, even if they had friends or relatives to help them get through it.

A small buffet of breakfast foods waited on a table by the door: coffee, bagels, and fruit. I reached for the coffee first and then, even though

I wasn't particularly hungry, I selected a whole-grain bagel and some slices of cantaloupe. As I headed toward a vacant chair, I noticed the generous plates of bagels and fruit balanced on other laps.

Look at me—I'm a healthy breakfast! our plates were proclaiming to the world. *This person doesn't have food issues—no sirree!*

The psychologist in charge of Family Day was familiar to none of us. She'd been invited in from another clinic. This way, she told us, if she brought up a particular issue, we wouldn't think, *She's talking about me!* And we could speak frankly to her, too, without wondering if our comments would come back to haunt us during the next family therapy session.

Family therapy. I spared a second of annoyance for Susan. Demonic possession—what kind of stupid topic was *that*?

The psychologist launched into a lecture on the way eating disorders change the brain. These changes can actually show up on MRI scans, making the brains of some anorexics physically different from the brain of a non-anorexic. The area of the brain that's different controls body image, and that means an anorexic truly can't see himself or herself the way healthy people do. So it doesn't do any good, the psychologist told us, to point out how skinny an anorexic has become. It isn't psychological, it's physiological: the brain itself won't be able to process that image.

As I scribbled notes on a little memo pad, I thought about how hard it was for me to understand my daughter. So it wasn't just my imagination after all: Elena's brain truly *was* different.

Next, the psychologist worked through a list of dos and don'ts. One of them reinforced what Elena had told me when I first came to visit her: "Don't mention physical appearance at all. Even a compliment can redirect the attention of an anorexic to body image, which is never a comfortable thing for anorexics to think about."

I remembered all the times I had complimented Elena's appearance. Then I thought about how quick we humans are to notice the *lack* of a compliment and misinterpret that silence as disapproval. Then I gave a sigh.

I thought, *This is just another one of those anorexia no-win situations.*

But the friendly attitude of the other family members steadied me. Some of them had been coping with their loved one's anorexia for over a decade, and yet they were staying positive. They were holding on to their patience and compassion, and they watched for little signs of progress.

"It's like a yo-yo," one veteran said. "It's up and down, but the lows don't go as low, and the highs are a little bit higher each time."

In fact, this group of family members seemed refreshingly normal, and that secretly amazed me. I realized I had been expecting to find a shadow in their eyes, some collective sign of remorse. Then I realized what an overwhelming load of shame I'd been carrying around with me for the last four years. It had started building up when Valerie had first begun to self-harm, as if those marks on her body were cut and burned into my body, as well, because I should have—I *would* have!—defended that body with my life.

Once again, my imagination showed me that image of the nasty dark stream of blood running down the sink. Meanwhile, Elena's voice was saying serenely, *I like scars.*

I gave a shudder of disgust.

Was it me? Had she done that just to get back at me because I wouldn't let her leave? She knew how painful I had found Valerie's cutting and burning.

"What do you do if your patient wants to leave treatment?" I asked the group. "What do you do if you just want to support her in treatment, but you find that you've become the enforcer, the one who's pushing her to stay?" *And that becomes the reason neither one of you can get along anymore?* I thought.

A veteran mother nodded. "That's a tough one," she said. And a father shared his experience about his daughter's prior hospital stay, when he and his wife had had to stand up to her repeated attempts to leave.

Nobody could really answer my question, but they made me feel better anyway. At least I wasn't the only one dealing with this.

After a couple of hours, Elena and the other patients joined our group: nine or ten rail-thin young women with their arms around one another for support. Taking turns, they read us their own list of dos and don'ts. Elena had chosen to read out this one:

"When your patient talks negatively to you, remember that sometimes it's just the eating disorder talking. Don't react. Give her time to re-center." She looked up at me. "For instance, if she says she wants to do something self-destructive, like stop treatment, just let her cool off for a while. She's just frustrated. She doesn't mean it."

And the other family members shuffled in their chairs, caught my eye, and gave me a smile.

After lunch, the psychologist split us family members into two groups and paired each group with the patients who didn't have family among us. This way, we could ask questions freely without provoking our relative or hurting her feelings, and our group of patients could speak freely in return.

My group held about ten family members and four patients, none of whom we knew. But, although we didn't know them, these patients knew us very well. They sat through group therapy sessions all the time and heard one another's history over and over.

I could tell that the patients in our group felt sorry for us. They genuinely wanted to help. They sat at the front of the room, facing us, and for an hour, they did their best to answer our questions.

"Why don't you want us to give you compliments?" a friend of a patient asked. "If you've been recovering, don't you want to know that the hard work is paying off? Don't you want to hear that you're looking healthier?"

A patient with her hair back in a sandy-blond ponytail spoke up. Although she was thin, she looked athletic, like a long-distance runner.

"That's easy," she said. "I equal good looks with my lowest weight, so if someone says, 'Hey, you're looking great today,' in my mind, I think, *You think I look good now? You should have seen me a month ago! You should have seen me five pounds ago. That's when I really looked good.*"

"But what if you know that the person saw you a month ago? What if I say, 'Hey, you're looking so much better now that you're at a healthier weight'?"

The girl shrugged, and her long plait of hair twitched like a horsetail flicking away flies. "That just . . . doesn't make sense," she said. She said this reluctantly but firmly, the way a polite Christian might react to a description of the birth of Buddha. "Even if you say that," she went on, "you can't make me believe it. I'll think, *Yeah, but he's wrong. He doesn't remember. I looked better a month ago.* Look, I *know* I look better when I've been running my miles."

She fell silent, and we fell silent, staring at one another across the gulf of our differences.

It's hopeless, I thought. *There's no way across. They can't get to us, and we can't get to them.*

"What I can't handle is all the lies," a father said. "I understand the not eating, but the constant lying—it hurts, and it makes me angry. My daughter should know that she can tell me anything by now. I'd give my life to help her. Then she lies to me over and over, stupid lies, lies I'm bound to find out are lies, like whether or not she finished her yogurt."

There was a pause. Then the oldest patient spoke.

"Just please remember," she said, "that we don't want the lies to hurt. It's not personal. But it's so hard to explain how this disease makes you feel. Let's say that I go out with my friends to a movie. I want to enjoy myself, relax, and forget life for a while. Most of all, I want to forget about my anorexia that badgers me all day long. But then my friends buy popcorn, and they try to get me to eat it.

"But if I eat five pieces of that popcorn, I won't even see the movie. I won't be able to think about anything else except how my self-control broke down. I'll be locked in a battle with my eating disorder voice for hours: 'Look at you, you pig, you can't stop shoveling food in your face!' I may not sleep that night. I may have to run five miles to shut that voice up.

"But I can't tell my friends that," she concluded. "There's no way they would understand. So I just say, 'I already ate before I came.'"

We family members sat silent for a minute. I thought, *That is one of the saddest, most honest statements I've ever heard.*

"You've been answering our questions," the father said next. "Is there anything you'd like to ask us?"

The patients stirred and glanced at one another. This wasn't something they'd prepared for. Clearly, it wasn't a part of past Family Days.

"I do have a question," one of them admitted in a small voice. "Is there ever a point when you can't take it anymore? When you just say, 'That's it!' and you stop loving us?"

And with a guilty flush, I remembered my anger: *That's* it!

"No," the veteran mother said firmly. "We never stop loving. Never." She was right. I felt it in my heart. She spoke for all of us.

After the hour was up, we filed back into the main room, and the patients joined their family members again. One girl sat across her father's lap, with an arm around him and an arm around her mother. She looked about thirteen, but Elena had already told me that she was in her twenties.

Her parents were wonderful people—relaxed, easygoing people. They looked like a pair of old flower children. Elena had told me that they'd driven across the country to rescue her from this latest health crisis. They had boxed up all her belongings and brought her and her things safely home.

Now, the three of them were relishing this moment as a family. They were all three smiling, quietly joking, glad to be together.

This is how I choose to remember this patient. She's dead now. She lost her fight with anorexia. I know that her parents grieve for her every day. But I also know, as the veteran mother said, that they will never stop loving. And I honor that love.

For the last item on the program, Elena had volunteered to be the subject of an IFS psychodrama. The psychologist explained to us that in this psychodrama, the various voices inside Elena's head would do their talking out loud so that we could all hear them. These aren't like the voices of schizophrenia, she explained: we all have different parts of ourselves that join our interior monologue. Maybe we could recognize the idea of a critical voice, the voice that comments on the things we do. Or some of us might have a scared voice, or even a happy voice.

I thought of my timid, fluttering Edward Gorey mother, trailing her handkerchief past flowered wallpaper and potted ferns: *What do we do?* I couldn't help wondering if anyone else in the room had a Victorian voice.

The psychologist went on to tell us that because eating disorders are so isolating, most outsiders don't have any idea how abusive and upsetting an eating disorder patient's interior monologue can be. Elena had worked with her therapist and friends so that the different girls could portray her inner voices. That way, we could get an idea what our patients were going through.

We all scooted our chairs into a circle again, and Elena sat barefoot in the middle of the group. She looked completely calm, but I could feel myself pushing into the back of my chair, as if I were in a car that was going too fast. Flutters of worry plucked at me, and that Victorian mother inside me woke up:

Oh, no! Oh, no!

Was I ready for this? Did I really want to hear this?

Elena looked beautiful, with her long brown hair down on her shoulders and her dark eyelashes demurely brushing her cheeks. This was her territory, physical as well as mental, and she was as relaxed as I was nervous.

Then, one by one, her voices came in to confront her.

First was the Critical Voice. The Critical Voice stood behind her and talked down at her, ignoring us completely.

"You little shit! You little whore! What makes you think anyone cares about you? You're not worth anybody's time! You failed at your job, you dropped out of school, your friends don't remember you, you're fat and ugly. You've screwed up your whole life, you stupid bitch!"

I couldn't believe it! My beautiful, sensitive child—was *that* what she had to live with every day?

Then came the Caring Voice. This wasn't directed at Elena, though. It had its back to Elena and faced the rest of the world.

"Please let me help you," it begged, holding out a hand to us. "I know what it's like to suffer. I'll listen. I want to help."

And I thought about Elena's endless compassion—compassion for everyone except herself.

Meanwhile, the Critical Voice continued its furious tirade:

"You little shit! You little whore!"

The Sad Voice joined them, so quiet that it could hardly be heard. It sat huddled in a ball by Elena's feet.

"I hurt so much," it moaned to itself. "I can't make the pain stop. I've lost so much. There's no point in going on."

That was the rape, I thought, almost in tears. I remembered my bright, bouncy, bubbly, happy little girl. I had dropped her off at boarding school . . .

And I had never seen her again.

Meanwhile, "I'll listen," the Caring Voice promised us gently.

"You've screwed up your whole life, you stupid bitch!"

Finally, the Eating Disorder Voice came in. It crouched protectively behind Elena's chair and spoke into her ear.

"Don't worry, I'll get you through this," it said. "You're not alone as long as I'm here. I've always been there for you. You don't need anyone else. I'm the one with the answers. We'll handle this ourselves, the way we've always done."

Isolation, I thought. *Perfection. That's the way she's always done it. My poor, poor wounded daughter.*

"You little shit!"

"I've lost so much."

"I know what it's like to suffer."

"You've screwed up your whole life, you stupid bitch!"

The voices became a shrill cacophony as each person said the lines over and over, an audible representation of the dangerous forces inside Elena's head. I turned away from the sight of my girl, my baby, sitting so composed in the middle of that horror. No wonder she cut, with all that pain boiling up inside her! How could anybody live a normal life with that?

Then the Eating Disorder Voice stood up, and she was the psychologist again. She thanked Elena, who smiled graciously as the group applauded, and she thanked us for coming to Family Day.

The program was over. We were free to leave.

Elena and I drove home in silence. My head hummed and whirled with all the new information I'd learned. I thought of my earlier decision: *I'm done! She's a closed book.* I thought of how I had thrown up my hands and told myself that no one could understand my daughter.

But that was the coward's way out. Understanding was possible.

It *had* to be possible—because it was necessary.

But how? I had tried, hadn't I? I'd tried, and I'd failed. Elena and I didn't talk anymore. We'd lost the energy to talk.

How could we bridge the gulf between us?

Understanding. My brain knows only one way to get to understanding. When I have a question I can't answer, I write a story. I watch my characters, and I learn from what they do. Over the years, my characters have taught me many things I'd never even begun to guess before working with them.

And Elena has the mind of a writer, too.

Since the Summer from Hell, Elena had wanted to write a memoir about her anorexia. She'd asked me every few months if I would help her. Each time, I had told her no, that this was her story to tell, not mine.

But was that really what was behind my no?

Wasn't I really just pushing all this away? Wasn't I just refusing to get involved? My telling her to write the story herself was a way of saying (to myself, at least): *This isn't my problem. This is somebody else's problem. And I have problems of my own.*

Now, as I drove, I turned my mind to look at my characters, one by one. Paul, my werewolf woodcarver, pale and sick with his deadly contagion, afraid for those around him. Kate, plucky and serious, determined to figure out a way to vanquish goblins. Poor little Izzy, the ghost without eyes who had been my wayward daughter Valerie. Martin, whose adventures had gotten tangled up in my own unhappy life.

As I'd written about them, I'd learned things that no one else around them knew. I'd discovered things—all kinds of things—that even *they* didn't know. I loved all my characters, even in their weakest moments. Even the villains had a chance to tell me their side of the story.

Had I been denying my own family this same closeness?

Elena and I reached the orphanage, and I parked the car in the horseshoe-shaped driveway. It was going to be a busy night here. There was only one spot left. In silence, Elena and I walked past grandparents talking on their cell phones, past a father pacing the hall with his fretful baby, past a trio of children running by with dollar bills in their hands to feed into the vending machine.

I unlocked our door. Elena walked in and dropped her backpack by her bed. "I'm glad *that's* over!" she muttered, stretching.

I was still standing by the door.

I should say it, I thought. But it was going to be hard—I could see that already. It would be harder than anything I'd ever tried. Maybe I couldn't do it. Maybe I didn't have enough of the gift.

And what would be the cost if I failed?

But then again, what was the other option? Keeping my head in the sand? Protecting myself? Leaving my own daughter to carry her burden of stress and pain while I played with my imaginary friends?

"Elena," I said, and there was something in my tone that made her stop and look at me. Probably I sounded like I was about to deliver one of those "mom" pronouncements that make children want to roll their eyes. Yes, that must be it because I could see Elena's face falling into her polite, distant mask.

And I thought, *I do not see how this is going to work.*

"Elena," I said, "you've asked me to help you write a book about your eating disorder. If you still want me to help you, I will."

CHAPTER THIRTY-FIVE

Elena lit up with real excitement for the first time in months. "Let's start right now!" she said. "Get your laptop." And she came over to sit on my bed.

I picked up my laptop and sat down facing her.

"Okay," she said. "Ask me anything. I'll tell you anything you need to know."

I couldn't help but feel touched at her faith in me. She really thought I could do this! So I opened up the laptop, and I thought about my daughter as if she weren't my daughter—as if she were one of my characters instead.

What did I need to know?

Everything.

"Okay, let's start with something that's really hard for me to get," I said. "Tell me about purging. What's it like? Have you done it often? When was the last time you purged?"

"The last time I purged was over a month ago," Elena said. "I can't purge at Clove House, but when we were at home, I purged almost every meal."

What? Almost every *meal*? Oh my *God*!

That was the mother in me. I could feel the panic and hurt clawing my chest. I could feel that helpless Victorian mother, wringing her hands and whimpering out her protests: *All those pizzas I ordered for you? The cake I made that you used to love? Why? Why do you do this to me? Why do you hate me so much?*

But the writer in me couldn't help but feel fascinated. And it was the writer who spoke.

"Almost every meal? Weren't you afraid we would hear you? The house was full of people. We must have been right in the next room."

"There's no way you'd hear me," Elena said. "I'm one of the best purgers I know because I learned from the best, Mona in boarding school. You could stand right next to my restroom stall, and you still wouldn't hear me. You'd swear I was talking to you the whole time."

Purging right next to me in a restroom stall? Carrying on a conversation and *vomiting*? My stomach twisted, but I fought down my feelings of disgust.

Notice the cool poise, the writer in me pointed out. *My character is speaking with real confidence. This is a skill she's mastered, and she's proud of that skill. It makes up part of her hidden world.*

"So, I'm trying to wrap my head around the experience," I said. "It's really hard for me to see the appeal. It's nasty! Whenever I throw up, I feel horrible and shaky, and my throat burns from the acid."

"Yes, but that's because you're sick. It's not like that when you purge. It feels great, actually. Any pain you're in, purging will make it disappear."

I wanted to shove this idea away with both hands and then stomp on it. But instead, I forced myself to be fair.

"It's true," I said, "that when I've gotten migraines, I've thrown up sometimes, and that stops the migraine immediately. I don't know why it does that."

"Plus, there's the whole ritual of it," Elena said. "There's the preparation for it: putting a towel around you, tucking your hair up. You put a little toilet paper in the bowl so no one will hear, and you get all ready."

My mind ran through this imaginary scene. As much as I didn't want to watch it happen, I could see the comfort my character was taking from it. She'd been raised on small rituals—the Sign of the Cross, grace before meals. And she liked them. Elena had OCD.

But then . . . I could feel my own throat tighten up. I felt water gather in my eyes.

"But you're getting ready to *gag*," I pointed out.

"Not really for me," Elena said casually.

That squashed my mental image. My scene was wrong. I had to pay attention.

"When you're new, you have to gag," she explained. "You stick your finger down your throat, and you purge a little bit, and then you stick your finger down your throat and do it again. Some people use other things so it won't mess up their nails. But the thing is, if you're a pro, you don't have to use anything, you can completely control the whole process. But when you're starting, you kind of take it slow, and you work at it . . ."

I was silent. More and more, I let this realization sink in: *My character worked very hard at this. She is a pro.*

The realization began to bear fruit. I caught glimpses of my character, younger, worrying about her nails, practicing to get this right . . . And ripping off fake nails when she ruined them?

No wonder I'd seen her yanking off her French nails!

The mom in me was standing by, mourning, wringing her hands, but the writer in me was hard at work now. The writer knew that only by watching, only by paying attention, would I gain that true awareness of character. One small trait would reveal another. This couldn't be rushed or interfered with. I'd only learned about my character Miranda's cutting by paying attention to the look in her eyes when she noticed a scrape.

Now, Elena was ticking off techniques, informative and practical, like a seasoned guide giving a lecture to a tourist.

". . . and some people purge by color . . ."

"By *color*?" I interrupted.

"Yeah, you eat things one by one, and you eat a certain-colored food first. Say, you eat a certain kind of veggie. And then, when you purge, you know when you get to that color that you've gotten it all out."

Okay, I had to admit, that was clever. Gross—horribly gross! But clever.

"It sounds very scientific," I said.

Elena laughed. "Well, we're not stupid!"

She was sounding so relaxed but so animated right now. I must have sounded like that when I was lecturing Susan on folklore. This was something very close to this character I was studying, very safe for her.

"Anyway, you control it, that's the thing," she concluded. "Some people purge just so much, but not more. It's up to you. It's the best feeling . . . It's more addictive than smoking."

More addictive than nicotine? Wait a minute! How could that be right?

"But what's addictive about it?" I asked. "Is it the thought that you're getting rid of calories?"

"No. It's just—well, think about it: you're prone to anxiety already, and your stomach is full and unsettled. And then you purge, and you feel nice and empty inside, and your stomach is settled down, and you wipe your mouth, and you check in the mirror, and you go through your post-purge ritual . . ." She pauses. "I used to purge just water."

Okay, that was just plain crazy! I couldn't understand it at all.

Or . . . could I?

Be fair!

My imagination brought me feelings from when I had been very nervous. I could remember my stomach feeling so unsettled that I thought I was going to throw up. If those nervous feelings were very intense, day after day, never letting go—and I thought of that Critical Voice, yelling down its vulgarities and insults—wouldn't *I* try anything I could to find a little relief?

No! said the mother in me. *No, no, no! Think of the* waste! *Think of the nasty acidic old used food!*

And I felt my stomach give a lurch.

"But still, vomiting . . . ," I protested.

"No," Elena interrupted. "Everybody thinks that, and it's wrong. Vomiting when you're sick is completely different. It's very uncomfortable, and you can't stop it. You can't *control* it—it's not anything like purging."

Control. I thought about that. I thought about this hidden skill, this secret sense of control.

But then I thought about something else. How hidden had it been, really?

"All those doctors I watched you talk to during the Summer from Hell," I said. "Did they know you purged?"

Did they lie *to me?* demanded the mom.

"Nah," Elena said. "Dr. Costello and the other hospital doctors probably thought they knew what they were looking for: dingy teeth, brittle nails, that kind of thing. I've always been very careful about that. It's the little things that give you away."

Quieted, the mom settled down, and the writer took over again. In my imagination, I saw my character going through her daily life, using her body like a mask, like a shield. She was watching over its details in order not to give away the secret life going on inside . . .

But at the same time, sadness was starting to well up inside me. It was exhausting, this strange new world I was having to see.

"Did you tell Dr. Petras?" I asked. "Is that why he diagnosed you anorexic and put you in the hospital?" And, even though I tried my best to stay in my writer's mind, I fidgeted at the thought. This was still a sore point with me.

I couldn't help it. I just despised that man!

"No, he didn't know," Elena said. "And I don't think he guessed, either. I didn't tell him very much. He just got lucky with his diagnosis."

Lucky?! shrieked the mom. But I shut her down.

"Well, what about the psychiatrists at the children's hospital?" I went on. "What about Dr. Costello?"

"No, I didn't tell them. They seemed to think that there were anorexics and bulimics, and the anorexics restricted, and the bulimics purged. They knew it wasn't that simple by that time, but it still seemed like a lot of them thought that way anyway."

This struck a chord with me.

"You know, I think I remember reading that back then," I said, "about the difference between anorexics and bulimics. It's one of the reasons *I* didn't think you purged."

"There *is* a big difference, but it doesn't have to do with purging," Elena said. "Tons of anorexics purge."

Elena and I worked all evening. She talked while I took notes, and if she wasn't as vivacious and alert as the old Elena, she fought off the sedation more effectively than she'd done in weeks. Then she took her evening pills and vanished into sleep while I lay awake, studying my notes.

This is amazing! I thought in a rush of excitement. *She's really committed to this! She really* is *letting me into her world.*

But it was a creepy world, a world that made my skin crawl.

I thought of the Critical Voice, harping away day and night. I thought of vomiting, turned into an addictive pleasure. I thought of teeth and nails, not as parts of a regular person, but as a kind of disguise instead. I thought of doctors, not as professionals who healed and helped, but as bumbling detectives to be fooled and put on the wrong trail.

Nothing that I touched in this new world was turning out to be the way I thought it would. A normal person couldn't survive here for five minutes.

My imagination called up scenes to show me, building them out of the comments tonight and out of the bits of information I'd learned over the years. Before, this information had been a source of worry for me. Now, it gave me important clues. I needed to see this strange new place. I needed to learn about the character who lived there.

Toilets became faithful allies in the quest for independence. Trash cans guarded secrets. Kitchens became a frightening, bewildering muddle.

This was a misty place, where details blurred and scenes swam in the fog of perpetual starvation—a fog I could relate to from my experience of serious blood loss. Touch and feeling, I remembered, had become stronger and more reliable than vision. Over time, touch must start to supplement sight in this foggy world.

Touch. Hands wrapped around the thigh meant victory. Hunger pangs meant reassurance. The curve of the collarbone turned into a kind of worry stone, to be touched and rubbed again and again.

Gingerly, I tested out my theories about this dim world, which rippled with unforeseen dangers and unusual suggestions. It was an austere place, that I could easily understand. There was no abundance here of any kind. Everything had to be measured out and rationed, from food to action to breath.

Little by little, the world I was building began to feel like the undersea world of the mermaids Elena loved so much.

This was a lesser world.

It was a fragile, attenuated existence.

It survived on borrowed light.

It was such a hard place for the delicate creature who drifted through it! No wonder so many of her brothers and sisters ended up dead.

The next morning, Elena fought off her drug-induced fatigue to continue the discussion of her memoir. "I'll leave you my journals," she said, taking them out of her nightstand drawer. "Read anything you think will help."

And, as she got out of the car at Clove House, she told me, for the first time in years: "Write lots!"

I drove home slowly, trying to think of how to write about what I was learning. The more I tested this world, the more like the bottom of the ocean it seemed, and I couldn't stifle my suspicion and concern at finding myself there. The cute daydream substitutions of the Disney mermaid's world—water for air, fish for birds, seaweed for grass—seemed like nothing more than a pretty fiction set up to hide the grim reality. Because what *was* the bottom of the ocean, after all? A dreary gray underwater wasteland that stretched for mile after barren mile.

Back at the orphanage, I brewed a double-strength cup of coffee. I brought it down the hall to my room, opened up my laptop, and tried to write. I conjured up my own daughter and studied her traits and attitudes as if I had only just met her.

Who is she? I wondered. *What does she have to say for herself?*

Elena had never put up with bullies. She had always had a chip on her shoulder. That cocky attitude appealed to me. I let it do the talking:

> For every woman who sighs to her girlfriends, "If I could just drop fifteen pounds"—check this, bitches, I'm proof that you could. For every girl who cracks on Day Three of the diet and wolfs that chocolate shake—tough for you, babe, here's what you could have had. I'm all your insecurities, the ones you try to pretend don't matter—but the minute you see me, they do.
>
> Hey, we all feel them. I'm just the one who's strong enough to do something about them. The

rest of you, you don't have the drive. You don't want it badly enough.

You're not willing to die.

I am.

Oh, God! I thought. *That can't be right, can it? That can't be what she thinks—not my little girl!*

Like a balloon deflating, the writer side of me faded away. It was the mother who was reacting now. I saw my daughter as a toddler, clutching my finger for support. I remembered her grabbing for Joe's and my hands and swinging on them, skipping, almost jerking our arms out of our sockets as she jumped as high as she could.

That exuberant little girl never simply walked anywhere. Everywhere she went, she danced.

And I found myself starting to type.

> My daughter is disappearing. Fading away. Letting go of everything she loves. My youngest baby, my little girl, is dying.
>
> What do you say when someone you love is standing on a building ledge? What can you do besides scream?

Tears were on my cheeks now. I wiped my eyes angrily. Why was I writing this? This wasn't helping me understand Elena!

But I couldn't stop myself. I kept typing.

> Every parent has nightmares. We try our hardest not to think about the worst thing that could happen. But when we hear a father interviewed on the news . . . When we read a family's released statement . . . When we catch sight of a milk carton photo, we think, *That could be my child.*
>
> Over the years, my worst fears for my daughter have crystallized into a terrifying daydream, a daydream so frightful that I have never told it to a

single human being until now. It has stayed in the realm of things too terrible to mention. I haven't wanted to bring it to life.

I stopped. Was I really going to do this? Was I really going to write it down? Because this was one of *my* secrets.

My daydream is this: I am receiving The Call. A voice is saying, "I'm so sorry. It's about your daughter," and I continue to hold the phone, but I can't hear anymore. It doesn't matter. I already know what the voice is going to say.

This nightmare scene has been with me for years. For decades, in fact. I'll see that news story, read about that grisly discovery, and The Call plays out in my mind:

"I'm so sorry. It's about your daughter."

And I know what's coming next.

In all the years that The Call has been with me, I've never imagined past this point. I've never figured out my reaction. Never even begun to consider the funeral. Never pictured myself living with the news, moving on, making sense of it all, healing.

"It's about your daughter." And after that, a hole that my thoughts can't get past. A bright red hole, endless, perfectly round, like the entry wound of a bullet.

"I'm so sorry. It's about your daughter."

And after that:

Nothing.

I pushed away the laptop and stumbled up from the desk. I forced myself to stare at the green field outside until its wavering image finally came into focus. Tufts of grass six or seven inches tall swayed back and forth in the breeze. Time to mow. Three songbirds flew past the window very quickly, in a tight jet-fighter formation. The dumpster in the back parking lot was filling up. The door to the orphanage kitchen was ajar.

This isn't going to work, I thought. *I can't hold these two different people in my head, the daughter who's cocky and oblivious and the mother who's desperately afraid. I'll go insane before this story is finished.*

But then the writer in me woke up and stretched again.

Cocky? Oblivious? Is that really true?

No.

Elena wasn't a clueless plastic Little Mermaid, shouting insults from the safety of her coral towers and deadly water-air. That wasn't my character. I didn't have her right yet. Before I could conjure her, I needed to learn more.

So I sat down with Elena's journals and notebooks and worked my way through them.

Elena had written beautifully about Drew Center, I discovered. Her fellow patients came to life on the page. And this episode with her friend Mona in boarding school was quite vivid. I was sure there would be a place for it.

As the hours passed, I skipped around, pulling folded sheets of paper out of notebooks and skimming their contents. Senior year was brief and laconic, as I had expected it would be. Elena's image was perfect by that time. Her shield was impenetrable. Even her journal couldn't get inside anymore.

And here, at the beginning of college, was a long list of impossible daily rules:

> *No junk food.*
> *Exercise every day.*
> *Study hard.*
> *Work hard.*
> *BE hard.*
> *No tears.*
> *No meat.*
> *No eating after 9 p.m.*

Get up at 6 every day.
Bed before 1 a.m.
800 calorie max on weekdays.
Weight day is Friday.
Days will be planned, and that plan will be followed.
Tidied room. No slacking. No laziness.
I will not be a failure!

I felt a stab of pain. This wasn't what Joe and I had wanted for our daughter as she embarked on her college career. We had wanted her to love learning and make lifelong friends. Where had she learned to be so harsh and strict with herself? Not even a monk could keep all these rules!

Yes, yes, the writer in me said, *but never mind that now. Look closer! What does this say about my character?* And my imagination brought me the image of Elena, writing down the list of rules, firm, purposeful, and satisfied.

I felt a little tug of self-recognition. I, too, liked to write down lists of priorities and rules. Of course, I also had the good sense to break them almost at once. Elena, it would appear, held on to hers. Was that better discipline? Or was it desperation?

I didn't know. I needed to see more.

I picked up another journal, the one I hadn't wanted to read. Reluctantly, I edged into the year we had all spent dealing with Valerie's depression. Elena's entries reflected my own thoughts at the time: turbulent, alternately furious and despairing. No, this was no perfectly poised mermaid, gliding triumphantly through her strange, poisoned world.

But maybe it was too soon. Maybe the eating disorder hadn't taken over yet.

I turned to the beginning of the next year. Let's see: where were we all then? Joe and Elena were already back in Germany. They had flown home without me. I was staying in the States for another week to get Valerie settled in at college . . .

The college she would run away from three months later.

I put my hands over my eyes. They were still wet, the eyelashes slippery with tears. Suddenly, I felt so exhausted that I wanted to curl up right there and pull a blanket over my head. I couldn't do this! Why did I say I would do this? It was too hard! Too hard to go back there . . .

But my writer's mind kept prodding me: *What about the character? This isn't about* you! *What about* her?

So I dropped my hands and picked up the journal again.

This past year was not a sweet sixteen, Elena had written, *but I did learn a lot about inner strength, about holding on.*

Inner strength—yes! This was a character I could bring to the world. She wasn't sassy and silly. She was a realist. She was fighting. She knew she had to hold on.

> *Resolutions? I have a few, some good, some bad. But*
> *right now, I am starving, my throat aches, and my*
> *hands are kinda shaking. I better lie down.*

So it *was* already here. The eating disorder was already eating her alive.

Then came the sentence that told me my character saw it all. She knew she wasn't floating through some coral wonderland. She saw the whole dreary, empty truth. I read it over and over while the tears ran down my face, and it was the saddest, simplest, clearest, wisest statement about anorexia nervosa that I have ever read. It stood like an epitaph for all Elena had lost, and like a verdict that summed up all she would have to suffer:

> *I miss so many things that were beautiful.*

CHAPTER THIRTY-SIX

Two weeks later, Elena was the one with the cold. Even though she had gained weight again during this stay at Clove House, each day seemed to suck away a little more of her strength. The only thing that brought her to life anymore was the memoir we were writing together.

But if the memoir had become Elena's lifeline, it had become my little slice of hell.

I had to understand things, and that meant I had to ask about things. That meant I was learning things that I would never have wanted to know—such as the truth about what had been going on during the Summer from Hell.

It began simply enough—but then, I was starting to learn already that I never knew how easy or how painful an interview with Elena would be. Elena was lying on her bed, with an arm up to block the light from the windows. I was sitting beside her with my laptop, taking notes.

"So, I mentioned in an email to a librarian that I'm writing your anorexia memoir," I told her, "and the librarian says she's afraid it'll reveal tricks. She says we don't need any more anorexics out there teaching today's teens new tricks."

Elena smiled—a grim, sad smile. "She doesn't have any idea what anorexia is."

"What do you mean?" I asked.

"It's a prison. It's twenty-four-hour-a-day life in a jail cell. We never get out, not even for one second. All we can do, all day long, is look for ways to survive. Nobody needs to teach us tricks. We brainstorm our own tricks all day long. When *real* anorexics compare notes, we've already figured out all the same tricks—and each one of us did it on our own."

Okay, prison, I thought. *That's very interesting.* I had already known about the walls that kept others away from my character. So those walls kept her in, as well.

And what about the blackouts? Were those walls, too?

"In the Summer from Hell, what about the dissociation blackouts you had? Were they an escape, or were they more prison?"

Elena thought about this while she blew her nose. "Not really either one," she said.

"I've read that a lot of eating disorder patients start dissociating in childhood," I continued. "Child abuse is one of the biggest factors. But you never had any blackouts before the Summer from Hell, when you were already seventeen."

And in my mind, I was adding . . . *Right?*

"A lot of anorexics dissociate," Elena said with her eyes closed. "It happened all the time at Drew Center. It can happen to anybody if you're freaked out enough. I was freaking out."

"I guess so," I said a little doubtfully. Anybody? I tried without success to imagine myself freaking out that much.

"We had a guy brought to the ER once," she continued. "He was dissociating just like I did, the thrashing around, the works. He was kind of a big guy, and he hadn't been able to pass his fitness test. That morning was his last try—if he failed, they were going to kick him out of the Air Force. His commander came in with him, and he wanted to know, 'Is this guy faking it?' 'No,' we told him. 'It's real.' It was the stress."

"The stress," I echoed, and then I couldn't help myself. "That bullying psychiatrist!"

"That psychiatrist probably saved my life."

Elena's voice was as calm as if she had mastered inner peace. I felt anything but calm. The writer in me slipped away, and the mother took over again. When I thought about what that man had made her suffer . . .

I set down my laptop and jumped up to walk the floor.

"I can't believe that," I said. "He did nothing but make you lose more weight."

"That's true, at the start," she admitted. "It happened when Dr. Petras weighed me. He weighed me himself that second time, when I came in for that second appointment. I had been hardcore deep in my disorder at boarding school, and the stress with Valerie hadn't helped either. But, early that summer, I was really busy. I had started to concentrate on other things. When I went in for that counseling session with him, and he read my weight out loud, I completely freaked. I had never weighed anywhere near that much in my life!

"So I started restricting again. I really did lose those eight pounds that month. And if he hadn't stopped me, I would have kept right on going, and I'm pretty sure I would have died. It's true that at first in the hospital, I lost even more weight, but I was where they were running daily EKGs, so they caught the heart damage early.

"After that, in senior year, even though I kept restricting, I worried about ending up at somewhere like Drew Center again, so I made sure my weight didn't go too low. He probably saved my life," she said again.

Dr. Petras, the hero. No! I couldn't live with that. I could handle the truth, I could look at this world without blinking—but I could *not* deal with that!

There had been that golden month of June, when the stress had gotten better and Elena had gained weight on her own. As she said, she had concentrated on other things. Maybe she was growing out of it naturally. She was enjoying life. She was even enjoying food. I *saw* her enjoying food!

After the Summer from Hell, she never did that again.

Not ever.

"He triggered you himself, reading your weight out loud like that!" I said. "He yelled at you. That man bullied you!"

"I was making a fool out of him," Elena said. "Nobody believed his anorexia diagnosis. I had told Dr. Petras about my restricting, but to everybody else, I acted like, *What?* The pediatrician actually told me he thought Dr. Petras was a crackpot. Nobody likes to be made to look like an idiot."

"Thanks to him, you started dissociating," I said. "His bullying knocked you right out of reality."

"It wasn't just dissociation," Elena pointed out. "There was the starvation, you have to remember that. A lot of the time, I was so weak, I really did faint."

I stopped to stare out the window. It was dusk already. We could see the sunrise once it cleared the trees in the neighborhood behind us, but it bothered me that we couldn't watch the sun go down.

My careful lists of questions that summer! I thought sadly. I had opposed that bullying moron so completely, with all my logic and reason. *Was he right?* I asked myself. *Can I live in a world in which that man was right?* And I felt myself give a shiver all over, as if flies had landed on me.

No! I would never believe that.

I could believe that Elena had had an eating disorder then, even a serious one. I could believe that she had needed professional help. But I would *never* believe that she should have been treated so cruelly. A rape victim, bullied and yelled at—*no!* That treatment had *no* place in a trauma victim's recovery.

That man was *still* a bully, and he was *still* a moron. He had *still* caused more harm than good. *That's* what I could live with! Yes, I could live with that.

Shadows gathered over the grassy playground. The birds were singing quietly. I turned my mind to my old lists of questions—to the other mysteries from that summer.

"But what about the weight loss in the children's hospital?" I challenged. "They were watching every bite, and you had the feeding tube and everything, and you still kept losing weight."

"Anorexia doesn't turn around in a day," Elena said. "Just like me in January, when I got here to Clove House: even on three thousand calories a day, I wasn't putting on weight. And besides, at the children's hospital, I only ate about half the food they gave me, and very little of the feeding pump stuff went in."

I turned in amazement to look at Elena. Was my daughter—my character—joking?

No, she didn't look like she was joking. She had a frown on her face. She had her eyes shut, and she gave a sniffle to clear her nose.

"But what about the anorexia protocol?" I asked.

"The techs who watched me eat? They were just nice girls. They weren't mental health nurses. They thought I was just like they were."

But . . . weren't you? I thought.

I needed to calm down. I was getting too involved again.

"So you did what?—with those nice girls there?" I asked.

"I hid food. I hid it anywhere I could. Plastic wrap. Pajama sleeves. I'd get up to come to the table, but I'd keep my fuzzy blanket wrapped around me. I could stick all kinds of food in there. That's why the real treatment centers never let their patients have loose clothes or a hoodie."

My mind boggled. I could feel it boggling. My imagination was pulling up images of Elena squirreling away a slice of tomato here, a piece of cheese there, a chunk of sandwich . . . right in the clothes she was wearing. In the blanket she slept under at night!

A grimace of disgust hardened on my face as I watched the imaginary film clips. I had to swallow my saliva.

That's nasty! It's all so unsanitary! I thought. *It's unsavory—that's what it is. Unsavory!*

But that was only the mother doing the thinking.

Look at the caution my character is showing! thought the writer. *Look at the attention to detail. There it is again, that careful attention to detail. That's a constant with this character. And think of the confidence it takes to engage in that misdirection, to distract someone right in front of you. The willingness to play with societal norms and rules like a magician: Nothing up my sleeve but a pickle spear!*

Elena was right: this was a *real* anorexic's trick. It wasn't anything someone had needed to teach her. It was an act brought on by sheer desperation. It wouldn't even occur to a normal person!

My imagination continued to bring me sample bits of film. It showed me Elena, cagey, casual, carrying on a conversation while she stuffed tomato slices and pieces of ham into her clothes.

Ugh!

But—now, wait a minute, this was interesting—it looked very much like a prisoner slipping a spoon or some other implement into his pants.

Is that why Elena watches prison shows all the time? asked the writer. *Because she sees herself as one of them?* And I made a mental note to find out more about that. It was a whole interview, all by itself.

"Okay, but the feeding pump," I continued, sufficiently calmed down that I could sit on the bed again and pick up my laptop to take notes. "That room at the children's hospital was pretty small. I slept within eight feet of you, and a nursing tech sat up by the door all night to make sure you didn't mess with the pump. So, what do you mean, not much of it went in?"

Elena's voice was stoic. "What can I say? If you want it enough, you'll be the last person awake."

What?! They fell asleep? The techs who were watching over my daughter—they fell asleep?!

I forced myself to take notes, just as if this were something I might forget later. As if it were something I would *ever* forget.

I needed to stay calm. I needed to stay objective.

"Yeah, but you must have had to wait for quite a while," I said aloud. "That means the pump had already been going for some time."

"I suctioned it out."

I fell silent.

Elena interpreted this as encouragement to continue her explanation. It wasn't encouragement.

"I suctioned it out," she elaborated, "with the syringe the nurse used to clear the line. She left it right next to the pump every night. No way would a mental health nurse make that mistake. I used it to pull a suction and let the feeding tube drain into the sink."

"You suctioned out the contents of your stomach," I said flatly.

I could feel my own stomach twisting, rising. I was going to be sick. This was . . . so horrible. So foreign! So utterly alien to health!

But look at the tenacity! said the writer. *Look at the willpower. Yes, it's foreign—now get over it! What's her reason?*

"Why?"

That was the most I could manage. I couldn't trust myself to say more.

"It's always been a phobia of mine," Elena said, "the thought that I'll be in a coma or something, and while I'm lying there helpless, they'll pump me full of calories till I'm huge. And I'll wake up, and I'll be three hundred pounds and not be able to do anything about it."

My imagination played out that image: lying there helpless, pumped full, huge.

And my writer's mind pounced: *The rape!*

I remembered the fourteen-year-old Elena, home from the boarding school—that intense, miserable, thin little fourteen-year-old whom Dr. Eichbaum had pronounced completely normal. That "normal" eighth grader was dragging me to the library . . . to check out books on babies.

What to Expect When You're Expecting.

At the time, Elena had told me she wanted to learn about childcare for babysitting, and I had supported her desire to learn whatever she wanted to learn, to pick up any book the library had to offer. I did ask a few gentle questions, of course. They didn't get anywhere. But then, what had my character said about Dr. Eichbaum's questions?

I lied my ass off.

That fourteen-year-old was carrying a horrible secret. She was terrified that she might be pregnant.

Helpless. Raped. Terrified. And maybe pregnant.

What does a mind do with a rape? What can it possibly do with such terror and disgust and shame? It buries the secrets, and like termites, those secrets eat their way out somewhere else . . .

Helpless—a coma. Assaulted—a feeding tube. Pregnant—pumped up into obesity . . .

And four years later, there was Elena at the children's hospital, lying helpless as the sitter and I nodded off. Pumped full of calories, absolutely petrified with terror and disgust and shame . . .

I couldn't think about this anymore. I couldn't talk about it anymore. I groped around in my mind for a distraction, something, anything—

"What about the puddings?" I asked.

Elena didn't move. She still had her hand over her eyes. Every now and then, she cleared the gunk out of her throat.

"What about them?" she muttered.

"Every day at the children's hospital, I brought you a pudding, and every day, you ate it. You acted like you couldn't wait. But at the same time, you were so obsessed with calories that you were passing out from the stress of having to eat. You were stuffing potato chips into your pillow case. You were staying up half the night to pump your own stomach."

And, in the back of my mind, I was waiting for Elena to protest these incredible statements, to sit up and laugh: *No, I wasn't!*

But instead, she just coughed and blew her nose again. "And?"

"And you anorexics can't bear to eat!" I said. "Five pieces of popcorn is enough to send you into a tailspin. It keeps you up all night, it sends you exercising, it brings your Critical Voice in to scream at you . . ."

As I said this, I knew what I wanted. I knew exactly what I wanted. I wanted Elena to say, *That's crazy, Mom! I don't think that way. You're being silly. You've got it all wrong!* And she would take me by the hand, and we would walk back to a normal life . . .

But Elena just said, "Yeah, so?"

I felt anger and confusion and pain rise up to choke me. It was all wrong! So wrong!

"And so, what about the puddings I brought you?" I snapped. "Did you just purge them?"

"No, I never purged the puddings."

"But *why?*"

I was really angry now. The puddings had made me angry. Those puddings represented everything I didn't know back then, despite my best efforts to learn. They represented everything that *still* made no sense.

"You count every calorie!" I said—but I realized I wasn't saying it, I was shouting it. "You watch every bite! Those puddings—they must have been *torture!* *Why* did you let me feed them to you? *Why* did you act like you wanted them?"

She said, "I did it because it made you happy."

I put down my laptop. I hurried off to the bathroom. I sat down in a corner on the tile floor, and I cried.

Those puddings were and are the saddest thing in this entire story. They were love and confusion and hurt and redemption. They were the gift of the magi.

Elena and I were on our commute to Clove House the next morning when I finally asked about Drew Center, that first treatment center—the one that had held her by force. I had been putting off talking about it, and I had to force myself to bring it up.

I myself could hardly bear to revisit those memories. Just the words *Drew Center*, spoken out loud, brought up in grim, ghastly detail that dark time, the lost time, when I had known my daughter was a prisoner and I had wandered all alone in that terrifying place inside my own head.

But, once again, Elena was calm about it in a way that I couldn't be.

"Institutions like that have to be careful," she said. "They could have been sued if they had let me out and I did something crazy. They were just covering their butts."

Good point, noted the writer in me.

But the mother promptly pushed it away.

"It was my decision, not theirs!" I said. "If they were concerned, they should have shared those concerns with me. But they didn't—they didn't share! They didn't educate me, and they didn't help me. They treated me like an enemy."

"Well, yeah, they did," Elena said. "But it wasn't personal."

The highway around me seemed to blur for a second, and I blinked and checked my mirrors. All good, no cars nearby, nothing to worry about.

It was just my mind, starting to boggle again.

"They—what?" I said. "They treated me like an enemy, but it wasn't *personal*? What do you mean, 'wasn't personal'?"

I glanced at Elena, and my writer's mind noted that my character's profile was nonchalant. Maybe *too* nonchalant, in fact: carefully, deliberately neutral.

"At Drew Center," she said, "they taught us that our families were the reason we had our eating disorder."

I could hear the screech in my voice: "They *what?*"

"They told us—*all* of us, not just me—that our families were the ones who made us sick."

The mother in me completely short-circuited. She was shocked right out of existence. She had frozen on that single screech:

What??

But time didn't stand still. Our exit came up, and I took it. I drove in silence, still hearing that screech in my head:

What??

Meanwhile, the writer in me did what she always does. She took in the evidence, and she started looking for patterns.

The careful generalities from the set of three psychiatrists. Their lack of information. Their look of polite disbelief.

Dr. Petras's angry voice: *I'm not going to argue with you!*

The hostility of the Drew Center staff. The rolled eyes and contemptuous voices.

Dr. Moore: *So, you don't want your daughter to be treated for anorexia.*

And that baffling note in the hospital system, the one that had denied Elena medical care: *This patient AND HER MOTHER . . .*

"It was the mother, wasn't it?" I said.

"What?"

"It was the *mother* who caused her daughter to have anorexia."

Elena was silent for a moment. Finally, she said, "I guess."

So there it was.

There it bloody well was!

While I was back at the hotel, agonizing over how to help my sick child recover, doctors and therapists at Drew Center were busy explaining to Elena that *I* had made her sick. That's right: the woman who had dropped everything and flown halfway around the world next to her stretcher. The mother—the cause of all her problems!

Did *any* of them have a single shred of evidence for that? Did *any* of them try to find out anything about me?

"Hey, can we stop for coffee?" Elena asked. A Starbucks drive-through was coming up.

I whipped into the lane and waited behind the other morning commuters. I drummed my fingers on the steering wheel. My whole body vibrated with emotion.

The child abuse case.

The *child abuse* case!

Oh, my *God*—!

"Those people hadn't even *met* me!" I said. "They made up their minds before they asked a single question. No, wait—they never *did* ask a single question!"

"It wasn't personal," Elena repeated in the same neutral voice. "They said the same thing to all the patients."

We arrived at the Starbucks window. I paid in silence and reached for Elena's coffee. It took all I had to keep from hurling it across the parking lot. The way I was feeling, it wasn't the best thing for me to have a sloshy projectile in my hand.

"Those *bastards!*" I said as I made my right turn back onto the street. "Those arrogant, preening, self-satisfied *bastards!* Blame it all on the mother, right? Lord knows *she* deserves it!"

"Mom," Elena said. "It doesn't matter. I didn't believe them."

Really?

While the mother in me continued to rave, my writer's mind examined this new piece of information. It studied the patterns. It tested the facts.

Elena's shift in attitude. Her distant expression. The bitter tone in her voice. It was all right there, as early as the very next day, on the car ride to Texas:

Chill out, *Mom! Dad, Mom doesn't trust me!*

"Of *course* you believed them!" I snapped. "What teenager in pain wouldn't? You're out of your mind with grief and anger, your sister's run away, you're locked up against your will . . . and then a doctor cozies up to you and says, 'Here, let me set you straight. Simple answer: your *mother* did it!"

"I told them they were wrong."

The writer's mind studied that: the conviction in my character's voice, the look of pained memory.

"Yes, you did," I agreed. "You defended your family, but that doesn't mean their crackpot nonsense didn't poison your mind."

And my imagination played out scenes of Dr. Moore and the other therapists, so smooth, so sure of themselves, tormenting that sick, desperate young woman with their trumped-up pseudoscientific theories . . .

The *suffering*! The *suffering* they had caused!

"They knew *nothing* about your family, those people!" I said. "Dr. Petras didn't ask us a single question, not one. I was tried, judged, and executed before I even stepped into his office. Before he even laid eyes on me!"

"Yeah, well," Elena said. "Dr. Petras had his own problems."

But I couldn't stop to hear this. I was still locked in a hell of my own.

"As if you and your sister weren't the most important people in my world! As if I wasn't by your bedside every night, reading to you. Reading to *you*—you used to read to *me* more than I read to you! Every book you picked up, you told me all about it. Every class you took, every friend you made, you came home and said, 'Guess *what*!' Did those doctors want to hear about that? Did they ask about the hours I set aside to hear about your day, to talk over what was going on in your life? And I didn't do it because it was some kind of duty, either. I *wanted* to be an audience! I *love* being a part of your life! I—I—there I was, worried out of my *mind* over you—and they all thought I was the *enemy*!"

"Not all of them," Elena said. "If it makes you feel any better, a lot of medical doctors think everything a psychiatrist says is bullshit."

But it didn't make me feel better. I wasn't listening.

"The riding lessons," I went on, "when you were little. I drove you half an hour each way and stayed there the whole time. *You're* the ones who asked for them. I didn't pressure you! I wanted you to learn what interested *you*! The folklorico dance lessons you begged me for—*I'm* the one who made them happen. And how many parents listen to every new song their child wants to play for them? How many times have you and your sister said, 'Hey, Mom, listen to this'? And I did. I do! I'm *glad* to! I want you to be able to talk to me! I want—I want to be a *positive* part of your *life!*"

Elena's voice was stoic: "You're a great mom."

Unfortunately for us both, I was listening this time. And this, of course, was the wrong thing to say.

I hadn't been a great mom. I had tried—God knows, I had tried. I had gone into this with the intention to be extraordinary. And I had been a *good* mom, I felt sure of that—a *good* mom. But a *great* mom . . .

Or had I?

Had I been a good mom—*really?*

My imagination obligingly found memories for me, dozens and dozens of them. Little snappy comments. Impatience. Frustration. Exhaustion. No time . . .

And my girls, my two little girls, with looks of disappointment, of dismay . . .

They were so precious, those little children! They were like flowers. Like stars! Those two little girls had deserved the *best!*

So maybe it was true. Maybe I *had* been a bad mom. The stakes had been so high! I had tried, yes—I had *tried.* But there, that bright, bouncy, goofy, happy little girl had gotten raped—gotten raped on my watch.

I sank to the bottom of a pool of misery and regret.

"Maybe if we hadn't moved to Germany," I mourned.

"Screw that!" Elena said. "I love Germany."

But I didn't care. I abandoned myself to that inky-black ocean of remorse.

"Maybe if you hadn't gone to boarding school."

Elena gazed out the window in silence.

"Mom, this is stupid," she said after a minute. "You know it's not your fault. Nobody believes that anymore, not even the psychiatrists who used to tell people that. The theory got discredited. Remember what Dr. Leben told me? Teenage anorexia comes from *outside* the family."

I surfaced again, boiling mad. No, not just boiling mad—almost hysterical. The suffering—the *suffering* they had caused!

"Do those bastards have *any* idea of the torment they put us through? *Any* idea of the damage they did in peoples' lives? There they are, coming in to treat a desperately sick child, sick with a disease that already isolates people—and what do they do? They teach that child to hate and fear the *only* allies who won't give up, the *only* people who would give *anything* to make things better!"

A school zone showed up. My leg muscles cramped with the effort to keep the car under the speed limit. I could feel each individual muscle in my jaw tightening down into my neck, into my chest, my shoulders, arms, hands.

"How many anorexics are *dead* today because they were taught not to trust their parents? How many anorexics didn't *survive* long enough to hear, 'Oh, sorry, we were wrong. Oops! That theory is discredited'?"

"They didn't know better," Elena said. "They were doing the best they could."

I pulled into the Clove House parking lot and stopped with a jerk.

"You know who does the best they can?" I snapped. "Witch doctors, that's who! Psychology is supposed to be a *science*! Really, you're going to tell me that *that* was the best they could do—pin one more problem on the *mother*? It was irresponsible and . . . and chauvinistic! And ignorant! And damaging!"

"Mom, calm down."

". . . and devastating! *Devastating!* In the sense of *laying to waste*! Like an army! Like locusts! Like a plague! Like ebola! Like—"

"*Mom!* You need to *calm down*." Elena said this loudly and slowly, like the nurse she hoped to be.

I paused for breath. I was panting, hyperventilating. Okay, she was right. I *did* need to calm down.

Elena climbed out of the car with her Starbucks cup in one hand and her backpack in the other.

"Love you," she said firmly, looking back through the window at me.

"Love you, too," I mumbled back.

On the drive home, I tried to calm down. I tried to concentrate on the sunshine. I tried to be in the moment. *Elena's right*, I told myself. *It's all in the past.* But the more I thought about it, the more distraught I became.

That poor child! She was all alone in that grim treatment center, that place replete with hostility and hideous rules . . .

And then, those bastards—those smug, arrogant *bastards!*—they made sure she'd *always* be alone.

I pulled into the horseshoe drive and forced myself to park carefully. I made myself walk at a calm pace down the hallways to my room. I made myself look into the offices and notice the smiling photos on desks.

But that's not what I was seeing inside.

My imagination was showing me a gray-faced eighteen-year-old: my traumatized daughter, trying to push herself by brute force and ambition through her senior year, alone—all alone, even in the house with her family around her.

They had taken a child with trust issues, and they had taught her not to trust. They had taken a child with anxiety, and they had taught her to fear. And during that senior year, I had seen it in her eyes: the suspicion, the scorn, and the loathing for us *both*—

—because, after what Elena thought I had done to her, she hated herself for being stupid enough to love me.

My throat closed up. I was grinding my teeth. My hands itched and twitched with the desire to smash themselves into walls.

You need to calm down!

But I didn't.

I unlocked my door, threw myself on my bed, and cried. I twisted and punched my pillow and sobbed and moaned. I howled for Elena, for all the poor patients like her, for all the poor mothers and fathers like me who had reached out to hug their beloved children—and found themselves hugging a cold-eyed stranger.

The gall of it! The sheer, breathtaking, monstrous inhumanity of it! To stand in front of a roomful of children you didn't even know and say, *Your family did it. Your parents made you ill. Your mother is killing you.*

How many children *died* from the heartbreak and isolation? How many children did they *kill*?

Those damn *murderers!*

MURDERERS!

Finally, I couldn't cry anymore. I had no more tears. My hands were shaking, and my head was pounding. Elena was right. I needed to *calm down*.

So I stood up and remade my bed. I washed my face. I pulled up the blinds, and I let in the morning sunlight.

Then I opened up my laptop.

And I wrote it all down.

CHAPTER THIRTY-SEVEN

A couple of weeks later, Brenda called Elena and me into her office for a special meeting. She said, "It's time to step down from all-day therapy."

I realized when she said this that when I had pictured this moment, I'd seen it as something like a graduation. Elena would shake hands all around and maybe make a speech. Then she would walk out into the world as a newly minted recovering anorexic.

But what the moment actually felt like was coming to the end of one of those moving sidewalks. It dove into the floor, and we found ourselves stumbling away.

"I don't feel any improvement!" Elena protested. "I still fall asleep all the time. What am I supposed to do?"

"You'll need to find an apartment nearby," Brenda told her. "Don't worry, it isn't as if all treatment stops. Three or four times a week, you'll come in for a couple of hours to meet with your therapist and nutrition-ist and do group therapy with the other patients. You'll practice going to grocery stores and preparing meals together."

"But I'm not ready!" Elena insisted. "Maybe if I had another few weeks to get ready, now that I know this is coming . . ."

"No, I'm afraid the insurance company won't okay any more time," Brenda said. "And we agree with them. You're at a healthy weight, and you've been in intensive therapy for six months now."

The ride was over. It was time to walk.

I left the session and went home to make lists: a series of comforting, nicely prioritized to-do items to pile up like sandbags against the anxiety

I was feeling. I ran the numbers and made sample budgets, and Joe and I spent hours on the phone, discussing them.

Numbers were safe. They represented safe things like poverty and bankruptcy. I knew this. In college, I had survived on very little. Air conditioning is only a nice-to-have item, and so is phone service. A bouillon cube, nestled in a pan of rice, makes the body think it's eating chicken . . .

As long as I spent my time on numbers, I didn't have to think about what really mattered, which was that Elena was nothing more than a zombie these days. When she sat down to watch a video, within seconds, she was asleep. She had begged me to buy her a computer game, but almost as soon as it would start, she would fall asleep. She didn't even try to read anymore. If she opened a book, she was asleep. I took her to see a movie she'd been excited about for months, and she nodded off within minutes.

Elena could barely stay awake long enough to take a shower. How could she stay awake long enough to embark on a normal life?

I marshalled my carefully prepared notes that evening, and I sat down with Elena on her bed. "So, I called the nursing schools nearby," I said. "Here's what Dad and I think we can manage. If you can get by with the furniture you brought back from Germany . . ."

A long sigh interrupted me. Elena was nodding off.

I prodded her awake again.

"Here are a few nice apartment buildings in the area," I went on as I pulled up photos on the laptop. "Now, this one is particularly good because it has protected parking and a night guard. It's set up especially for single women."

I waited for a comment, but there wasn't one. Elena's eyes were blinking—focusing and unfocusing.

"Anyway, I think you ought to give this place a call," I said, trying my best to sound positive and optimistic.

"Can't you call them for me?" Elena begged. "I'm so sleepy! Besides, I don't know what to say." And she curled up like a shrimp right there, with the laptop sliding off her lap. Within a second or two, she was unconscious.

I fought back panic. This was so unlike Elena! Why was Clove House doing this to her? The drugged sleepiness was depressing her as much as the eating disorder ever had. If it left no room for self-destruction, it left no room for joy or initiative, either.

Elena was right: how was she supposed to function like this?

I didn't have answers. I had *none* of the right answers. But what could I do? All I could do was keep going.

"Sure," I told her sleeping form. "I can give them a call."

The next afternoon, Brenda gave Elena a pass so she could look at a couple of the apartments I'd called. I drove her around, and we walked through them together.

The places looked perfect to me. They looked really cute. I remembered my excitement and enthusiasm over my first college apartment, how I'd decorated it with two-dollar art posters and served my friends cups of tea . . .

But Elena wasn't excited, and she wasn't enthusiastic. She didn't even seem to be looking around. She was waiting by the door before I could even finish asking the building manager my questions.

"This isn't going to work," she told me flatly.

"But—why?" I spluttered. "It's perfect! Your furniture will work great in there, you can walk to nursing school—they even have one spot left in the protected garage! I know you're worried about snow and ice, but . . . but . . ."

But Elena didn't actually look worried about anything. She didn't look as though she felt anything at all. When was the last time she had discussed an apartment and nursing school with me?

Back when I had come to Clove House the first time.

Now, Elena was beyond worries, wakefulness, anything. She sat like a lump in the passenger seat, eyes closed, head sagging against the window.

She muttered, "Maybe I should just do treatment at home."

What?

"But, Elena, think! You're doing good work here . . ."

I waited for her to argue with me, but she didn't bother. "This is bullshit, Mom," she murmured finally.

That Edward Gorey mother in me was beside herself, fluttering her handkerchief and wringing her hands. But the writer in me was calm and straightforward. *My character is telling the truth*, it noted. *This is bullshit. No one can live an independent adult life in this kind of condition.*

So I called Brenda, and Brenda called us in for another special meeting in her office. "Elena, leaving or staying in treatment at Clove House has to be your decision," she said. "You have to figure out what you're going to do."

Okay, I thought. *That's good. I can see that it's good. It's important to force Elena to interact with her future.* Because, as far as I could tell these days, Elena wasn't interacting with anything.

I looked at my daughter. In spite of the weight gain, she didn't look better to me this time. The hollows in her cheeks had filled out, but her whole body looked yellow and puffy, and her eyes looked old and sick. Even now, during one of the most important moments of her life, she was blinking away fatigue.

"Well . . . ," Elena said. "I think maybe it's best if I go home with Mom and do my outpatient treatment with Dr. Leben at Sandalwood."

There, I thought. *We have a decision. Elena has interacted with her future.* And once again, I began to make lists in my head: *extend the insurance override to cover costs at Sandalwood, call Dr. Leben to see if she has an opening . . .*

But Brenda didn't speak. She just stared sternly at Elena.

The moment stretched on and on.

"Well . . . ," Elena muttered, "maybe I should go ahead and stay here . . ."

"Good!" Brenda said. "It's settled then. I'll give you another pass so your mother can take you to visit the local colleges."

Was it Elena's and my recent conversations about Drew Center that made me feel so upset at this? Yes, I could see that Elena's decisions were suspect, but this was pure manipulation. If she needed to stay there so badly, why tell her it should be her choice?

"She's so drugged!" I said to Brenda, almost beside myself with frustration. "She hasn't participated in any of this. She can't stay awake long enough!"

"Mrs. Dunkle, we've talked about this," Brenda said. "It's important that Elena get relief from her self-harming urges."

"Yes, but she has no urges of any sort! She has no interest in life!" And I thought of my bright, nervous daughter, of her rapid speech, the quicksilver emotions dancing across her face: *Guess* what!

"It's an adjustment," Brenda said. "Mrs. Dunkle, it isn't as if Elena will be out on her own. She'll still be here for ten to twelve hours a week. If we see that it's too much for her, we can put her back into full-time treatment. Now, Elena, I'm going to write you a pass. Why don't you and your mother go visit the nursing schools?"

And I left with my somnambulant daughter again, my head in a complete whirl.

Back into full-time treatment? But—when would she get *better*?!

The minute we got into the car, Elena told me she wasn't going to colleges. "Not today," she said. "Let's go back and look at the computer again. You can explain the budget to me. I'll pay attention. And I can do things there . . . Make calls . . ."

What could I do? Could I force my adult daughter to walk into a nursing school?

"Okay . . . ," I said.

But when we got back to the room, all she did was crawl into bed and close her eyes.

I begged her. I shook her and nagged her. "You can't just lie here!" I said. "It's the one thing I can't allow. I'll help you do *anything* else!"

But Elena lay without answering. She didn't move.

"Look at how much you need to get done," I whined. "Think about your recovery!" And there it was, that hand-wringing mother again: *Please, darling! We need to* talk!

"My recovery? My recovery is a joke."

And, while the mother in me continued to wail, the writer took in that simple declaration. *My character is a realist*, the writer said again.

We were running out of time. I could feel it. We were sliding over a cliff. I lay awake that night, and my imagination showed me that cliff edge, getting closer and closer. Elena's last week in treatment was almost over. We had to do something—*anything*!

"Did you know," Elena said bitterly as she got into the car the next evening, "that I won't even keep my same therapist and nutritionist? Clove House has staff who work with inpatients and staff who work with outpatients. This is bullshit. I'll be starting all over again."

"Yes, but it's a good program," I protested, and I despised myself for the feeble, whimpering tone in my voice.

"How do *you* know?" Elena snapped. "*You* don't know the outpatient people. It could be a complete waste of time!"

And, although I said every positive thing I could think of, I thought, *That's what I'm afraid of, too.*

I felt crushed by the responsibility of it all. I spent each day that week moving heaven and earth. On the laptop, on my scribbled pages of notes—even in my own imagination—I tried to weave together a future for Elena.

But after all my numbers and budgets, after all my plans and visits, we ended up packing the car.

I hadn't known this on Friday morning, when I had dropped Elena off at treatment. But when I picked her up that afternoon, it was a fact of life. It wasn't just the one last fight Elena had had with her therapist. It was the result of too many unknowns.

"Why do we have to pack *now*?" Elena sighed as she emptied drawers. "I'm so tired! Why don't we just leave in the morning?"

This was the most practical thing to do, of course. I could get some rest and wake up ready for the long road ahead. But as I looked around at the familiar walls, at the familiar view out the windows, I realized just how much I hated this place. It had been my shelter in a time of great need. It had also been the scene of some of the saddest, worst, most horrible moments of my entire life.

"No," I said, "let's hit the road. I'd like to see how far we can get tonight."

I left Elena packing while I took my printer to the car, and as I carried it out into the sunlight and found a place for it in the backseat, I felt my spirits soar in a veritable frenzy of fierce, unapologetic joy. At least—at least—tomorrow was going to be *different*! It wasn't going to be another one of those dull, drab, hideously depressing days that dragged along in plodding monotony week after week after week and changed only in the amount of pain they brought me.

I found myself smiling broadly at the cheerful volunteer as I paused at the front desk to check out. "We're going home!" I told her.

Home! I wanted to shout that word over and over until the halls rang with noise—those pained, hushed, sickly-silent halls.

Maybe this is going to work out beautifully, I thought as I hurried back to take another load out to the car. *Maybe Elena will give the Sandalwood therapists another try. Maybe—maybe—things will finally get* better*!*

Then I opened the door of our room and found Elena asleep next to her half-full suitcase, and my heart sank into my toes once more.

Anyway, I thought, *what choice do we really have?*

The moving sidewalk had ended. And we were stumbling away.

CHAPTER THIRTY-EIGHT

Joe and Valerie sounded a little panicked when I called and told them the good news. I had caught them completely off guard.

Of course, they were happy we were on our way home—of *course*!

"But you know Gemma's still not sleeping, right?" Valerie said. "You know I couldn't clean, right?"

And I could hear the exhaustion in her voice.

"I need to get to the backyard," Joe said. "The lawn mower won't start, and I haven't had time to fix it. With the HVAC problem at the big VOQ, I've been gone a lot."

And I could hear the exhaustion in his.

"It's okay," I told them both. "Don't worry. I'll be home soon. I'll take care of it, don't worry."

But they did worry. And they kept calling—anxious calls.

Just so I knew: the freezer door wouldn't stay closed. Dylan the fish still wouldn't eat. The trash cans were full. There wasn't much in the way of meals. The laundry—they should probably get to the laundry. The bills had been piling up. Clint had just gotten back from Georgia, and his stuff was in bags all over the house. They couldn't put it in the garage. Simon was still in the garage, and still in the cone.

"I've taken him back to the vet," Joe said, "and so has Valerie. We've tried a bunch of different things. But he keeps tearing himself up, ripping his neck open the second the cone comes off."

Poor Simon!

"He's pretty much destroyed the garage," Joe added bitterly. "The place absolutely reeks."

"Well, it's okay," I said. "I'll work it out. It'll just be good to be home."

Long hours later, with a feeling of happy optimism, I parked next to the Korean invasion. But what I walked into wasn't home. It was a sad-looking, beaten-up, dusty little house that seemed to be bursting at the seams. Gemma's toys and walker and playpen had taken over the living room, along with old fast-food cartons and random piles of junk mail. Odd new stains had bloomed across the carpet.

"Ohh," I said, looking around.

"I know. I'm sorry, Momma," Valerie said. "But hey, wait till you see Gemma again. She should be waking up any minute. You're not going to recognize her!"

Genny, the ratty old terrier, came bouncing up to me and danced on her hind legs. Given the sad changes in my house's interior, she looked downright stylish. Which reminded me . . .

"How's my blue boy doing today?" I asked Valerie as I patted the dog.

"Well . . ."

The majestic blue minidragon I had left in his aquarium now looked like a pale sardine.

"Good lord!" I burst out. "Dylan's got fin rot! The poor guy's fins are *gone*!"

"Oh! Hey, they are!" Valerie said. "I'm sorry, Momma, I didn't notice."

Poor Valerie—of course she wouldn't have noticed. My older daughter was also pale and droopy-eyed. Having acted as a single parent to an infant daughter still waking up a couple of times a night, Valerie had been living with a pretty rigid set of priorities. And Joe's job was like a buzz saw: people called from a couple of continents and a fair collection of islands to demand his attention every day.

I couldn't expect an overworked, overtime-working manager and a brand-new mother to notice changes in a fish.

Out in the garage, things were even worse. Simon was frantic with boredom and discomfort, and the place smelled like a bad gas station toilet. I sat on the concrete step by the laundry room door, stroked the big cat's dirty fur, and agonized.

What was I going to *do*?

Even though the wound had healed up nicely, Simon's neck had stayed injured somehow. There seemed to be a constant itching in the area of the bite. The vet had tried creams and courses of pills, but nothing had made the slightest difference. Only the cone could keep Simon from tearing himself apart, and because of the cone, he couldn't go outside.

Now, I pulled the dirty white cone off Simon's neck. He purred and rubbed his dusty head against my knee, and loose fur went flying up in clouds. Then he hopped up onto a stack of boxes and began to dig at the healed-up wound.

I stood up to pet him and distract him, but Simon wouldn't stop. I held his back foot so he couldn't scratch anymore, and he started twisting to try to reach the spot with the other foot. So I put his cone back on, sat back down on the step, and called the vet.

"Mrs. Dunkle, at this point, there's not much left for us to try," he said. "The last time I saw it, the injuries had healed up with no sign of infection."

"The fur is back to normal," I agreed. "Could it be nerve damage then?"

"It certainly could," the vet said.

"Meaning that it won't improve," I summed up. And we were both silent for a few seconds, thinking about that.

"There's a test we can do," the vet said. "It's a special test that we send off to Houston. It takes a tissue sample and tests it for every kind of skin problem you can think of. I think it's around six or seven hundred dollars. I can look it up and get an exact price."

"But that test," I said. "Haven't you already given him the treatments we'd try for those skin problems anyway?"

"A good number of them, yes."

"Are there any other treatments we can try that we haven't tried yet? Can't we just skip the test?"

"Well, at this point, we get into really complicated things. And without an idea of where we're going—with healthy-looking skin, healthy blood values, no symptoms but the scratching—I just don't see a way forward unless we do that test."

I stroked Simon's big head and scratched his ears inside the cone.

"This isn't the kind of year," I said, "when we have that kind of money lying around. We've had some big medical bills."

"I understand," the vet said. "Believe me, I do."

The garage got quiet. Outside, not too far away, a lawn mower began its monotonous drone.

"If we *knew* it would help . . . ," I said at last. "But it sounds like you've already tried the basic treatments. Six or seven hundred dollars, and probably nothing to show for it. I just can't justify it on a gamble."

"I understand," the vet said again. "I've made these kinds of decisions myself."

And there was silence again.

Simon sprawled next to me, purring, on the cool concrete, and I ran my hand down his dusty side. I remembered when Elena and I had chosen him as a kitten: the one black kitten in the whole litter. The only one who had purred.

The vet was waiting for me to say it. I didn't want to. But I had to.

"When can I bring him in?"

We set up a time for the following morning, and I put down the phone. Simon wriggled on his back on the concrete and looked up at me from inside his white cone. Execution by lethal injection at ten o'clock tomorrow morning, and I couldn't even let the poor guy have a last night out of the cone. He'd tear himself up. He'd have his neck in tatters.

I stroked his soft fur.

Dead cat purring.

With a lump in my throat, I gave Simon a last pat, climbed to my feet, and walked back inside. The kitchen was an unspeakable disaster. The counters were jammed. Swirls of pet hair, gray with dust, gathered in the corners of the floor. The freezer had popped open again—probably needed defrosting.

But at least . . . at least . . . my family was back together. Valerie was here, and Gemma was here, and Clint had just gotten back, and Joe would be home from work soon. And, after sleeping straight through on the drive home, at least Elena was up and walking around.

Now Valerie headed toward me from the back hallway, her tired face animated and purposeful. Clint and Elena trailed behind her into the living room.

"Hey, Momma, we've got an idea for where to put everybody," Valerie said. "Next time Gemma wakes up, we're going to move her crib into the media room. Then we'll put Elena's furniture back in her room, and I can stay in the office, with the air mattress."

"But what about the media room furniture?" I asked.

"That's what I wanted to talk to you about. We need to move the PS3 and the flat-screen out here. We can put the big living room chairs in the garage and turn the sofa around over here, and then if we want to play a game or watch a movie, we won't wake up Gemma."

"Okay, but . . ."

But the fact is that I hate a screen in the living room. Not once in the girls' entire lives had there been a screen in the living room. A living room is for people, not machines.

Valerie was right, though. We were running out of rooms. A media room was a luxury we couldn't afford anymore. I glanced around the living room, piled to the window sills with trash and displaced belongings, and my shoulders sagged with discouragement. Cleanliness appeared to be a luxury we couldn't afford, either.

"So, we're going to get started, okay?" Valerie said. "Clint, grab the other side." They heaved, and a sedate wingback chair rose from the floor and levitated its way across the room.

"Wait!" I said. "Not the garage. Let's not move things now. Tomorrow, you can put things into the garage."

They stopped and looked at me again—a careful look. Valerie said, "You mean you called the vet?"

"Ten o'clock in the morning," I answered, and then I hurried away from those sets of sympathetic eyes.

If only I'd never let that stubborn cat outside!

I remembered the bouncy kitten Simon had been. Why did all the bounce and happiness have to die in my house?

With a lump in my throat, I went back into the filthy kitchen and started unloading the dishwasher. "I'm sorry, Momma," Valerie said, following me. "Dad and I did our best, we really did. I went out and sat with Simon every day."

I nodded briskly. "I know that, honey."

But her comment reminded me of Dylan, my ailing fish. He needed to be my next priority. So I abandoned the dishwasher only partly emptied, grabbed my purse, and drove to the pet store.

Fifty dollars' worth of fin rot drugs, an aquarium vacuum, and filter inserts later, I was cleaning up Dylan's home as well as I could while the little guy huddled under his favorite plant.

Poor pale sad little fish! He was so changed from the lovely and confident creature I had left behind two months ago. Back then, he would swim onto my hand and perch there like a bird. Now, I wasn't sure he could even swim.

When everything was as clean as I could make it and the water values were right again, I poured in the fin rot treatment—the maximum dose since this was such a drastic case.

Poor Dylan didn't even have fins left to rot.

As I worked, I tried not to look anywhere but at the aquarium. The bathroom was unspeakable, too: empty toilet paper rolls, dust and dog hair in the corners, and a layer of cast-off clothing underfoot. The bathtub was gray, and the sink was so crusted with fallen makeup and dried toothpaste that it had lost its original color.

I can't stand a lot of different kinds of dirty, but a dirty bathroom is the worst. A filthy house gives me a sense of physical desperation akin to claustrophobia. It feels as if chaos is raining down on me, as if I'm drowning under piles of trash—as if the earth itself has vomited all over me. So, as I cleaned Dylan's aquarium, I had to pause every now and then and take deep breaths.

Priorities! I reminded myself firmly. *It'll be all right in a couple of days. Just hit one thing after another—one thing after another.*

Then I walked into the media room, where Valerie and Clint were playing with Gemma. And my grandbaby was happy and beautiful. She was blooming with health.

I picked her up, and my arms wrapped around her, and my whole body relaxed. Gemma and her immaculate clothes and her pink, perfect skin positively glowed with care and loving attention. The chaos in the house hadn't touched her at all.

My imagination pulled up memories for me of another baby being carried through a dusty, gray-tinged house: baby Valerie at this same age, also pink and perfect and blooming with health, with dirty dishes and dirty clothes piled up all around us.

Yes, I thought. *Yes, I remember.*

Valerie had done the right thing. This was what had needed to happen during the months when I was gone. And she and Clint didn't have much time together, either. In another week, he would be in basic training, getting yelled at and stressed. I could leave them alone to have a few happy days.

I'll get to it, I thought. *It's not a big problem. Dirt isn't fatal.*

Next morning, I got up early with Joe. While he ate his bowl of cereal in preparation for another long workday, I told him about my worries at Clove House.

"Elena never got traction," I said. "She was a zombie more or less the entire time."

"I thought things were going badly," Joe said. "You weren't telling me much. You try just to tell me the good stuff."

"In that case," I sighed, "it's a wonder I told you anything at all."

Joe frowned. "Maybe the sleep is a kind of dissociation. Maybe she's avoiding the stuff that makes her uncomfortable."

"That wouldn't explain why she nods off during movies, too," I said. "She begged me to take her to see this one ballet. Then she got so sleepy that we ended up having to leave halfway through."

"I guess they were trying to get her to the point where she wasn't angry all the time."

I thought about that last day, when Elena had called me up, absolutely fuming over something Brenda had told her.

"Well, if that was the plan, it didn't really work."

After Joe left, I spent a while in the smelly garage with Simon. I took off his cone and held him to keep him from scratching. "Sorry, big boy," I whispered to him as he rolled back and forth across my lap. "We would fix you if we could, but we don't know how to fix you." Then I pondered that statement, dreary and dejected.

Wasn't that the story of my life?

With a *crack*, the door to the house pushed open. "Momma," Valerie said. "You need to come see this."

It was Dylan. A clear sheet of skin had peeled off his side and was hanging down loose.

"Oh, my God!" I said.

"It's got to hurt," Valerie agreed mournfully. "Fish may not feel much, but they're bound to feel *that*."

She was right. Of *course* she was right! It was appalling—appalling!—that a creature in my house should be in so much pain. Poor little Dylan, my dragon boy! He had to be put out of his misery right away.

With trembling fingers, I searched "fish euthanasia" on the Internet. Thank God for thoughtful hobbyists everywhere.

"Okay, clove oil," I told Valerie. "And vodka. I'll be back."

I found the clove oil in a tooth repair kit at our neighborhood drugstore, along with cotton balls, a dental mirror, and some temporary cement. I was surprised to find a liquor store open at eight thirty in the morning, and they were probably surprised to find that I desperately needed a bottle of vodka.

Then again, maybe they weren't.

I sped home and snagged the poor betta in a measuring cup. He didn't do any of the things fish normally do to escape. He probably couldn't imagine that his life could get any worse. Then I cleared off a few square inches of counter space in the unholy mess of my kitchen and dumped him out into a cereal bowl.

Elena was up by this time, nursing a cup of green tea. Clint came wandering into the kitchen.

"Mom's killing Dylan with vodka," Valerie informed him.

"Oh!" Clint said amiably. "I guess if you've gotta go . . ."

Meanwhile, I was busy dismantling the tooth kit. Two drops of the clove oil were supposed to put Dylan to sleep. But how would I know if he was asleep? It's not like fish have eyelids.

I knew, all right. The two drops of clove oil laid poor Dylan out flat on his side. I poked my finger into the water and stirred him around gently, but he didn't move. He was probably already dead.

I remembered the day when I had picked him out in the pet store, the handsomest, strongest betta there, and my heart broke for the beautiful little life that had floated so gracefully through mine.

Valerie came up behind me. "Is it time to flush him?"

"He doesn't get flushed," I said. "We wait another"—I looked at the clock—"five minutes. Then we replace part of his water with the vodka."

And I followed my painless-death recipe to the letter, even though I felt sure he was already gone.

Deep breath. Time to take Simon to the vet. No negative thoughts or feelings, now. It wouldn't be fair to pass along bad vibes to a helpless animal.

"We're so sorry, Mrs. Dunkle," the receptionist said soberly when I came staggering through the door with Simon's heavy cage. "Room 2 is all ready for you. You can go right in." And I was grateful that the vet and technician came in at once and didn't keep us waiting.

Simon strolled about impatiently and bumped our hands with his head while we once again went over our lack of options. The sight of the big cat, so strong, apparently so healthy, set up an odd cognitive dissonance within me. I couldn't see how it could possibly be true that this big bruiser of a cat needed to die. But in the short car ride, Simon had already scratched his neck bloody again, and I had to hold his back foot to stop him from doing more harm.

Nerve damage. Joe had taken pictures of the savage bite into the black cat's neck, down to the shiny gristle-covered bones.

"Are you ready?" asked the vet.

And just like that, Simon's broad-shouldered, brawling days were over.

I drove home with my hand resting on his white cardboard coffin. They had barely managed to wedge him inside. When Simon had first come home with me as a kitten, his family had found him a white cardboard box for the ride. That had been only a few years before Valerie's overdose and the Summer from Hell.

It seemed to me in those sad moments as if my family's collective life had been contracting ever since those grim years, like lifeboat survivors throwing the weaklings overboard. First I had thrown overboard my story characters, who still tried to visit me from time to time, but I couldn't clear my mind enough to deal with them anymore. Then Dylan had gone, and now Simon.

They had been too demanding and too delicate. They had taken risks. They had asked too much of my strained abilities: attention, protection, loving care.

I brought the coffin into the jumbled, trash-strewn living room. It joined the rest of the debris from our fractured lives. "Clint," I said, waving vaguely at the box, "I need to ask a favor."

He stood up at once. "Sure thing."

Gemma was awake. I claimed her from Valerie, and while Clint was out back digging a hole large enough to hold a cat and a fish, I sat down with my grandbaby to get reacquainted.

This isn't a contraction of our lives, I reminded myself. *This is a wonderful addition to our lives. Gemma and Clint are both wonderful additions.*

But then again, that was Valerie's doing, not mine.

Gemma had grown so much in the two months I'd been gone that she was already bored with just lying in my arms. Now she wanted to wriggle around and pull up on things. She stiffened her little body and tried to stand up on my lap.

"Hey, Elena!" Valerie said, poking her sister, who had curled up in one of the armchairs. "Crib! Move it! Let's go!"

Elena muttered something inaudible, but she opened her eyes and got to her feet, and the two of them headed off down the hall.

I stayed behind with my granddaughter on the dusty, hair-covered couch, and looked into her wide blue-gray eyes. *"A, B, C, D, E, F, G,"* I crooned, bouncing her in time with the letters. But around *Q*, my voice turned husky, and by *S*, I had to stop.

It's perfectly ridiculous, I told myself, *to cry in the middle of the ABCs. Think of the vet: he has to put down animals all day long.*

Valerie emerged from the hallway and balanced a long slab of slatted crib against the cluttered piano. "Gotta put it out here while we move Elena's mattress."

I stroked Gemma's fine flyaway curls. Her hair had lightened up. I, too, was a blond baby. Was it just wishful thinking, or did Gemma look a little bit like me?

Elena came out with another piece of crib to stack against the first.

My phone rang. I propped up Gemma with one hand while I swiped the answer button with the other. The gentle voice of my sister-in-law was on the line.

"Hi, Godmother," she said, and I could hear the smile in her voice. "I was supposed to call you last week—*but* . . ."

My brother and sister-in-law had been talking about coming down for a visit, something they do a time or two a year. It isn't the easiest thing for him to leave the produce farm, or for her to pull their four children away from homeschooling. So, since they hadn't chosen firm dates—and since I'd been dealing with everything else—I hadn't paid too much attention. That was all their vacation planning had been so far: just talk.

Up to this point, at least.

"We're about halfway there," my sister-in-law told me, and I could hear the happiness in her voice. A vacation—getting away from the farm and the stacks of papers to grade—the chance to visit people she was fond of . . . "I'm sorry we're not giving you much warning, but you don't need to feed us. I've got things for supper right here in the motor home. Is it all right if we stay in your driveway tonight?"

Even while making these apologies, my sister-in-law's voice didn't lose its happy warmth. She knew what the answer would be. If there's a person on this planet I adore, it's my sister-in-law. She's my godchild, too. I would do anything in the world for her happiness, she knows that. Anything in the world.

I cast a frantic eye around my chaotic living room. Clint came walking in the back door, having propped the dirty shovel outside, to take the cardboard coffin with him and see if it would fit. Valerie and Elena sidled by me, lugging an armchair between them. The flat-screen teetered in the middle of the coffee table, along with half-empty soda cans and the remains of Subway sandwiches. A pile of dirty laundry was spilling out of Elena's suitcase on the floor by the cluttered piano bench.

It was horrible. It was unspeakable! And, once again, I fought down that feeling of claustrophobia, as if I were being crushed alive in a loaded garbage truck.

"I—I—you know I just got home yesterday," I heard myself babble. "I—we—I haven't—I don't know—"

For the first time, my sister-in-law sensed that something was wrong.

"You know it doesn't matter how the place looks," she assured me. "We're just looking forward to seeing you."

That was true. That was absolutely one hundred percent true. I could welcome my brother and sister-in-law in my pajamas, and they wouldn't mind. They love me as sincerely as two humans possibly can.

And yet—and yet—

A strong odor of urine curled around me from the open garage door. That stain on the floor—was that Big Red? Was it going to come out?

When my brothers and their families come to see me, I do my very best to spoil them. I cook big meals and every dessert I know they like. It matters to me what my big brothers think of us. I want them to feel proud of us, to feel that we're doing well.

"Coming through!" called Valerie, and she and Elena walked a headboard past me on its way to the garage. "Okay," she said to her sister, "let's take a smoke break."

"But . . . they're moving furniture!" I said helplessly into the phone. "There's not even anywhere to sit!"

"We won't be there for another couple of hours," my sister-in-law said.

Another couple of hours in this place. What could I get done in a couple of hours? Ruined food in the freezer, God knows what in the fridge, a guest bathroom with dirty clothes for a carpet, a dead fish on the kitchen counter . . .

"I just put down our fish," I heard myself say. "Our cat's dead. Clint's digging a grave."

I barely heard her efforts to persuade me. I was looking at my whole life through her eyes. It wasn't just the dust bunnies and carpet stains. It was the army of brown pill bottles by the breakfast table. It was the big white poster board sticking up out of our mound of suitcases, a sample of Elena's art therapy, with a four-letter word scrawled across it in black paint.

For one split second, I imagined my brother's family—that calm, quiet, thoughtful family—walking through the door of this house. My brother and sister-in-law don't raise their voices. Their four children are the most easygoing youngsters I've met. They would stand together in the middle of my living room, and they would look around and take it all in. There are happy, productive, I've-been-too-busy-to-sort-this-all-out dirty houses. And then there was the kind I had. No one would mistake this kind for the other kind. Not even the youngest child.

If my family saw it—if they walked through that door and saw it—then they couldn't possibly unsee it again.

I couldn't bear to let that happen.

"I'm not ready!" I cried in despair. "If you come later this week . . . If you go to your sister's house first . . . There's nothing clean here. There's no place to *be*! It isn't just that the cat's dead and the freezer doesn't work. It's everything, the whole place, the whole house!"

Stunned and small, my sister-in-law's voice murmured good-bye. I sat there with my squirming grandchild while my imagination played it out for me: the abrupt, shocked stillness inside the motor home. My brother would be staring straight out over the steering wheel, disappointed and angry. He would doubtless remind his wife that she should have worked out the details sooner, as he had doubtless been reminding her to do. The children would be puzzled. They would be asking unfortunate questions. And she would be the one who would have to answer them, her vacation suddenly grown meager.

Who could blame a busy farm wife for failing to plan? And how could she have planned for this anyway? In her wildest dreams, she couldn't have imagined that her godmother would turn her away. She couldn't have planned for this kind of pain.

I bounced Gemma recklessly on my knee while her baby face blurred and the chaos distorted around me. Then I wiped my eyes, stood up, set my grandchild on my hip, and walked out to the backyard to find the others.

"I'm going to Whataburger," I said. "What does everybody want?"

CHAPTER THIRTY-NINE

With the PS3 in the living room, I couldn't write at home anymore. The sound of exploding zombies seemed to find me wherever I went. So, once I had imposed order and my house was no longer filthy, I began exploring new places to write Elena's memoir.

The library, I thought. *A library will be perfect!* I'm a librarian by training, and I worked as a university librarian for years, so I had happy dreams of sitting at a library carrel, typing away on my laptop. How could this solution not work?

But it didn't.

I tried three different libraries, but none of them worked.

Day after day, I started Elena's story over. I pulled up a clean, blank page, and I hurled sentences at it. For an hour or so, everything would go well. Then my thoughts would stop finding connections.

I would start deleting the things that were wrong. The sentences would break apart. The words would capsize into the endless white.

And at the end of the day, I would find myself staring at a clean, blank page again.

I moved that useless, empty file from one computer to another. I changed screens and put on my reading glasses, as if the problem were as simple as the font size I'd chosen—as if, with one little tweak, I could bring the whole thing into focus. And now, here I was, bouncing from library to library, as if the problem were as simple as that particular mix of patrons—the particular hiss of a whisper or the scrape of a library chair.

But I knew that wasn't what was wrong. It was that the story hurt. It hurt me so much that I could hardly bear to be in the same room with it.

It hurt me so much that putting my hands on the keys seemed to generate an electric shock. It was sending me, step by step, methodically and meticulously, through every single one of my worst memories.

Normally, when I write, I forget who I am in this world and become the god of another. I set tasks for my characters to achieve and watch over them as they struggle. Because I hate boredom, I create amazing things for those characters to find along the way: a magic plant made out of starlight, wizards who wrap themselves in mist, or a living cat of clear glass whose paws chime gently as he strolls across the floor.

When I write stories, I forget that I'm working with words. I don't see the computer screen anymore. I see monsters, hear shrieks, feel soft threads of moss, and smell the sharp, clean scent of snow. I don't stay in this world. I fall out of this world into a *new* world, a place I've designed myself—a place that is under my complete control.

But I was in Elena's story. Elena's story was in my world. When I wrote it, I couldn't escape.

When I wrote her memoir, I fell out of my world . . . into my world again. I closed my eyes, forgot the computer screen, opened them in that other reality . . . and saw my computer screen again.

I was transported to a place . . .

That was right here.

I was like a bird on a string. I was like a frog trying to fly. I would get a running start and slam into a brick wall.

Over and over and over.

One morning, having made my way through every room of the house over the course of the past week, I was back at the local public library again. I rubbed my toes along the tops of my flip-flops on the floor under the table, cracked my knuckles, and reread what I had written so far.

It was my character, Elena. She was talking about her memoir.

> So, the way this book should go is the way things
> go in those after-school specials—you know, the
> ones with the two best girlfriends who do every-
> thing together. And they have the good times—cut

to scene of girls laughing and eating cotton candy at the carnival. And they have the bad times—cut to scene of girls throwing up behind the dumpster while flashing lights indicate that the cops are closing in.

And then, tragically, suddenly, like we didn't know it was going to happen all along, one of the girls (a) overdoses, (b) gets pregnant, (c) goes to jail, (d) drives drunk and ends up in a wheelchair, (e) dies dies dies dies dies.

And the other girl gets her act together.

It isn't that easy, of course. It requires several scenes of school counselors and teachers looking solemn, a tearful group hug with parents and siblings, maybe a short film clip of a doctor's office, perhaps a few scary seconds of a judge. And then, sooner or later, there's the scene where the girl has to be all boring and watch her friends go off to party without her. Oh, yeah, it's a long, hard process of recovery, taking at least five minutes of film time, but it pays off in the end with the glowing graduation speech:

God bless us, every one!

Well, I had a best friend, Mona. We did everything together. We cried together. We cut class together. We ate and ate and overate, and then we purged together.

And now my best friend has a job, and a life, and a healthy baby girl.

Where the hell does that leave *me*?

Anger and bitterness built up inside me as I read. *The world wants anorexia to be so easy*, I thought. *Well, this isn't an easy disease! It isn't just fooling around with green tea. It isn't just a diet gone wrong.*

Deal with it, world! Deal with it!

But then my writer's mind stopped me. Was this really Elena's voice? Was that my character speaking? Was that really Elena? Or was my character standing there, silent, while her author wasted time ranting again?

Because God knows, these days I was feeling angry and bitter.

Elena was doing badly. After all our labor and sacrifice and savings and time apart, after six months of around-the-clock treatment—at the end of it all, Elena was doing very badly. She hadn't gone through with her plan to work with the Sandalwood staff. Furious nagging from me had forced her to pick a psychiatrist, therapist, and nutritionist more or less at random off our list of preferred providers, but none of them had much experience with eating disorder.

Elena barely interacted with us these days. She barely even held her new niece. All day and all night, she did almost nothing except sleep. The powerful medications Clove House had put her on left her feeling nothing at all, and her new psychiatrist, overbooked and overworked, was seeing her for only about fifteen minutes a month. Time after time in these rushed, hectic, brief appointments, the psychiatrist declined to make changes, so Elena was still on massive doses of sedatives.

Even worse, she hardly ate these days. And what she ate was never enough.

So here I was, trying to write Elena's memoir while she slid back into the danger zone. Why had I said I would do this? It was causing me nothing but pain. The closer I came to Elena's character, the more she made me doubt that she would ever find a way to recover.

Tell the truth: strangely enough, that's the motto of the fiction writer, whose stories take place in worlds that don't exist. And the more I learned—the more I read through Elena's agonized poems and journal entries—the more painful my quest for her truth became.

My hands are frozen blocks of ice, she had written right after the Summer from Hell.

> *I am so cold*
> *all the time.*

I hope when I die
the dirt wraps me like a cocoon,
soft and dark
like fainting,
but a deeper smothering
than that.

Sitting there in the library, stepping on the tops of my flip-flops, I read those lines from three years before. Then I thought of Elena on the couch last night, curled up under her fuzzy blanket. She had looked like she was in a cocoon then. And she wouldn't wake up to eat dinner.

Had *anything* changed for the better in the three years since the Summer from Hell? Had *anything* good happened during the whole six months of full-time therapy?

A group of teens passed me, giggling and shoving. They looked happy . . .

That was it! This place wasn't working out. I couldn't work under these conditions! I hit the sleep button and folded up my laptop.

A coffee shop, I thought as I got into my car. *Of course! I'll try a coffee shop.* After all, coffee shops are practically a habitat for writers: they sit at their little tables, frown magnificently down at their computer screens, sip their lattes, and create exquisite prose. So I drove to the nearest coffee shop, purchased my very own latte, and attempted to create some exquisite prose of my own.

Lately, I'd been working on short monologues, attempting to find Elena's true voice behind the incessant jabber of my own fears and worries. I chose topics and tried to write about them from Elena's point of view.

Treatment, I thought now as I sipped my latte. *What does my character— that is, my daughter—say about treatment?*

As I stared at the white screen and the blinking curser, I flipped my right hand over and held it palm up. This was a habit I'd acquired from a library school professor. She told us she did this whenever she was thinking about how to classify something. The answer, she told us, should not be too broad and not be too narrow—it should fit into the palm of a hand.

Now, as I stared at the screen, my open hand waited for that perfect answer. What words would fit Elena's attitude toward treatment centers? What writing would match who she was—who she *really* was?

The palm of my hand began to fill up with words.

> I wish we did something crazy for treatment. I wish I could tell you:
>
> > *Today they strapped wires to my arms and sent electricity through me, and I smelled smoke and heard a crackle in my ears, and orange and purple spots appeared in the center of my vision, and afterward I had to lie down with a hot water bottle pressed to the back of my neck while I trembled and shook for a couple of hours.*
>
> Because then you'd say:
>
> *That's horrible! You were so brave! You're working so hard to get better!*
>
> But that's not what I can tell you.
>
> Instead, I have to say:
>
> *We had ice cream for afternoon snack.*
>
> And you say:
>
> *Mmmm! Ice cream!*
>
> You say:
>
> *I love ice cream!*
>
> There is nothing I can say to make you understand.

I closed my hand around that answer. It felt right to me. It felt real. And it made me want to cry for my miserable, miserable child until the little wooden table in front of me floated away on a wave of tears.

At that moment, the music blaring out over the coffee shop speakers changed. A woman's voice started telling me a story. She sang in malicious triumph about slashing up her cheating boyfriend's pickup truck. With a feeling of relief, my imagination turned to her.

Where is she? I wondered.

My imagination brought me images of a dim parking lot at night: lumpy, crumbly, poorly laid asphalt. I saw black potholes cratering down to the dirt. Light glittered off broken glass.

Where am I? I wondered.

Outside a windowless honky-tonk bar.

That honky-tonk—what is it like?

Like a view through binoculars that comes into focus, the scene before me began to clear. I saw a squat, square, one-story cinderblock building, with a string or two of those old big-bulb Christmas lights tacked up along the frame of the scuffed-up door. There was a sign beside the building up on a thick iron pole, the kind of sign with those black plastic moveable letters:

FRI 1 7TH, RAPSCALLIONS

$1 DRAFT BEER

And there was the young woman who was singing to me. She didn't care who saw her. She was striding toward that shiny custom-painted crew-cab pickup in her favorite pair of tight jeans, a leather jacket, and Lucchese cowboy boots. She had a baseball bat in one hand and a pig-sticker knife in the other.

Then she took a wide swing at the left headlight: a loud, musical shower of glass.

Yes! I cheered. *Let the consequences fall where they may!*

And then the woman—let's call her Amanda—she sees her ex come charging out of the bar. And her ex—let's call him Brad . . .

Another song came on over the loudspeakers. Another person wanted to tell me a story. But I closed my laptop, threw away my latte, and walked out.

Exquisite prose in a coffee shop? Who were they *kidding*?

I drove home through the hazy late-summer heat and turned the last corner. Such a litter of small, smudged Hyundais clustered these days outside the tired ranch house! Four Hyundais in four different colors.

Each, more or less, with its own designated parking place. One Hyundai was missing: the silver one. Joe, of course, was at work.

And one Hyundai—the tan one—was pulled into a clumsy tangent with the curb. It was facing the wrong way—again!

That was Elena's car. Late at night, she had roused herself from her stupor and gone out with friends. Now, worries fluttered up and clutched at me. Had Elena been drinking, even with all her meds? Was she drunk when she drove home last night?

And why was the tan Hyundai even here? Elena was supposed to be at her therapist's appointment!

Valerie was kneeling on the living room floor next to Gemma's exercise bouncer. She glanced up and saw the look in my eyes.

"I tried," she told me. "She wouldn't budge."

I marched past her and pushed open Elena's bedroom door.

For a few seconds, the darkness disoriented me, and I couldn't immediately register whether anyone was there. Shutters and shades kept Elena's room in a state of perpetual twilight.

"Elena!" I barked, snapping on the light.

"Ugggghhh . . . ," groaned the bed by way of answer.

I stepped gingerly across sliding mounds of brightly colored laundry. Elena's closet appeared to have burped its contents out into the room. The closet itself was open and empty of everything but some boxes, a few pink plastic hangers, and a red satin prom dress held up by one white loop.

"Elena!" I said again, prodding the one living mound in the room. It was sharing the bed with half a suitcase's worth of underwear and pajama sets, two blankets, three pillows, Genny, and Tor. The old terrier rolled a cautious eye up at me, decided she didn't need the drama, jumped down, and walked stiffly from the room. The old cat gave a stretch, flipped onto his back, and closed his eyes again. He was going to ride it out.

Various groans and snarls had been rising steadily from the mound of purple blanket. Now it gave a sudden lurch, and Elena's face appeared, creased from the wrinkles on her pillow.

"*What?!*" she demanded, rubbing her eyes. "Leave me alone! I just got to sleep!"

"It's noon," I said. "You've *been* asleep. You slept through your therapy appointment!"

"Oh." Elena blinked for a few seconds. "Why didn't you wake me up?" she asked.

I felt my frustration rising in a suffocating wave. And here I was, shouting already: "Why is it *our* job to wake you up?"

"Fine, forget I asked then," Elena grumbled. "I can't stand that lady anyway."

"*You* picked her! So find another therapist you like!"

"I will. When I wake up." And Elena rolled over. She muttered, "Why do you always have to yell at me first thing every morning?"

Why? Why did *my* life have to be like this? Why did it have to run like this, day after day after *day*?

"It is *not* the first thing in the morning!" I said. "Your sister and father and I have been up for hours! You missed another appointment with Bea, and that means we have to pay another seventy-five dollars for *nothing*. You know the insurance company doesn't pay their share when you miss an appointment!"

Elena grumbled into her pillow at this. It might have been an apology or an admission of guilt.

Then again, it might not.

"And another thing. You parked facing traffic again. They've already left us a warning. Next time, it'll be a ticket! *Why* is it so hard for you to turn your car around? Were you drinking last night? Were you drunk?"

"*No*, I wasn't drinking!" Elena cried, and when she did it, I realized that her loud, angry voice was only matching my own. "I was spending a little quiet time with Meghan. We were eating *Mexican food*, if you have to know!"

She spit out the words *Mexican food* with pained and vicious hatred, in the tone of voice I might use for maggots in the trash can. Implied but still included in her virulent hostility were the tacos last night, all meals on all nights, and me, for being the person who made her eat.

It seemed, during the course of these last few weeks, that all food had become my fault again, even if I wasn't there to serve it to her. I fell silent in the face of such resentment. How did her therapists stand it?

In the silence, Elena rolled over and hitched the blanket up to her chin. "Turn out the light," she muttered.

"But—no! Elena, you have to get up. You need to"—I hesitated, then decided to brave it out—"You need to eat some breakfast! You need to take your morning pills, or you'll get withdrawal symptoms again—God only knows what they're doing to your brain! You need to park that car *correctly*, and you need to call up Bea and reschedule."

And before she could sit up and rip into me again, I picked my way back across the loose laundry and out the door.

"Come on, Genny, you need to go outside," I said to the little terrier as I came back into the living room. I went outside with her and sat on the patio and thought gloomy thoughts while she trotted and nosed her way around the yard.

The back door opened. I looked up, hoping for an olive branch, but it wasn't Elena, it was Valerie. She had a pack of cigarettes in one hand and a Shirley Jackson novel in the other.

"I don't suppose she's eating," I said as Valerie fished for her lighter. She shook her head and concentrated on that first long, luxurious drag.

"Nope," she said, and then exhaled in a steady gray stream. "She's back in her room again."

I sat there for another minute, building courage for the next salvo, until my desire to say the angry things I probably shouldn't say exceeded my desire to avoid a fight. Then, once again, I marched inside, pushed open the bedroom door, and flicked on the light.

"Mom! Turn it out!"

"You need to get up."

"I did everything! I parked the car. I called Bea. Tomorrow at eleven thirty."

"Did you take your medicine?"

"*Yes*, I took my medicine!"

"Did you eat your breakfast?"

Silence.

"You need to get up, Elena. You need to eat. You need to do *something*"—I kicked at the laundry—"with this messy room."

Elena pulled the blanket over her face.

"I'll do it later, I promise," she said. "Meghan and I ate a huge meal at four o'clock in the morning. That makes it breakfast."

She subsided into a mound again. I stood in the doorway, struck with pain. Now that she wasn't yelling and I was no longer angry, the Elena in this room and the Elena in my laptop suddenly felt frighteningly close.

"Please get up," I tried in a softer tone. "We miss you! We haven't seen much of you lately. Come out to the couch and spend some time with us. You can tell me how Meghan's been. I haven't seen her in ages."

The mound on the bed quivered slightly.

"Meghan's okay," it finally said.

Could this inert lump really be my quick, bright daughter Elena, the girl who could turn a five-minute trip to the drugstore into three different thrilling, gossipy stories lasting ten minutes apiece? "Mom! Guess *what*!" She would be so excited she would almost be jumping out of her skin with the need to tell.

And I could never guess.

"I've been trying to work on the memoir," I said. "There's something I need help with."

The blanket quivered again. But that was all.

This had worked longer than any other appeal. It had worked even better than time with Gemma. Elena wanted her memoir to happen as much as she wanted anything in the world. But for the last couple of weeks, even this appeal hadn't worked.

"I'll help later," her muffled voice said at last. "I'll get up and help you with it. Promise I will. Just let me sleep for an hour."

I left the room. And I didn't see her for the rest of the day.

Late that night, after Joe had already gone to bed, I was walking through the house, collecting dishes for the dishwasher. I paused in the hallway. From behind Elena's closed door came laughter. There was a certain sound, playful and confiding, in the tone of her voice. Elena was flirting with someone on the phone.

At least she's awake, I thought, walking away.

A few minutes later, her bedroom door opened, the bathroom door shut, and the shower came on. Elena was up at last.

Maybe she would finally help me with the memoir. That was good. Since leaving the coffee shop, I hadn't done a thing. So I started the dishwasher, picked up my laptop, and settled down in the living room to wait.

Genny came galloping in from the backyard and jumped up into my lap. Valerie walked in behind her, yawning.

"This woman is a genius," she said firmly, holding up the Shirley Jackson book. "I'm reading this for the fourth time. Every sentence is amazing."

"Too right you are," I agreed. "I'd die happy if I could have written her last novel."

Valerie put the book down on the coffee table. "So. I'm off to bed. And why are you still awake, woman? Didn't Dad go to bed, like, an hour ago?"

I stretched and sighed. "Your sister's up. Maybe we can finally get some work done."

Valerie pulled out her phone and looked at it. "At eleven o'clock? Screw that! Make her get her work done tomorrow morning."

She disappeared down the hall, and I heard the door to her bedroom slide shut across the carpet and click into place. Of all of us, Valerie was the quietest at shutting a door. She was the one who had to live with the consequences if she wasn't.

Genny put her fuzzy head down on my knee, and huffed, and I scratched her wiry coat. Maybe it would be a good thing that Elena and I would have this time together after everybody else was in bed. In spite of the nagging and yelling I did, she was still wonderfully candid about the details of her illness when we worked together on her story. That honesty impressed me as much as it saddened me.

But when Elena came into the living room, it was clear that she wasn't ready to work. She was wearing a minidress so tiny that I could only stare.

Where had *that* thing come from?

"Oh, hey," she said, surprised but not pleased to see me, and she went over to her purse and hunted for her keys.

I pondered various comments and rejected several.

"So, you said you'd help me with the memoir," I started off in as neutral a tone as possible.

"Oh, yeah. Can we do that tomorrow? I'm headed over to Lisa's. She's having a bad time."

"Lisa's," I echoed, trying to catch her gaze with mine, but her eyes kept sliding past my face. "Look, I don't want you to go, Elena. Not this late. And certainly not looking like *that*."

Elena tottered by me on high heels into the kitchen and came back with a bottle of water. Her legs were like matchsticks. The dress was made to hug a rear end, but there was no rear end there to hug.

"It's just Lisa," she muttered. "It's the only thing I have that's clean."

Maybe, I thought.

"You haven't eaten all day!" I pointed out.

"That's the other reason I'm going. I told her I'd stop by McDonald's and pick something up." She paused in the doorway, and her voice softened. "Really, Mom, it's just Lisa. Just for an hour. We'll eat and everything, don't worry. And I'll help you with the book tomorrow. I promise."

I spread my hands. "Elena, I can't believe you. I'm not this stupid, really. You weren't talking to Lisa, and you're not going to see Lisa—not dressed like *that*, anyway."

Elena drew herself up and folded her arms. They were like matchsticks, too.

"Just because I tell you things," she said, "now you think you know everything about me. You know I used to make a habit of telling lies, so now you disbelieve everything I say! I wouldn't have started this book with you if I knew you'd end up calling me a liar all the time."

"This has nothing to do with your memoir," I said. "It has to do with *now*. I know you're not going to Lisa's because you were talking on the phone with a guy. That's when you decided to get up and get . . . dressed."

Elena threw up her hands in a fury. Her dark eyes were huge in her thin, pinched face.

"So *now* you're listening in on me?" she said. "How do *you* know who I'm talking to? Have you been monitoring my phone calls?"

"No. I was walking by. And *no*, I don't have to listen in! It's your tone of voice. You only talk to guys like that. Don't treat me like I'm a moron!"

"Oh, yeah, well, thanks, Mom, you guessed it, you're absolutely right—I'm *actually* going to turn tricks to support my meth habit!"

Genny had been listening with her head up and one eye fixed sadly on my face. Now she jumped down and trotted out of the room.

"Very funny!" I said. "You lied about where you're going, and you lied about picking up food. Can't you just for *God's* sake tell the truth?"

"I didn't lie! I *am* going to pick up food!"

"Elena! You don't have any money!"

Elena stopped, surprised, and reached into her purse to flip open her wallet. "Where's the twenty I had?" she cried suspiciously.

"Oh, *I* wouldn't know!" I cried back. "*I'm* just a person who lives in the same house with you and spies on you and monitors your phone calls! But if I had to *guess*—now that I know *everything* about you—I'd say that you used it last night to buy *Mexican food*!"

Valerie's face appeared around the hall door frame.

"Listen, you two!" she hissed. "In case you didn't notice, it's the middle of the night, and some of us actually have to get up in the morning! Momma, why are you even doing this? You know she's not going to listen. She's going to do whatever the hell she wants. Elena, if you want to go out dressed like a total skank, *by all means*! That is *totally* your God-given right. But I swear to *God*, people, if you wake up Gemma, I will murder you!"

I felt my face go hot, and I dropped my voice to a whisper.

"Oh, Valerie, I'm so sorry. You're right. I'm sorry we woke you up. But don't say 'swear to God.' It's wrong. And, Elena," I continued, turning back to the piano bench—

But Elena wasn't there.

I heard the click as the front door shut behind her.

CHAPTER FORTY

When I got up with Joe at six the following morning, Elena wasn't home. When Valerie came out at eight thirty, groggy from having been up at three in the morning, and handed me a sleepy, happy, freshly changed baby, Elena wasn't home. She wasn't home at nine thirty, either, although the sun had been up for hours and every normal person had long since gotten up, had coffee, and driven to work or to school or (in my case) started the washing machine.

I dialed Elena's phone and got no answer. How many times had I told her to send me a text if she wouldn't be coming home?

By ten o'clock, I had dialed her phone at least a dozen times.

My overactive imagination started feeding me images: Elena's car in a drainage ditch. Elena's car crashed into a tree. *Mrs. Dunkle, I'm so sorry. It's about your daughter.*

Of course she was safe. Of course she was just asleep somewhere.

Elena's slender hand flopping over the side of a fifty-five-gallon drum. A lock of Elena's dark hair sticking up out of loose earth. *Mrs. Dunkle. It's about your daughter.*

Writing was out of the question. I did small, meticulous things. I unloaded the dishwasher. I started cleaning out the fridge.

Why did she *do* this to me? Didn't she have the slightest regard for my feelings? *I'm so sorry, Mrs. Dunkle. I'm so sorry . . .*

At ten thirty, I sat down at the kitchen table, and I dialed her number over and over. On the ninth or tenth time, the line picked up.

"H'lo . . . ," grunted a husky voice.

"Elena! I've been trying to reach you!" I snapped, relief fueling my anger. "You said you'd be home last *night*!"

"Oh . . . Sorry, Mom," muttered the husky voice. "I fell asleep."

"Well, get up!" I said. "Your appointment with Bea is at eleven thirty, and the office is half an hour away. And you'd *better* not miss this one!"

Fifteen minutes later, Elena stumbled through the door. She was barefoot, her hair was tangled, and her makeup was smudged. Her tiny dress smelled like a beer keg.

"H'lo," she muttered, dropping her purse onto the piano bench.

"How much did you drink last night?" I demanded. "Are you even good to drive?"

Annoyance flashed across her puffy face. "*Yes*, I'm fine to drive!" she said. "You should be glad I didn't drive last night! I was responsible."

Without a word, I turned back to the fridge. Its disorder was so much less frustrating. A few minutes later, I heard the front door shut.

I finished the fridge and carried the bag of trash out to the garbage can. Then I sat down to have a cup of tea.

Elena wasn't dead in a ditch. We wouldn't get another no-show bill from the therapist. The sun was shining, and my kitchen was looking good. These things were enough to push the day into positive territory.

I had learned not to ask for too much.

My cell phone rang. I glanced at it as I answered. It was Bea, Elena's therapist. "I'm putting your daughter into the hospital," Bea said. "She needs immediate psychiatric treatment."

Long ago, in another life, such a statement would have bowled me over and left my world in tatters.

Today, I felt hardly a flicker.

"That sounds like a very good idea," I said. "Things have been deteriorating these last several weeks. Which hospital are you going to use?"

Bea's voice was stiff. "I don't know. I'm going to call an ambulance."

Long ago, I wouldn't have known the implications of that. Nowadays, I was a veteran. I immediately went into full planning mode.

Ambulance, I thought. *Emergency services, covered in full; hospitalization, another five hundred dollars if she's there five days, but no—we've already reached our yearly catastrophic max. Let's see, I'll need to cancel her nutritionist's appointment on Friday.*

"Okay," I said, grabbing a pen and starting a list on the Post-it pad on the fridge. "Her insurance card should be in her wallet. Just make sure the EMTs see it and take her to one of the hospitals covered by our plan. That would be . . . well, I don't have a list with me, but it needs to be a preferred provider."

And I should call from my side, too, I thought, *just to make sure the EMTs get it right.*

I jotted down a note: *CALL, CHK IF HOSPTL PREFERRD.*

"I can't promise that," Bea said.

I paused in the act of drawing a box around my note.

"I don't understand. What do you mean?" I said. "You can't promise you'll show her card to the EMTs? They'll ask for it."

"Mrs. Dunkle," Bea said, "I mean that I'm not promising you *anything.*" And for the first time, I registered the fact that her voice was absolutely dripping with rage.

What? my stunned brain asked. *What just happened?*

"Look, Mrs. Dunkle," Bea continued with icy fury, "if you want to be a part of this decision, then you'd better get over here right *now.*"

"I'm half an hour away," I said automatically.

"Then be here in half an hour!" And the line went dead.

I stared at the phone in complete amazement. She had actually hung up on me!

"What's that all about?" Valerie called from the living room.

"I don't know," I said. "Elena's therapist. She says—she's putting Elena in the hospital. She seems to be mad at me."

In a daze, I got up and looked around for my car keys. I had brushed my teeth this morning, right? I found my shoes and slipped them on. My phone? It was still in my hand.

Valerie blocked my way to the door. She was holding Gemma in her arms.

"Momma, what's going on?" she said. "Who's mad?"

"Honestly? I don't know. I . . . I guess I upset Bea somehow." And in my mind, I reran the conversation. "She said she was putting Elena in the hospital, and I said fine, just make sure it's a hospital on our insurance. And then she said," and I imitated the angry voice, "'I'm not promising you *anything*.'"

A reckless light shone in Valerie's eyes. "I'm coming, too," she said. "Let me grab my wallet. I'll do the driving."

We pulled up at the bland suburban house where Bea held therapy sessions. The living room was her waiting room, and a guest bedroom was her office. We opened the door of that living room to an astonishing sight: Elena, lying on the couch with her head on Bea's lap.

"Come in!" Bea called imperiously.

I obeyed in a dream, astounded by the tableau before me. Bea was looking down tenderly at Elena and stroking her tangled hair. After waiting for the moment to reach its full dramatic effect, Bea softly and sorrowfully pronounced, "I have never met a child so full of self-hate."

And her eyes rose accusingly to mine.

"Woman," I said.

She blinked. "What?"

"Woman," I repeated. "Not child. She'll be twenty-one in a month. Calling her a child just exacerbates the problem."

Bea's eyes flashed with anger. She was an impressive white-haired woman herself, a veteran therapist of many years, and she knew exactly how to convey what she was feeling.

"*I'm* telling you that your daughter is suicidal with guilt," she said, "and *that's* what you have to tell me—that she's not your *child*? Well, for your information, this *child* has been sobbing for almost an *hour* about how she can't win her mother's approval no matter *what* she does!"

Beside me, Valerie stirred and made a strangled sound.

I held up my hand to stop Valerie from speaking. Valerie was angry, but I wasn't angry. I just felt old and jaded and tired.

I understood everything now.

Elena had seen this woman all of three times, and she had played Bea like a con artist plays a chump. I had seen Elena work her mind games with the therapists at Clove House. My daughter was a force to be reckoned with. Bea might be clever, and she might be a veteran, but I had already gathered that she didn't normally handle young adults. She clearly had no idea how tricky they could be. Elena had gotten under her skin.

"So, would you like to know," I said in what I sincerely hoped was a pleasant manner, "what Elena has done lately to earn my disapproval—no matter *what* she does? She's refused even to pretend to eat with her family anymore. She won't even attempt to eat at all, although we offer to buy her any food she thinks she could stand. She won't leave her room, where she lies in bed with the lights off, and it's not as if all we do is yell at her, either—we beg, we plead, we offer her books and movies, but nothing gets her out of bed.

"Now, last night, after refusing to budge all day, she got up at midnight to go out on the town. She lied to me about where she was going, she lied to me about who she'd be with, she drank alcohol, which mixes in a dangerous way with her meds, and she didn't let me know she was safe. Finally, at ten thirty this morning, I managed to reach her on her cell phone. Up till then, I thought she might be dead in a ditch."

Elena didn't move throughout this whole recital. She lay perfectly still with her face hidden under her tangles. Bea didn't stir, either. But she had stopped stroking Elena's hair.

"Now," I concluded, "why don't *you* tell *me*? Which one of those accomplishments is supposed to win my approval?"

It was a very neat summation. I should have felt scornful and triumphant. But I didn't. I just felt tired.

Bea looked me in the eye again. Her gaze was less fierce now. I think the light was beginning to dawn. But Valerie could control herself no longer.

"I can't *believe* this!" she burst out.

Bea transferred her gaze to Valerie and summoned her dignity again.

"And who are *you*?" she asked.

"I'm that little shithead's sister!" Valerie said. "Really, Elena? *Really?* You let somebody believe your screwed-up life is all down to *Mom*? You've done some seriously shitty things, but this is right up there."

Elena's silent form quivered slightly at this but gave no other sign of life. Bea raised her eyebrows and put her hand around Elena's shoulder.

She said, "Well, I don't think talk like *that* is going to help."

But Valerie wasn't about to be shut down. Her brown eyes were shining, and her mouth was curved in a cynical smile, but I could see that she was beside herself with rage. Her words flowed out in a torrent now, over Bea and Elena both.

"The *one* person who has put up with your shit!" she said. "The *one* person who would do anything for you! The *one* person you had, all your life, who you knew would put aside *everything* the minute you needed her!"

Valerie's defense gave me a little breathing room. Now I could sort out the hospital problem.

Psychiatric care, I thought. *Do we need an ambulance or not? I think not. Waiting room . . . How long will we be there? Maybe I can make better use of our time by calling the insurance company from there. But maybe we need precertification, and what if they call her right in? No, I'd better check before we go to make sure we're good. And what about Genny—doesn't she have her appointment for shots this afternoon? I'd better call and cancel. Call vet . . . Pack Elena a suitcase . . . Make sure to pick up hamburgers for while we wait . . .*

"Like it's supposed to be *her* fault you screwed up!" Valerie was saying. "Like you didn't do *every single thing* she taught us not to do! Hey, *I* was an idiot, *I* know my way around psych wards, but at least I didn't blame *other* people for the shit *I* did!"

The glare had left Bea's eyes. She had figured it out. That was good: one item off my to-do list. At these words, however, Bea gave a little shake and said, "You mean, you were in an institution, too?"

"Eight weeks in England with the rich and famous," Valerie affirmed. "Tea and crumpets on the lawn every afternoon."

"Anorexia?" Bea asked.

"Depression," Valerie answered calmly. "I burned and cut the shit out of myself. A lot of it, right there at the hospital."

She held Gemma with one hand while she stretched out the other hand. Once again, I saw the shiny lilac dots of the burns.

They've faded out so well, I thought. *You'd hardly even know they were there.*

Bea studied them. Then she turned to me. "That must have been very painful for you," she said.

Was it? I found myself thinking in surprise. *Was it painful?*

My imagination found the memory and played it for me: Valerie walking into the kitchen, humming softly, oddly excited and jubilant. And her hands . . . the oozing round sores on the backs of her hands . . .

It was as if a crack had opened up in the earth at my feet—a crack that went all the way down to hell. Violent anguish shot through me. I had had no idea that I could still hurt so much.

The next instant, rage came boiling up inside, the closest feeling to hate that I'd ever known. How *dare* this woman try to touch my injured feelings! She'd made herself *part* of my injury now! That little drama she'd played, ordering me into her presence—and, once she'd found out that she was wrong, to come schmoozing up to me and actually force me to *feel* . . .

I lifted my head, and I glared her down.

"Well," Bea said, shifting a little and sighing, "I still think it's a good idea for Elena to go into the hospital. She's in a very poor frame of mind."

An hour and a half later, I was sitting with Elena in the waiting room of a very large and very busy hospital. At least fifty other people were waiting there, too. One man was waiting in handcuffs, with police.

When I had woken up this morning, I hadn't had this in mind for my day. But things were starting to improve: at least now we were sitting down. For the first fifteen minutes, there had been no free chairs, and both of us had had to stand.

Elena and I hadn't spoken to one another on the way home. After what she had put me through that day, I hadn't even bothered to suggest that she eat breakfast. But after she had changed clothes, she'd brought a bowl of cereal over and sat beside me while I'd made my insurance calls. Now she was reading a book while I people-watched. A waiting room is a great place to meet new characters.

"Listen to this, Mom," she said.

Half of my brain listened to the passage she read out while the other half thought back fondly over all the thousands of times in her life when I'd heard that invitation. Valerie and Elena were both huge readers, devouring several new books a week, and they often read out passages to me. Elena had probably given me summaries of three-quarters of the books she'd read.

Or, at least, she *had* been a huge reader—back when she'd had a life.

After a little conversation about the book Elena was reading, she began to share amusing stories with me about the party last night. Lisa had been involved in it in some way, so her statements to me hadn't been complete lies.

"My friend Steph's roommate had a party last week," she said, "but Steph's in summer school, so she decided she'd be good and stay in her room and study for her exams. She kept the door shut and studied all evening. She didn't come out and have a single drink. Around midnight, she needed to go to the bathroom, but the party was going full force. She didn't want to attract attention and have someone call for her to come drink with them, so she tiptoed across the hall to the bathroom without turning on the light. She took one step into the bathroom and fell flat on her face. A guy was lying on the floor in there; she fell right over him.

"Steph got a concussion and broke her nose; they had to call nine-one-one. And the guy she tripped over—of course, *he's* fine. So, she's sitting there, holding a towel up to her nose, she's bleeding all over her shirt, and she yells at the guy, 'Why were you lying down in the bathroom?' And he says, 'Because I wasn't feeling good.' And she says, 'Yeah, but in the dark?' And he says, 'The light hurt my eyes!'

"So now Steph's back in class, and she's got two black eyes and a broken nose, and she says everybody wants to know what happened. So she says, 'I fell in the bathroom,' and they giggle and say, 'So—a party, right?' And she says, 'Yeah, but I didn't drink!' And they say, '*R-i-g-h-t*, sure you didn't drink!' 'The one time I'm good!' she says."

I laughed. This felt like the old Elena, the one I missed so much. I hadn't heard her talk like this in ages. And then it hit me: Elena had missed her medication that morning—all those powerful, mind-altering, mood-stabilizing drugs.

Elena was watching a young Hispanic mother with two children. The baby was the sick one. Its black eyes were bright with fever, and it gave a weak, exhausted cough every now and then. I could tell that the mother hadn't slept lately. Her eyes fixed and drifted in a stare of self-hypnosis.

The toddler sitting next to her wanted to be in her lap, too, where the baby was, so he scaled her periodically, using handholds and toeholds, in the manner of a small rock climber. Each time he reached a certain point, she detached him and plopped him back down on the seat beside her.

"So, what did you want to ask me about the book?" Elena said. Even though all I had was a fragment of a manuscript, she always called it *the book.*

"Recovery," I said. "Talk to me about recovery. What does that word mean to you?"

Elena didn't answer right away. She continued watching the young mother with the baby.

The toddler had reached his maximum altitude again, placing one sneaker on his brother's blanketed form. His mother disentangled him and moved him to his seat. But she didn't scold him. Her hands were gentle.

At last, Elena said, "I don't know."

When the topic of recovery had come up before, it had been in the middle of arguments. But we weren't arguing now. So I waited.

"I guess, at first, I hoped that recovery would mean that my critical voice would shut up," she said. "It yells at me all the time. It's like living with a witch. But now, I don't know what I hope for. I don't hope for anything, I guess."

My heart sank. But I wasn't surprised.

"I think," she continued, "that recovery means doing the things you know you have to do, even though you don't want to do them. You build up your willpower. You know you have to eat breakfast, so you do, even though your critical voice is yelling. You know you have to eat a snack, so you do. And so on, and so on, every day. You make yourself buy food, and you make yourself eat it. It never stops being a struggle."

"So, for me," I said slowly, trying to internalize this bleak picture, "it would be like—I don't know. Like going on a very severe diet, where everything I wanted to do was the opposite of what I did."

"Does your critical voice call you a bitch if you go on a severe diet?"

"No," I said. "I mean, I don't know because I've never done crazy diets, but my critical voice doesn't usually call me names."

"Then no," Elena concluded. "That's not what it's like."

And we fell silent again.

The toddler had given up mountain climbing for the moment. He'd turned his attention to his mother's ring. He was holding the ring with both small hands and turning it in the light, even though it was still on her finger. This involved a certain amount of impossible bending, but his mother accommodated him without protest.

The baby in her lap stirred every now and then and opened its mouth as if it wanted to cry. But all that came out each time was a little cough.

"What about your friends, then?" I said. "What do you think they'd say recovery was like?"

"They don't know, either," Elena said. "I've never met a real recovered anorexic."

"Not one? Don't they bring them back to give pep talks or something? If you don't meet them, how are you supposed to know what to aim for?"

A note crept into Elena's voice. Bitterness? Sadness?

Maybe fatalism.

"They haven't recovered," she said. "None of them. There's Sheila: she's been in treatment off and on since 2004. She never finished high school. There's Paula: she's been anorexic since her car accident. Five months of full-day therapy didn't change a thing. There's Stella: since leaving Clove House in April, she's been in the hospital twice. She didn't sign up for classes this fall, either. She hides out in her room all day."

This sounded like somebody I knew.

"There's Erin. She's been at Clove House four times already. Each time they send her home, she gets worse until her heart starts showing damage, and then they put her back in again. I don't know a single anorexic who's gotten a job. I don't know anybody who's managed to finish school."

"What about your friend, the master's student?"

"Dropped out. Her parents had to move her back home."

"What about Mandy? She looked great the last time I saw her. She actually was at full, normal weight."

"Clove House kicked Mandy out of the part-time program last month because her attitude was so bad. We keep track of one another, but nobody knows what happened to her. We haven't heard from Mandy since."

I could feel a chill rising through me, as if ice had been piled around my body. It was all I could do not to shiver and rub my hands. I wasn't asking interview questions anymore, I was starting to argue and plead. I took a breath and willed myself to calm down.

"Okay then, what about your anorexia books?" I said, trying to keep my voice neutral. "All those memoirs and biographies you've read that I won't read—they're bound to talk about recovery."

"They talk shit," Elena said in a matter-of-fact tone. "They go along for a while, maybe telling the truth, maybe not, and then all of a sudden, it's rainbows and unicorns. I don't know those people. I don't know whether they were ever like me. Show me a person who says she's a recovered anorexic, and how do I know she ever felt the way I feel?"

I could understand that. The writer in me could feel the truth of that.

"What I'm waiting for," Elena continued sadly, "is for one of my friends to recover. I still haven't seen that happen."

The toddler finally gave up climbing and exploring. He sat down flat on his rear in the chair and started to whimper. The young mother roused herself at this and gave him a smile. He stopped crying, but he went right back to climbing.

"Maybe it has to be you," I said. "Maybe they're all waiting for you."

"What makes me so special?" scoffed Elena.

Besides everything? I thought to myself.

"You're extraordinary," I said. "How many people do you think could have tackled boarding school in a foreign language? None of the other English-speakers there mastered German—only you and your sister. How many high school students could have handled volunteering at the ER? You handled everything there from infant death to battle fatigue."

"We call it PTSD, Mom," Elena murmured, but I could tell she wasn't really listening. "They're all back, you know," she continued in a low voice. "All my friends. They're already back."

"Back where?" I asked.

"Back at Clove House. They go on crash diets as quick as they can, and then they get back in. It's all they used to talk about, some days, how much they were going to lose to get back in once they got kicked out."

"But I thought they all hated that place!" I protested—maybe with more force than I should have. I took a second to bring my voice back under control. "Why would they work so hard to get back in if they hate it as much as they say they do?"

"We do hate it . . . ," Elena said slowly. But I could see it in her eyes. Elena wanted to go back, too.

Go back to *what*? Not to recovery. That much I was sure of. Elena's feelings about Clove House didn't have anything to do with recovery.

Did *any* of her feelings have to do with recovery?

As if Elena guessed what I was thinking, she gave a little shrug. "They're my friends," she said.

A staff member in blue scrubs came through the door and called out a name. It wasn't our name, and it wasn't the name of the baby with the cough, either.

"This is bullshit," Elena said. "That therapist was a fruitcake. I don't need to go into the hospital, and I don't want to. School registration starts tomorrow. Classes start next week. I have things to do. Let's get out of here, and can we go by Whataburger? I want a Number One combo meal."

She knew me so well. Just as she had done with Bea, she was playing on all of my weaknesses. She was saying all the things she knew I wanted to hear. Even now, after everything I'd learned, I couldn't help hoping that she was ready to make a fresh start.

We left and picked up our Whataburger order. With an inward sigh, I chose chicken tenders. I had put on eight more pounds so far this year, but I didn't want to look like I was afraid of food.

"I want to get my room cleaned up," Elena said as we walked into the house. "Hey, Val, didn't you want to go to Babies"R"Us?" And she headed over to the mob of pill bottles. "I feel like death. My head is pounding. Did I forget my drugs this morning? Hey, don't let's eat in here, let's watch a *Futurama*."

Watching television helped Elena get through the ordeal of eating. How sad to think of a burger and fries as an ordeal.

While we moved the various white paper bags and large plastic cups to the living room, Elena and Valerie discussed what Valerie needed at Babies"R"Us. But by the time the *Futurama* episode was over, Elena was starting to blink with sleepiness.

"I think I'll go nap for an hour," she muttered.

"But what about your room?" I prodded hopefully. "What about going to the store?"

"In an hour," she said as she trailed across the living room, fluttering her fingers good-bye. "I'll be up in an hour, I *promise*."

We didn't see her again until noon the following day.

CHAPTER FORTY-ONE

Three months after Elena and I came home from Clove House, the nutritionist she was working with called me up.

"Mrs. Dunkle, I have good news!" she said. "Elena gained two pounds this week!"

"But . . . ," I said. "How is that even possible?"

"Well, she did very well on her meal plan last week," the nutritionist answered, nonplussed. "It's clear that she's been working hard . . . What do you mean, how is it possible?"

"Elena didn't follow the meal plan you sent home," I said. "Not at all."

"Oh! But she gave me a food diary, all filled out . . ."

"And she ate very little. She didn't even *pretend* to eat more than one meal a day, not to mention the possibility of purging."

"Oh. Well, I don't know. I take her weight on the same scale each week. Maybe it's possible that she's eating, Mrs. Dunkle, and you're just not seeing it."

No, it isn't, I thought. *No, it isn't possible.*

I was on my way to pick up Elena from that appointment. Once again, she had started talking me into driving her around. The way I saw it, it was better than having her sleep her life away at home, and she was so drugged and gaunt that I worried about her endangering herself and others. What if she passed out behind the wheel?

I pulled into the parking lot, and Elena slid into the front seat.

"Did you hear?" she asked. "I gained two pounds!"

I stared at my daughter. She looked worse than I had ever seen her look before.

Elena's hair was weedy and dry. It tangled constantly. The skin of her gray, gaunt face was scaly. It sagged in little wrinkles over her cheekbones and pinched in around her temples. Her dark brown eyes were sunken and lifeless, and she looked closer to forty years old than twenty. I stared at her and thought, *My beautiful daughter isn't beautiful anymore.*

"So," I said casually, "what *is* your weight these days?"

Elena named a number only three pounds off her ideal weight.

And I can fly, I thought sadly. *Who do you think you're kidding?*

But I didn't say a word out loud.

We drove to the grocery store. Elena wouldn't have gone there on her own, but if she was riding with me, she had to put up with it. She trailed behind me around the store, exhausted, begging me to hurry up.

I took my time.

"We should get a cake!" Elena announced suddenly. "To celebrate my two pounds."

Once more, I stared at her.

Did she mean it? Would she actually eat?

"Absolutely!" I said. "Any cake you like."

So Elena hauled me to the bakery and studied the cakes with interest. Remembering her former love of fudgy chocolate cakes, I pointed out several of those.

"No, I want that one," she said.

"That one?" I said in astonishment. "But that's . . ."

I didn't finish the sentence, but the disconnect between reality and my day grew even wider. Elena's choice was a "Disney princess" cake, the kind that looks like a doll. A plastic doll of Cinderella was poking up out of the center, and the round blue-frosted cake was her gown.

It was the kind of cake designed to appeal to preschoolers or early grade-schoolers inviting their whole class to their birthday party. It certainly wasn't the choice of your typical twenty-one-year-old.

But there was a *slight* possibility—*very* slight—that Elena might actually eat some of it. I would give a great deal to make that happen.

"Any cake you want," I repeated with hollow cheerfulness, and I purchased the plastic princess cake. When we got home, I cut a slice for Elena, Valerie, and myself. To my surprise, it turned out to taste fantastic.

Fork in hand, Elena talked ninety miles an hour while Valerie and I ate our pieces of cake. Finally, she took a couple of nervous bites and then told us she didn't feel well.

"But save my piece," she said. "I'll eat it later."

Valerie and I watched her go. Then Valerie got up and cut us each another piece of cake. She said, "So, Clint says, now that he's graduated, they should assign him to a tech school pretty soon."

This was a constant hopeful refrain around the house these days. Like me, Valerie is an optimist.

I had been very impressed at how well she and Clint were handling their separation. During the eight long weeks of his basic training, they had been able to talk on the phone only twice. Nonetheless, Valerie had stayed upbeat and relaxed. We had had endless cheerful conversations about babies and baby care, and if she was lonely, she had kept it to herself.

Clint's graduation had been a grand, beautiful ceremony, but afterward, he had been able to spend only two days with his family. On our way back to the car after dropping him off at the dorms, we had passed a young woman who was sobbing as her new airman said good-bye.

"Look at that!" Valerie had said scornfully. "Like he needs that, with everything else he's got going on! I wouldn't do that to Clint, no matter how bad I felt. That's not what it takes to be a good Air Force wife."

Now Clint was coming home each weekend while he waited to be assigned a specialty. But once he went into tech school, he might be far away again, and it might be months before their family could be together.

"Does he have any idea what they might choose?" I asked.

"No," Valerie said. "The tests don't just spell it out. They look to see how you do, and then they look to see what they need. But here's the thing: most tech schools are only about three months long. That's not too bad. And if they send him to learn something really complicated, they'll send Gemma and me, too. They do that with the longer schools."

Three months! I thought. *I'd hate that!* And I remembered how depressed I'd been, away from Joe and the rest of the family at Clove House. But that wasn't what I said out loud.

"Three months will go by quickly," I said.

"Yeah, they will," Valerie agreed. "I just feel bad for what he's missing out with Gemma. He missed her learning to roll over when he was in Georgia. He missed her learning to sit up when he was in basic. He's already pretty much guaranteed to miss her first Christmas, and if they keep messing around, he'll miss her birthday, too. I just wish they'd get off their butts and send him *somewhere*."

That was on Monday. On Wednesday, Elena's alarm went off and once again failed to wake her up. It was so loud that the whole house could hear it, including Gemma, who started to cry. But somehow, right next to it, Elena still slept on.

In the bedroom, trying to write, I listened to it blare. Then I heard Valerie yell. Then I heard Elena yell.

Good, I thought. *That means she's up.*

Half an hour later, I walked into the living room. Valerie was on the floor with Gemma, feeding bright plastic balls into a toy contraption. With a *whoop*, the balls popped up into the air: red, yellow, blue, green. Each time a ball popped up, Gemma gave a scream of delight and made a swipe for it.

I paused to watch for a minute. Gemma was growing up so fast! Valerie handed her a purple ball, and Gemma held it in both her chubby little hands and brought it up to her mouth to taste it.

Then I noticed that Elena's purse and car keys were still on the piano bench.

"Where's your sister? I thought she got up thirty minutes ago."

"I haven't seen her," Valerie said.

"But the alarm went off!"

"Yeah, and it kept going off until I went in there and made Her Highness stop it. But you know that doesn't mean anything."

And that, of course, was true.

I pushed open the door to Elena's room. Immediately, Genny jumped down from the bed and trotted out. She wasn't the brightest little dog in the world, but she had learned the routine by now.

"Elena!" I said, shaking the blanket.

"Nnnnnn!" it protested.

"Elena, you're going to be late for class!"

Again! I thought. But I didn't say it.

Elena rolled over and announced with perfect composure, "Class is canceled. The professor called. She's sick."

"The professor called," I echoed. "She called *you*."

"Mm-hmm," Elena muttered, her face in the pillow.

"A class of ninety students, and she called *you* to say she was sick. Get up, Elena! You can't miss class again."

"I will," she murmured mechanically.

But I didn't believe it. I kept shaking her. "I'm not stopping until I see you sit up."

Muttering darkly, Elena sat up.

There! That wasn't so bad. I walked back out and sat down next to Valerie and Gemma. My granddaughter greeted me with a happy gurgle and handed me the purple ball, now slippery with baby spit. Her eyes were lightening up and changing color, with green flecks and blue flecks. They *did* look a little bit like mine.

Half a minute later, Elena appeared in the living room doorway. "What the *hell*!" she cried. "You let me sleep too late!"

Valerie and I exchanged a look.

"My alarm didn't go off!" Elena continued, frantic. "It didn't go off! You didn't wake me up! Thanks a *lot*, you two!"

A second later, the bathroom door slammed.

"I'm going back to work," I told Valerie, standing up. "I have writing to do. I am *not* driving your sister to school."

Fifteen minutes later, I was in the car, driving Elena to school.

Elena was in her pajamas. Once upon a time, she had assured me that many college students go to class in their pajamas. Once upon a time, I had actually cared. Nowadays, pajamas out in public were the last thing I worried about.

Elena looked out the window and sighed. "Oh, school, how I hate thee!"

My cynicism vanished in an icy blast of fear. The hair actually prickled on my arms. Of all the things this sad creature next to me could say, this was the one statement *least* like my daughter.

Elena loved school. She had loved it from the very first day of preschool. She was absolutely passionate about learning. Her curiosity extended to everything in the universe. I had never once seen her bored.

Dear *God*! What had happened to my daughter?

That afternoon, I sat down at the kitchen table and ate the last piece of Disney princess cake. As it turned out, Elena hadn't had more of it than those two bites. Her partially eaten piece had stayed on the counter until its blue frosting had dried out. Finally, I had thrown it away.

While I ate, I opened up my laptop and reread what I had written on her memoir that morning.

> When you recover . . .
>
> Yes, of course, anorexics support one another in recovery. But they don't, on the whole, understand it very well. Recovery is like death: a closed door, a complete unknown. A lot of anorexics never make it through that door.
>
> Treatment—now, that's something anorexics come to know backward and forward, and they enjoy meeting up with their friends at the treatment center. "Are you going back in?" they say. "I'm going back in, and Leslie's there, and Tracy's there, and Jenna's coming next week. Come back to treatment, we all miss you so much!"
>
> But recovery . . . that's a different matter.
>
> Not good. Not bad. Just unknown.
>
> When you gain weight, you don't look like an anorexic anymore, and that means you don't belong in the club. You can't meet back at the treatment center when you're at a healthy weight.

Hence the question anorexics ask one another as they're sitting around the treatment center, sipping their Boost Breezes:

"How much weight are you going to lose the month you get out?"

I read this little snippet, and I thought of all the things I knew about Elena now. I took out a sheet of paper, and I made myself stay cold and calm. I didn't let myself be a mother about this—that feeble, fluttery mother. I made myself stay in my writer's mind.

What did I know about my character's time since she had left treatment? What had she done in the last three months?

The sheet of paper started filling up with bad news.

- weight: as bad as before treatment, maybe worse

- mindset: definitely worse now—before, at least she wanted treatment

- habits: same as before treatment

- health: very bad, at least as bad as before

- medication: takes it, doesn't try to abuse it or overdose— but it isn't helping

After I was finished, I read it through, then drew a line underneath it and summed it up:

- WORSE THAN BEFORE!

And in January, they said she was weeks away from dying!

I stared out the window at the bright, beautiful day. My writer's mind—I needed my writer's mind for this. I needed my imagination.

Where are we? I asked it, just as I had asked it thousands of times before. *Where are we? What is my character doing?*

The answer came back:

My character is coming to the end.

When I had first offered to help Elena write her memoir, what I was really trying to offer was a happy ending. That's what I offer my characters, after all. I don't like sad endings. In the back of my mind, I had had the silly idea that if Elena were in a story of mine, Elena would find her happy ending, too.

And maybe even Elena thought that.

Characters have story arcs. They do stupid things, but they learn, and they grow—at least, that's what's supposed to happen. But no author can force a character to do anything if that character doesn't want to do it.

I consider it my most sacred duty to be true to my characters. I want to see them do well. But sometimes, the only thing a writer can do is be with a character while that character fails. We're our characters' only witness—the only one who really understands. We have to be honest and fair right through to the very last minute. We have to watch. We have to watch right to the end.

When it came to my daughter, the mother in me wanted to make excuses. She wanted to see hope and fresh starts wherever she could. The mother in me saw every request for fast food as a step toward recovery. She saw every request for a ride to school as a chance to get out and meet new people—a chance to gain a new interest in life.

But the writer in me—she knew what was going on.

I stared at that piece of paper, and I didn't cry. I didn't wring my hands or have hysterics. I found my cell phone, and I called Joe.

"Let's meet for lunch," I said.

We left my car in the parking lot, and Joe drove us to a restaurant near his work. At first, neither one of us spoke. Joe knew better than to ask for updates. The most innocent question—"How's your day going?"—could lead to painful surprises.

Finally, when we were parked next to the restaurant, I said what I had come to say:

"Elena isn't going to make it."

That sentence hung in the air, and I heard it echoing in my mind. But I didn't feel anything at all. Years and years of titanic struggle had brought me to this moment. I had hoped—how I had hoped! I had seen hope everywhere I could.

Now I could see only the reality:

The end.

Joe burst into tears. "Do you think I don't *know* that?" he said. "That's why . . . that's why I don't like to be the one to wake her up for dinner. Because I know . . . I know that one day soon, I'll walk into her room, and she'll be *dead* . . ."

And he sobbed out loud and ran his hand over his face while I went hunting through my purse for a tissue.

". . . She'll be dead," he went on when he'd gotten a little calmer, "lying right there on her bed. I can see it like it's already happened! Every time I stand outside her door, I see it."

And he broke into sobs again.

I put my arm around Joe's shoulders. *So I'm not the only one*, I thought sadly, *who lives with a mental image of the death of my daughter*. Joe's image was different from mine, but I couldn't say that it was wrong. It was right, in fact. It was exactly right.

Joe drew in a breath. "I don't *want* her to die! I don't want my daughter to *die!*" And that's when I said the other thing I had come to say.

I said, "I have a plan."

Inside the restaurant, we talked it over. I had realized that Elena might be detaching from life, but she was still attached to her comforts. She might not eat, but she still gave me a list of shampoos and scrubs to buy at the store.

"She doesn't like risk," I pointed out. "The routine of the house makes her feel secure. It's giving her the security she needs to set up everything so that she can die in peace."

Joe nodded. "She's using us to help kill herself."

"So my plan is this," I said. "We take it away. Each week she fails to improve or gets worse, we take away something else. We don't let her just close her eyes and go to sleep and lose it all. We make her feel that loss step by step. Phone, car, computer, hot water, everything we're providing for her. We take it all, if that's the way she chooses to go."

Joe's brows creased together. "Until when?" he asked.

"Until she has to die under an overpass bridge."

I said it—the most horrible thing a mother could possibly say. I said it, and I felt nothing at all. Pain, panic, and fear were nothing but the flip side of hope, and Elena had learned how to use that hope against me. She played on my hope just as she had played on Bea's protectiveness. It was a luxury I could no longer afford.

"Under a bridge," I repeated firmly, "with nothing but the clothes on her back. No home to hide in, no car to crash, no shower, no safety, no nothing."

As I said it, my imagination showed me the whole horrible scene: my daughter, skeletal, dehydrated, curled up high in the little space between the bridge beams and the slope of the embankment, alone and unattended, taking her last rattling breaths.

I made myself stay with it. I didn't look away.

This plan was the last, best hope we had. So far as I could tell, it was our only hope. But if we let ourselves feel that hope, we wouldn't be able to bear the cruelty of it. We wouldn't follow through. And if Elena didn't believe that we would follow through, she would go right ahead and ignore us—and die.

So it was her death against our death now: death at home or death under that bridge. We had to see our goal just as clearly as she saw hers. We had to work toward that goal, that death—that awful, uncomfortable death. Only then did we have a chance that she might back down.

No hope: *that* was our only hope.

The line between Joe's brows remained. "Under a *bridge?*" he echoed, and I heard the pain and bewilderment in his voice.

Maybe Joe could have a little hope, then. He probably needed it.

"*If* that's what she chooses," I said. "She can turn this around at any time. We'll set it up so that she can earn her privileges back as soon as she starts putting on weight."

Joe thought about this for a few minutes.

"It's the only chance we have," he said. "We can't help her die. That's what we're doing now." He picked up his fork but put it down again.

This conversation wasn't exactly helping our appetites. "But she's falsifying her weight," he pointed out.

"I thought of that," I said. "She's bound to hit a limit in the ways she can add weight to herself during weigh-ins. She can't exactly stick her feet in cement."

"And considering how far the weigh-in weight is from reality right now," Joe said, "she should be hitting that limit pretty soon."

I pulled out a notepad, and during the rest of the meal, we brainstormed our penalty scale. We set down three weights for Elena: a "green" weight, which was her ideal weight, according to Clove House; a "yellow" weight, which was five pounds under the ideal weight; and a "red" weight, which was anything below that. Losing weight moved Elena down the penalty scale. Gaining weight moved her back up.

This was what it looked like when we were done:

- GREEN WEIGHT: no penalties apply.

- YELLOW PENALTIES:

  1st yellow week: grace period (no change in penalty scale).

  1. I lose my debit card and the right to regulate my own smoking. My parents will provide 6 cigarettes a day provided I complete my food plan and food diary.

- RED PENALTIES:

  1st red week: grace period (no change in penalty scale).

  2. I lose texting features on my phone.

  3. I lose my MP3 player.

  4. I lose movie rental privileges.

  5. I lose Internet capability on my computer.

  6. I lose three cigarettes from my daily ration and drop to 3 cigarettes a day.

7. I lose smoking privileges (i.e., go cold turkey).

8. I lose my computer.

9. I must start paying $50 a week for rent. Failure to do so results in a move down the penalty scale.

10. I lose my car. I will be given bus fare if I can show the routes I intend to take.

11. I lose my house key. I must arrange for someone to be home to let me in. Failure to observe this penalty results in a move down the penalty scale.

12. I may not be home from the time my father leaves in the morning till the time he returns at night (7:00 a.m.–6:00 p.m.). Failure to observe this penalty results in a move down the penalty scale.

13. I must move out and finance my own life and education. I may take the car, registered in my name, provided I have paid for six months of automobile insurance. My parents will not cosign any leases or loans with me. I will have one month from the date of this penalty to save up money and move out.

When Joe came to the end, he sighed.

"The Clove House people said not to focus on weight or numbers," he said. "But I don't see what else we're supposed to do."

"Clove House's advice hasn't gotten anybody in this family very far," I pointed out. "And they made her sign several contracts with them."

"She's going to hate this," he said. "She's really going to hate it."

"That would be progress," I said. "Hate is better than what she's doing now. What she's doing now is letting go. But I know she'll fight it. It's the disorder above everything else at this point, and this directly challenges the disorder. She'll say anything. She might even *do* anything. We'll be the enemy—no two ways about it."

"I hate being the enemy," Joe said sadly.

"If we back down on this," I said, "it'll mean she can go right back to sleep. We have to mean this because Elena means it. She knows that she's dying."

"She has to," Joe agreed.

"Well, if Elena can accept the reality of dying in her bed, then we have to accept the reality of packing her stuff up and pushing her out the door. It's our reality against her reality, and our reality has to win. She has to know that overpass bridge is waiting for her."

"I know," Joe said. "It's the only way."

And again, I heard the pain in his voice.

This is going to be very hard on Joe, I thought. *He isn't made for this. He can get angry and yell, but he can't resist tears. He can't be mean on purpose.*

So it would have to be me.

I would have to be mean on purpose.

CHAPTER FORTY-TWO

That evening, Valerie and Joe and I sat down together, and we called Elena out to sign the contract. Valerie was prepared. She had had us wait until Gemma was up. "This is going to get pretty loud," she predicted.

I went in to wake up Elena. "You need to come out here," I said.

"What?" the mound of blankets answered. "I'm not hungry."

"It isn't dinner. You already slept through that. You need to come out here." I left and sat back down on the couch.

We waited. But Elena didn't show up.

This time, Joe went to fetch her, and this time, she came out. "What?" she said angrily when she saw Valerie and me waiting on the couch.

She already knows, my writer's mind observed. *She knows what's going on here.*

"Elena, we need you to read this, and we need you to sign it," Joe said, and he handed her the contract. Elena tossed it aside without a glance.

"What is this?" she demanded. "I'm not reading anything!"

"It's a contract that says that you'll gain weight," I said. "If you don't gain weight, you'll lose privileges week by week: phone, computer, car."

Elena glared at me. "I'm not signing anything!"

"Then you can pack up and move out," I said.

Cue the expected eruption.

"You know I don't have anywhere to go! You know I'm sick! You're blaming me. You're blaming me for being sick!"

"We aren't!" Joe said. "Elena, we just want to help."

"Like *hell* you want to help!"

I didn't say anything.

Once upon a time, I had lain awake nights, thinking, *How do I say this? How can I make her understand?* Once upon a time, I had spent my days agonizing and engaging and explaining. For years and years, I had hoped and struggled. I had moved heaven and earth.

Now, there was only the reality—the *single* reality: Elena was going to die. But she was *not* going to do it here.

Meanwhile, the fight was in full swing. "So, you want to know what it's like not to have a daughter? Fine! I'm not your daughter anymore. I can't believe you're doing this! You're *blaming* me! You're *blaming* me for getting raped!"

"Elena, no! That's not true! That isn't the idea here!"

Once upon a time, that would have been my voice raised in entreaty, my voice full of hurt and love. Now, it was Joe's voice. And I was silent.

She'll say anything, my writer's mind observed. *She'll sacrifice anything to the eating disorder. If she's willing to sacrifice herself, her hopes and dreams, everything she ever wanted, then don't think she's going to spare the rest of her family.*

"You want to get rid of me?" Elena said. "Okay, fine! I'll go back to Clove House. I'll go back into treatment."

To treatment. But not to recovery, said my writer's mind. *She doesn't know what recovery is.*

Joe and I had already discussed this. He was ready with the right answer. "If you want to go to treatment," he said, "there's Sandalwood right here in town."

"I'm not going to that place!"

"Then you're not going back to treatment."

Suddenly, Elena turned on me, livid with fury. Her glare was so intense, it was like a physical blow.

"This is *your* idea!" she said. "Dad wouldn't do it. I know Dad wouldn't do it! *You* put him up to it. I hate you! I'm *done* with you! I'll never speak to you again!"

She grabbed the pen we'd laid out and signed the contract with a dramatic flourish. Then she left the room. We heard the slam of the bedroom door.

In the silence that followed, my writer's mind warned, *She won't keep that threat never to speak to you again—*

But it would be more pleasant if she did.

As soon as Elena's alarm went off the next day, she was out of bed. But she made sure I wouldn't be enjoying this victory. She felt betrayed—completely betrayed.

"I know this is your fault!" she said. "I *know* Dad wouldn't do this to me. Well, you'll get your wish—you'll get rid of me. You'll know what it's like to lose a daughter. Once I find a way to get out of here, I'm never coming back!"

Then she swept up her purse and her car keys and stalked out the door to go to class. She was through asking me for rides.

As soon as she left, Valerie came out of her room with baby Gemma in her arms. Her cheerful expression was gone for once.

"Clint called. His tech school is going to be five months long!" she said. "It's the longest tech school can be before they send the family along, too. Clint's not going to graduate and get his first assignment until April of next year."

April! My heart bled for them both. Valerie and Gemma had first moved in with us last March. That meant over a year of long-distance marriage.

"Well, you know your dad and I don't mind," I said as I reached out to take baby Gemma onto my lap. She pulled herself into a standing position and held on to my hands. Her little body bent and swayed like a flower in the wind.

"Don't take this the wrong way," Valerie answered. "We're grateful, really. But to be honest, I can't wait till I can get out of here. I feel like I'm trapped inside an *Intervention* episode that starts over every day."

"That's pretty much exactly what we're in," I said with a sigh. "Which reminds me: do you want to help me intervene a little bit more?"

"Will I get yelled at?" Valerie asked with typical practicality.

"No, probably not—probably just me. I want to go through Elena's clothes and get rid of the inappropriate sizes. I bought her a whole new wardrobe last spring when I went out to visit her, but she won't touch any of it. Her old sizes are still around, and they're making her want to stay thin."

"And they're making her look like a tramp," Valerie said.

Valerie and I spent an hour combing through every item of clothing in Elena's room while Gemma sat in the middle of the pile and grabbed up fistfuls of silky fabric. Then Valerie and I went through all the laundry bins. When we were finished, we had three black garbage bags full of clothes.

"I'll drive them to Goodwill right now," I said. "They'll make someone very happy."

"*And* they'll make her look like a tramp," Valerie said.

Elena came home and immediately shut herself up in her room. In her exhaustion, she didn't notice that the piles of clothes were gone. This should have felt like a reprieve to me, but it didn't. I felt like a child who had spilled nail polish on her mother's favorite dress and hidden it at the bottom of a closet.

Sooner or later, Elena was bound to notice what I'd done. And those clothes—Elena had loved those clothes! Some of the items had been with her for years. They had precious memories bound up in them.

When she realized they were gone, she was going to feel real pain. After all the pain she had already gone through, I hated the thought of adding more. Had I done the right thing? Was I helping her recover? Or was I being the person she thought I was—was I being the evil witch?

The contract had been necessary. But was this necessary?

She said she would get rid of those clothes the day we left Clove House the first time, I reminded myself. *She had plenty of time to do it. She broke her word.*

But that didn't change the way I felt.

All that evening, I paced from room to room. I carried soda cans to the kitchen and loose pairs of shoes to the bedrooms. I tried to make myself look as if I were tidying the house. Actually, I was waiting for the bomb to drop.

Should I wake her up and tell her? No, she would certainly see that as gloating. I would just have to wait until she noticed—and blew up.

You'll know what it's like to lose a daughter!

I already knew how that felt.

I miss the old Elena, I thought mournfully as I put dishes in the dishwasher. *I miss my fellow storyteller.* I remembered her laughing, her dark eyes dancing: "Guess *what!*"

That Elena was gone for good.

A couple of weeks later, the nutritionist called me for her weekly update. "Mrs. Dunkle, I'm afraid I have bad news," she said.

Elena had lost weight again, for the second week in a row. It was time to start cutting off privileges.

"You know, I'm pretty sure I've got shopping to do," Valerie said when I told her. "I think Gemma and I need diapers or something." And she put the baby into the car and left.

Once again, I paced the house, pretending to put things away. I agonized over what we were about to do. Texting was the first privilege to go. Of all the penalties, it was the least harmful to Elena's goals. But cutting off texting meant isolating Elena from the only friends she had left. And isolation was the hallmark of anorexia.

Are we helping? I asked myself. *Or are we just pushing her closer to the end?*

Well, if nothing else, we would be showing her that we meant business. That easy death in her room wasn't going to happen. It would be our way: the overpass bridge. She had to believe that. She had to *know* it.

We had to know it.

When we told her we had turned off her texting, Elena came completely unglued. "I can't control what I weigh!" she said. "I've been eating! There's nothing I can do!"

As she said that, my imagination pulled up a memory for me of a hostile nurse at Drew Center all those years ago. She had a clipboard in her hand. *Towney. Dunkle. Your family member is not allowed to have visitors. She didn't gain weight today.*

You're punishing her for something that's out of her control, I had told that nurse. And I had been so angry that I could remember shaking with rage.

Tell the truth—the writer's creed. I looked this truth in the face. This was where we were now. This was who we had become.

Joe tried to reason with Elena. I didn't. I'd already spent days and months and years trying to talk. It hadn't done any good then, and it wouldn't work now. There was nothing left to say.

So, while Elena shrieked, and Joe talked, I went to my desk in the bedroom and started working on bills. Numbers and receipts seemed like safe company. Plusses and minuses. Those were truths I could handle.

But Elena followed me.

"Dad wouldn't do this if you weren't here!" she told the back of my head while I typed in numbers. "He's sorry for me, I can tell. This is *your* idea! *Your* fault! You're not sorry, you're happy. You *love* this!"

Oh, yes, I thought. *I surely do love this.*

"You're spiteful and evil! You're the most invalidating person I know!"

I didn't bother to answer.

I was surprised at how calm I felt. The more she yelled and screamed, the more numb I seemed to be. I didn't turn around. I went right on typing numbers.

Eventually, the fight moved off, like a thunderstorm. I could hear the rumblings in the distance as it raged on without me.

Finally, it spent itself in tears.

There, I thought, *that wasn't so bad. It wasn't any worse than it always is. A little louder, maybe, and a little closer together, but basically, the same accusations.*

When Elena finally realized that her favorite clothes were missing, I was standing in the kitchen, putting away groceries. Valerie was standing at the end of the counter, talking to me about dinner. I had just come back from the store.

That was when Elena stormed in:

"Where the *hell* are my clothes?"

Enough time had passed by then that I had forgotten to be anxious about this moment. And by the time it came, I had heard enough shouting and ranting that I didn't feel anxious anymore. What pain could I be causing Elena that she hadn't already felt by now? And by this time, what pain could she cause me?

So, when I spoke, I once again felt nothing at all. "We got rid of your extra-smalls," I said.

And Elena came unglued.

Again.

Since Valerie was present for this particular battle, she tried to intervene and defend me, but I didn't think I needed it. I continued putting away groceries, as if Elena were nothing more than a toddler having a tantrum.

Hateful phrases bounced over me: "What you've done . . . Hate . . . Lose a daughter . . ."

It was all starting to feel pretty normal.

". . . Never loved me . . . Bitch! You only pretend to care . . ."

"Hey, don't call Mom a bitch!"

Maybe Elena was right, I thought as I found a place for a box of cereal. Maybe I *did* only pretend to care. Before, no matter how bitterly Elena and I had fought, I could always feel it: how much I cared, how *desperately* I cared. I could feel that love and longing to see her get better.

But now, I didn't feel it. I didn't feel a thing.

Before, when Elena had yelled, it was only because she was in pain, and that was the only way she could let me know. And before, when I had yelled, it was only because I was afraid for her, and nagging was the only way I knew to show it. Elena had yelled because she hurt, and I had yelled because I loved her—to wake her up and show her the danger I saw.

But now, in the middle of this barrage of accusations, I didn't feel the fear, and I didn't feel the worry.

This time, I didn't even feel the love.

"What kind of mother *are* you?" Elena wailed. "You don't feel anything for me!"

Maybe it was true. Maybe that love was finally gone. Because I looked at this hateful woman standing in my kitchen, and I didn't feel anything at all. It was as if I were standing outside myself, walking and talking on autopilot, while the part of me that mattered was off in a corner somewhere safe, watching us like a boring show on television.

"You love your books more than you love me!"

Did I? Maybe so. Maybe that was why I felt this coldness, this emptiness.

"You're enjoying this. You *enjoy* seeing me . . ."

Enjoy it? No, I could take it or leave it. I reached into a bag and started stacking canned goods.

". . . Never cared! When I did my IFS psychodrama, you were the only person in the room who didn't cry!"

The IFS psychodrama. My imagination found the memory and played it for me. Parents and patients in a circle. Elena, so beautiful, sitting on a chair in the center. "You bitch! You whore!" raged the Critical Voice, while I marveled at the calm look on Elena's face. My poor daughter! She had to listen to that. To suffer like that! My poor baby . . .

And suddenly, I wasn't watching us on television anymore. I was inside the moment, and that moment held more pain for me than I had ever thought I could feel. With no warning, I went from feeling nothing to standing inside an ocean of pain. It was indescribable. It was hand-on-the-hot-burner pain. Valerie's pain—Elena's pain—my pain—Joe's pain—they flashed straight through me and scorched me to the heart.

In an instant, I had my car keys and my purse. In seconds, I was out the door. I was in the car, out of the driveway, and down the street.

And I drove.

Oh, I didn't drive crazy. I'd been a mother too long for that. I kept my eye on my mirrors. I yielded to hopeful motorists waiting to merge into traffic. But I didn't answer the phone, and I didn't turn around.

I just drove.

Fifty miles away, I stopped to put gas in the car and return Valerie's frantic calls. Poor Valerie! I could hear the ragged note of worry in her voice. "Are you all right?" she said.

Am I all right? I wondered with a spectator's casual interest. And in answer, the pain sizzled through me again, like lightning jetting out my fingertips.

"I need to go now," I said. "I need to drive."

"Where are you going? Tell me!" she begged.

But I didn't answer. I was already pressing the button to hang up.

I drove through one big city after another, looking around at all the new construction, studying the rush-hour motorists with curiosity. I drove through the big grassy meadows between the big cities and sighed over the brand-new suburbs spreading across the fields like mange. I drove past ancient interchanges that had once marked important towns—towns that had since shrunk and shriveled off the map. I didn't think or worry or rage or cry.

I just drove.

A couple of hours later, I pulled off an exit ramp to purchase a burger and fries. As I exited the freeway, I couldn't help smiling at myself. Running away! What a childish thing to do. Really, what had come over me?

But the second I pulled into a parking place and reached for the ignition key, that whirlwind of pain surrounded me. It was agony. It was flames. It was white-hot needles. I got back onto the freeway.

And I drove.

Late that night, I called up my oldest and dearest friend. "Would it be all right," I asked, "if I came by for a visit?"

"Sure, Clare. You know I'd love to see you. When were you thinking of coming by?"

"Well, I'm . . . Let's see. I think I'm about ten minutes from your house now."

I was six hours away from home.

CHAPTER FORTY-THREE

My oldest and dearest friend welcomed me that night as if nothing out of the ordinary had happened. If her brown eyes looked shocked and her eyebrows once again asked questions, she knew to save them for another day. And as for me, I settled down in her guest bed with a feeling of simple contentment.

I had always run to her when life was caving in.

The next morning, over coffee, she finally asked me, "So, do you want to talk about it?"

I did. I talked. I told her what happened. At least, I think I did. I was hooking together words and arranging sentences, but I didn't seem to be able to listen to myself. I couldn't focus on the conversation at all.

Look at that sunshine! I thought as my lips moved and my tongue moved and the orderly processions of words moved out of my mouth. *Bright blue sky—it's a nice clear day today.*

And my oldest and dearest friend just looked at me, puzzled and worried. Did I look like that?

No, I felt a smile on my face. What was that smile doing there? It seemed to be in response to something I'd said. Had I made a joke? Had I said something funny?

My imagination reached for the tape of the last few seconds. It had movement, feeling, sight—but no sound.

Hmm, I thought. *Something seems to be wrong with me.* But I couldn't feel that anything was wrong. If anything, I felt better than I had in weeks.

Joe called and told me that the girls were going out of town for a few days. Valerie was taking Gemma to see her other grandmother, and she was bringing Elena along. I could hear his voice on the phone, repeating, "So you're safe. You can come home now. It's safe."

But of course I'm safe! I thought with amusement. *Why wouldn't I be safe?*

The pain of the day before wasn't even a memory.

I hugged my oldest and dearest friend good-bye, smiled at the worried look on her face, said something—I didn't know what—the tape was blank again—and got back on the road.

Something's wrong with me, I thought idly. *Something's different. I'm a little broken right now.* But the thought didn't particularly worry me.

Valerie called from her car to check in and tell me how sorry she was. She sounded stressed and anxious. She passed the phone to Elena, and Elena said she was sorry, too. Elena sounded as if she were reading a script.

And when I answered them, I sounded as if I were reading a script, too.

Joe and I spent a quiet evening. It was very quiet, in fact. He tried to talk to me, but I couldn't seem to think of anything to say.

"Are you all right?" Joe asked after a while.

"I'm fine," I said. Because I was.

"Then why aren't you talking?" he asked.

"I don't need to talk," I said. Because I didn't.

"I want you to pack a suitcase and call your mother," Joe said. "I think you need a break."

So I drove the seven hours' worth of gray concrete freeway up to north Texas ranch country, where my parents live in a little three-bedroom house on my brother's produce farm.

Joe was right. This was safe territory for me. This was very safe. I knew just what I would find when I arrived. My older brother, whip-thin and weather-beaten, in his daily uniform of white shirt and blue jeans, would be out on one of the tractors he's salvaged from garage sales. Or he might be on the phone discussing course loads because he's also a computer science professor at a California university. The produce farm in Texas is just his hobby—a hobby that comes with backbreaking daily labor. He and my father put up almost every building on the farm, including the two-story air-conditioned workshop and garage.

His wife, my godchild, would be puttering around the kitchen, checking on loaves of bread, or possibly brewing a batch of beer, while her four children came to her one by one with homeschooling questions. Or she might be stripping down and reprogramming another computer. My sister-in-law went to MIT on full scholarship. She has a PhD in computer science, and before she retired, she was a computer science professor, too.

But regardless of which role they were filling at the moment, dirt-under-the-nails farm couple or sophisticated academics, they would welcome me warmly: that I knew. My sister-in-law, the same one I had turned away from my door, would never turn me away from hers.

I called my mother from the highway to let the family know I was coming. They knew that Elena had been ill. What I said to my mother now, I didn't know. Once again, I couldn't seem to pay attention to the words coming out of my mouth.

It's old news to me, I thought as I watched the interstate roll by while orderly processions of words marched into the phone. *No wonder I can't focus on it anymore. It's boring to me by this time.*

. . . Or maybe I'm just a little broken.

I got out and unlocked the big cattle gate and drove up to my parents' white house. "Greetings!" called my mother from the door. My parents have gotten a little shorter and a little more stooped over the years, but they still make a handsome couple. My father has a chestnut sweep of hair across his forehead, even though it's heavily frosted with white, and his mischievous gray eyes and pink cheeks would look right at home on Santa Claus. My mother, small and girlishly pretty, still has a dancer's ankles, and her white cotton candy hair sweeps back into an elegant French twist.

The sight of them brought me instant contentment. Joe was right. It was good that I was there.

On this island of peace, this place of windswept meadow grasses and wildflowers I'd known since I was a little girl, I could let the gentle routines of family life pick me up and carry me along. I could sit down to the big meals that my mother and my sister-in-law cooked, and I could kneel down with them at night to say the rosary.

My family almost never argues. I've never heard my parents raise their voices. The most they do—and this my mother does regularly—is crimp their eyebrows together into The Frown.

"Do you want that second slice of cranberry bread?" my mother asked my father as he was stirring sugar into his tea.

"Do I want a well-priced blasphemy for my head?" he echoed in amazement. His hearing is bad, but he doesn't do much about it—largely, I think, because it provides him such amusement.

And my mother gave him The Frown.

"Yes," she said with dignity. "Yes, that's exactly what I asked."

For a week, I lay low there and licked my wounds. I sat with my parents at the kitchen table next to the windows with the humming-bird feeders, and I talked about everything and nothing: Japan during World War II, genetically modified food, German house construction—anything but what was going on at home. I walked through my brother's greenhouses, and I listened to his brilliant and creative farming ideas. I followed my busy sister-in-law around her large well-equipped kitchen and listened to her stories about homeschooling. And every couple of minutes, one of their four children appeared at my elbow and said very politely, "You know what, Aunt Clare?"

Guess what! echoed the voice of the young Elena in my mind—the daughter who was surely lost to me forever.

What did I say to my family about Elena? I had no idea. Whenever her name came up, I could feel myself speaking—sometimes vigorously. But I retained nothing of what was said—

With one exception.

I think it was my last night there. My sister-in-law, my mother, and I were sitting at the supper table after the children and the men had left, and our conversation was ranging over topics of education.

I think I was saying that I didn't attempt to regulate my children now that they were grown. Valerie and Elena knew right from wrong, I said, whether or not they chose to pay attention to it. They were women now—grown women—and they and I were separate human beings. I brought things to their attention, but I was no longer interested in being their police.

My mother disagreed with this approach, and so did my sister-in-law. "As long as they're in *my* house," they said firmly.

I looked at my sister-in-law, her face serene and sure, her arms still accustomed to the feel of hugging small, adorable bodies. And then I thought of Elena, shrunk down to bone and gristle, dying in her bedroom at home.

"You have no idea," I said.

In an instant, my sister-in-law's beautiful face changed to stricken sorrow. "Oh, Clare!" she gasped. "We made you cry!"

The next instant, she was around the table and was holding me in her arms.

"Oh, Clare, Clare, I'm so sorry! We made you cry."

Was I crying? I didn't feel it. I felt as dry and dead as dirt. What I'd just seen on my sister-in-law's face—pain, regret, love—should be my feelings, too. But I couldn't feel them. I didn't feel anything.

I was severed from my feelings.

The almost-an-argument was over. My sister-in-law would no more say another word to hurt me than she would think of turning me away from her door. But inside that warm, heartfelt hug, I couldn't shake this strange sense of who I had become.

I had pretended all week to be normal, but I was not like my normal, healthy family. I was like the prophet who has seen things no one should have to see. I had traveled out to some terrible country where my sister-in-law—God forbid!—might one day have to follow. And so, once again, I delivered my message—the truth from that terrible place:

"You have no idea. No idea."

When I got home, Joe wanted to know if I was feeling better. I thought so. I didn't see why not.

The girls were back home, but they were giving me some room. Valerie watched me carefully. Elena was quiet.

Joe said, "Do you think you'll get some writing done today? We could use the money from that Holt book."

That sounded like a good idea. Why shouldn't I do some writing? So, after breakfast, I carried my laptop into the bedroom again and piled all the pillows up against the headboard. Then I leaned back against them and opened up my latest Word file.

This file contained Elena's memoir. I read the last few pages I'd written, but they didn't seem to have anything to do with Elena or me.

I stared at them for a while, but I couldn't think of anything to add.

That seemed odd.

I had no memory of how to do this.

The problem is that I'm too close to this story, I thought—although I felt very far away. *I'll write a new story. I want to write my mermaid story now.* I'd been planning to write it for some time.

So I went looking inside my imagination for the mermaid.

But there was nothing inside my imagination. It was an empty room. Nothing moved there. Nothing lived there. It was just dead white space—white like the blank Word page in front of me.

Once upon a time, a mermaid had lived inside my imagination, and I had daydreamed a story for her. How long it had been since she went missing, I couldn't say.

Tor scratched at my bedroom door and meowed, and I welcomed the interruption. But he jumped onto the bed and curled up and fell asleep, and it was just me and my Word file again.

The problem is that I haven't thought about my mermaid in a few weeks, I concluded. *I need to bring her back into focus.* So I brainstormed a page of ideas about mermaids, based on the mermaid who used to be inside my head.

But when I read through those ideas, they were as dry as class lecture notes—dry and boring.

The inside of my imagination was boring. Nothing moved there now—not even dust.

During the difficult days of Elena's senior year, six months after the Summer from Hell, Elena had asked me to write her a book about mermaids. Busy with poor Martin, I hadn't done that, but I had written her a page about one. I found that page now and pulled it up on my laptop and read it while Tor twitched slightly in his sleep.

> When you ask about the ocean, I do not understand you. I only know that once I could fly. I soared above the reefs and sands of my world, and wonderful creatures soared with me. Like your birds, they were bright and colorful. Like your birds, they gathered in flocks. They sang, and I sang with them. I was never afraid.

When you speak of tails, I grow confused. Tails
are for your world, for elephants and monkeys. What
I had was a broad sail to tame the wind. With it I
could swoop and dip and twirl through my blue sky,
and I needed nothing else to make me happy. You
know of such sails, but you turn them into brooms
and tell yourselves that the women who ride them
are hags. You are afraid of those women. You are
afraid of me.

When you speak of dark waters, of struggle, of
drowning, I begin to understand. Once I was light
and could dance like a bubble. Now I am crushed
down to the ground. In your world, my body is as
clumsy as a crawling sea star, as heavy as a boul-
der dragged under the mud. I lie immobile, helpless,
anchored by chains I cannot see, while you spurn me
with the narrow blades of your feet.

You have taken my tail, but you have not given
me wings.

I reread the simple paragraphs. I couldn't really remember writing
them. I couldn't remember being the kind of person who *could* write them.
I absorbed their graceful images and compared those images to the dull,
empty room inside my head.

Nothing lived there anymore. Nothing could possibly live there.

It seemed impossible that those words had come from me.

In a state of disbelief, I jumped up from the bed and went to find my
books. I brought the whole stack of them back to my bedroom and shut
the door again. I opened a book and read the first thing I saw.

The silent woodcarver glanced up quickly to study
Lady Mary. His lean face was the color of bones,
and his eyes were the clearest, brightest green. There
was caution in those eyes—intelligence, too—and
he stared after the old woman hungrily, as if he were
learning her by heart. One long, penetrating glance,

and he was working at his carving again as if he had never stopped.

I was in the garret of our German house, I thought, *when I wrote this paragraph. I was staring at the ceiling of the bedroom at night when I first saw my werewolf's green eyes.*

But, to save my life, I couldn't remember *where* the werewolf had come from—how it had felt to bring his character to life. And when I looked inside my imagination, he wasn't there anymore. All I found was a memory of him from the book, going through the motions that were trapped on its pages.

It was a good thing, I realized sadly, that my werewolf's story was written down. Otherwise, I'd never get to see him again.

One by one, I went through my books, but all that moved were their pages. The lives I had caught there—the lives that had been so much broader and deeper than the books themselves: every single one of them was gone.

Last of all, I picked up my very first book, the one with my oldest child-characters in it. If anyone could live for me, they would.

I flipped it open at random.

> Kate felt them shift as if the horse had stumbled. She took her eyes off the pursuing moon and glanced ahead. They were on a level field, but the horse's racing feet were sinking into it as if it were quicksand. He was not slowing his gallop; if anything, he was running faster, his legs invisible below the earth. In another few seconds, Kate's feet were gone, too, and just as if the field were a mist or sea, only the horse's head plowed along above it. Now the horse's head was gone, and the ground was rising up around her, lapping at her without waves until it reached her chest and then her neck. She screamed in terror, the goblin's arms clamped tightly around her as she threw back her head for one last glimpse of the moon.

I remember writing this, I thought. *I remember thinking that I wanted something interesting to happen.* And now this paragraph was down here on the page.

But *how* did it get here? *How* did I see this scene? I didn't know what had happened to bring it to life.

Once, I had sat in a corner and watched my characters as they went about their busy days. I couldn't stop watching them even when I wanted to. They had never once left me alone. The inside of my mind was like a bus station, crowded with imaginary life. I had put only a few of the many things I saw there down in the pages of my books.

But now, there were no more characters left inside my mind. There weren't even statues of characters. There weren't even pictures on the walls.

It was white—dead white, like an empty page.

I used to be a writer, I thought as I felt the books' hard boards and ruffled the pages and ran my hands over the slick covers. *These books are proof. They have my name on them. I used to be a writer.*

And I put them down and went off to load the dishwasher.

Valerie came to find me to chat, and I listened to her with pleasure. But after a while, she broke off and grew quiet.

"Hey, are you all right?" she asked with a frown.

I was matching socks as I talked to her. It felt pleasant to do mindless work.

"Sure, I'm fine," I said.

This was absolutely true. The pain I had felt while running away was something I couldn't quite remember. It seemed to have vanished down the cracks between my bones.

"If you say so," Valerie said suspiciously. And she picked up her book and went outside.

I told Joe about this little conversation that night as we were brushing our teeth. "I guess I still hurt," I said philosophically. "So do you. We all hurt, we just don't notice it anymore."

"I notice," Joe said sadly, and I spared a few seconds to feel sorry for him, the way I might feel sorry over an item in the newspaper. But I felt a little complacent, too. I was glad I didn't have to feel like that.

"So, did you get any writing done?" Joe asked as he hung up his shirt. "Do you think you'll be getting that manuscript to Holt before the end of the year?"

I couldn't very well explain to Joe about the day I'd spent reading through old files—about how the last few sentences of a broken-off story should feel like a signpost pointing which way to go, but instead they felt like crude wooden crosses that said HERE LIES.

I couldn't tell Joe that I used to be a writer.

"I didn't get very far today," I said.

"On what? On Elena's memoir? You need to ditch that memoir."

"On anything, really," I said.

Joe stood by the closet door, and he frowned at me, too, as I walked around the room, straightening things up. But I wasn't frowning. No longer was I split between two worlds, between reality and make-believe. Instead of seeing ghosts or goblins hanging in the air, I saw the small, neat room before me.

It was a relief, really. It felt good to have a grip on the real world.

"What's the Holt book going to be about?" Joe asked. "I'd like to read a chapter if you've finished one."

This generous offer made me smile.

Once upon a time, long ago, I had positively pestered my family to read my stuff. I had printed out chapters and met Joe at the door with pages in my hand. Once upon a time, long ago, my girls would pause a dozen times a day to read the latest paragraphs over my shoulder. "Write lots! Write lots!" they shouted as they raced off. And I did write lots.

Once upon a time, I couldn't stop writing. I couldn't turn off the nonstop movies I saw behind my eyes. I couldn't quiet down the mob— the zoo!—of characters milling around inside. *Me next! Me next!* they had clamored.

Now, as I squared my books into a neat stack, I paused to take another look inside the white room of my mind.

Not even the goblin King was there.

And if he was gone, there was truly nothing left.

CHAPTER FORTY-FOUR

When I got up the next morning, Elena was already out of bed. She had been out of bed quite a bit the last few weeks. The lineup of pill bottles had changed, too. She was seeing a new therapist, who was working with her new psychiatrist. Certain powerful drugs were now gone.

Was Elena eating more? I didn't know.

Was it my business? She surely wouldn't think so.

But when Elena asked me for a ride to her new therapist's office, I was perfectly happy to provide it. In fact, I was perfectly happy to fill up my time with all kinds of routine tasks. It would be an opportunity to get out and run some errands. It would help me use up the day.

There was no need to hold on to writing time anymore.

So I drove Elena to her new therapist's appointment and ran errands while she was there. Then she called, and I swung back by to pick her up. Driving was such a nice, safe, enjoyable activity: I moved my hands a little bit, and the world went by. I hardly had to do a thing.

Elena opened the car door and sat down in the passenger's seat in silence. In silence, I drove us to the grocery store. Once, I would have begged her for details about her day. Once, she couldn't have stopped herself. But those people—those long-ago, far-off people: we weren't those same people anymore.

As I pulled into the grocery store parking lot, Elena cleared her throat and said, "The therapist agrees with you." She said this in a formal tone, as if I were her professor instead of her mother.

"Oh?" I said without particular interest. After all, it would be impolite to say nothing.

"Yes," Elena said. Then she elaborated as carefully if she were giving a business presentation, "I told her that I was very upset with you and that contracts are bad for anorexics because they force us to give up control. That control is all we have left to count on, I told her. But she said you were right to take drastic action. She said that psychological treatment is expensive, and I've only got insurance for another year. This is an opportunity, and I'm running out of time to use it."

"I see," I said. "Well, what do you think?"

"I don't know," Elena said.

A year ago—six weeks ago—my heart would have leapt at this. I would have seen it as a fork in the road, a chance for a fresh start. I would have launched into a passionate appeal. I would have pinned all my hopes on it.

But now, I found a parking space and turned off the ignition. "I'll be about twenty minutes," I said. "You can wait in the car if you want."

"No, I'll go in," Elena said.

She trailed me around the store as I checked items off my list and moved them into the cart. Once, I had studied her every look and gesture in the grocery store, and I had put in the cart anything she had glanced at. But today, I didn't. I had my list, and I worked my way through it.

I was standing next to the frozen meat when she spoke again. "I've made my decision," she said. "I'm going back into treatment."

Six weeks ago, I would have burst into tears of relief. I would have hugged her and told her I knew she could do it. But now, I looked around the freezer cases. It was always so cold over here. I'd wanted chicken thighs, but all they had were bags of drumsticks.

"Did you hear me?" Elena said.

Did I? Yes. Then why was I not answering? Treatment meant weight gain even if it meant nothing else. Weight gain meant a reprieve of a few months from finding her dead.

My heart should leap with joy and relief.

But it didn't.

"You can't go back to Clove House," I said as I opened the freezer door and pulled out a bag of drumsticks.

"I know that," she said. "I'm going to go to Sandalwood, across town. And this time," she added, "*this* time, I'll make it work."

Wasn't that wonderful? What was wrong with me? Why wasn't I brimming with excitement? Why wasn't I walking on air?

"I won't do the calls for you," I said as I dropped the icy bag into the cart.

"No, I'll call, as soon as we get home."

And that's exactly what Elena did. She drove herself to the intake interview and arranged to be admitted the following week. And she drove herself to school to withdraw from all her classes.

When the reality of this finally dawned on me—when I finally realized that this was, in fact, going to happen, that my child was going to seek help again and work to find a way back from the brink—I did a thing that nobody understood. Least of all, me.

I lay in bed all day long and cried.

"Are you okay?" Valerie wondered, coming in to check on me.

"I guess," I sniffled. I honestly had no idea.

Elena came to the door. "Look, if you don't want me to do treatment, I won't," she said. "I thought you'd be happy."

"I *am* happy," I sobbed. "Just shut the door on your way out."

Joe came home and sat beside me. "I think you're just feeling relief," he said.

"Maybe so," I gulped, wiping my eyes.

But it didn't feel like relief. It felt as if a room-size lead-gray block of misery had pinned me down to my bed.

"You'll feel better in the morning," Joe said. "Elena's going to be away at therapy all day, and you and Valerie can just spend time playing with Gemma."

"You think so?" I asked.

I didn't think so. I couldn't see that happy day, myself. I saw myself staying there, hiding there, while Valerie worried and Joe got more and more exhausted and depressed and I never wrote another book. And if I didn't write that Holt book, sooner or later they were going to want their advance money back, and what were we going to do then?

The next morning, Joe and Elena left to go to their respective workplaces—Joe to the office and Elena to Sandalwood. After they were gone, I finally ventured out.

Valerie and Gemma were in the living room. Valerie was sitting on the carpet by the hearth. Gemma was standing on wobbly legs and, hand-hold by handhold, making her way around the coffee table.

"Hey, Momma," Valerie said. And Gemma gave a happy cry and waved at me.

"Look *out!*" I cried, grabbing Gemma's free hand.

"Okay . . . ," Valerie said. "What was that about?"

I felt too shaken to answer.

I had seen it all: Gemma was waving at me, and then her free hand slipped, and she toppled sideways and clonked her head on the corner of the hearth. The corner brick hit her right in the temple, and when we lifted her up, there was blood. And then there was wailing, the waiting room, the MRI . . .

"We need to get padding on these corners!" I said. "We need to do that today. The electrical outlets. We haven't done the outlets!"

"Seriously?" Valerie said. "Momma, she's never out of our reach. How is she going to get something into an outlet?"

But I was seeing new images: Gemma, finding a pin in the carpet and sticking it into that outlet over there. I could hear her shrill screams and see the burn. Only, in the next instant, I saw her *eat* the pin instead, and it was so vivid that I started scanning the carpet for pins, even though I couldn't remember the last time I'd seen one in this house.

"Your uncle stuck a bobby pin in an outlet when he was two," I said.

"Yeah, and he became an electrician."

How can she be so cavalier about this? I thought indignantly. I was shadowing Gemma around the coffee table now, like a spotter in a gym nastics competition.

"Let's go get childproofing stuff," I told Valerie. "I'm buying."

"It's your money," she said with a shrug, and she stood up and found her keys.

But being in the car was even worse. I didn't just see the traffic. I saw exactly how every *other* car on the road would end up hitting *our* car. The busy street was like a coach's whiteboard, with big blue arrows all over it: that van pulls out *here*, and that gray Mazda turns left *now*, and that banged-up pickup truck slams on its brakes *now* . . .

"Watch out!" I said as Valerie made a swift right turn.

"Have I ever had an accident?" Valerie pointed out.

"You *could*, though," I said. And then, "Okay, I'm sorry. I guess I'm just a little edgy."

But over the following days, and then weeks, I realized that I wasn't just a little edgy. Edgy didn't begin to describe it.

"Oh!" I gasped as Joe was driving down the freeway.

"What?" Joe demanded, on edge because I was on edge.

"Nothing . . . I just thought that car next to us was coming over into our lane."

Not true. What I'd really seen was that the car came over, Joe swerved, there was a massive smack and a shock, and the world went spinning as the SUV behind us caught the corner of our bumper. Then came the view through the spiderweb cracks in our windshield of an eighteen-wheeler barreling down on us. I could hear its brakes screaming, see its massive grille, as we sat, stopped dead in the center of the freeway, facing the wrong direction . . .

All that, in milliseconds. It had happened so fast, it was the sight of the eighteen-wheeler that made me gasp.

For months, I had been haunted by that Edward Gorey mother, with her feelings of fluttery panic and feeble cries. Now, she had swallowed me whole. I wasn't just living *with* fear anymore. I was living completely *inside* fear. And the feeble cries were my own.

"Oh, my *God!*"

"Clare, would you just stop it with the *Oh my Gods*? It's a broken glass! It's no big deal!"

But that broken glass *was* a big deal because I had seen Joe's lacerated hand that didn't happen, and the severed thumb tendon that didn't happen, and the emergency room visit that didn't happen—all in the time it took the glass to fall.

I barely seemed to register that things were getting better. Elena was back in treatment, having her ups and downs, but she was working hard. She was doing a new kind of therapy called DBT, and it seemed to have clicked with her. Little by little, she was filling out and starting to look normal again. She was even sitting down to meals with us.

Clint was doing well in tech school, too. Soon, Valerie and he would be ready to move to their first assignment. Valerie was a joy. Gemma was a dream. And Joe's job might be grueling, but he was in charge, and he relished the challenge.

My family was doing well again. But if my family was doing so well, then why was I doing so badly?

My nerves were shot, I told myself. My nerves were completely shot. I had heard that expression before and thought I had known what it meant. Only now did I understand.

And it wasn't just danger that got to me, either. It was . . . well, everything, really.

At the grocery store: "I *knew* they wouldn't have the right kind of tuna! I *knew* I should have picked a different recipe!"

Or, when Joe called from Japan: "I *knew* you were going to forget something if you put off packing! *Now* what are we going to do?"

Oh, no! Oh, no! What are we going to do?

So stressful were these wails of terror for me and everyone around me that I tried to stop things before they got that far. I spent my days checking, analyzing, examining, and planning for everything before it had a chance to go wrong. And since my disaster footage warned me ahead of time about everything that possibly *could* go wrong, my advice was absolutely flawless.

All my family needed to do was listen to that flawless advice. Then nothing bad would *ever* happen.

"It's forty-five along here. They have traffic cameras here, you know."

"Don't stop to talk now—get that dog to the backyard! She's been in all night, you know."

"If you park over here, it's easier to get past that traffic, and it's a simple right turn out of the parking lot."

"Did you remember your wallet? Your phone? Your ID? Your lunch?

Your passport? Your meds? Extra diapers?"

As the weeks unrolled, my entire family started sending me subtle clues that I had morphed into a madwoman.

"Whoa, there, Mamacita!" Valerie said. "Deep breath! It's just a misplaced debit card. I've already ordered a new one."

"You know what?" Joe said. "I don't think I'll park way out here. I think I'll do something *crazy*."

"You're being kind of a B, Mom," Elena said. "It's menopause, isn't it?"

Maybe it was.

But all I knew was that I had lived with so much pain that I seemed to have hit some kind of limit. Like our insurance payments, I'd hit my catastrophic max. Before, I had been cautious and overprotective, but now, I was this terrified, shattered person who saw pain coming from every direction. And I couldn't take it. I just couldn't take it. I couldn't bear one more little tiny bit of stress. I stopped reading books, and I stopped watching movies because I couldn't bear to witness any more suffering.

"So, do you have a chapter for me to read yet?"

"*No!*"

It was a Saturday in December, and Elena was home because Sandalwood's program didn't run on the weekend. Joe was gone—Guam this time, I think—and I was shut up in the bedroom, trying to write. Joe was right, I needed to try again. I *had* to try again. Besides, there was no reason not to try.

Elena wasn't dying anymore. Gemma was happy and healthy. Clint was earning praise from all his instructors. Valerie was her usual sunny self. Joe was back to sending me photos of interesting exotic places.

Everything was fine. My family didn't need me right now.

Everything was *fine*.

I didn't have to work on the memoir. I could write whatever I wanted. I could write something fun, something that wouldn't take me back into the past. I could go somewhere completely new and different, somewhere I'd never been before.

So I sat down on my bed, picked up my laptop, and pulled up a blank Word page. And I asked—just as I've always asked:

Where am I now? What am I seeing?

Slowly, a scene came into focus.

There was a mansion. It was near a wide river—the Hudson River, maybe. It was early spring, and there was a hard frost. When the sun came up, the short grass would be white, but right now, it was still a ghostly light gray.

The sky was clear, a bright clear brown with just a single strip of salmon-orange cloud in the east. And there was a pool of water in the short grass near the mansion—a perfectly round, deep, glass-smooth pool, catching the dawn light in a color like pink pearl . . .

But wait! Wait! What am I doing here? What am I doing? That's not right! That's crap!

What did I know about mansions on the Hudson? Nothing! I'd have to research that first. I needed books of architecture . . . history . . . No, that wouldn't be good enough, I needed to make a research trip! And did clear skies look like that? Did frost look like that? Did calm water reflect that light? I needed to see frost again! That trip needed to be in the spring! I needed to find a pool!

Oh, what am I even doing, thinking about stuff like this? I don't know what I'm doing! It won't work. This isn't going to work!

Okay. Blank out the mansion and the frost. I could figure that out later.

There was a girl standing by the pool. She had long blond hair. The dawn just gave her pale oval face a touch of rose. I could see her bare feet on the light gray frost of the grass. She smiled. And, even though it was cast-iron cold outside, she dove gracefully into the water . . .

But wait! Wait! In what*? What is she wearing?*

Was that a shift? A nightdress? Did it have lace? Machine or hand lace? What was the difference? I needed a book on lace! Was she wearing a corset? What kind of a corset? I needed photographs . . . costume books . . . novels from the time period . . . old movies . . .

Oh, what's the use? What's the use*? This isn't going to* work*!*

Slowly, I came back to the safe view of the walls of my bedroom. I was hyperventilating, stiff with terror, as stiff as a board. I sat there panting, then talked myself into unclenching my shaking hands. I put the laptop back into sleep and folded it up for the day.

Word count: two hundred and ninety words.

Misery overwhelmed me. I pulled up the covers and burrowed down into their warmth. All I wanted to do was sleep. As long as I slept, I couldn't hurt, and I couldn't fail. As long as I slept, nothing bad could happen.

Voices. Loud voices. I tried to stay asleep, but the voices were pulling me back.

Laughter. Loud laughter.

Right outside my door!

Why were they yelling and laughing like that? I wanted to *sleep*! I wanted to stay *asleep*!

In a frenzy, I jumped up and slammed open the bedroom door. "I'm trying to *sleep* in here! Do you *mind*? How about showing a *little* consideration? Do you think you can do that? Well? *Do* you?"

My brain captured a single image: Valerie and Elena sitting on the floor together, staring wide-eyed at me, their laughter frozen into shock.

I turned around, slammed the door, and threw myself back on the bed.

And yes, I was fully aware of the irony.

CHAPTER FORTY-FIVE

Six weeks later, I was driving Elena through morning rush-hour traffic. It was January again, a year after Elena's first admission into Clove House.

January. A new year. A fresh start.

Elena had been attending Sandalwood's treatment program for three months now. She was on much less medication these days, and that had been a rocky process for her and her care team there. The opposite of sedation is excitement—fight or flight. Elena had gone through lots of fight-or-flight moments as her body had learned to give up those powerful drugs.

For the first month, Elena had driven herself back and forth to treatment, but that hadn't been ideal. When those fight-or-flight moments had come up, Elena had grabbed her car keys and bolted. I got regular calls from Dr. Leben back then: "Elena's on her way home. Try to talk her into coming back."

So Elena had asked me to start driving her to treatment. "That way, I won't have a getaway vehicle," she said. I had been driving her in now for the last two months: thirty minutes there and thirty minutes back, twice a day.

Once upon a time, a commute like that would have played havoc with my busy schedule. It would have interrupted my writing and thrown everything off. It would have become the reason I let myself fail.

Now, it was the most pleasant part of my day.

Elena and I had stayed careful with one another for weeks. Each of us, for excellent reasons, saw the other person as the greatest threat to her happiness. As weak as we both were, if we had had the chance, we probably would have drifted apart, and that sense of threat between us might have hardened into animosity.

But the commutes had brought us together. They threw us together in one small space, and they let us both do something we enjoyed. I got to drive, and Elena got to tell stories.

This morning, as we inched past a big drugstore, Elena said, "Did I tell you what Jamie's grandmother says about those places? She thinks they're secret gambling dens. 'The parking lots have *so* many cars in them,'" she quoted in the grandmother's high, wavering voice, "'but when you get inside, you hardly see *anybody* in the aisles.'"

"Hey, she's right!" I said. "I never thought about that!"

"'Where *are* all those people?'" Elena went on, mimicking the grandmother. "'*I* think there's a craps game in the back!'"

I laughed.

"I just love her," Elena said. "You can never tell if she's going senile or just messing with your head. When I was there last week, they had these really cool dessert plates out, the kind with a raised pattern, a big fruit. The grandmother was sawing away at the plate with her knife—an empty plate. And the mom said, 'What are you doing, Mother? I haven't cut your cake yet.' And the grandmother said"—and here Elena went back into that wonderful, wavering voice—"'*Oh!* I *thought* that pear was very hard!'"

I laughed again. Even though my shot nerves still kept me from picking up a book these days, small stories like these were feeding a hunger that was starting to grow inside me. Little by little, they were pulling me out of my shell.

"When I'm old," Elena mused, "I want to be exactly like that. Wonderfully weird, keeping everybody guessing."

My imagination started to assemble a reel of film. Elena, old. Elena, white-haired, with a dancer's ankles like her grandmother, and a lift to her chin that showed that you'd better not mess with her. My daughter, old. My daughter, surviving. Surviving . . .

Instantly, I felt a stab of pain from my shot nerves.

Don't think about it! Don't!

I took a deep breath and focused on the cars in front of me.

We made it past the drugstore and its full parking lot and craps game, and the traffic broke loose and picked up speed.

"So, I need to ask you something," I said. "About the memoir."

"Let's hear it," Elena said.

Lately, I had started working on Elena's story again. My imagination wasn't quite an empty room now—more like a foggy street. Characters, half dream and half daydream, had begun to walk out of the mist as I was falling asleep at night. But I didn't trust them yet. I didn't want to get to know them. I couldn't bear to lose them again. So, as painful as it was to go back through those bad memories, Elena's story felt like the only writing I could do.

I had begun doing my interviews again on our commutes, trying once more to discover my character. And Elena told me anything and everything I asked. It never ceased to amaze me how candid she was. Her fearless honesty was the opposite of my huddled, pain-filled hesitation.

Elena still thought I could do this.

She still thought I could write.

"The Summer from Hell," I said now. "Senior year. I didn't end up helping at all. If I went back, knowing what I know now, how could I have helped you? What could I have done differently?"

"Not much," Elena said with brutal and impartial honesty. "Maybe commit me. But then I never would have spoken to you again—and I mean *never*. If someone were to turn me in back then, I'd never have forgiven them."

Like the contract, I thought—it was a miracle that she was working around to forgiving me now . . .

Immediately, I felt that jolt of pain again, like the stab of pleurisy that keeps the breaths careful and shallow:

Don't think about it! Don't!

I turned my attention back to those earlier days.

"Take Anna Anton," I said. "She tried to tell me what was wrong. She called me from boarding school and told me you wouldn't eat."

"Anna Anton was a bitch!" Elena snapped.

"She said you were ill and didn't want to live," I said. "That was true. I drove all afternoon, I had a frantic meeting with the housemothers . . ."

"And I had to work my butt off to get you all calmed down! . . . She was a bitch," Elena said again.

Implacable resentment, my writer's mind noted. *Irrational, implacable resentment.*

I fell silent.

"There's this novel I read," Elena told me, "where a girl's best friend tells her school counselor she needs help, and she winds up getting put into a hospital. But at the end of the book, the two of them make up. Well, that would never happen with an anorexic."

"You can't be sure," I protested.

"I am sure," Elena said, and my writer's mind noted her air of calm assertion. She wasn't upset anymore. This wasn't just resentment. "If someone had had me committed in high school, I would never speak to that person again, *ever*—period, dot. You, Dad, my closest friends—I don't care. I might forgive them, and I might even understand it. But the friendship would be done. Dead. Done."

"But you needed help in high school!"

"Yep."

"If you'd gotten it then, it would have been the best thing for you."

"Yep."

"And . . . Anna Anton was trying to get you that help."

"Anna Anton was a bitch!"

This is another one of those anorexia things, I thought, *that doesn't make sense.*

But that wasn't fair, and a writer has to be fair. So I amended that thought:

Maybe I don't have the right angle on this yet.

When I got home from the commute, Valerie was up. She was walking slowly—very slowly—across the living room. Gemma walked along beside her, keeping a death grip on Valerie's index finger.

Gemma gave a happy cry when she saw me, and I bent down and held out my hands.

"Come on!" I said. "Come to Grandma!"

And Valerie pulled her hand free.

Gemma stood there for a second, wavering a little, her big blue-green eyes on my face. Then she dropped to her hands and knees and zoomed over to me.

"So close!" I said as I scooped her up. "You'll be walking any day now, and then your mommy's going to have to run to keep up with you."

Valerie followed us into the kitchen. "Speaking of, I had an idea."

"Let's hear it!" I said as I filled up the coffeepot.

"I'm thinking about getting a three-month lease on an apartment near Clint's school," she said. "That way, we'd be able to see Clint in the evenings and on the weekends. He's missed out on so much of her babyhood already. I don't want him to miss out on her first birthday."

"But will a place let you get a three-month lease like that?" I asked.

"I've been doing some calling, and yeah, they will if you're military. They'll even let me break it if we've got orders."

I thought about this as I measured out scoops of coffee. I'd gotten used to having the two of them with me. It hadn't occurred to me that I might be losing them so soon. But I sneaked a glance at Valerie. My sunny daughter was finally beginning to droop. She hadn't exactly had the happiest year of her life here.

"Do it!" I said. "I'll help." And I did help, even though we quickly figured out that it meant I'd be towing a trailer across three states.

I was absolutely petrified about that trailer. I had nightmares about it for days. As I towed it home, I listened to every rattle and slowed down for every little dip in the road. My imagination sent me flashes of everything that could go wrong: a tire going flat, the hitch coming undone, the trailer dragging me into a ditch . . .

But I stayed upbeat and hid my fear. Valerie needed me to do this. She needed me to do it—

And that meant that I could.

The trip was completely uneventful. It even wound up being fun, and Clint was beyond thrilled to have his family back. I left Valerie and Gemma in their new apartment, surrounded by boxes and toys, and Gemma took her very first steps before the week was out.

By the time Gemma was walking, Joe and I were able to park our cars in the garage again. The media room was a media room once more; the office went back to being an office. And even though I missed my family now when I dropped Elena off at treatment in the morning, the peace and quiet did my shattered nerves good.

One evening, when I picked up Elena from the treatment center, she pulled a piece of paper out of her backpack. "Connie read us a poem today in spirituality," she said. "I asked her for a copy because it made me think of you."

"A poem?" I said, pleased.

I love poetry. My mother and I have shared countless poems with one another over the years, and so have Elena and I. My favorite poem is "Morning Song of Senlin," by Conrad Aiken. It became my favorite poem when I first read it in fourth grade. I've read it many times since and never regretted my choice.

"Who wrote your poem?" I asked Elena.

"Daniel Ladinsky," she said. "It's from his book *I Heard God Laughing*."

God, laughing. My imagination brought me images to match that thought. Sunrise over the ocean, with the noisy, boisterous rolling of the surf. Wildflowers, whispering and chuckling and bowing in the wind. Lightning, and the boom of thunder—a grand, victorious *Ha-ha!* Strong, lovely images.

And then she read,

> There is a Beautiful Creature
> Living in a hole you have dug,
>
> So at night
> I set fruit and grains
> And little pots of wine and milk
> Beside your soft earthen mounds,

And I often sing.

But still, my dear,
You do not come out.

I have fallen in love with Someone
Who hides inside you.
We should talk about this problem—

Otherwise,
I will never leave you alone.

I was quiet with the poem for a minute. I let the words soak in and find their places.

"When I heard it, I thought of you and Dad," Elena said. "I thought about what it was like for you, being the parent of an anorexic. This is what it's like, this poem. I understand that now. I understand how hard it was for you to save me."

Tears welled up in my eyes.

How funny that I should seem this way to my daughter. I saw it from the other way around. This person persisting, coming to sit beside the cave and sing, was how my daughter seemed to me. I had become so terrified of life, so timid about emerging from my shell of fear. It was Elena, day after day, who came with news from the outside world. She brought me gentle, happy truths, like the story of the funny grandmother, and she brought me big, hard truths, like the story of her eating disorder.

She was so brave, my daughter. She was absolutely fearless. Even now, with this poem, she was reaching out to me, and she made me want to come out of hiding.

Tomorrow, I decided, *I am absolutely going to write!*

The next morning, after our commute, I sat down to play one game of FreeCell—but really to work up my courage to write.

See? I'm already on the laptop, I thought as I organized the cards in tidy sequences of ace to two. *I can open up Word. It won't be that bad. It can't be that bad.*

The phone rang. It was Sandalwood: Jen's number. Jen was Elena's therapist.

Mrs. Dunkle, I'm so sorry. It's about your daughter.

No, of course that wouldn't be what Jen would say! That was completely ridiculous! But still, my hands shook as I answered the phone.

Elena left the treatment center. Elena cut herself. Elena is in the emergency room . . .

No, no, no! That wasn't what Jen had said. She hadn't even spoken yet! "Hello?" I said into the silence.

"Mrs. Dunkle," Jen's firm, capable voice said, "could you and Mr. Dunkle come in for a special meeting this afternoon?"

Oh, no! What is it? What's happened now? What are we going to do?

"Of course," I said, trying to control the panic in my voice. "Three o'clock? That sounds fine."

And when I called Joe, I could hear the panic in his voice, too.

Writing was out of the question. I shut down the laptop, and my imagination played out every disaster that could possibly have occurred.

Elena's insurance is refusing to pay. Elena isn't making progress. Elena is taking herself out of treatment. We need her on suicide watch . . .

Joe stopped by to pick me up, and we drove to Sandalwood in silence. In silence, we filed into Jen's empty office to wait. A special meeting with the therapist can mean just about anything. It can be horrible: *Your daughter is having strong urges to self-harm.* Or it can be exciting: *Your daughter is ready for half days.* So Joe and I sat side by side, trying not to hope, trying to gather our courage.

It's when you let down your guard that the ax falls.

It's hard to prepare for the special meeting. There's how to sit, for instance. Upright and attentive? Or will that look too much like fear? Leaning back into the couch, relaxed? Or will that look hardhearted? And then there's the whole problem of which expression to put on. Where to put the purse. What to do with the hands.

I had tried to prepare. God knows, I had tried to prepare. But not a single one of my imaginary disasters came within miles of the truth.

In a dream, I heard myself say, "You think she needs a *what*?"

Calmly, Jen repeated herself:

"I think Elena needs a snake."

It had to do with the self-harming urges, Jen explained. She and Elena were working on distraction skills, and they'd been trying certain tactile distractions like strings of beads, as well as a favorite perfume to smell. But late at night, when Joe and I were in bed, those urges were still getting the better of Elena. She thought a snake might help, and Jen agreed with her. Playing with a snake would be an excellent distraction.

Future disasters immediately started to play themselves out in my head: a snake slipping around the edge of Elena's room and sliding under the door, a snake getting stepped on, a snake scaring guests . . .

Too painful! Too risky! What are we going to do?

"But what about Tor and Genny?" I protested out loud. "Can't they distract you?"

"They just sleep," Elena pointed out—which was certainly true.

Joe was doing much better with his expression than I was. "Well," he said, "if you think it's worth a try . . ."

A snake lying neglected and ill, skin half shed, covered in mites . . .

Darling! Darling! No! Let's talk *about this!*

"But—I don't have time to take care of a snake!" I said.

"You won't have to, Mom," Elena said. "I'll take care of him."

"That's what you said about Dylan," I muttered. And at the thought of my poor lost blue dragon, I felt even worse.

Jen gave Elena a pass for the afternoon, and Joe drove us to the pet store to take a look at snakes. For once, I wasn't scanning the traffic and backseat-driving him to death. I was still watching snake footage. A cute, tiny mouse, huddled down amid wood shavings, quivering in abject terror . . . The pounce, the squeeze, the long, painful trip down the tight gullet . . .

"No one in *my* house," I burst out, "is going to *eat* someone else in my house!"

"Mom, snakes don't have to eat live prey," Elena said. "In fact, it's better if they don't. No live prey. I don't want to see that, either. Okay?"

That was a relief. I did feel a little better.

Joe and Elena walked through the pet store while I loitered behind, mulish and out of sorts. Near the reptile terrariums, Joe corralled a young man with a name tag to ask him about snakes.

"How about a corn snake?" the young man suggested. "We have some nice young ones." He picked up a plastic box and stirred the aspen-shaving litter with a pair of tongs, and two little brown snakes shot up out of the shavings and began weaving back and forth like a pair of tiny cobras.

He gasped and almost dropped the box. "I'm not really the snake person," he confessed.

"*Is* there a snake person?" Joe asked.

The snake person was paged. She turned out to be a tough-looking young woman with short blond hair and a frank, confident manner.

"You might think about a boa," she suggested.

"Ugh," I said faintly.

I had known a boa once. He was a nice snake, but he was also a muscle-bound monster. He was like one giant roided-out bicep.

Body builders make me queasy.

Meanwhile, Elena was still studying the plastic box. She said, "Look at this little red guy."

Behind the two aggressive young brown snakes, a third snake was looping along lazily. He was the most peculiar color: salmon orange, with dark red spots down his back.

He was quite unexpectedly beautiful.

"That's an albino corn snake," said the snake person, fetching him out with the tongs. She wasn't quite right about that, but never mind.

Elena spread her fingers and watched the little red snake weave his way among them, the tip of his tail curled tightly around her thumb.

It wasn't that I disliked snakes per se. I had always loved the feel of snakes, like fine smooth plastic. I reached out and took the slim red snake on my palm, and with him came a bright, busy crowd of memories.

Funny hognose snakes, playing dead. Big black king snakes, sunning on the gravel drive. Water snakes, swimming at the head of their V-shaped wakes. Garter snakes with yellow racing stripes.

Tiny blind snakes, pink and shiny, like a more perfect earthworm . . . How old was Elena the first time I had showed her a blind snake? Emerald-green grass snakes, elusive and beautiful, the elf of the Texas snake world . . .

Texas has a lot of snakes.

Tor had once dragged home a massive garter snake by the very tip of its tail. That snake had been distraught at the rough treatment. It had flung itself back and forth with impotent fury. I had made Tor let it go, and it had flashed away in an instant. It was astounding how fast that snake had moved without feet.

That's such a strange mode of travel! I thought yet again, interested in spite of my bad attitude as the little guy navigated carefully from finger to finger. *Imagine: a life without feet!*

The little snake wasn't panicking or flailing, he was just looking around. He had a docile nature. "He's a picky eater, though," the woman warned—to Elena's great delight.

"I'm bonding with him already!" she said.

But my mind wasn't through playing disaster footage yet. It flashed to the image of a listless reptile, immovable in its terrarium, afflicted with some mysterious, expensive ailment . . .

What do we do? What do we do?

"What do we know," I said, "about keeping a *snake*?"

"You could buy our corn snake book," the woman said.

In the end, we brought the little snake home, along with the corn snake book, aspen chips, red and blue light bulbs, misting bottles, drift-wood, a hollow ceramic "rock," daytime and nighttime lamps, an under-tank heater, frozen mice, interchangeable water dishes that couldn't tip over, and a twenty-gallon terrarium—in all, several hundred dollars' worth of snake and snake paraphernalia because *no* animal—not even an animal I opposed—would know hardship or want in my house.

Once Elena had the corn snake moved into his terrarium, none of us could take our eyes off him. He looked so beautiful, and somehow primitive and ancient at the same time, like a work of aboriginal art.

This is what Elena does so well, I thought, remembering the poem she had read to me. *She tells me sad stories I don't want to hear, but then I never want to forget them. She drags me into adventures I don't want to have, but then I don't want them to stop.*

She was so brave! She made me want to be brave, too.

The next morning, Joe had another plane to catch. Well before dawn, I drove down wide-open highway to the airport and pulled to the curb by the terminal doors. It was so early that the airport hadn't really gotten going yet. The two old porters, standing by the curbside baggage check-in counter, looked ready to fall asleep.

"See you in two weeks," Joe said, giving me a hug. "*Please* write me something I'll want to read."

He had refused to read Elena's story. I didn't blame him.

I'm going to miss this hug while he's gone, I thought. Joe is so tall and big compared to me that he can rest his chin on the top of my head. When I'm in his arms, I can't see anything but his shirtfront and his shoulders and his arms as they reach past to wrap around me.

A hug from Joe is a wonderful place to be.

I left the airport, made a detour to a nearby drive-through for a wakeup cup of coffee, and drove home through the empty predawn streets. When Elena and I would drive this stretch of road in a couple of hours, it would be a zoo, but for the time being, it was nice and quiet, just the way I liked it. I sipped my coffee and made a resolution: I *would* write something Joe would want to read. And I'd start right away. That couldn't get too depressing. I'd have only an hour of writer's block to face before taking Elena to treatment.

So, when I got home, I shut the door of the bedroom, and I opened up my laptop. For the first time in weeks, I thought about my mermaid again.

Where is she? I asked, just as I always had. *Where is she? What is she doing?* And, as the scene coalesced, I began to type.

> "Look what I've brought," Rain said, holding the door open with one foot as she bent to pick up the rattan tray. Mama stirred under the sheet and opened her eyes. A fragile beauty still hung about

Mama's delicate features, but time and worry had taken their toll. Wrinkles pressed close to Mama's mouth now, and her eyes glittered with fever.

"They aren't with you, Rain? They aren't?"

Rain pushed the door shut with her hip.

"No one's there, Mama," she said. "It's just me."

No one was ever there.

I grimaced with annoyance. A sick mother, lying in bed. A weak, sick, fear-racked, paranoid mother—wasn't that lovely!

Stupid overactive imagination!

I blew out my breath and took a sip of coffee. *Look again,* I told myself. *What is the* mermaid *like?*

And once again, I began to type.

But Rain was never sick. She was strong. And life was beautiful. Real life was more beautiful than any fairy tale could ever be. The fly-specked window and unpainted walls around Rain suddenly seemed unbearably precious. They were landmarks in the flow of this beautiful life. They said, *We are here, and you are here, at this exact moment.*

This is me, Rain thought. *This is me, in the middle of my life. I am standing in a room in a town in the middle of a territory so young, it's not even a state yet. No matter where I go, I'll carry this town with me—it and everywhere else I've ever been.*

Wait! What town? What territory? Where is this? Oh, no*! What are we going to* do*?*

Did we still have an atlas? Could I find maps of the time period? Would I need to use real names of towns? What if the towns hadn't been founded yet? How would I know I was wrong? What did our library system have? Could I get a list of Western towns and their founding dates?

Oh, no! Oh, no! Oh, no!

Then I read the paragraphs again, and my worry subsided.

I thought, *I like this girl!*

Rain crossed and recrossed the room, doing the mundane chores her mother was too weak to do. Quietly, I settled down in the corner to watch. Rain put away laundry. She tidied the bare space. She didn't mind the boring work.

But when nighttime came, Rain took her mother's medicine bottle and crept out of the house.

Of course! I thought. *She's going to find water.*

Rain and her mother were mermaids, after all. No wonder her mother was sick. She must need so much water per day, week, month, or else she would start to get sick. And not just water, I realized, getting excited now. It would have to be *living* water—*flowing* water. Rain must be going out to find a stream or a creek—even a little spring.

And I pictured a tiny spring nearby with a few green ferns gathered around it, maybe back in the pine-covered folds of the land I could see behind the town.

But *that* isn't what my imagination pictured—

Because that isn't where Rain went.

My mermaid girl turned and walked downhill, down the side of the steep Western ridge. It was nothing but desert scrub and dusty earth, dim under the light of the moon. Far below, I could see more desert, spreading out wide and flat. I could see fuzzy cactus down there, catching the moonlight.

But . . . *why is she doing this?* I wondered. *There's no water here!*

Or was there?

> Water was closer now, wandering blind and searching for a way out. Rain felt it, traveling along deep cracks in the sloping ground beside her.
>
> A sapling grew at an angle out of the hillside, its tender, rustling leaves betraying the secret that lay at its roots. Rain knelt down beside its slim trunk and dug into the ground.

"Here," she sang under her breath. "Here! Come this way!"

The groundwater . . . Rain was calling the groundwater!

Water hurried. It seeped out around the trunk to wet and cool her hands. A tiny trickle welled up and began to thread its way down the hillside.

"More!" Rain urged. And more water came. She could feel it feeling its way to her through the tons and tons of rock.

Of course. Of course! Water came to her call!

The ground beneath Rain's feet shook as she scrambled aside. Another few seconds, and rocks bumped and tumbled out of the way. The sapling bent horizontal, thrashing in the current. Then it shot off and out of sight.

Water sang a wordless song of triumph as it burst out of its grave. Rain sang with it, dancing, and bent to thrust her hands beneath its cold, shining arc.

Water and she never stopped moving. Water and she were always on their way.

Tears were in my eyes now. Tears rolled down my face as I watched this beautiful, joyful young creature dance in the moonlight.

I didn't see it coming, I thought. *I didn't see it coming! She surprised me!*

My timer went off. Reverently, I saved the Word file. It wasn't a white page anymore. It was a home.

She's alive, I thought as I wiped my wet cheeks. *She's actually alive!*

Then I set aside the laptop, and I went to wake up Elena.

"Hey," I said, shaking her, and my old terrier lifted her head from a fold of blanket and gave me a careful look.

But, "Hey," Elena mumbled back almost amiably. She didn't have much trouble waking up anymore.

"So, I wrote a chapter of the mermaid book this morning," I said, sitting down on the bed.

"Mmm?" inquired Elena, face-down in her pillow.

"The mermaid did something I didn't expect."

"Mmm!" Elena said.

But she didn't know what that meant, how that sentence should be accompanied with trumpets. And that was all right. It was part of my other life. It belonged to my other world.

"Come on now," I said, reverting to my role in *this* world. "Got to get moving. Time to get up!"

Scruffy little Genny stood up, stretched stiffly, and jumped down. But Elena rolled over with her eyes still closed. She murmured, "I just need to finish this dream first."

"I'll give you five minutes," I said. "Get to dreaming."

So I popped the top off Mr. Snaky's cage, and I misted it and changed his water and admired his vibrant oranges and reds as he traveled footless along my arm. "Who's a pretty snaky?" I crooned to him, running a finger down his silky back. "Who's my big strong boy?"

And Tor strolled in to ask for his breakfast. And Genny trotted in circles, panting, wondering who I was talking to.

And my daughter—my bright, fearless daughter—finished her dream.

EPILOGUE

Elena stayed in treatment at Sandalwood from October to March before she felt ready to resume college. She enrolled in summer school and promptly fell in love with learning all over again. Once more, she was bursting with information to share. She even told me jokes in sign language.

The following year, Elena applied to nursing schools and was accepted everywhere she applied.

The month after the painful breakup described in the first chapter of this book, Elena called me to say that she was traveling to Baltimore to visit an old friend.

"He's the only one who's stayed in touch from my state university days," she said. "He knows you're in Germany and Clint and Valerie are in Nevada, and he says he doesn't want me to be alone over the Thanksgiving holiday."

I knew the young man already from Elena's stories of university life. Like Elena, he had boundless curiosity, a sharp mind, and oceans of ambition. He was a bright, humorous, gentle person with old-fashioned Texas manners, and he didn't have a mean bone in his body.

"That's great!" I said. "You know he's in love with you, right?"

"Mom, we're just really good friends."

After the holiday, she called me up again: "How do you *know* these things?"

It's simple. I think of Elena, and I ask myself: *What bright young man wouldn't love her?* Answer: *Nobody!*

That's how I know.

A year after this holiday, almost to the day, the two of them got married. I have never seen Elena looking happier than she looked on that day. She absolutely glowed with happiness.

In order to be with her new husband, Elena decided to put her nursing career on hold. His job requires constant travel, so she has settled down to keep house in a hotel suite. Elena, turning away from quantifiable perfection to nurture a loving relationship—that's an idea I like to run barefoot through every now and then.

Naturally, this transition wasn't without its tearful moments. Elena could have sold her finest fish for an excellent price, but she gave them away instead—all one hundred and thirty-six fish—on the condition that the least valuable ones would be treated as well as the best ones. She and her husband still have her little dog with them in the hotel. Her cat, Leela, came to Germany to live with Joe and me, so once again, a black cat snoozes nearby as I write.

I rewrote Elena's memoir, *Elena Vanishing*, three agonizing times. Each time I revised it, I reminded myself that once it was finished, I would never have to go back there again. But when Chronicle Books bought it, my agent called me up.

"They'd like another memoir," she said. "A memoir from your point of view this time. They think it would help other parents."

So I went back there. I wasn't sure I could, but I did.

"I'm looking forward to reading this one," Valerie says on the phone. "I can relate, being a mom and all." She and Clint now have a family of four: Gemma and her little brother.

Baby Gemma is already five years old. And she does look a lot like me.

Valerie and Elena stay in touch daily, and so do their husbands, who have become good friends. We share videos and photos back and forth, and the girls call the house almost every single day. When the phone rings, Joe and I drop everything to get to it. We talk about anything and everything going on in their lives, except for the quarrels they may be having with their husbands. For all I know, neither one of them has any quarrels. After all, both of my sons-in-law are amazing.

Each day, as I hang up the phone, I think once again about how lucky I am—except, there's no such thing as luck. My life is so much richer because of the way my girls share their days with me, and I don't take that kind of attention for granted. My daughters have families now—priorities that outrank me. They have full, happy, and demanding lives.

So I savor each call. I celebrate each moment they share with me as the precious gift it is. Because how much longer will these two busy women be able to fit me into their days? How much longer will Valerie and Elena be able to spend this kind of time with me?

Forever, I hope . . .

I hope.

AFTERWORD

This book is an accurate description of how I dealt with my daughter's eating disorder. No part of it is intended to be a guide for how others should live. Many of the things Elena chose to do were extremely dangerous, and some of the things my husband and I chose to do were also dangerous. The contract we made Elena sign, for instance, that tied her weight to a list of privileges, could easily have driven her to suicide instead of to treatment. If you or someone you know has an eating disorder, please do not take any part of this book as a suggestion for how to handle your own journey to recovery.

If you are dealing with an eating disorder, the one thing I will advise you to do is to seek professional help. Please, do not try to manage an eating disorder on your own. These are serious, life-threatening conditions. And please, do try to educate yourself with up-to-date information. Eating disorders are complicated, and the professionals who deal with them are trying out new approaches all the time. In the years since my daughter's eating disorder began, we have seen treatments and theories change radically.

If you are just starting this journey, I suggest you visit the websites run by the National Eating Disorders Association (NEDA) and the National Association of Anorexia Nervosa and Associated Disorders (ANAD). Their websites will help you find the latest resources available, and the caring staff and volunteers who monitor their helpline and forum can help connect you to the information you need. They will tell you what I am telling you: Recovery is real. You don't have to lose hope.

ACKNOWLEDGMENTS

Warmest, most heartfelt thanks go first to Elena Dunkle, my daughter and coauthor on her own memoir, *Elena Vanishing,* for the incredible courage she displayed in sharing the details of her illness with me. She turned the greatest burden of her life into a gift to the world.

Special thanks to my daughter Valerie, who comes across as a hero in this book because she is; to my patient, long-suffering husband, Joe, who had to watch me live through these awful events again and again as I wrote; to my dear sons-in-law, Clint and Matt, who have always been a part of this family, even when they didn't know it yet; and to my grandchildren: you are this family's greatest joy and brightest hope.

Daniel Ladinsky, the author of Elena's favorite recovery poem, "We Should Talk about This Problem," which is quoted in this book, turned the chore of obtaining the reprint permission into a joyful, life-affirming communication. And Erin Murphy, literary agent extraordinaire, believed in me, and she believed in this memoir. She even made me believe in it, too, and that's the greatest gift an agent can give a client.

I had just sent a note to my editor to tell her that I couldn't write this book. Then I spent an amazing evening with fellow YA author Jennifer Ziegler, and she gave me the strength to try again. I don't know how she did it. Fairy dust may well have been involved. She and her equally amazing author-husband, Chris Barton, have been my cheerleaders throughout this process. Dear friends, this book exists because of you.

And to Ginee Seo, my unbelievable editor at Chronicle—what can I even say? You had the second sight necessary to see what this book could be, even when that wasn't what I was giving you. A lesser editor would have burdened me with demands and suggestions. You didn't. You found the words to release me. You freed me to find this book inside myself, and I wrote it down for you.

Magic exists. You people are magical. I love you all.